More Praise For

Neuromyths

The activities of the brain, the most complex machine we know, underpins all aspects of our life from birth to death—including our education. Understanding of the brain has been growing at a fantastic rate and findings from neuroscience are increasingly being used to enhance educational outcomes in classrooms and other informal settings. This field is full of "neuromyths"—beliefs that are incorrect but widely accepted and often used to support educational practice. Tracey Tokuhama-Espinosa dispels these myths. In this well-researched and readable book, she identifies neuromyths in Chapters 1-10, presents their origins, and explains how they are wrong.

This clear exposition is a primer on these false beliefs and will be an eye-opener for anyone working in education.

—**Pankaj Sah, P.h.D.,** Director, ARC Science of Learning Research Centre (SLRC), The Queensland Brain Institute, University of Queensland

Neuromyths is a must-read for instructors and instructional designers in K-12 education, higher education, and professional development. Dr. Tokuhama-Espinosa provides critical insight that addresses common misconceptions and misunderstandings about the brain. The convergence of Mind, Brain, and Education principles and tenets with debunked neuromyths is powerful, thought-provoking, and transformational.

—**Kristen Betts, Ed.D.,** Clinical Professor, Drexel University

Tracy Tokuhama-Espinosa's excellent book, *Neuromyths*, makes a significant contribution to the body of literature in neuroeducation by identifying commonly held misconceptions about learning. The book identifies a host of neuromyths, explains the origins of each, and describes how researchers know them to be false. *Neuromyths* does more than the book title suggests. In an accessible way, Tokuhama-Espinosa shares research on a myriad of topics relevant to the teaching and learning process. This book is a must-read for educators at every level, from early childhood teachers to university professors.

—**Mariale Hardiman, Ed.D.,** Professor, Johns Hopkins University School of Education, author, *The Brain-Targeted Teaching for 21st Century Schools*

NEUROMYTHS

ALSO BY TRACEY TOKUHAMA-ESPINOSA

Five Pillars of the Mind

Making Classrooms Better

Mind, Brain, and Education Science

NORTON BOOKS IN EDUCATION

NEUROMYTHS

Debunking False Ideas about the Brain

Tracey Tokuhama-Espinosa

W. W. Norton & Company
Independent Publishers Since 1923
New York • London

Note to Readers: Models and/or techniques described in this volume are illustrative or are included for general informational purposes only; neither the publisher nor the author can guarantee the efficacy or appropriateness of any particular recommendation in every circumstance.

For information about permission to reproduce selections from this book, write to Permissions, W. W. Norton & Company, Inc., 500 Fifth Avenue, New York, NY 10110

For information about special discounts for bulk purchases, please contact W. W. Norton Special Sales at specialsales@wwnorton.com or 800-233-4830

Manufacturing by LSC Willard
Book design by Vicki Fischman
Production manager: Katelyn MacKenzie

ISBN: 978-0-393-71323-7 (pbk.)

W. W. Norton & Company, Inc., 500 Fifth Avenue, New York, N.Y. 10110
www.wwnorton.com

W. W. Norton & Company Ltd., 15 Carlisle Street, London W1D 3BS

1 2 3 4 5 6 7 8 9 0

This book is dedicated to all the educators I work with around the world who seek to better understand the science in the art of teaching.

CONTENTS

TABLES AND FIGURES

NEUROMYTHS

ACKNOWLEDGMENTS

I would like to thank Paul Howard-Jones, Sanne Dekker, Jelle Jolles, Suzana Herculano-Houzel, Michael Shermer, Elena Pasquinelli and Daniel T. Willingham for their inspiration as teacher educators and Myth Busters, *par excellence*.

To John Bruer, whose critical skepticism has helped the field move forward and inspired us all to be cautiously optimistic.

Thanks to John Hattie for helping mine so much of the new evidence we can now use to definitely put some of these myths to rest. Kudos to Robert Marzano for keeping his head above the fray and sticking to the data.

Appreciation to the OECD and Andreas Schneider for launching the battle against neuromyths decades ago.

Sincere thanks to the wonderful editors at W. W. Norton for all they do to make science meaningful to teachers. Thank you, Deborah Malmud, Carol Collins, Mariah Eppes, and Kate Prince.

INTRODUCTION

Teachers care deeply about their students and about doing their jobs right, and many spend a lot of time immersed in new and improved ways to teach because they want to stay abreast of the latest and greatest the profession has to offer students. However, some of the information that reaches teachers about the brain and learning is less than perfect. So, how can teachers know what is good information about the brain and what should be avoided?

I have wondered about this question for decades. Ever since John Bruer (1997) suggested the challenges of using neuroscientific insights to inform education,[1] researchers have struggled to establish the precise role of **learning sciences**—the natural (biology, chemistry), neural (i.e., neuroscience, educational neuroscience), and social sciences (i.e., psychology, sociology)—in teacher education. Over the past 20 years we have constructed new evidence using these learning sciences that offers multiple ways to improve teacher practice, yet not all teachers receive quality training in this area. To get closer to an answer and a solid recommendation for educators, in 2006 I gathered a Delphi panel of experts related to Mind (psychology), Brain (neuroscience) and Education (pedagogy and didactics) Science (MBE) to determine what, if anything, was worthy of making its way out of the brain lab and into our classrooms. I conducted a 10-year follow-up to that study, which ended in 2017. More than a hundred invitations were sent to experts on all continents, 41 of whom complied. These experts came from 11 different countries and from all branches of the learning sciences. They were asked five questions. The panel members provided studies and peer-reviewed articles to support their viewpoints as they argued for the inclusion or exclusion of ideas. After reviewing more than 80 "brain-based" concepts in four rounds of debate, all the panel members accepted only six as being "true" for all brains (these are now known as *Principles*). That is, without exception, all human brains, independent of age, subject matter, or culture, adhere to these six Principles.

TABLE 0.1. MIND, BRAIN, AND EDUCATION PRINCIPLES 2017

Principles in Mind, Brain, and Education Science (2017)	
Principle 1	**Human brains are as unique as human faces.** While the basic structure of most human brains is the same (similar parts in similar regions), no two brains are identical. The genetic makeup unique to each person combines with life experiences (and free will) to shape neural pathways.
Principle 2	**Each individual's brain is differently prepared to learn different tasks.** Learning capacities are shaped by the context of the learning, prior learning experiences, personal choice, an individual's biology and genetic makeup, pre- and perinatal events, and environmental exposures.
Principle 3	**New learning is influenced by prior experiences.** The efficiency of the brain economizes effort and energy by ensuring that external stimuli are first decoded and compared, both passively and actively, with existing memories.
Principle 4	**The brain changes constantly with experience.** The brain is a complex, dynamic, and integrated system that is constantly changed by individual experiences. These changes occur at a molecular level, whether simultaneously, in parallel, or even before they are visible in behavior.
Principle 5	**The brain is plastic.** Neuroplasticity exists throughout the life span, though there are notable developmental differences by age.
Principle 6	**There is no new learning without some form of memory and some form of attention.** Most school learning requires well-functioning short, working, and long-term memory systems and conscious attention. However, procedural learning, habituation, sensitization, and even episodic memory can occur without conscious attention.

The panel also identified 21 concepts, which are also true but have a high degree of human variation, which are known as *Tenets*. The Principles and Tenets in MBE serve as the foundation for a new teacher education curriculum.

TABLE 0.2. MIND, BRAIN, AND EDUCATION TENETS 2017

Tenets in Mind, Brain, and Education Science (2017)	
Tenet 1	**Motivation influences learning** (however, what motivates one person and how may not motivate another in the same way).
Tenet 2	**Emotions and cognition are mutually influential.** Not all stimuli result in the same affective state for all people.
Tenet 3	**Stress influences learning** (but what stresses one person and how may not stress another in the same way).

Tenet 4	**Anxiety influences learning** (but what causes anxiety in one person may not cause anxiety in another).
Tenet 5	**Depression influences learning** (but what causes depression in one person may not cause depression in another).
Tenet 6	**Learning is influenced by both challenge and threat as perceived by the learner.** What a person finds challenging or threatening is highly individualized, as are their reactions to the stimuli.
Tenet 7	**Reactions to facial expressions are both universal and highly individualized:** they reflect human instincts, personal experiences and reactions to cultural expectations. (Exception: autism spectrum disorder.)
Tenet 8	**The brain interprets tones of voices unconsciously and almost immediately,** however, the reaction to the tones of voices is based in part on prior experience and therefore individualized.
Tenet 9	**Humans are social beings who learn from and with each other.** Social interactions influence learning. Different people desire different amounts of social interactions around learning.
Tenet 10	**Attention is a complex phenomenon comprised of multiple systems** (supporting functions such as metacognition, self-reflection, mindfulness, and meditation, as well as states of high alertness, selective attention, and focused attention), which work to different degrees in different relationships with one another.
Tenet 11	**Most learning does not occur linearly,** but rather advances and retracts based on stages of growth, reflection, and the amount of repetition to which one is exposed.
Tenet 12	**Learning involves conscious and unconscious processes,** which may differ by individuals based on their training and other individual experiences. Learning is also described as **implicit** (passive or unaware processes) and **explicit** (active or aware processes).
Tenet 13	**Learning is developmental (nature and nurture) as well as experiential (nurture):** a person's age, cognitive stage of development, and past experiences all contribute to learning and do so differently for each person.
Tenet 14	**Learning engages the entire physiology:** the body and brain interact to play a role in learning processes.
Tenet 15	**Sleep and dreaming influence learning in different ways:** sufficient sleep permits the brain to pay attention during wakeful states, and dreaming contributes to memory consolidation. The amount of sleep and dreaming individuals need can vary based on culture, circumstances, motivation, genetics, and learned sleep hygiene practices.
Tenet 16	**Nutrition influences learning.** Basic nutritional needs are common to all humans, though there are variations in the frequency of food intake and some dietary needs, which are unique to individuals.

Tenet 17	**Physical activity influences learning,** however, different individuals need different amounts of physical activity to perform optimally. Interspersing physical and cognitive activity may improve learning.
Tenet 18	**Use it or lose it:** Brains that remain active cognitively help development and can also stave off cognitive decline in the aging brain. However, individual variations, including experiences and genetic predispositions, influence the final outcomes of interventions.
Tenet 19	**Feedback about learning progress influences learning outcomes.** Feedback itself can be a source of learning. The type, frequency, and use of feedback can influence learning outcomes, which can also vary by individual.
Tenet 20	**It is easier to retrieve memories** when facts and skills have been **embedded in individually relevant and meaningful contexts**, (however, what is relevant or meaningful varies by individual).
Tenet 21	**Brains detect novelty and patterns** (however, what is novel or a pattern to one individual may not be novel or a pattern to another).

The evidence cited by the panelists in their review is open to the public for scrutiny on ResearchGate and the final results were based on more than 1,000 studies conducted between 1997 and 2017.[2] It is encouraging that many teachers see the Principles and the Tenets as quite intuitive as they reflect many best practice activities already incorporated in great schools. But a word of caution is needed.

The Delphi panelists warned against simplistic interpretations and cautioned that each of these short statements has volumes of research behind it. It is not enough to use these statements as mantras, but rather, teachers must learn about the evidence that substantiates the claims. Rather than adhering to slogans or maxims, they suggest teachers do a deep dive into the research underlying each concept in order to truly bridge the divide between educators and neuroscientists to improve student learning. Part of the Delphi panel process was to generate an open-source mini-library for each statement so evidence can be available for all to review and critique.[3] The panelists were concerned that if the Principles and Tenets do not become part of formal teacher education, they will likely be watered down, and risk turning into new myths, which would defeat the purpose of integrating neuroscience into teacher education. This means that it is not enough to know the Principles and Tenets by heart, but rather, it is important to know *why* they justify best practice in teaching. The risk is real because neuromyths have a certain allure about them.

WHY WE LOVE MYTHS

A myth is an elaborate tale that prods the imagination. All cultures use stories to explain complex phenomena. The Greeks' King Midas or the Norse myth of Thor help teach about the downfalls of greed, the rewards of persistence and strategy, and in some cases, are used to explain things we experience but don't understand. Myths are reflective of the level of scientific sophistication of their times, and still persist in abundance today. Like ancient Greek myths, current neuromyths are entertaining stories that try to explain complex phenomena, in this case, brain functioning. Neuromyths are sometimes based on fiction, misunderstandings, misbeliefs, misconceptions, or misinterpretations about how the brain learns. Thankfully, neuromyths are not only entertaining, but they can also teach lessons.

HOW DID WE GET HERE?
A BRIEF HISTORY OF HOW (WE THINK) WE KNOW THE BRAIN

The history of science is full of amazing celebrations. Thanks to the imaginative conception of "germs" and the ability to see them with microscopes (credit to Robert Hooke, whose writings in 1665 inspired scientific microscopy), epidemiologists can stop water and airborne diseases in their tracks. Thanks to vaccines and pasteurization, microorganism-contaminated foods are less common, and diphtheria, measles, smallpox, tetanus, typhoid, and polio are less frequent threats.[4] Thanks to advances in technology, we less often die of ulcers, abscesses, or fevers (because of penicillin and Alexander Fleming's work leading up the Nobel prize in 1945). The history of humanity has never seen such healthy bodies as we have today.

In more recent times, scientific celebrations have gone from saving bodies from disease to maximizing the potential of brains and minds. Dmitri Mendeleev's 1869 invention of the periodic table of the elements began our understanding of how different neurotransmitters can combine to either enhance or impede learning.[5] Friedrich Miescher's work[6] led to James Watson's and Francis Crick's[7] discoveries of DNA, showing how humans govern their own fates by passing on their genes and managing their environments in a balance of nature and nurture.[8] Wilhelm Conrad Röntgen's 1895 work with x-rays gave us a first insight as to what goes on inside the body and brain, which was followed by nuclear magnetic resonance imaging[9] that extended beyond views of damaged organs to being able to watch healthy brains actually strengthen neural networks of learning.[10] As science improves, knowledge improves. Human potential advances with each new insight and discovery. With each new finding, some myths about the brain emerge and others cease to exist. While it often looks like two steps forward and one step back, humanity has always inched toward a better understanding of itself.

One of the most interesting insights that can be gleaned from this quick review of the history of science is how technological advances change people's visions of their worlds. It is understandable that before good scientific tools were found, people believed that the gods were responsible for everything, from the weather to illness. Being "cursed" for bad actions or choices was a natural consequence in which disease served to mediate morality. Given the limits of science at different periods in history, it was easy and even reasonable to believe that "bad air" (*mal aria* in Medieval Italian) from the swamps caused thousands of deaths in the 1400s, rather than being carried by mosquitoes. Insufficient information can lead to logical but erroneous hypotheses, which are generally corrected over time thanks to advances in technology that allow us to "see" more than meets the eye.

More than two thousand years ago, limited by technology but not by imagination, the Greeks looked at the patterns in world order and tried to map them onto the human condition. They believed that *humors* found in four liquids in the body (blood, phlegm, black bile, and yellow bile), were aligned with the four elements (earth, water, fire and air) and the four seasons of the year (Winter, Spring, Summer, Fall). Stable health depended on a good balance of humors, elements, and the seasons. This explanation gave way to the belief in the gods' (and then to God's) work, and that in turn was complemented with scientific explanations. In the two-steps-forward-one-step back shuffle, some of these original thoughts remain today. For example, Aristotle's belief that all new learning occurs through sense perception has withstood the test of time and is currently supported by new technologies. This means two things: Not all old ideas are wrong, and that to have a good idea, one has to test multiple hypotheses.

Throughout history, human imagination has been a double-edged sword. On one hand, it pushes new discoveries, but for every newly established scientific fact, there are often multiple erroneous hypotheses, which must be corrected along the way or risk becoming myths. Thomas Edison is credited with saying: "I have not failed. I've just found 10,000 ways that won't work,"[11] implying that error is part of invention. Unfortunately, if errors or partial truths get circulated long enough, they can lead to a false echo chamber of repetition and suggest "truth" where none exists. For example, even though the *humors* have been discredited for centuries, some still believe in the myth that blood types (blood being one of the four *humors*) can determine personalities.[12] A quick Google search finds more than five million websites related to this topic, meaning this myth is slow to die.

In science, there are actually no truths, but rather *evidence* or *lack of evi-*

dence, which fluctuate based on improvements in technology and better and more research studies. When there is sufficient evidence, scientific knowledge grows, myths can be definitively categorized and blocked from use, and we all benefit. What is a myth and what is evidence-based relies heavily on good technology and quality research. The growing interest in the brain and learning has occurred so rapidly over the past two decades that gaps in understanding have emerged. Many teacher training programs still do not offer enough information about the brain, leaving teachers vulnerable to neuromyths. This leads us to modern times.

HUMANS ARE GETTING SMARTER OVER TIME, *BUT . . .*

The Flynn Effect is a phenomenon that shows humankind has become smarter over the years,[13] at least as far as intelligence tests are concerned. The average kid is doing better on IQ tests, children are entering kindergarten knowing more letters and numbers than their peers of a generation ago, and humans around the world in both developed and developing countries are benefiting from their "enhanced cognitive environments."[14] Part of the reason people are getting smarter is thanks to the sheer amount of information available, often at low or no cost, easily accessible and plentiful over the Internet. Others say it is due to the need for more complex problem solving and new uses of the information available.

While people seem to be reaping many benefits from having so much information at their fingertips, this has also caused the proliferation of additional neuromyths. Like a small child in a candy store, some adults believe that *quantity* (the sheer number of websites that exist) often competes with *quality* information that comes from good research. This creates a new challenge in education. Whereas my generation had to rush to the university library for a copy of the class textbook to do the homework—signifying a *deficit in access* to information—the current generation is bombarded by information but doesn't always choose the right sources, signifying a *deficit in criteria* for identifying good information. The second problem is arguably more serious, as quality, not only quantity of information, is what moves science and education forward.

Changes in technology have helped humanity learn collectively at a quicker pace, but this has also posed problems for many who were never explicitly taught digital critical thinking skills. While there are gallant efforts to try to curb the spread of "fake news" and to teach skills to identify poor information,[15] misinformation will continue to spread until basic thinking skills are both modeled by teachers and taught in schools explicitly. This means teachers today need to learn a new set of research skills, which have not yet made it into all training programs.[16] Teachers are now faced with the challenges of helping kids separate the wheat from the chaff in order to avoid myths, and judging multiple sources of information quickly and across disciplines. However, teachers themselves are often limited in these skill sets through no fault of their own, as the flood of information is relatively recent. Teachers' preservice digital literacy is just beginning to creep into university education programs and, as of 2018, there were still only a handful of degree programs in the United States that required that teachers learn about how to manage the massive flow of information their students will grow up with effortlessly. The average teacher in the world is 40 years old, meaning they received their training about 20 years ago when the Internet was just in its infancy.[17] It is no surprise that the overwhelming amount of information on the Internet and published in the popular press causes teachers and others in the community to doubt what is "true" (has evidence behind it), and what is a neuromyth. Teachers have never before been asked to critique so many claims about the brain and learning and to judge the quality of the information being presented as they are now. This is an explanation for why so many teachers believe neuromyths. However, it is not an excuse for allowing them to continue.

THE PREVALENCE OF NEUROMYTHS

It's hard to stay up to date on a subject as dynamic as the *brain and learning*. The field of educational neuroscience published around 380 articles in 2016, with findings from the broad topic of general cognition to very precise neural networks for decoding phonemes to read or recognizing numerical symbols to do math. The field of Mind, Brain, and Education science (MBE) had about 1,000 publications in 2016 that considered the broader implications of findings about the brain and learning, such as how a person's internal sense of time affects their ability to learn, or how social interactions and emotions affect cognition. The umbrella field of the "learning sciences" published more than 7,000 articles in 2016 and touched on the broader definition of learning across species.

Teachers are responsible for the best learning possible in their classrooms, and this often means they have little time to read often highly technical peer-reviewed journals, despite knowing that this information can potentially help them do their jobs better. Bridging neuroscience and education is a hot topic—after all, the brain is the organ of a teacher's professional existence. Two very different offspring have resulted from teachers' needs for information about the brain, their sincere interest to learn, and the reality of limited time.

On the one hand, there is a booming industry to offer teacher professional development on the brain and learning around the world. The allure of the brain

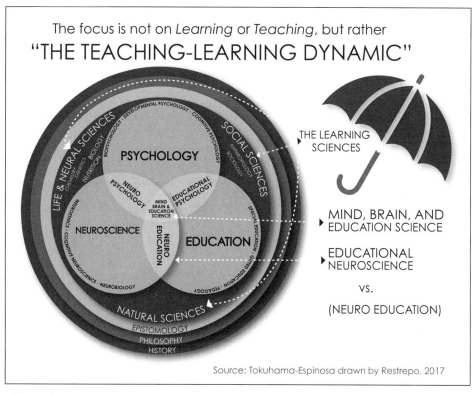

The focus is not on *Learning* or *Teaching*, but rather

"THE TEACHING-LEARNING DYNAMIC"

Source: Tokuhama-Espinosa drawn by Restrepo, 2017

Figure 0.1: *The Learning Sciences as an umbrella concept under which Mind, Brain, and Education Science, Educational Neuroscience, and Neuroeducation*

and the "sexiness" of neuro-*anything* have led to a mixed bag of information for teachers. Unfortunately, the research shows that one-off conferences do little to change teachers' fundamental beliefs about how humans learn, gain intelligence, or thrive in our classrooms.[18] Even explicit instruction debunking neuromyths does not significantly reduce belief in those myths.[19] This means that more than a professional development conference is needed to bridge the gap and eliminate myths from teacher practice. This leads to the second offspring.

On the other hand, now we see the development of a new type of professional— an MBE scientist, or "learning scientist," who seeks to work at the intersection of neuroscience, psychology, and education. Among MBE professionals there are at least three types of researchers. Some do *original* research, some do *collaborative* research, and others do *translational* research. Those in translational research try to bridge communication gaps among neuroscientists, psychologists, and educators. Part of this translation means interpreting the findings from neuroscience for educators, and from classroom settings to laboratory researchers. Quality translational research is the key to dispelling myths.

While born of the same necessity—improved scientific literacy for teachers—these two offspring often look like rivals as they send mixed messages. On the one hand, the translators want us teachers to understand that the brain is the most complex organism in the universe[20] and on the other hand, the conference organizers want us to believe that we can learn techniques in a one-hour session that "maximize the potential of all learners in a classroom." Both cannot be true. Teachers must embrace the complexity of the brain and trust more in the translators than the "brain-based" commercial ventures, or they risk missing the opportunity to modernize the teaching profession by becoming learning scientists. Neuromyths present a wonderful opportunity to advance this purpose. Howard-Jones[21] writes:

> The study of neuromyths and how they develop may provide a valuable source of insight into the challenges of interdisciplinary communication between neuroscience and education, and into how these challenges might be addressed. Understanding the cultural distance to be travelled between neuroscience and education—and the biases that distort communications along the way—may support a dispassionate assessment of the progress in developing a bridge across these diverse disciplines and of what is needed to complete it.

Working together to dispel neuromyths can serve as common ground for neuroscientists, psychologists, and educators.

The growing interest in the brain in teacher education has revealed gaps of understanding that must be addressed in order to improve the use of high-quality information and eliminate the neuromyths. Both initial teacher education in universities and continuous professional development through conferences, courses, and books need revision. The inclusion of courses on brain and learning concepts such as plasticity, memory, attention, cognition, and emotion is being discussed by some leaders in higher education for new teacher formation.[22] However, teachers who are already in the classroom also need to update their knowledge base.

Unfortunately, a little knowledge *is* a dangerous thing. It seems that nearly all teachers have some misunderstandings about the brain.[23] Rather than get good information from universities, many teachers often receive professional development from commercial bodies that do little to eliminate neuromyths, and sometimes even promote them. When presented with 32 statements about the brain, Dekker and colleagues found "on average, teachers believed 49% of the neuromyths, particularly myths related to commercialized educational programs."[24] Just like Greek myths, many of these ideas have intriguing story lines and draw the reader into an interesting plot. *Do we really just use 10% of our brains? Can we really learn to multitask?* But unlike Greek myths, the lessons come from an explanation of the backstory, rather than from the intriguing plots and headlines.

Myths do harm: They create the wrong environments in our schools, limit the potential of our students, and reduce the human capital of our societies. While it might sound cliché, expectations of teachers have changed in modern times. Teachers need to be the guardians of new scientific knowledge, and help translate scientific findings into their classrooms. The evolving profile of the modern educator is more complex than ever and requires new competencies, including the ability to judge the quality of research as it relates to the brain and learning. One of the most effective ways to improve education and student learning outcomes in the shortest possible amount of time and with the fewest resources is to educate teachers about neuromyths.[25]

Staying up to date is part of any job, and this is a particularly big challenge where science is concerned. Research must become more palatable to teachers, which means a greater role for translators, who help neuroscientists understand real classrooms, and real classroom teachers understand the lab. The changing profile of educators means that teachers are no longer average citizens to be lured by newspaper headlines, but rather *learning scientists* who understand the quality of evidence behind claims. As part of the new learning science community, teachers should permit themselves to be entertained, but also to be wary of exciting headlines such as "Lobes of Steel",[26] "Extreme parenting: does the baby genius edutainment complex enrich your child's mind or stifle it?",[27] and "All Gas and No Brakes"[28] about adolescent brains. This book hopes to contribute to a new researcher-practitioner model that requires teachers to be more skeptical consumers of data, and arms them with better tools to do so.

Neuromythical beliefs are found at all levels of education, from preschool to university, and there is evidence they abound all around the world in about the same measure. According to Howard-Jones, "this prevalence may reflect the fact that neuroscience is rarely included in the training of teachers," meaning that teachers aren't taught "to be critical of ideas and educational programmes that claim a neuroscientific basis."[29] Teachers around the world are in need of better training to avoid myths and better understand the brain, for the simple reason that it is the organ through which all learning occurs. A big part of understanding the brain is learning what it is, and isn't, capable of doing. This book is meant to assist students in teacher training programs, experienced teachers, and concerned citizens to identify and dispel myths that *can* do harm in education.

WHAT IS A NEUROMYTH?

The word "neuromyth" is a compound word that joins *neuro*, as in the cells related to the nervous system and the brain, with *myth*, as in "a widely held but false belief or idea,"[30] effectively *false beliefs about the brain and/or its functioning*. Howard-Jones writes that "the first use of the term neuromyth was attributed to the neurosurgeon Alan Crockard, who coined it in the 1980s when he referred to unscientific ideas about the brain in medical culture,"[31] and that myths are often "biased distortions of scientific fact."[32] The Centre For Educational Neuroscience at the University College of London says neuromyths are often "teaching practices, ideas, or techniques that do not actually have a scientific basis in neuroscience."[33] Neuromyths are misunderstandings or misconceptions about the brain and how it functions that can limit human potential.

WHERE DO NEUROMYTHS COME FROM?

While all myths result in bad information, they can originate from many different sources. Myths exist because humans want things to be easy (complexity is rejected; reductionism; oversimplification of findings). They also emerge due to lack of scientific literacy and/or expert knowledge. Distortion of scientific facts also leads to neuromyths, as do misinterpretations of experimental results and confirmation bias. Many unscrupulous businesses use myths, which are the offspring of scientific hypothesis but proven untrue, for commercial benefits. Some popular press reports repeat myths because they are often based on partial truths and because they have sensationalist value. Some myths cited in scientific articles are true for animals, but there is little evidence they are true in school children. Some myths were true using old technology, but not with better imaging techniques. Others are based on good, but sparse evidence, or come from a confusion of correlation vs. causation (the belief that one thing causes another rather than that it simply occurred at the same time), or on absence vs. existence (believing that a damaged area of the brain uniquely correlates to lost skill sets). Some myths are an overgeneralization of findings based on small samplings, or research done on adults but not on children. There are also myths that can appear true in lab contexts, but not necessarily in real schools or homes. And the flames of all myths are fanned by *bandwagonitis*,[34] in which people jump on board, just because others have.

WHY NEUROMYTHS DO HARM, BUT CAN BE ALSO BE OPPORTUNITIES

The primary reason neuromyths are considered problematic in education is because they actually *do harm*. Telling girls they don't have the same potential for learning science or math as boys, *does harm*, as does telling someone she has a learning style incompatible with the teacher's teaching style. Believing that intelligence is fixed rather than fluid *does harm*. Neuromyths are negative influences on quality education because they create false barriers to learning. That said, every problem has the potential to be an opportunity.

Neuromyths provide an opportunity to learn about scientific inquiry and can serve as prime teaching moments. There have been calls for teachers to receive more rigid education in research methodology and scientific literacy to improve the chances of avoiding myths.[35] Neuromyths need not only be the subjects of inquiry—they can also serve as the means by which to instruct about good research practice.

Many people think that the myths of yesterday are the truths of today, as if science is slowly but surely proving humans' inability to identify a falsehood, but rather the opposite is true and "today's myths were yesterday's facts."[36] In 2008, there were 29 neuromyths that the experts found in the literature, and just 5 well-established facts.[37] In 2016, there were 44 neuromyths and 6 well-established facts,[38] and research for this book in 2018 yielded more than 70 neuromyths.

It was fascinating to note that few concepts identified as neuromyths, or as being well-established facts in 2008, changed categories in 2018. However, many things that were considered intelligent speculation were moved to being neuromyths. This means it is very hard to earn the labels of *well-established* or *neuromyth*, but those concepts in the middle (*probably so* or *intelligent speculation*) are prone to change, thanks to better technology and more studies. Once something is labeled a myth it is nearly impossible to change status.

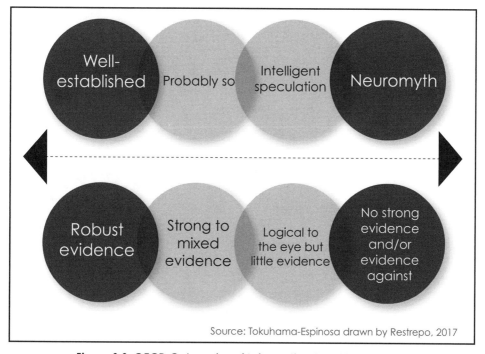

Source: Tokuhama-Espinosa drawn by Restrepo, 2017

Figure 0.2: OECD Categories of Information Read by Teachers

TABLE 0.3 NEUROMYTHS IN 2006, 2016, AND 2018

Type	Neuromyths	Year of Publication			
		1997, 2002, 2007[1]	2006–2008[2]	2016–2017[3]	2018
Myths about Intelligence	1. Mental capacity is hereditary				X
	2. Intelligence is fixed, not fluid				X
	3. There is no such thing as genius				X
	4. Most people use about 10% of their brains	X	X	X	X
	5. Listening to classical music makes you smarter: The Mozart Effect		X	X	X
	6. Male and female brains are designed for different types of skills	X	X	X	X
	7. There are brain differences based on race		X	X	X
	8. Vaccines cause Autism				X
Myths about Brain Architecture and Structure	9. The left and right hemispheres of the brain are separate systems for learning	X	X	X	X
	10. Short bouts of coordination exercises improve integration of left and right hemispheric brain functions	X	X	X	X
	11. Some people are more "right" brained and others are more "left" brained	X	X	X	X
	12. There is a "localizationism" of academic skills in the brain				X
	13. Brain parts work in isolation		X	X	X
	14. Keeping a "cool head" (thinking without emotions) improves learning		X	X	X
	15. Feelings are produced in the heart and thinking in the brain				X
	16. Creativity is in the right hemisphere of the brain				X
	17. Your brain will shrink if you don't drink six to eight glasses of water a day		X	X	X
	18. The bigger your brain, the smarter you are				X
	19. Brain scanners "see" thinking				X

Type	Neuromyths	Year of Publication			
		1997, 2002, 2007[1]	2006–2008[2]	2016–2017[3]	2018
Myths about Teaching and Learning	20. Individuals learn better when they receive information in their preferred learning styles		X	X	X
	21. The Theory of Multiple Intelligences is validated by neuroscientific research		X	X	X
	22. Intrinsic motivation is driven by external reward				X
	23. Teachers' subject knowledge and instructional strategies are more important than student relationships				X
	24. Students should be rewarded all the time to elicit dopamine				X
	25. Students should be given positive reinforcement to speed learning processes				X
	26. Students must be exposed to new information between three and seven times to learn it effectively		X	X	X
	27. Unstructured discovery learning is preferable to structured, teacher-centered instruction		X	X	X
	28. Intelligence tests measure intelligence				X
Myths about Human Development	29. Humans are born with a "blank slate" and they will learn if knowledge is simply provided		X	X	X
	30. Humans are born with all of the neurons they will ever have	X		X	X
	31. Everything important about the brain is determined by the age of three	X	X	X	X
	32. Brain development is complete by the time a person reaches secondary school			X	X
	33. Human learning progresses linearly			X	X
	34. Learning problems associated with developmental differences in brain function cannot be remediated with education			X	X
	35. The "terrible twos" and "crazy adolescence" are inevitable and always negative		X	X	X

Type	Neuromyths	Year of Publication			
		1997, 2002, 2007[1]	2006–2008[2]	2016–2017[3]	2018
Myths about Learning Environments	36. Humans need enriched environments in order to develop their natural potential	X	X	X	X
	37. Violent video games have no effect on behavior			X	X
	38. Using the Internet makes you smarter/dumber				X
	39. Learning is independent of the learner's history				
	40. "Brain training" is supported by neuroscience				X
	41. All knowledge has to be actively constructed by a learner		X	X	X
	42. Self-perception is less important than IQ in academic achievement			X	X
	43. Brain activity depends entirely on sensory input				X
	44. Playing computer games keeps your brain young				X
Myths about the Mind-Body Balance	45. Your brain uses 20% of the body's calories, so sugary drinks help cognition			X	X
	46. Dietary supplements improve cognition				X
	47. Omega-3 pills enhance the mental capacity of children in the general population			X	X
	48. When you sleep, your brain shuts down			X	X
	49. People can learn in their sleep	X	X	X	X
Myths about Brain Plasticity	50. Critical periods limit learning parameters	X	X	X	X
	51. You can't grow new brain cells		X	X	X
	52. Brain damage is always permanent				X
	53. Neural plasticity is due to good pedagogy		X	X	X
Myths about Memory	54. The brain has unlimited memory capacity		X	X	X
	55. Memorization is unnecessary for learning and undesirable in modern education		X	X	X
	56. Memory is in a single network in the brain (keeping a phone number in memory until dialing, recalling recent events, and remembering distant experiences all use the same memory system)			X	X
	57. The Learning Pyramid: People only remember 10% of what they read				X

Type	Neuromyths	Year of Publication			
		1997, 2002, 2007[1]	2006–2008[2]	2016–2017[3]	2018
Myths about Attention	58. The brain can "Multitask"			X	X
	59. Learning can occur without attention				X
	60. Attention is a single network in the brain (orienting towards a loud noise, concentrating on reading a passage in a book and deciding what is important all use the same attention system)				X
	61. Children are less attentive after sugary snacks			X	X
	62. Attention is unaffected by sleep				X
Myths about Language, Bilingualism, and Multilingualism	63. Language is located in the left hemisphere of the brain		X	X	X
	64. Adults cannot learn a foreign language as fast as a child				X
	65. Children must acquire their native language before learning a second	X	X	X	X
	66. Children learn skills effortlessly, including foreign languages				X
	67. All language functions use the same brain networks (recalling the meaning of a word, being able to sound out a word, and interpreting the emotional intention of a written word use the same brain networks)				X
	68. Crawling is necessary for literacy				X

Source: [1]OECD, 1997, 2002; [2]Author, based on 2006–2008 Delphi Panel on Mind, Brain, and Education; Alferink & Farmer-Dougan, 2010; Howard-Jones, 2014; Pasquinelli, 2012; [3]Author, 2016–2017 Delphi Panel on Mind, Brain, and Education.

More myths are a sign of more discoveries and an indication of human imagination at work. Once recognized, however, the lessons they share should be learned.

WHAT TO EXPECT IN THIS BOOK

This book is about how the brain learns best, based on the most recent information from Mind (psychology), Brain (neuroscience), and Education science and focuses on eliminating neuromyths that harm our educational practice. The 2017

Delphi panelists agreed that teachers' belief in neuromyths was one of the greatest, if not *the* greatest, barriers to improving education. At the 2016 International Mind, Brain, and Education Society meeting in Toronto, the leadership lamented the same: The single greatest difficulty in improving teacher practice was teachers' beliefs in neuromyths. This worry was echoed by The Wellcome Trust[39] in the UK and the OECD[40] in Paris. More than 200 books and articles have been written about neuromyths, but to date, few academic programs train teachers in how to avoid them. This book is a resource to help improve teacher practice based on MBE guidelines by first eliminating myths and then using evidence-based practices to structure better classes.

To approach the dozens of neuromyths that are out there in an orderly way, we've divided them into 10 large categories: myths about **intelligence** (Chapter 1); **brain architecture** (Chapter 2); **teaching and learning** (Chapter 3); **human development** (Chapter 4); **learning environments** (Chapter 5); the **mind-body balance** (Chapter 6); **brain plasticity** (Chapter 7); **memory** (Chapter 8); **attention** (Chapter 9); and **language**, bilingualism, and multilingualism (Chapter 10).

Chapter 11 looks at effective practice to avoid myths in the future. The book closes with reflections on teacher education in the future, and offers teachers tools to improve their practice. The big takeaway from this book is that while myths might be fun and entertaining, they can also teach us valuable lessons that are key to better teacher education.

We begin with a look at Myths about Intelligence.

1 • MYTHS ABOUT

INTELLIGENCE

MENTAL CAPACITY IS HEREDITARY

Perhaps the most classic question in psychology is whether you are who you are due to your nature (genes), or nurture (environment). Were you born with behavioral traits, or did they emerge from your interaction with the world around you? Humans have contemplated this since the Greeks, into the Enlightenment, and it continues today.

Where the Myth Comes From

The question about whether intelligence comes from your genes or the environment has existed for centuries. Darwin's *Theory of Evolution* (1859) and the belief in the survival of the fittest assumes that the best genes are the ones that come out on top. *"The Inheritance of Intelligence,"*[1] *"The Relative Influence of Inherited and Acquired Traits in Determining Intelligence, Achievement, and Character,"*[2] and *"The Genetics of Intelligence"*[3] were all articles from the early 20th century that leaned toward the belief that mental capacity is hereditary and cannot be changed by experiences, such as schooling. Other studies in the not-so-distant past[4] showed rat intelligence seemed highly dependent on genes, so why not human intelligence as well? The argument in favor of genes reached a peak in the 1990s, when questions were asked about what percentage of intelligence was gene-based in Herrnstein and Murray's *The Bell Curve*.[5]

So, while we can look forward to a future in which science discovers how to foster intelligence environmentally and how to use the science humanely, inherited cognitive ability is now extremely important. In this sense, luck continues to matter in life's outcomes, but now it is more a matter of the IQ handed out in life's lottery than anything else . . .[6]

There were quick reactions to the claims that nature weighs more than nurture in determining cognitive outcomes,[7] which sought more politically correct ideas about human potential. These later publications argued for the vital role of environment in gene potentiation and the general nature-to-nurture interplay that leads to intelligence. While the jury is still out on an exact percentage of nature vs. nurture, more recent titles suggest the belief in *Nature via Nurture*.[8]

What We Know Now

We now believe that the construction of intelligence is complex. Mental capacity is not entirely hereditary, nor entirely dependent on the environment. We have limited evidence that richly stimulating environments can make great learners out of people born with low intelligence[9] and robust evidence that environments devoid of normal stimuli can keep people from reaching their genetic potential. What is clear is that the environment and experience, as well as schooling, social-educational policies and free will, can modify outcomes that benefit the individual and society.[10] Positive school environments can make up, to a certain extent, for poor homes.[11]

It is also clear that intelligence is not purely hereditary, and that mental capacity is not only represented in intelligence. Mental capacity can be improved with learning, even if native intelligence cannot. Extra training does not increase intelligence,[12] but it can help improve skill sets and academic outcomes, and make an individual appear smarter.[13] We also know that children are not condemned to the brains they are born with. Thanks to a better understanding of neural plasticity, we know humans can and do learn throughout the life span. According to Doidge, "we are all born with a far more adaptable, all-purpose, opportunistic brain than we have understood"[14] in the past. While hereditary traits are important, they are not destiny.

INTELLIGENCE IS FIXED AT BIRTH

The belief that people are born either smart or not is related to the previous myth that mental capacity is inherited. If you think cognitive abilities are inherited, you weigh in heavily on the side of nature, and the idea that a person gets his or her cognitive abilities through the parents' genes ("you are your biology"). This way of thinking leads people to believe that everything about them, including intelligence, is settled by their genetic makeup, what Carol Dweck has called a "fixed mindset."[15] This is in contradiction to a flexible or growth mindset, in which the individual believes he or she has control over all aspects of life, including becoming smarter. Headlines such as *Intelligence Genes Discovered by Scientists*[16] lead people to believe that cognitive abilities are inherited, and therefore, cannot be remedied by education or other life experiences. Dweck's work shows that:

> students who believed their intelligence could be developed (a growth mindset) outperformed those who believed their intelligence was fixed (a fixed mindset). And when students learned through a structured program that they could "grow their brains" and increase their intellectual abilities, they did better.[17]

This means that improving learning outcomes is dependent on the individual's belief that mental capacity can be changed. This gives credence to John Hattie's major meta-analysis of hundreds of meta-analyses showing that a student's self-perception as a learner influences learning outcome, independent of intelligence levels.[18] If you think you can learn, you will; if you don't think you can learn, you don't even try.[19]

But nature vs. nurture remains a complex question. The work of Robert Plomin and Ian Deary of King's College, London[20] considered 11,000 pairs of twins, and Polderman and colleagues' work in the Netherlands looked at "virtually all published twin studies of complex traits" covering 14,558,903 partly dependent twin pairs.[21] Despite being incredibly comprehensive, these studies do not definitively answer what percentage of intelligence is based on genetics.

One of the reasons this question is so complex is because it is easier to identify genetic influences on intelligence than it is environmental influences. Genes involve traits inherited from a mother and a father, which are complex in and of themselves, but even more multifarious are environmental influences that can include almost anything: school size, socioeconomic status, breastfeeding, water fluoridation, culture, bullying, number of siblings, music lessons, housing, nutrition practices, sleep habits, number of books read during childhood, and so on. Environmental influences are much harder to measure.

Where the Myth Comes From

Once it was understood that at least some of intelligence comes from genes, it became easy to accept that "intelligence is mostly inherited,"[22] even though that has not yet been determined. Also, it is clear that intelligence is a human trait. Gregor Mendel's principles of inheritance, first published in 1866, are still shared in nearly all basic biology classes around the world; his experiments with pea plants demonstrated just how predictably traits pass from generation to generation. This means that many people are exposed to information about heritable traits. Most do not receive equal exposure, however, to information about environmental influences. Thus, this myth is due in part to information bias.

There are multiple studies that question whether or not fluid intelligence can actually be improved. Does cognitive training improve intelligence itself, or just working memory skills? If the definition of fluid intelligence *includes* working memory, then training does help. Fluid intelligence is "the ability to reason and to solve new problems independently of previously acquired knowledge," according to Jaeggi and colleagues, and it "is critical for a wide variety of cognitive tasks, and it is considered one of the most important factors in learning."[23] Reasoning and problem solving (part of fluid intelligence) both rely heavily on working memory.[24] This means that the myth originates in part from how we define *intelligence*.

What We Know Now

We now know that both nature (genes) and nurture (environment) play roles in shaping cognitive abilities, and that it is likely that nurture has the greatest influence in the early years, but that the environment plays a greater role in later life.[25] And we also know that high-quality educational interventions can remediate the deficits caused both by nature and by nurture to maximize the potential of students.[26] We also now know that fluid intelligence is comprised of multiple elements, including working memory, attention, and the ability to reason and problem-solve, which can all be improved with training.[27] This shows that intelligence is fluid, not fixed, and that people can become smarter with training.

THERE IS NO SUCH THING AS GENIUS

Genius refers to exceptional intellectual abilities as well as to creative thinking.[28] Since Galton's time, hereditary genius has been explored based on evidence from "the whole organic world,"[29] which seems pretty convincing. Being "gifted" is also often related to the concept of genius.[30] For many years it was believed that one had to be born a genius to achieve that status, until K. Anders Ericsson came along. Ericsson[31] suggested that with enough practice, anyone can *appear* to be an expert, and that the illusion of genius could be attributed to simple hard work. Ericsson suggested that with around 10,000 hours of rehearsal of a musical instrument, for example, a person could appear to be a gifted musician. For the past decade, the running theory is that hard work and practice are the only things geniuses have over regular people. However, this is wrong.

Where the Myth Comes From

The "*My Fair Lady* concept," in which anyone off the street can be molded into a high-class personality, along with the Horatio Alger belief that anyone can grow up to be anything, promotes this myth. While this view is encouraging and instills a sense of hopeful optimism, it is a myth nonetheless. The belief that genius is nothing more than lots of practice by average people was born of an incomplete reading of Ericsson's work and the desire to believe that everyone has the potential to be gifted. While everyone can improve, not everyone is a genius.

What We Know Now

There are true geniuses in the world, at least as measured by scores on intelligence tests.[32] One in 1,000 people is highly gifted, and about one in 100,000 is exceptionally gifted. We now know that while some people can achieve levels of expertise through guided rehearsal, as Ericsson suggested, a small number of people, roughly one in 100,000, can be classified as hereditary geniuses.

MOST PEOPLE USE ABOUT 10% OF THEIR BRAINS

One of the most prevalent myths in the popular press is that we use only 10% of our brains. This has been mentioned in more articles out to debunk myths than any other.[33] Unfortunately, despite efforts to eliminate the myth, even college-educated students believed this myth.[34] *The Skeptical Inquirer*[35] writes:

> That tired Ten-Percent claim pops up all the time. Last year, national magazine ads for U.S. Satellite Broadcasting showed a drawing of a brain. Under it was the caption, 'You only use 11 percent of its potential.' Well, they're a little closer than the ten-percent figure, but still off by about 89 percent.

The prevalence of the 10% myth appears regularly in TV ads, newspapers and magazines and shows only small signs of decline.

Where the Myth Comes From

There are several probable roots of this myth. Back in the 1800s, Harvard psychologist William James is said to have suggested that humans are using only a fraction of their potential, which is one possible source. Another likely culprit is technology. When neuroimaging was first used in numerous studies at the end of the 1990s, it was common to "see" just small areas of the brain illuminated during the experiments, and some people presumed this meant that just a small portion of the brain was being used. Another thought is that "the 10-percent myth became popular with the self-help teachings of Dale Carnegie, as a way of helping people think about how to realize their own potential."[36] Others suggest that the 10% myth is linked to people selling ways to unleash psychic power.[37]

What We Know Now

There is no study that definitively identifies a percentage of the brain being used. However, the most up-to-date brain imaging available shows intricate networks throughout the brain in most tasks. Beyerstein[38] offered evidence to eliminate the myth by noting that if just 10% were used, brain damage would have to be limited to those few places, when we know that in actuality, brain damage has been documented in every part of the brain. He also suggested that brain scans show activity (blood flow, electrical and chemical changes) in all areas and that the brain is the most demanding organ in the body, using 20% of the body's energy while occupying 2% of the body's weight, which would be unlikely if only 10% of the brain were being used. He also argues that both PET and fMRI neuroimaging shows that the brain is active even during sleep and that no area is completely inactive. There is evidence of broad network activity rather than simple "localizationalism," where small, specific parts of the brain are used. He also argues that microstructural analysis would have offered evidence of disuse if it existed, and that synaptic pruning would be evident in autopsies. These explanations show the fallacies in believing we use only 10% of our brains.

LISTENING TO CLASSICAL MUSIC MAKES YOU SMARTER: THE MOZART EFFECT

The belief that classical music makes people smarter was born from decades of speculation about the links between cognition, music, and natural rhythms in the brain. The earliest inklings came from the Greeks, but the first lab trials were suggested in 1988. Gordon Shaw and Xiaodan Leng of the University of California at Irvine, hypothesized that higher-order thinking could be stimulated through music.[39] These theoretical papers were followed by published experiments on 36 college students.[40] The students were divided into three groups. The first listened to Mozart, the second group listened to a relaxing tape, and the third had 10 minutes of silence. The students who listened to Mozart "scored 8 to 9 points higher on the spatial IQ reasoning subtest of the Stanford-Binet Intelligence Scale" as compared to the other groups.[41] The benefits of this enhanced spatial reasoning lasted only 10 to 15 minutes (the time of the testing). To see if additional exposure would extend the benefits of spatial reasoning, 84 college students were exposed to Mozart over five consecutive days. After the second day, the results were similar to the first findings. Furthermore, Phillip Glass's piano music did not have the same effects as Mozart, emboldening the authors to suggest that there was something special about Mozart.

The findings were so dramatic that they were immediately suspicious. The Mozart Effect's grand claims were soon put to the test as dozens of scientists tried to replicate the findings. In 1999, *"Prelude or Requiem for the 'Mozart Effect'?"* Chabris[42] explained results from a first meta-analysis that showed that the small benefits of music exposure could be attributed to "enjoyment arousal" but not to the complex neurological explanations offered by the original authors.

Despite the evidence to the contrary, individuals, schools, and whole governments continue to invest money in the Mozart Effect, and the pseudo-phenomenon receives lots of press. Chip Heath of Stanford University and colleague Adriana Bangerther in Switzerland found that "the Mozart Effect received the most newspaper mentions in those U.S. states with the weakest educational systems,"[43] meaning that the less prepared the school system, the more gullible. The *Yale Scientific: The Nation's Oldest College Science Publication* noted that there were multiple cases of low socioeconomic status (SES) school districts which adopted playing classical music to small children.

> In 1998, Governor Zell Miller's budget proposition allocated $105,000 to buying classical music CDs for every newborn in the state of Georgia. In 2000, a South China Morning Post article read that "babies who hear Così Fan Tutte or the 'Mass in C Minor' during gestation are likely to come out of the womb smarter than their peers," and the Times of India has referred to the Mozart effect as "music curry for the soul." Although the idea that listening to classical music increases intelligence has become popular worldwide, most scientific evidence fails to support such a connection.[44]

Not only is this a case where a myth does harm, but it removes much-needed resources from other school programs.

Where the Myth Comes From

It is attractive to believe that something as simple as classical music exposure for a few minutes can improve reasoning, recall, and learning in general. The initial positive results fueled excitement and soon turned into *bandwagonitis*. Some follow-up studies showed slight positive results, but these were caused by temporary arousal due to novelty and/or a type of placebo effect in which wanting something to work increases the probability of positive results.

What We Know Now

In 2010, a meta-analysis of these efforts was documented by Pietschnig and colleagues entitled "Mozart effect–Shmozart effect: A meta-analysis." In this paper, the authors summarized nearly 40 studies and found only a slight improvement with music versus no music, and a negligible difference between Mozart and other types of music. They concluded that "on the whole, there is little evidence left for a specific, performance-enhancing Mozart effect."[45] We now know that the initial premise that "syncing" the brain to musical rhythms based on "predictions of a structured neuronal model of the cortex"[46] has not yet been proven, however the use of music to arouse attention can offer limited benefits in the short term.

MALE AND FEMALE BRAINS ARE DESIGNED FOR DIFFERENT TYPES OF SKILLS

The first musings about differences between males and females was based on the intelligent speculation that if men and women are different from the outside (their bodies), they must also be different on the inside (in their brains). Darwin[47] writes:

> . . . *sexual selection apparently has acted on man, both on the male and female side, causing the two sexes to differ in body and mind, and the several races to differ from each other in various characters, as well as from their ancient and lowly-organised progenitors.*

The first study actually showing some physiological difference was in 1854, with Emil Huschke's finding that men's frontal lobes were slightly larger (1%) than women's. (It escaped people at the time that almost every part of a man's body is slightly larger than a woman's.) The belief that men are naturally smarter than women paralleled other misconceptions from the 19th century, including the idea that whites are smarter than other races, and that certain countries were meant to dominate the world. All these notions have since been overturned, thanks to science. In fact, there are greater differences among all women and among all men, for example, than between men and women.[48]

Where the Myth Comes From

From an historical standpoint and based on limited technology, it is easy to see how this myth came about. As I wrote in a journal in 2009:

> It is logical to presume that just as men and women's overall physiology differs that parts of the brain differ as well. Neuroscientists have offered the most information in this area, while psychologists have debated the genus of differences between genders, and educators have worked hard to eliminate them. Neuroscientists have noted that a small area of the prefrontal cortex, a part of the limbic system (the hypothalamus), and the corpus callosum are larger in women. On the other hand, a small area of the amygdala related to arousal and threat response is larger in men.[49] Also, men's brains are slightly larger than women's on average. However, there are no conclusive studies showing that these physical differences translate into different learning abilities.[50]

The myth is primarily due to intelligent speculation, in which the presumption seems logical, but buckles under the weight of the evidence.

What We Know Now

There are a handful of physiological differences between men and women, but no conclusive differences, with the exception that male brains tend to be slightly larger than female brains, and size does not matter where learning is concerned.[51] The most robust studies show slightly different neural networks between men and women, but no differences in aptitude or intelligence based on these different networks.

THERE ARE BRAIN DIFFERENCES BASED ON RACE

Since the times of the first eugenics debates (*eu* meaning "good and *genics* from genes) around the early 1800s, there have been suggestions of stronger and weaker species and members of each species. A small number of white, male scientists debated intellectual superiority by race in the 1800s, in much the same way as gender and intelligence were discussed. The findings proved more political than scientific, however. Racist acts, such as those committed by the Nazis in the name of cleansing the human race, were justified by the belief that some races should rule others.

Where the Myth Comes From

The idea came from Francis Galton, Charles Darwin's half cousin, who shared the belief in natural selection and survival of the fittest. Intelligence tests, designed by whites for white contexts, "proved" that other races were inferior. Those against these racist tests were not in power, meaning their arguments did not serve the dominant science of the time, leading to a self-fulfilling prophecy. Blacks and other minorities did not have the mental capacity to learn, therefore, they were not given the opportunity to do so, leading to a circular pattern of under-education. Colonialism, slavery, and racism are justified by this myth. In World War I, early IQ testing purported the superiority of whites, creating the first serious reflection on the root causes behind differences in scores.

What We Know Now

We now know that test bias, general education, and nutrition due to circumstances of poverty can be behind differences in IQ test scores. Richard Nisbett's address "All Brains Are the Same Color" tried to politely respond to Arthur Jensen's suggestion that the 15-point difference between blacks and whites on IQ tests was mostly due to genetics. An adoption study carried out by Elsie Moore at Arizona State University considered black and mixed-race children who had been adopted by middle-class families (either black or white) and found no difference in IQ between black and mixed-race children. Furthermore, she found that children adopted into well-off, high-socioeconomic-status white families, independent of their race, had higher IQs by about 13 points, meaning that environment was the mediating factor,[52] not the race of the individual.

It has been suggested that pursuing race as a line of research takes away resources from other areas of study and causes tensions, leading to *Nature*'s editorial "Should Scientists Study Race and IQ? NO: Science and Society Do Not Benefit."[53] The debate on resources to study race continues, though the evidence now weighs in heavily on the side of nurture rather than nature.

VACCINES CAUSE AUTISM

In 1998, *The Lancet* published an article linking the measles, mumps, and rubella vaccine with autism. This article was soon retracted as being erroneous, but already had garnered acceptance from many readers. This in turn planted seeds of doubt in the minds of the general population and led to a hysteria connecting vaccination to autism. Autism has no single cause. Dozens of unproven theories and no firm answers caused the general public to latch on to this idea because there is no evidence to the contrary. Despite the quick reply of the medical community to reject this idea,[54] many people still believe this.

> *Concerned parents of autistic children are drawn to this idea because during child development, the first symptoms appear around the time that children receive vaccinations. But in several countries, removing the additive to vaccines that is said to cause autism, thimerosal, has had no effect on rates of autism.*[55]

Unfortunately, the myth about vaccines and autism continues to show up in the press, and some parents choose to skip vaccinations for their children, putting them at risk for curable diseases.[56]

Where the Myth Comes From

The myth comes from both mistaken correlation-causation findings (symptoms of autism arise around the time of vaccinations), and from the lack of a definitive cause of autism. Older theories about the cause of autism ranged from the "Refrigerator Mother" Hypothesis of Autism[57] to suggestions of over- or under-doses of lead, mercury, and/or vitamin D. Aamodt and Wang[58] note that "autism is a partially hereditary disease, and is caused by the inheritance of multiple 'bad' genes. However, the identity of those genes is not yet known."[58] *The Lancet* study filled a void for people anxious to find a cause.

What We Know Now

There are dozens of theories of what causes autism, dividing the scientific community. However, there is one agreed-upon finding by the majority, namely that vaccines are definitely not the cause. Just because there is correlation (signs of autism tend to be recognized around the time a child gets his first immunization) does not mean causation (that the vaccine caused autism).

It is likely that autism is neither wholly inherited nor wholly environmentally triggered, but rather a combination of the two, as is true for so many disorders. Some researchers focus on answering the genetic contributions to autism,[59] while others try to figure out the ambient triggers,[60] and yet others focus just on how to classify the thousands of studies a year that relate to this question.[61] To date, however, there is no final word on the cause of autism.

WHY THIS IS GOOD NEWS FOR TEACHING

A teacher's job is to maximize the potential of all the students in the class, independent of background. John Hattie[62] notes that a teacher's unconscious prejudices about his students influence their learning outcomes. This occurs in part because the teacher unwittingly treats his students differently and has different levels of expectations for different groups. Teachers can change learning outcomes by elevating the expectations of learners. It is great news for teachers to understand that, independent of the level of native intelligence of an individual, mental capacity can be improved with good schooling and quality teachers.[63] The good news for teaching is that intelligence is not fixed, but fluid: Good teaching can make a difference in reaching intellectual potential, partially by helping students believe in their own ability to learn.[64]

Practical Application of MBE:
Believe in the Role of Plasticity and in Your Students

Students excel when they themselves and their teachers believe their intelligence is ever changing. Teachers who believe their job is to help each student reach their potential know how to adjust learning experiences and differentiate instruction for the best results.

Students who think their teachers think they can learn do learn. Students who believe, erroneously or not, that their teachers think their intelligence is inflexible will likely not even try, and therefore complete a self-fulfilling prophecy.

To improve classroom outcomes, teachers should take the time to have honest conversations with each student and help them find even small successes daily.

It is also good news that teachers now know that true genius case be in their midst, and that everyone uses more than just 10% of their brains. It is also great news that resources can be channeled into evidence-based practices, rather than relying on quick fixes, such as classical music, which should be celebrated for other reasons, but not touted as shortcuts to learning.

It is also great news for teachers that half the world—females—has finally been given equal footing for intellectual activities. This was unheard of 150 years ago. Intellectual parity among the sexes is a powerful message, which helps young girls believe in themselves. Similarly, it's great news that race (something a teacher has no control over) is not as important as environment (something a teacher does have control over). Finally, it is also good news that the rejection of the belief that vaccines cause autism has led to the development of a new branch of neuroscience, called neurodiversity. Neurodiversity seeks to celebrate the variability in humanness and classifies autism as just a slightly different kind of brain. The neurodiversity movement has led to a great openness to all types of differences in the human brain.[65]

We now turn from Myths about Brain Architecture and Structure.

2 • MYTHS ABOUT

BRAIN ARCHITECTURE AND STRUCTURE

THE LEFT AND RIGHT HEMISPHERES OF THE BRAIN ARE SEPARATE SYSTEMS FOR LEARNING

One of the most cited myths is that the right and left hemispheres of the brain are separate systems for learning, rather than an integrated system.[1] Some go so far as to claim that the "right brain" is creative, spatially oriented, and emotionally intelligent (i.e., *The Right Brain: A New Understanding of Our Unconscious Mind and Its Creative Power*[2]); while the "left brain" is highly structured and hyperorganized (i.e., *"The U.S. Is a Left-Brained Society for Right-Brained People*[3]). Roger Sperry[4] can be credited with the initial labeling of different functions for the two-brain theory. He declared that, "the split brain behaves in many respects like two separate brains providing new research possibilities."[5] Sperry, along with David Hubel and Torsten Wiesel, won the 1981 Nobel Prize in Physiology and Medicine for work on brain hemisphere lateralization functions. The neat separation of the brain into different types of functions in different halves of the brain (or in the "two brains") was a clean but erroneous division of labor. "Dichotomania," or the desire to categorize every human ability into either a left or right brain[6] arose out of this initial research but was soon found to be nearly impossible to substantiate, as there was rarely just one hemisphere involved in human skills division. Despite dozens of different publications showing this is inaccurate,[7] this myth still persists today.

Where the Myth Comes From

When public autopsies were first performed for group diagnostics and critique in England in the 1660s, people's imaginations were captured by the fact that there seemed to be two halves of the brain, somewhat walnut-shaped, and slightly different in form.[8] The two hemispheres of the brain were also compared with the pairs of body parts (arms, hands, legs, feet, eyes, ears, and so on), and intelligent speculation made it clear that one (right or left) should be dominant. This led to a mania to determine hemispheric dominance for different skills (i.e., music,[9] perception of verbal stimuli,[10] foreign accents[11]). In a related phenomenon, people with damage to one side or another of their brains often lived normal lives, with the exception of one lost skill set or another, leading physicians of the time to presume that each half had separate functions.

What We Know Now

An example of lateralization for brain function comes from language. For more than 150 years, scientists have known that most people have Broca's and Wernicke's areas in the left hemisphere of the brain, and that these are key "hubs" to express language and to construct sentences.[12] However, it is less known, but also a fact, that other functions, such as the correct intonation of words, reality and delusion interpretation, and the appreciation of humor and sarcasm, use far greater right hemisphere activity.[13] Additionally, certain percentages of people (5% of right-handed people and 30% of left-handed people) have either cross- or bi-lateralization of Broca's and Wernicke's areas. This means that "researchers should not rely on handedness as an indicator of cerebral lateralisation for language."[14] We now know that there are complex networks in the brain, rather than single-area or hemispheric responsibilities.

> . . . *there are many learning systems in the brain, most based on skill areas, not on left and right hemisphere division. According to Bruer,[15] the right-brain, left-brain claim is an "educator's myth"[16] and is used as a convenient way of boxing instructional theory.[17]*

Additionally, we know that people can survive with just half a brain and develop most skills with just *one* hemisphere, with often unperceivable differences (see Battro's *Half a Brain is Enough*[18] and Immordino-Yang's "A Tale of Two Cases: Lessons for Education from the Study of Two Boys Living with Half Their Brains"[19] as examples). This indicates that while lateralization suggests one hemisphere might "naturally" be more dominant for hubs of one skill set or another (as in Broca's and Wernicke's Areas), if needed, the other hemisphere can possibly take over that function.[20]

SHORT BOUTS OF COORDINATION EXERCISES IMPROVE INTEGRATION OF LEFT AND RIGHT HEMISPHERIC BRAIN FUNCTION

Commercial exercise programs for newborns, toddlers, and preschool children lure parents into thinking they need to invest in getting their children's brains in sync, as if they were born out of sync. Some primary school districts pay lots of money to tell the children they need to move their hands in a figure eight in order to coordinate their left and right hemispheres and keep their brains fit.[21]

Teachers around the world were asked if they believed that short bouts of coordination exercise can improve integration of left and right hemispheric brain functions, and a disturbing number said this was so.[22] Many commercial programs and a lot of informal recommendations from parenting magazines suggest that more "brain breaks" are needed in educational institutions. According to the book *Energizing Brain Breaks,*[23] these are said to help improve attention, and headlines such as "Move Your Body, Grow Your Brain"[24] are difficult to resist, as they sound deceptively simple to fulfill and reap immeasurable benefits.

Where the Myth Comes From

The mysteries of the brain are enticing, and quick fixes to the complexities of learning are attractive. Many articles written in the 1960s and 1970s discussed the "lateralization" of functions in animal brains, leading people to intelligently suspect that humans must also have two different brains devoted to specific tasks. It followed that these separate systems of learning would need to be integrated somehow for efficient learning. This was later proven untrue in all animals, including humans.

What We Know Now

While exercise is beneficial for human growth, we now know no exercise is needed to join the right and left hemispheres of the brain before learning can occur, as this happens naturally. Short bouts of exercise are good, not because they unite the hemispheres, but rather because they can improve attention. While there is some evidence that small, short bouts of aerobic exercise help,[25] brain breaks like touching your fingers together while singing "Itsy Bitsy Spider" do not show the same results. Giving your brain a break by permitting free mind-wandering is also helpful in refocusing attention but coordinated bouts of activity do not result in smarter students.

Saying that short bouts of coordination exercises can improve integration of left and right hemispheric brain function is wrong on multiple levels. First, teachers have been conned into believing that somehow their students' brains are not in sync and that the left and right hemispheres need to be coordinated before learning can occur. We now know that neither short bouts of exercise nor the joining of hemispheres is needed before thinking and learning can occur, and there is no evidence that the hemispheres are not already as connected as they need to be to perform well.[26] Several programs have been sold to entire governments (as well as school systems, individual institutions, and teachers) to help teach how to trigger brain activation through physical activity. This results in a loss of funds that could be better spent in other areas.

While many states have begun to adopt short bouts of exercise to combat obesity, they make no claims that this is beneficial to the brain, and in fact, limit their claims to saying things like: "Providing short physical activity breaks during the school day increases physical activity in students."[27] None of the articles in favor of short bouts of exercise that have been published in peer-reviewed journals mention hemisphere integration, while most speak of body weight and obesity, and a handful mention improvements in attention.

It should also be noted that exercise is beneficial to overall health and that regular, *consistent* exercise can help learning, so long as it is sustained over time. However, it was shown that in healthy, sedentary, young adults "a single bout of exercise did not affect recognition memory and resulted in increased perceived stress levels," and had nothing to do with coordinating hemispheres.[28] Furthermore, studies "reported no correlation between physical activity and academic performance in children and a recent systematic review of 30 relevant studies reported no significant improvement in cognition with physical activity or exercise in adults," meaning the jury is still out on the precise amount and type of exercise that leads to the best results for school kids.[29] Howard-Jones's literature review in 2014 showed that studies had either no effect, or a small positive effect in equal numbers, but no negative effects, meaning recommending physical activity is definitely appropriate, but like the other studies, no specific recommendations can be made.

SOME PEOPLE ARE MORE "RIGHT BRAINED" AND OTHERS ARE MORE "LEFT BRAINED"

The idea that some people are more "right brained" came with the commercialized hype that spatial abilities, creativity, imagination, and general artistry are gifts of that hemisphere. According to the blogs, popular press magazines, and websites on the topic, people who are "left brained" seem more orderly, structured, and math-minded. Some tests claim to be able to categorize individuals into "left- or right-brained" personalities with just a few key questions[30] and suggest that right-brained students are more likely to "read while lying down," "write fiction," "like mystery stories," "lose track of time," and are often athletic and good with people.[31] While there are still a handful of business and education journal articles that mention "right- and left-brained learners," the neuroscientific world has all but rejected this premise.[32]

Where the Myth Comes From

The "right-" versus "left-brained" myth emerged in part from the idea that most humans are right-handed (between 7 and 11% of people in the world are left-handed), and the fact that the left hemisphere of the brain controls the right side of the body and vice-versa. The thinking was that as most people are right-handed, they must also be "left-brained." This means the "right-brained" (left-handed) people are in the minority, as are their skill sets. The belief that "right-brainers will rule the future" thanks to their ability to innovate[33] has sparked a number of business-focused books.[34] This led educators to think about the "neglected right hemisphere" and the need to "activate" it[35] in order to try and use our "whole brains."[36]

What We Know Now

There are no "right-brained" or "left-brained" people. Humans have only one brain with two hemispheres that are used together in most functions. Evidence from the Connectome Project and BrainNet shows whole-brain activity[37] joining hubs or nodes in different hemispheres to create integrated networks, even with activities once believed to be isolated in one hemisphere, such as mathematics and language.

THERE IS A "LOCALIZATIONALISM" OF ACADEMIC SKILLS IN THE BRAIN

The idea that different memories are neatly stacked in different parts of one's brain is comforting, albeit erroneous. Rather than embrace the complexities of memory circuits, many people would rather believe that "Math Has Its Own Brain Region."[38] Compartmentalizing skill sets makes them seem more manageable. Unfortunately, many teachers believe in this localized view of the brain.[39]

"Math" is not in X part of the brain, and "art" ("history"; "science"; "literature"; and so on) in another, but rather information is distributed throughout the brain in complex networks. It would be much easier to think that there are single, precise areas dedicated to each academic subject area, but the brain developed long before academia divided learning into subject areas. There is no such thing as "triggering" math areas of your brain, or language areas of your mind, but rather multiple circuits of each academic area are constructed across hemispheres.

In a 2013 literature review, we identified 16 different neural networks that expanded into 109 pathways which were needed before a person could begin to read.[40] We also identified in the literature that to be able to do simple addition well, a child needs initial number sense, secondary number sense, coding of abstract to tangible symbols, coding of Arabic integers, anagogic quality, triple code, symbolic production, forms, shapes, geometry, ordinality, sequence, repetition, and regularity, among other networks. Each of these networks branches out into even more precise pathways. Initial number sense alone, for example, is related to multiple brain areas (key hubs): angular gyrus, anterior cingulate, anterior cingulated cortex, basal ganglia, central-parietal cortex, cerebellum, frontal lobes, fusiform gyrus (right), hemispheres (right and left), horizontal segment of the intraparietal sulcus, interparietal sulcus and intraparietal sulci (bilateral), lateral anterior intraparietal sulcus, and parietal and lateral occipital regions.[41] Both pre-reading and early math skills are made even more complex by also requiring well-functioning sensory perception (being able to see and hear correctly); graphomotor skills (to write), and well-developed networks for memory, attention, and executive functions. This means that it is impossible for "math" or "reading" to be in a single place in the brain. "Localizationalism" is promoted by the desire for simpler answers. The brain, however, defies simplistic reductionism.

To visualize this better, Figure 2.1 shows the explanation offered by Mingrui Xia and colleagues at Beijing Normal University about the ways that new neuroimaging techniques eliminate any doubt about the complex networks involved in thinking and the rejection of "localizationism." Figure 2.1 is from the BrainNet Viewer program that emphasizes the location of hubs and nodes that link to create complex neural networks for skills.[42] Studies such as these make it clear that human cognition is complex and supported by extended brain networks rather than specific regions.

Where the Myth Comes From

Due to the limits of technology at the time, many brain scans done in the 1980s and 1990s appeared to pinpoint specific areas of the brain when individuals did specific activities. This led people to think that a single area of the brain was responsible for the entire skill. These main areas are now called "hubs" or "nodes," and in more sophisticated brain imaging, it's now easier to see how signaling

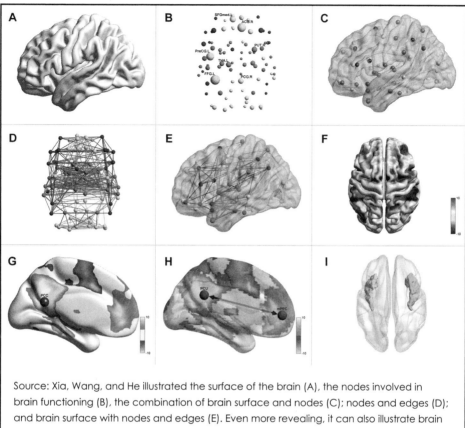

Source: Xia, Wang, and He illustrated the surface of the brain (A), the nodes involved in brain functioning (B), the combination of brain surface and nodes (C); nodes and edges (D); and brain surface with nodes and edges (E). Even more revealing, it can also illustrate brain surface and volume files for volume-to-surface mapping (F); brain surface, nodes and volume files for volume-to-surface mapping with nodes (G); brain surface, nodes, edges and volume files for volume-to-surface mapping with nodes and edges (H); and (I) brain surface and volume files for regions of interest construction. [49] Used with permission of the authors.

Figure 2.1: *BrainNet Viewer: A Network Visualization Tool for Human Brain Connectomics*

passes through those areas with frequency, rather than this single area of the brain being where X takes place. For example, the angular gyrus seems to be a key hub for arithmetic, and Broca's area seems to be a key hub for language. However, math and language are not located just in those little spots of the brain, but rather crisscross these hubs frequently in elaborate networks.

Some headlines generalize "math," "language," or "art" abilities without breaking down their sub-elements, leading readers to believe that entire academic fields can be located in one hemisphere or another (or even a single part of the brain). Titles like "Is Math Lateralised on the Same Side as Language?"[43] or the presumption that art is located in the right hemisphere (*Drawing on the Right Side of the Brain*[44]); or that *The Left Brain Speaks, The Right Brain Laughs*[45] mislead the average person into thinking that one hemisphere controls entire domain areas of thinking. The myth that academic subjects are in a specific area of the brain is also related to the belief that brain parts act in isolation. Despite the understanding that reading, math, art, history, physical education, and all other academic subjects involve multiple competencies, some still believe that each subject has a special spot in the brain.

What We Know Now

We now know that learning is more complex than once thought, and that aspects of cognition (memory, attention, executive function, among others) and academic subjects cannot be found in a single part of the brain. Learning competencies are located in multiple networks and hundreds of pathways in the brain. Additionally, skill sets can almost always be broken down into smaller sub-elements, and each element represents a different (albeit sometimes overlapping) network.

BRAIN PARTS WORK IN ISOLATION

The belief in hemispheric dominance paralleled a belief that different parts of each hemisphere had different roles to play in cognition, movement, learning, personality, and overall character. Once it was found that Broca's area was linked to expressive language in the 1860s, it was presumed that other areas of the brain were responsible for other skills, such as math, empathy, or creativity. This was confirmed, to a certain extent, by the practice of lobotomies, which were conducted to remove parts of the brain responsible for seizures. It was once believed that the frontal lobes caused seizures in epileptics, and that once these were removed, the seizures would stop. While this did occur in several cases, it wasn't until decades later that it became clear that epileptics could have seizures triggered in just about any part of the brain, not just the frontal lobes. Independent of this later finding, initial surgical successes led to the idea that certain parts of the brain were responsible for seizures and other brain functions. Other experiments in the 1800s used electrical stimulation, which enhanced memory in some patients.[46] Back then it was thought that if the precise area for stimulation could be found, any type of learning could be improved.

The focus on distinct parts of the brain and their specific roles was also tightly linked to the belief in the heritability of intelligence. People expected that, just as physical traits were passed on from father to son, so were intelligence and the physiology of the brain. As the lateralization of hemispheric skills was popular for a time, so was the idea that we could someday pinpoint exactly what part of the brain could or should be stimulated to improve a specific skill set or personality traits.[47]

Where the Myth Comes From

The idea of "localizationalism" stemmed from the late 1800s belief that different parts of the human brain represented different functions and personality traits. This idea was born of a time when few people actually had the opportunity to see real brains, and the primary promoters of this idea were people who measured external bumps and crevices on the skull (often at circus events) and then claimed they represented a certain trait (broad foreheads meant intelligence, and so on). Phrenology, promoted by Franz Joseph Gall, suggested that the brain was divided into 27 different faculties, and each functioned on its own accord.[48] This belief helped explain why some people might be very good at math but have lousy social skills, for example. The thought was that people were born with limited potential for certain skill sets (subfaculties of the brain), and that they could, at most, live up to their maximum potential. If they were, for example, born with little brain space for language abilities, they could be forgiven for being poor speakers, as the heritable traits were not their own doing. Thankfully, we have evolved from "localizationism to neuroplasticity."[49]

Most current studies look at the complex and intricate networks of these systems, rather than suggesting localizationalism. Unfortunately, the belief that parts of the brain work in isolation continues even today, as some medical students are taught functional neuroanatomy. Some texts proclaim that certain brain parts are responsible for certain functions rather than being key hubs or nodes, despite evidence for circuits rather than localizationalism.

What We Know Now

We now know that there is almost nothing a human does that is triggered by a single part of the brain. Rather, the brain works with complex neural networks that join thousands and often hundreds of thousands of different neurons and glial cells in a single task spread out in different parts of the brain.[50] While it is true that proximity is a good indicator of neuronal activity, sometimes neurons from different areas of the brain are part of the same network.[51] This does not mean that we reject area specialization completely, but we now know that the special areas of the brain we once thought were *responsible* for a certain action are more modernly referred to as hubs, nodes or key areas or parts of the brain through which the network circulates.

KEEPING A "COOL HEAD" (THINKING WITHOUT EMOTIONS) IMPROVES LEARNING

The belief that learning and cognition can be separated from emotion is reflected in the ways we give advice to each other: "Think about it with a cool head before you make a choice" or "Don't make any rash decisions before you think about this calmly." We tell people to not "get too emotional" before launching into a decision because we presume that logic and feeling are counterbalancing functions in our brains. Learning cannot and should not be isolated from the social-emotional context, nor can reasoning and decision making be divorced from emotion and feeling. When polled, around half the teachers in my training sessions believe that emotions are unrelated to cognition and thinking. While touted as opposites, cognition and affect are actually complementary forces in learning.

Where the Myth Comes From

The heart and the head are often treated as separate entities. Learning and cognition are associated with the brain, rationality, and unemotional reactions to situations. Since learning takes place in the mind/brain, it is hard for many to imagine how social and emotional contexts *external* to the individual can have any influence. Others believe that if thinking is going on inside your skull, why should it be influenced by matters of the heart? Some also believe that emotional sensation and cognition are two completely distinct ways of approaching the world, one being in the gut and the other in the brain; one being right-brained, the other left-brained; one being rational and the other irrational. This misunderstanding is often reflected in cartoon graphs of the brain, in which the right and left hemispheres play distinct roles in human behavior.

Emotions and the degree of control we have over them have been a subject of speculation since the Greeks. Aristotle is credited with saying: "Anyone can become angry, that is easy, but to be angry with the right person and the right degree and at the right time and for the right purpose, and in the right way, that is not within everybody's power and it is not easy,"[52] suggesting people need to learn to manage their feelings in order to work well in society. Theories about emotional intelligences in the early 1990s, starting with Salovey and Mayer[53] and then popularized by Goleman[54] suggested that EQ (emotional quotient) might be more important than IQ (intelligence quotient) in life achievements. This led to a host of books and training programs that, more often than not, *contrasted* emotions with cognition, or explained emotions as a personality characteristic to be dominated and tamed. Many of these programs suggest that learning to self-regulate and manage emotions is a conscious process, decided upon rationally. The myth derives in part from this belief that people can somehow turn their emotions off and on at will, and that emotions and cognition are in different compartments of the brain.

What We Know Now

The literature on cognition and emotions overlaps when discussing decision making,[55] motivation,[56] and consciousness.[57] This means that emotion and cognition bridge how we think about the world, the conscious choices we make and the motivation we have for learning new things. We also know that it is not always possible to rein in emotions, that cognition is highly influenced by emotions, and that there is no decision or learning without emotion.[58] Our actions, including learning, are based on choices, and our choices are heavily dependent on emotions. We now know that sensory perception and attention, both of which play key roles in learning, are highly influenced by emotions due to changes in neurotransmitters released in the brain. This means that what we can know is influenced by how we feel about it.[59]

FEELINGS ARE PRODUCED IN THE HEART AND THINKING IN THE BRAIN

"Think with your head, not with your heart!" we are often coached, as feelings get in the way of action. Or in the opposite case, "Show some heart!" we yell, as if deciding to do something in the head is not enough to get results. The belief that feelings are produced in the heart and thinking in the brain suggests that the heart is capable and responsible for feelings. While this is a beautifully romantic interpretation, the truth is that all feelings *and* all thinking occur in the brain.

Where the Myth Comes From

The myth emerges from the roles of the mightiest organs in the body, the heart and the brain. The iconic image of the beating, red heart, pumping with love and overcoming obstacles, gives people the false impression that the heart is what makes a person feel, a belief that goes back at least to the ancient Egyptians who also saw the heart, not the brain, as the seat of the soul.[60] The myth is caused by a lack of scientific understanding of how emotions produce feelings, which are actually generated in the brain and the mind.

What We Know Now

We now know that emotions are triggered by neurotransmitters (chemicals and hormones) in the brain, and the way we feel is the psychological interpretation of that emotion.[61] That is, feeling and thinking are both generated in the brain. People also believe that the skin is what senses, the eyes are what sees, the ears are what hear, the nose is what smells, and the mouth is what tastes. However, the truth is "[w]e see with our brains, not with our eyes," as Paul Bach-y-Rita says in Norman Doidge's book, *The Brain That Changes Itself.*[62]

The heart is necessary for life, but the only organ that makes us feel is the brain. The way that senses enter the brain has been studied for decades,[63] but it was only in the past few years that emotions and brain functioning came under deeper scrutiny,[64] and even more recently that a better understanding of how the complex array of emotions in the brain is perceived and used to understand its own surroundings and what this means for learning.[65] We now know that all feelings are generated by the interpretation of sensory perceptions combined with memories: The brain is the organ of all feeling, not the heart.

CREATIVITY IS IN THE RIGHT HEMISPHERE OF THE BRAIN

Along with the erroneous belief that language was only in the left hemisphere and spatial abilities in the right, some suggested that creativity—something that relied on spatial imagery—must be a right hemisphere function as well.[66] This was fueled by multiple illustrations showing rainbow divergent thinking right hemispheres next to mathematically proportioned square, logical thinking hemispheres on the left.

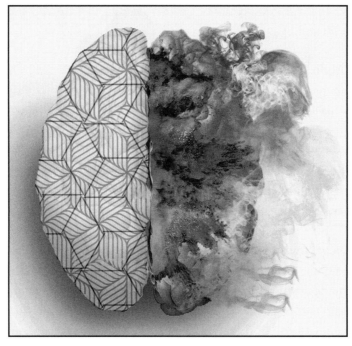

Figure 2.2: *Left-Brain, Right-Brain Myths*

All unanswered questions beg a range of hypotheses. Just where creativity might be in the brain has been in question for decades, if not centuries. After Sperry's Nobel Prize in 1981, researchers scrambled to identify exactly which brain functions did what. Harpaz's 1990 article "Asymmetry of Hemispheric Functions and Creativity: An Empirical Examination" published in *The Journal of Creative Behavior*, cited studies from the 1960s and 1970s. Harpaz declared that the right hemisphere "appears to be dominant in **synthetic**,[67] **nonverbal**,[68] **complete, whole unit**,[69] **spatial**[70] and **time-dependent**[71] functions" and was, therefore, responsible for creativity.[72] After 1981, researchers spent the next decade shoring up the arguments for creativity in the right brain, only to be challenged by different definitions of creativity and better imaging showing its broader reach and multiple, complex networks.

Where the Myth Comes From

The myth of the creative "right brain" comes from claims that science, math, and logical thinking are in the left hemisphere, and creativity in the right,[73] which in turn were born from Sperry's Nobel Prize–winning work in 1981 on brain lateralization. Until recently, the imprecise measurements rendered by brain imaging technology in the 1990s and early 2000s led to the promotion of this myth.

What We Know Now

The most current understanding of creativity is far broader and involves multiple brain functions and structures, as well as different neurotransmitters. According to Heilman's studies;[74]

> [i]nnovation requires disengagement and divergent thinking primarily mediated by frontal networks. Creative people are often risk-takers and novelty seekers, behaviors that activate their ventral striatal reward system. Innovation also requires associative and convergent thinking, activities that are dependent on the integration of highly distributed networks. People are often most creative when they are in mental states associated with reduced levels of brain norepinephrine, which may enhance the communication between distributed networks.

Creativity is also being studied as it relates to the default mode network, or the ways the brain is active when it is at rest.[75] Beaty and colleagues "suggest that the ability to generate creative ideas is characterized by increased functional connectivity between the inferior prefrontal cortex and the default network, pointing to a greater cooperation between brain regions associated with cognitive control and low-level imaginative processes."[76] This means creativity is not limited to right hemisphere functions and may not be related to "active" skill sets at all, but rather to what the brain does when it is not focused on anything in particular.

Creativity, like intelligence, is an extremely complex mental process. Locating it in the brain can be done only by first deciding which theory of creativity you adhere to, then breaking down creativity into its many sub-elements (disengagement, divergent thinking, risk taking, novelty seeking, associative and convergent thinking, cognitive control, and imaginative processes, among others) and identifying studies that establish each of these neural networks. This is a monumental task that has yet to be undertaken.

YOUR BRAIN WILL SHRINK IF YOU DON'T DRINK SIX TO EIGHT GLASSES OF WATER A DAY

Water and good hydration are important for physical health and for the brain to function properly. The suggestion that the brain is consistently dehydrated is worrisome, however, because if true, it would mean that children are not learning for lack of something as simple as water. According to the Harvard Medical School, water is necessary and does many important jobs, including carrying nutrients and oxygen to your cells; flushing bacteria from your bladder; aiding digestion; preventing constipation; normalizing blood pressure; stabilizing the heartbeat; cushioning joints; protecting organs and tissues; regulating body temperature; and maintaining electrolyte (sodium) balance.[77] That said, there is no evidence that children in our classrooms are less hydrated than is optimally recommended. Extreme cases of dehydration can cause learning problems: "When dehydration reduces body mass by more than 2%, it has been consistently reported that mood is influenced, fatigue is greater, and alertness is lower."[78]

Researchers Benton and Young wondered if slight water deprivation could also cause problems, as most people do not live in conditions in which they are deprived of water, unless they are athletes or live in very hot environments. After reviewing hundreds of studies on the topic they confessed that information on children was difficult to come by, and there was only one meta-analysis, conducted in 2006[79] that found an "association between hydration status and the cognition of children" but could not find any intervention studies. In fact, there was only one study within the meta-analysis that looked at this, and it took a correlational approach.[80] This study was undertaken "in a school in the Israeli desert, where the outside temperature was 35 Celsius [95 Fahrenheit]."[81] The researchers found that the dehydrated children actually performed better than the hydrated children on one of the five cognition tests, meaning that the evidence for dehydration adversely affecting learning is far from overwhelming. There are only four studies, according to Benton and Young, that show some benefits of drinking water, including one in which students rated "themselves as happier after drinking water."[82]

Recommendations about water consumption range from "4 to 6 glasses" to "8x8" (eight glasses of eight ounces) and even 8 to 10 glasses each day in the popular press.[83] Most doctors, however, recommend that drinking when you are thirsty is the rule of thumb; common sense should rule. Howard-Jones[84] writes:

> *although a daily intake of 6 to 8 glasses of water is a contentious recommendation with its own mythical origin[85]—and there is no evidence for underperformance among schoolchildren who fail to meet it—studies[86] have shown that dehydration can influence cognitive function. This finding may help to explain why more than a quarter of UK teachers who were sampled in a study believed that failing to meet this quota would cause their brains to shrink.[87]*

Additionally, it was found that drinking too much water can be as problematic as not drinking enough. Hyponatremia (caused by taking in too much water) can cause cells to flood because of low sodium levels, leading to water intoxication that can cause seizures, coma, and death in extreme cases.[88] Excessive intake of water can lead to debilitating health problems. Light over-intake of water in school can lead to multiple trips to the bathroom and missing class instruction.

Where the Myth Comes From

As the brain is mostly water[89] it seems logical to presume that drinking water helps keep the brain in the right balance for learning.

> *. . . about seventy-five percent of the body and brain is water. Some researchers suggest that allowing students to drink water in class helps restore the body to its natural state. This presumes that the body is "out of balance" due to a lack of water, which in some cases may be true. Some teachers encourage their students to drink in class. It has been argued, however, that students seem more alert after having a drink of water not because they needed to re-hydrate their brains, but rather because the water break provides a chance to refocus.[90]*

This means that it is intelligent speculation to think that water intake can influence learning, as both the brain and the body are composed of 70 to 75% water. However, evidence shows most schoolchildren are not dehydrated enough to recommend more water intake than they desire.

What We Know Now

This myth comes from knowing that severely dehydrated brains do not function well, and the presumption that extra water should therefore be beneficial, which is not true. We now know that too much water can be as harmful as too little water. It is also clear that insisting that children drink water can cause them to go to the bathroom with such frequency that they miss important class time. We also know that people who drink water when they are thirsty normally drink enough to keep their bodies and brains in balance. Drinking "8x8" glasses of water is an unsubstantiated belief based on intelligent speculation.

THE BIGGER YOUR BRAIN, THE SMARTER YOU ARE

The concept of "size matters" has been debated in many contexts and over many decades. Attempts to correlate physiological differences with intellectual superiority began to crumble when evolutionary evidence made it clear that Neanderthal man had a larger brain than contemporary *Homo sapiens*. Neanderthals died out, partially due to their inability to problem-solve and develop language, something *Homo sapiens* achieved with smaller brain mass.[91] Size, it appears, does not matter in terms of mental prowess. More important than sheer size is the actual *use* of the brain, which is evidenced by neural plasticity and increased white matter tracts.

A 1928 study of children showed "the relative capacity-intelligence coefficients are clearly insignificant with the possible exception of North European mixed boys, and one-fourth of them are negative,"[92] meaning there was an understanding more than 90 years ago that brain size does not determine intelligence, yet the myth persists. There seems to be little dispute with the findings that *abnormally* small head size can be correlated to intellectual deficits,[93] but small head size is not related to differences in intelligence. Additionally, it was found that small head size due to premature births can be remedied to a certain extent by breast feeding[94] and stimulation indicating that neuronal connections, not initial head size, is what matters.

However, some studies show that brain volume does relate to intelligence.[95] Lange and colleagues[96] have disputed these studies, however, noting that brain volume alone is insufficient in reaching conclusions about IQ. "The relations between total and regional brain volumes and IQ can best be discerned when additional variables known to be associated with IQ, especially parental education and other demographic measures, are considered concurrently."[97] Their study of children aged 4 years, 10 months to 18 years showed that parental education "has a strong association with IQ in children that is not mediated by total or regional brain volumes."[97] That is, having a big brain without proper environmental stimuli is not enough (just as having a small brain with lots of stimuli is probably also not enough). While there is evidence that brain volume and IQ have a correlation,[98] it is also true that this is reduced thanks to changes in improved environments.[99] This is supported by those who point to cases of exceptional intelligence with average-size brains, as in Einstein's case.[100]

Where the Myth Comes From

The myth emerged from animal studies. Initial studies considered that cats are smarter than insects, and monkeys are smarter than cats, therefore intellectual ability is correlated with brain size.[101] However, this argument grows weaker when we consider dolphins or elephants. Additionally, cow brains are larger than monkey brains, but cows do not exhibit higher intelligence than monkeys. Sperm whales have brains seven times the size of human brains, however they do not demonstrate superior intelligence either. This myth was born of incorrect correlation of general animal body size to presumed brain size. However, even when corrected for neuronal density within the brain instead of just head size, the evidence remains weak. A new measure, the "encephalization quotient" emerged.

The "encephalization quotient" (EQ) takes into account the relationships among body size to shape, anatomy, and physiology or "allometric effects of widely divergent body sizes,"[102] and places humans near the top of the list. Unfortunately,

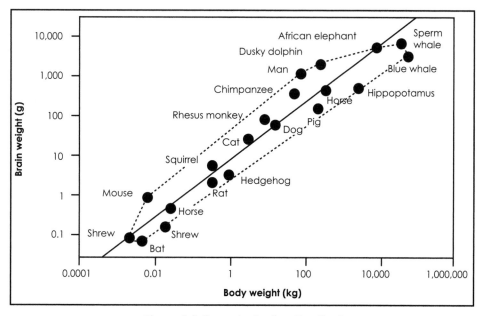

Figure 2.3: Encephalization Quotient

this too has recently been challenged.[103] Some of the relationships include body fat, and as women have more body fat than men, the calculation shows that this measurement is also imprecise. According to the formula, some interesting observations about men and women surface.

While a man's body fat percentage ranges between 18 and 25%, a woman's ranges between 25 and 31%. The deviation of the regression brain-to-lean-body-mass weight ratio allows for balancing the EQ of men and women. Thus, "a man with a brain size of 1,273.6 cm³ and a lean body mass of 67.58 kg (86.09 kg × 0.785) would have an EQ of 6.40, while a woman with a *cc* of 1,131.1 cm³ and a fat-free mass of 53.20 kg (73.89 kg × 0.72) would have an EQ of 6.66.[104]

This results in a general superiority of women. While the encephalization quotient is still under scrutiny, it appears to be better than simplistic measures of "bigger is better." Showing, by any measure, that women should be smarter than men is also not a popular finding in science fields, in which more men preside, suggesting that confirmation bias might also be at fault in the persistence if this myth.

What We Know Now

We now know that, like all things human, there is a range of acceptable brain sizes. Brain volume anywhere between 1052.9 and 1498.5 cm³ in men and between 974.9 and 1398.1 cm³ in women is normal.[105] Correlations of brain size to intelligence are dubious because multiple other factors, including body fat, come into play in calculating size in this way. Pietschnig and colleagues' work concluded "that it is not warranted to interpret brain size as an isomorphic proxy of human intelligence differences."[106]

We also know that some of the first precise brain studies are relatively recent,[107] and estimates of brain to body mass also show that bigger is not necessarily smarter.[108] Additionally, brilliant women such as Marie Curie, who won two Nobel Prizes, was just 5 feet tall, with an estimated brain mass smaller than average. Her very small head and reduced brain volume offer some evidence that it is not true that the bigger the brain, the smarter the person.

BRAIN SCANNERS "SEE" THINKING

There are hundreds of intriguing headlines that combine with the general feeling of Big Brother watching your every move to result in the myth that we can somehow "see" brains thinking. Headlines like *Brain Scan that Shows Researchers What You Are THINKING About* are even more disturbing[109] and declare, "brain scans now allow researchers to know exactly what a person is imagining."[109] Other headlines like, *"Mind-Reading Computer Instantly Decodes People's Thoughts"*[110] and *"This Camera Records the Thinking Brain"*[111] sound amazing, but less so when you see that they relate to mice studies and spatial memory, a sub-element of complete cognition.

Where the Myth Comes From

"Can a Brain Scan Tell What You're Thinking?" is the million-dollar question.[112] As we develop better technologies, surprising findings emerge almost monthly, and depending on how they are shared with the public, they are easily misinterpreted as meaning more than they actually do. For example, in his TED Talk, Christopher De Charms explains MRI imaging of parts of the brain used to move a hand. This is not thinking, but the title of his talk, *"Looking Inside the Brain in Real Time* suggests that "we can look at his mind" as he shows his colleague's MRI scan, which can mislead people to think they are seeing "thinking." De Charms says that we can learn to manage our pain better and avoid pills, psychiatrists, and surgery by controlling our bodies with our minds. While much of this is positive and can often be true, it can be argued that it is overreaching to think that "you will be able to look at *all* the aspects that make you yourself, *all* your experiences."[113] While it is true that technology is marching forward, it is probably unrealistic to think "all" of this will be available soon.

While sensationalist, the video is based on serious work by Nathan Spreng at Cornell University[114] that celebrates the complexities of thinking by considering agreeable and disagreeable descriptors, and the context in which social exchanges occur. By piecing together multiple images across variables, Spreng and colleagues suggest they get an idea of what people are imagining. While this is not thinking per se, the actual research was far less sensationalistic than the headline it earned and far more interesting to serious researchers.

In another extreme example, Grabianowski[115] writes that there are *"Six Ways Science Can See Into Your Brain,"* which is actually a nice summary article about imaging techniques electroencephalogram (EEG); computerized axial tomography (CAT); positron emission tomography (PET); magnetic resonance imaging (MRI); functional magnetic resonance imaging (fMRI); and magnetoencephalography (MEG). This article seems to go hand in hand with another, *"Brain Researchers Can Detect Who We Are Thinking About,"*[116] which explains how imaging techniques work. The belief that brain scanners can see people's thinking is due to lack of scientific literacy and/or expert knowledge about the limits of technology. In general, these headlines simply overextend the actual research findings. This is not their fault, however, as that is the job of a headline. The fault is in not reading beyond the headline, which is the reader's decision.

What We Know Now

Each brain imaging machine can, at best, measure a single dimension (electrical, chemical, or structural) of one sub-skill set (e.g., symbol to sound correlation; semantic memory; identifying mistakes in word spelling; mental rotation, alerting system, and so on). No imaging machine can measure thought, only a sub-element of a thought. The truth of the matter is that we now know that the act of thinking involves perception (all the sensory systems working together), memory, attention, executive functions, domain area networks, and other complex mechanisms to result in a single thought. "Thinking" is not a single firing in the brain, but rather the combination of dozens of networks (and thousands of connections) working in synchronous rhythm. While we can detect the neural networks that are important in each of these mechanisms, we cannot actually tell what they mean collectively. That is, we can see the networks related to semantic retrieval of information, but not necessarily the exact word "dog" as someone thinks of it.[117]

It's now clear that there are many different pieces to a single thought and that "the distinctive cognitive demands of each stage [of thinking] will produce a brain pattern that can be used to estimate temporal boundaries of that stage."[118] This means that, to actually see thinking, multiple simultaneous images would be needed. The closest we have to seeing this "big picture" of thinking is the Connectome Project,[119] which gives us images of neural networks. But a neural network is not a thought. It is easy to understand how the public can be misled by the alluring headlines that seem to promise a glimpse into individual thinking, but this technology does not yet exist.

WHY THIS IS GOOD NEWS FOR TEACHING

Eliminating the myth of hemispheric dominance is helpful because it shows that the human brain is far more malleable that once thought. There are no parts of the brain for math or language, but rather multiple areas of the brain and dozens of networks that are relied upon to memorize, pay attention, empathize, and interact with the world. It is great for teachers to know that networks, not localizationalism are at play because this can lead to more precision in both activity choice and the diagnosis of learning delays. For example, children must be able to decode sound to symbol, retrieve words from semantic memory, and correctly pronounce words in order to read aloud (among a dozen other sub-elements of reading). Each of these skills involves different neural networks, which are supported by dozens of pathways. Rather than thinking about stimulating "the reading part of the brain," we can now be more precise in helping kids with specific sub-elements, such as working memory, phoneme development, or pronunciation. Targeting interventions increases their chances of success in the classroom.

Practical Application of MBE: Break Down Learning Objectives and Plan According to Goals

Before choosing a strategy, great teachers should have a clear learning goal in mind (*what knowledge, skills, and/or attitudes are they out to develop?*); know how they will measure it (*what evaluation tools are the most appropriate to measure the goal?*); and then decide what activity, strategy, methodology, and resources to apply (*how can knowledge about how the brain learns best be used to select the best tools to reach the goals?*).[120]

Great teachers understand that all domain-area learning (reading, math, science, and art, and so on) requires multiple neural networks and hundreds of neural pathways in the brain. Once teachers clarify what their objectives are—and which neural pathway should be stimulated—the choice of classroom activity becomes clearer. For example, if a teacher's goal is to help a student's level of reading comprehension (which depends on neural pathways for semantic memory, among others), she can then devise the appropriate learning activities (such as vocabulary games).

Great teachers choose the activities that best help their students reach their learning objectives.

Great teachers take advantage of the real relations between the mind and body to stop wasting time doing the wrong kinds of exercise for the wrong reasons and continue doing physical activity for the right reasons. Rather than using class time for brain breaks, kids would be better served by school, state, and national policies that motivate healthy physical routines inside and outside class with regularity and throughout the school years and in K-12 settings.

It is also great for teachers to have an appreciation of creativity as a complex brain function, similar to intelligence, which is distributed throughout different brain areas and networks. This understanding hints at the trainability of creative skills, and the ability of students to acquire and develop creative traits. Rather than labeling kids as either creative or not, children can learn to think divergently, take risks, and use imagination, thus developing the building blocks of ingenuity.

Finally, knowing about the architectural myths of the brain frees teachers from wasting time on aspects of learning over which they have little control. For example, we can trust kids to know their own bodies, which will let their brains know when they want and need more water. Rather than worrying about whether a student is "right-brained" or "left-brained," teachers can spend more time thinking about the inner workings of the brain and how great teaching impacts neural networks. As the limits of neuroimaging make clear, teaching remains as much an art as it is a science: We need great teachers to facilitate this process, since machines cannot (yet) see exactly how this works.

3 • MYTHS ABOUT

TEACHING AND LEARNING

INDIVIDUALS LEARN BETTER WHEN THEY RECEIVE INFORMATION IN THEIR PREFERRED LEARNING STYLES

Asking students to reflect upon how they learn best is a great way to develop metacognitive skills; however, pigeonholing them into a category, style, or type of learner based on their answers to a short questionnaire is irresponsible. One of the most prevalent neuromyths is that people have "learning styles," and when they are taught in their preferred style, they learn better. The roots of learning styles rest in the positive struggle to increase differentiation in classroom models, but they have been abused and stretched well beyond the evidence.[1]

The term "learning styles" has been used to cover a broad range of profiles, including preferences for sensory modalities (visual, auditory, kinesthetic, or VAK), and intelligences.[2] Pashler and colleagues'[3] review found more than "71 different schemes" called learning styles,[4] which explains their broad reach, meaning debunking this myth will take time. While attending to different needs and differentiating classroom instruction are good ideas, telling a student his "style" of learning is *x* can do harm and actually stunt his learning. All this persists without even a single study to prove learning style categorization actually works.

The struggle to debunk this myth has been attempted in multiple publications that indicate there is little or no data that can support the investment and use of learning styles.[5] The biggest "negative" related to learning styles is that both teachers and students believe that their academic achievement is tied to a style that is not really in their control, but rather is innate. Titles like *"Students' Learning Style Preferences and Teachers' Instructional Strategies: Correlations Between Matched Styles and Academic Achievement"*[6] seem to suggest that success in the classroom is predetermined by one's style and that of the teacher, rather than on teaching, free will, or a student's self-perception as a learner, which do have evidence behind them.[7]

Where the Myth Comes From

Each of the different types of learning styles has its own story, but the history of personality studies is related to many of these types. The original use of the term "learning styles" began with a focus on special education and people with different learning needs,[8] but has expanded to cover students with all different levels of potential in the classroom. We now know that "learning styles" was a good first attempt at understanding the many complexities of the brain, and useful in promoting the differentiation movement,[9] but limited in terms of evidence.

The MindTools webpage says: "the VAK [Visual Auditory Kinesthetic] Learning Styles Model was developed by psychologists in the 1920s to classify the most common ways that people learn," but a Google Scholar search between 1920 and 1930 could not find any studies that considered "learning styles" or "visual, auditory, kinesthetic" learners. Others suggest that the myth likely was an outgrowth of work by famed psychologist C. G. Jung. Jung considered different archetypal personalities, as well as people who experienced their world either primarily as extroverts or introverts, and who were either thinking-feeling or sensation-intuitive.[10] Jung's theory was used to construct Katherine Cook Briggs's and her daughter Isabel Briggs Meyer's famous "Meyers-Briggs Type Indicator," first published in 1943, administered by the Educational Testing Service in 1962, and commercialized in 1989.[11] The Meyers-Briggs uses a series of self-reflection questions to identify the way(s) a person experiences the world (primarily through sensation, intuition, feeling, and thinking) and is widely used in business and education. Other personality theories morphed out of this, and include Keirsey Temperaments,[12] McCrea's and Costa's Five Factor Model,[13] and Goldberg's Big Five theory.[14]

The literature on learning styles grew away from personality theories and into its own in the late 1970s and early 1980s. One of the first articles to try to justify the existence of learning styles came from Riechmann and Grasha,[15] who spoke of "A Rational Approach to Developing and Assessing the Construct Validity of a Student Learning Scales Instrument." Others, like Kolb[16] linked *experiential learning* theory to the learning style inventory, widening the net of this catch-all phrase. This means that "learning styles" have been used to cover just about every new approach to learning that developed from the 1970s to the 2000s.

According to Stephen Hughes,[17] a medical researcher, there were 2,650 textbooks promoting "learning styles" in 2012 and, worse yet, professional practice guidelines for physicians promoting their use. Whole educational institutions, governments, and even academic societies have bought, literally, into the myth. While everyone celebrates the idea of differentiating practice and instruction to meet individual needs, few believe that a questionnaire with 20 to 50 items can accurately define an individual or get to the roots of how people differ in their learning processes. Unfortunately, people want things to be simple. Pashler and colleagues suggested: ". . . if a person or a person's child is not succeeding or excelling in school, it may be more comfortable for the person to think that the educational system, not the person or the child himself or herself, is responsible,"[18] pointing to reasons people believe in the myth.

Willingham and colleagues write that people believe in learning styles for many reasons, two of which they find particularly interesting. First, people believe what they think "scientists" have proven and, feel it's not their place to challenge this evidence. Second, there is confirmation bias, as "teachers are exposed to a plethora of materials that purportedly respect students' learning styles, materials that often claim a scientific basis for their design."[19] These two reasons suggest there is a circular reasoning for this myth's existence.

What We Know Now

We now know that the investments (money and time) in learning style analysis and training are better spent in other areas, as Dunn and colleagues warned more than three decades ago:

> . . . there are great dangers in the misuse of learning style concepts. Specifically, we must avoid turning these ideas into stereotypes used to pigeon hole individuals. Furthermore, we should not deny students the opportunity to develop themselves fully by only exposing them to educational environments that match their strengths.[20]

The modern-day problem is that using learning styles *does* often pigeonhole people into one type of instructional design or another as exemplified by multiple university webpages dedicated to new student orientation and study skills support. While well meaning, these tools convince some students they are incapable of learning one thing or another because the teaching style and his or her learning style did not coincide.

LaLopa's clever reflection *"The Difference Between Bigfoot and Learning Styles: There May Be Better Evidence to Support the Existence of Bigfoot"* alerts us to the lack of research support for learning styles. Despite a decreasing belief in learning styles among university professors,[21] for-profit programs still exist,[22] taking time away from evidence-based interventions and money from quality professional development initiatives.

Pashler and colleagues meticulously thought through the criteria for proving or disproving the existence of styles and concluded that "any credible validation of learning-styles-based instruction" would require an experimental design that included categorizing students into learning styles, randomly assigning them to multiple instructional methods, and then having all the students sit the same final exam and comparing the results. "Finally, in order to demonstrate that optimal learning requires that students receive instruction tailored to their putative learning style, the experiment must reveal a specific type of interaction between learning style and instructional method . . ."[23] Their study, published by *Psychological Science in the Public Interest*, summarizes by saying:

> We conclude therefore, that at present, there is no adequate evidence base to justify incorporating learning styles assessments into general educational practice. Thus, limited education resources would better be devoted to adopting other educational practices that have a strong evidence base, of which there are an increasing number.[23]

The visual, auditory, and kinesthetic (VAK) theory of learning, which maintains that individuals have a dominant sense through which they perceive information, lacked support from the start. People cannot limit perception to a single sense. The brain is extremely efficient. All new learning comes from the senses as the brain hungrily seeks as much information as it can from all its perception modes, all the time. Even if you wanted to, you would not be able to "turn off" one of your senses. While you might have a preference for a sensory modality based on past experiences and rehearsal in a certain context, those preferences change with each circumstance. You might think you are a "visual" person until you go to a music concert, for example.

We also know that there is no correlation between cognitive preferences (learning styles) and domain area aptitudes.[24] That is, one would think certain styles could be better equipped for certain types of learning, but there is no evidence for this.

More and more academic institutions are taking a stand on the side of evidence and rejecting the incorporation of learning styles in their practices. Titles like *"The Myth of Learning Styles: What Medical Educators Need to Know"*;[25] *"The Emperor's New Clothes Revisited: Learning Styles in Medical Education"*;[26] and *"Teachers Can Untangle the Truth from Myth in the Classroom: Using an Interdisciplinary*

Approach to 'Developing the Brain'"[27] hopefully signal the decline of this particularly persistent myth.

THE THEORY OF MULTIPLE INTELLIGENCES IS VALIDATED BY NEUROSCIENTIFIC RESEARCH

The Theory of Multiple Intelligences authored by Howard Gardner in 1983 revolutionized education by challenging teachers to think of the many ways a person can be intelligent, rather than the traditional idea that one was either "smart" or "not smart." Gardner's original theory[28] suggested seven intelligences (linguistic, logical-mathematical, visual-spatial, body-kinesthetic, musical-rhythmic, interpersonal, intrapersonal), and in 1997 he accepted an eighth, naturalistic.[29] To be considered, an intelligence should meet all eight criteria explained in 1999:[30]

1. The potential for brain isolation by brain damage
2. Its place in evolutionary history
3. The presence of core operations
4. Susceptibility to encoding
5. A distinct developmental progression
6. The existence of idiot savants, prodigies, and other exceptional people
7. Support from experimental psychology
8. Support from psychometric findings

The first point, "the potential for brain isolation by brain damage," is what led people to presume that the Theory of Multiple Intelligences (MI) was grounded in neuroscience. However, Gardner himself acknowledges that his is a psychological theory applied to education and did not originate in neuroscience, nor is the evidence to support his theory found in neuroscience. He emphasizes that intelligences are not in a single piece of the brain (a harkening back to localizationism), but rather complex neural networks. He clarifies:

> . . . *the several levels on which MI theory examines intelligences—as composites of fine-grained neurological subprocesses but not those subprocesses themselves, as biopsychological information processing capacities, and as the bases on which an individual can participate in meaningful activities in the broader cultural milieu.*[31]

This means that "visual-spatial intelligence" for example, would not be found in a single spot in the brain, but rather all of the networks of *subprocesses* known and presumed to exist in visual and spatial understanding and their correspond-ing pathways. Gardner suggests that "each intelligence comprises constituent units" and stated that "there are several musical, linguistic, and spatial subin-telligences."[32] In later work, Gardner called these "supermodules" that organize 50 to 100 "micromodules,"[33] noting that there are complex sub-elements to each intelligence. Whether we speak of *subprocesses, subintelligences,* or *micromodules,* Gardner's eight intelligences are multiplied in complexity once disaggregated into their sub-parts and would potentially require the documentation of hundreds of corresponding pathways, something not yet attempted.

Furthermore, Gardner establishes the important interaction among the eight intelligences to complete an individual, meaning that the whole person, not just the subsets of his or her various intelligences, should be the focus of our classroom endeavors.[34] Parsing out elements of a person ("he is a musical learner," "she is logical mathematical") does not serve the goal of teaching to the whole child[35] and does harm when an individual sees himself as the label of a single intelligence.

Where the Myth Comes From

Many have criticized the Theory of Multiple Intelligences (MI) for lacking neurosci-entific backing,[36] despite the fact that Gardner himself says he suggested a theory, not a prescription for schooling or a neuroscientifically substantiated intervention. Though people have interpreted his work as being a playbook for instruction, this was never his intention. Michael Posner wrote one of the few papers addressing the possible neural correlations underlying the various intelligences. In his paper, presented at the American Educational Research Association in 2003, Posner clar-ified that there are "examples of how real world actions may draw upon multiple neural systems and thus related to multiple forms of intelligence."[37] He also indi-cates: "It is also important to note that these networks have not proven to be as separate as though they were in different brains. Indeed, each node in these net-works communicates with other nodes of the network and with other networks."[37] This paper was an early hint at the complexity of trying to establish evidence for the multiple intelligences, and postulated that there were likely overlapping net-works in the different intelligences. There is a great amount of overlap in skill sets in nearly identical neural pathways for symbol interpretation of language and of math, for example.[38] Initially, Gardner himself inadvertently helped perpetuate the myth of different systems when he wrote: "MI theory demands that linguistic processing, for example, occur via a different set of neural mechanisms than does spatial or interpersonal processing."[39] To his credit, these earlier statements were modified after advancements in technology confirmed some of Gardner's original ideas related to sub-processes rather than separate networks:

Indeed, findings from neuroscience lend support to the call for increased spec-ificity in the classification of intellectual capacities. As Gardner pointed out in the original publications[40] it is likely that musical intelligence comprises several sub-intelligences relating to various dimensions of music, such as rhythm, har-mony, melody, and timbre. An analogous comment can be stated for each of the other intelligences.[43]

Gardner and colleagues suggested that "one test of MI theory would be whether the sub-intelligences within each intelligence correlate more highly with each other than they correlate with sub-intelligences within other intelli-gences,"[41] as this would be a much more accurate way to measure outcomes neu-roscientifically. However, this parsing of sub-processes would be a very complex undertaking: ". . . the number would quickly become unwieldy and virtually untranslatable to educators."[41] This means the myth exists in part due to the desire to avoid complexity.

In 2017, a paper was published entitled, "The Neuroscience of Intelligence: Empirical Support for the Theory of Multiple Intelligences?"[42], in which the authors review 318 studies in neuroscience and piece together evidence for the multiple intelligences by joining together many sub-processes for each intelligence under the umbrella of each of the eight intelligences. This is a significant task and advances the conversation in important ways. But while the evidence presented so far is an excellent start, it is incomplete. For example, in mapping neural correlates for math, there are at least 16 sub-processes that have been documented to date, including magnitude estimation and symbol to quantity understanding, among others,[43] which were not considered in the 2017 study.

What We Know Now

The Theory of Multiple Intelligences is just that, a theory, albeit a very good one that has rocked the foundations of education for the past four decades. The sheer complexity of the MI makes it untestable: ". . . the general processing complexity of the brain makes it unlikely that anything resembling Multiple Intelligences the-ory can ever be used to describe it."[44] However, this is actually one of the reasons to celebrate Multiple Intelligences, as it has moved society away from thinking of intelligence as binary (smart or not smart), and as being something easily mea-surable, which it is not. Daniel Willingham writes in his article "Reframing the Mind: Howard Gardner Became a Hero Among Educators Simply by Redefining Talents as 'Intelligences'"[45] that Gardner feels a majority of psychologists still favor a singular view when it comes to measuring and evaluating human intelligence.

We now know that there is no neuroscientific empirical evidence to back

Gardner's theory, and definitely no research that supports it without unifying hundreds of distinct pathways. We also know that dividing intelligence into multiple realms has often confused some teachers, who believe, mistakenly, that one intelligence can substitute for another. "Gardner also writes that intelligences are not fungible; the individual low in logical-mathematical intelligence but high in musical intelligence cannot somehow substitute the latter for the former and understand math through music."[46] This means the myth has also been perpetuated by a misunderstanding of the theory itself.

Gardner argues that the Theory of Multiple Intelligences is based on empirical findings,[47] just not from neuroscience. He and many of his followers suggest that this does not detract from the theory's usefulness or worth, but simply means the complexity of the theory is not testable with current technology in the field of neuroscience.

INTRINSIC MOTIVATION IS DRIVEN BY EXTERNAL REWARD

One of the best motivators to learn is personal satisfaction.[48] But where does this internal drive come from? Many believe that students are motivated to learn because of what the people around them do, called extrinsic motivation.

Starting in the 1970s, it was popular to believe the key to success lay within the now famous *self-esteem movement*.[49] This has proved, to a certain extent, to be validated by more recent research: A person's own belief in his or her ability to learn actually influences learning outcomes.[50] What has not panned out in the research is the belief that the development of positive self-esteem in children depends upon praise and positive reinforcements from adults and peers. So, what *does* makes a child believe in herself?

In a very mistaken interpretation of the research, teachers began giving children stickers and rewards for everything they did to "boost their self-esteem." This misguided practice not only led to disingenuous acts of rewarding kids for simply fulfilling basic expectations ("You followed the instructions? Congratulations! Here's your sticker." "You didn't get into a fight today? Congratulations! Here's your sticker."), but also delegitimized sincere feedback and praise for effortful improvement. This operant conditioning thinking led to a revival of external rewards to get kids to do things in schools, which in turn led to the eventual understanding that intrinsic motivation is not always driven by external reward. (The more than 7,500 teacher resources for sticker rewards options on Amazon. com alone indicate how many teachers have been persuaded that giving out stickers will keep kids on track.)

External rewards can take many forms, including positive praise and feedback, tangible rewards (such as a sticker, candy, money, or praise from parents or peers) or pressures (being tape-recorded or watched to be sure you comply or fined for bad behavior).[51] People can be extrinsically motivated in introjected fashions, such as going to school because of societal or cultural expectations, but the best way to instill motivation is through positive intrinsic forces (resolving a real-life problem of personal interest, learning to play music for the pleasure it gives, or being allowed to choose how and why to approach an assignment)[52] as this is the only way to assure potential transfer or future use of the learned competency.

Where the Myth Comes From

Many teachers believe their sole job is to keep kids motivated and on task, as reflected in numerous teacher guides (*Motivating Students Who Don't Care: Successful Techniques for Educators;*[53] *Practical & Easy Ways to Motivate Your Students (A+ Teacher Idea Book);*[54] *50 Quick Ways to Motivate and Engage Your Students*[55]). While it is true that students perceive a teacher's own level of motivation through social contagion,[56] it is not true that rewards—or punishments—need to be connected to the student-teacher relationship. It would be simpler to believe that teachers held all the bargaining chips for motivation in their own actions, but this is not true.

Every student comes to class with a lot of personal baggage; his own motivation for schoolwork is influenced not only by what the teacher does, but also by what his past experience has been with the subject, what he ate (or didn't eat) for breakfast, his relationships with his parents and peers, and how much he slept (or didn't) the night before, among a host of other factors. Motivation is not as simple as offering a reward. Teachers need to better understand the complex mechanisms of motivation to better leverage their role in student learning. While the teacher is the determining factor in establishing the right learning environment by demonstrating his or her enthusiasm for the subject matter and genuine concern for the students,[57] external rewards are not necessarily part of the magic formula to guarantee student motivation.

What We Know Now

We now know that autonomous motivation, or intrinsic structures for motivation, are much more powerfully associated with positive self-concept and academic achievement than external rewards.[58] In a sense, being an autonomous learner is its own reward. Self-determination theory tries to unite the best ways of using external motivators for intrinsic motivation, and suggests that teachers leverage the balance between what they can do for the students and what the students must do for themselves.[59]

In school-age populations, it is clear that punitive, externally driven motivators are associated with lower levels of intrinsic motivation for things like prosocial behavior, meaning that they are less desirable than intrinsic motivators.[60] Bear and colleagues' research[60] showed that helping students find their own intrinsic motivators—taking them on a walk and having them identify problems in their neighborhood they want to resolve and celebrating their success with them, for example—is more powerful than just supplying external praise.

According to Augustyniak and colleagues' article, "Intrinsic Motivation: An Overlooked Component for Student Success,"

> *Students with greater levels of intrinsic motivation demonstrate **strong conceptual learning**, **improved memory**, and **high overall achievement in school**.[61] These students are more likely to experience a state of **deep task immersion and peak performance**.[62] Studies have also shown that students with higher intrinsic motivation are also **more persistent**.[63] In fact, intrinsic motivation is a powerful factor in **performance, persistence to learn, and productivity**.[64]*

Clearly, intrinsic motivation is effective in spurring student achievement. But perhaps most important of all, the research clarifies that the teacher's role is confined to creating the circumstances under which the best learning occurs, rather than providing rewards themselves. Students need to learn to identify their own motivators, rather than relying on teachers for motivation.

TEACHER'S SUBJECT KNOWLEDGE AND INSTRUCTIONAL STRATEGIES ARE MORE IMPORTANT THAN THEIR RELATIONSHIPS WITH STUDENTS

The quality of a teacher's technical skills—knowledge of the learning content, pedagogy, didactics, and classroom management—influence the level of student learning, but there is a misconception that they are more important than student-teacher relations. Many believe that knowledge of content, such as mathematics, for example, and knowledge of strategies to teach that content, make a good math teacher. This is only partially true. There is now evidence that the learning environment and the quality of student-teacher interaction can have an even greater impact on student learning outcomes.[65]

It is clear that "good" learning environments aid learning, just as "bad" environments hinder learning.[66] But just how much of this is due to teachers and their relationships with students? The conversation about the role of good environments, either due to management,[67] or engagement[68] weighs heavily on teachers' decisions about student groupings, choice of activities, communication, and student-teacher interactions. What is less clear is how the teacher's relationships with the students influences their learning outcomes.

Where the Myth Comes From

For many years, "knowing" was enough: What a teacher knew (content knowledge) determined his or her status in a school—the more knowledgeable in a domain area, the better qualified the instructor. Information about the influence of affect on cognition has emerged only in the past 25 years,[69] meaning that what many teachers intuited as being true—emotions influence learning—now finally has hard evidence to support it.[70] This carries over into how teachers interact with their students. How a student feels about his potential to learn influences his actual learning, and the teacher plays the most important role in influencing this self-perception.[71] Personal interest in students was frowned upon just several decades ago in the Victorian age:[72] A teacher's role was originally just to instruct and to discipline. While some highly intuitive teachers realized that students live up to the expectations of their teachers, high or low,[73] it has only recently become common practice to take students' feelings into consideration when thinking about quality learning experiences.

What We Know Now

There is evidence that teachers can use "social contagion" to influence the environment.[74] The field of social cognitive neuroscience seeks to understand how people influence each other on three levels: "*the social level*, which is concerned with the motivational and social factors that influence behavior and experience; *the cognitive level*, which is concerned with the information-processing mechanisms that give rise to social-level phenomena; and *the neural level*, which is concerned with the brain mechanisms that instantiate cognitive-level processes."[75] Social contagion can explain, to a certain extent, how the teacher can influence the emotions and motivation level in a classroom.

When we speak of "good learning environments" these are dependent on the way the teacher manages the "feel" of the classroom setting through social contagion.[76] Do we smile because we are happy, or are we happy because we smile? Both![77] We now know that teachers have a very big influence on whether the group feels comfortable and to what extent other players in the class can influence the level of social contagion, good or bad, felt by the group. In fact, the teacher can "manage" the emotional state of the classroom; passion (or boredom) for the subject is contagious.

STUDENTS SHOULD BE REWARDED ALL THE TIME TO ELICIT DOPAMINE

Classical conditioning teaches us that people associate one condition with another. Some will remember Pavlov and his dogs, in which a bell was associated with food; eventually, the dogs would salivate whenever the bell was rung, even if food was not present.[78] Classical conditioning has been used in education for centuries to connect external rewards to learning outcomes. In positive form, this means something like giving a child a sticker when he achieves academically; in the negative, it can mean grounding a child (or taking away recess or the TV) as punishment if he fails academically.

In the 1950s, the first studies showing the relationship between motivation and addiction reported that the reason that classical conditioning works is based on the "dopaminergic loop" or reward system in the brain.[79] The press has reported so much on dopamine that it is known as "the media's neurotransmitter of choice."[80] The feeling of being high on drugs triggers the same mechanism as being intrinsically consumed by your own creativity or drive to learn something, which are all tied to intrinsic motivation. Teachers are told to get kids naturally motivated by stimulating the dopamine in their brains in order to achieve optimal learning.[81] The rationale is that teachers are responsible for creating the right conditions for dopamine release in the brain.

Dopamine is trending as the most popular neurotransmitter. And why not? . . . The craving you have when you smell the coffee brewing in the morning—thank dopamine. That elation you feel throughout your body when you fall hopelessly and deeply in love? Again, dopamine. The thrill of a shopping spree at the mall, the desire for the second and third glass of wine at dinner. You guessed it, dopamine. Dopamine seems to be everywhere giving people a little rush of pleasure and energy when we need it most. So, what's the harm? It's a natural, biologically based chemical that provides energy and motivation. . . . The increase in motivation and energy that dopamine provides can be a good thing, but when your brain gets wired to compulsive behaviors that stimulate the dopamine reward pathway (addictions), then your life can be as out of control as the poor rat in Skinner's Box.[82]

The truth of the matter is that dopamine is first and foremost triggered by fundamental needs, such as pleasure, food, and sex—not the top three things associated with school. It is also known that the search for pleasure overrides other needs. Olds and Milner[83] found that rats opted for stimulation of pleasure centers in the brain rather than eat, and others showed they would prefer to ingest cocaine for the pleasure sensation until they died, rather than meet their basic survival needs.[84] This view of dopamine as fundamental to addiction is hard to square with the view of dopamine as the heart of learning.

But there is a link. Recent studies indicate that "reward motivation promotes memory formation via dopamine release in the hippocampus prior to learning,"[85] and that dopamine is important for episodic memory consolidation.[86] It is clear that dopamine facilitates reward systems and some memory systems, and so, indirectly, motivation and learning. However, it is a leap from there to specific classroom interventions. There is no real research to date on how teachers can use this information. But there is a widespread misinterpretation that good *teaching* equals *dopamine*, which equals *motivation*, which equals *learning*. Just because dopamine aids some kinds of memory and motivation does not mean that teachers can increase dopamine levels through their teaching.

There are six presumptions here, five of which are not necessarily true, and one of which (the last) is definitely not true: (a) motivation is always expressed through dopamine release; (b) learning only occurs with positive motivation; (c) memory and learning are dependent on motivation; (d) fun is equal to motivation; (e) fun is necessary to learn; and finally, the idea that (f) teachers can control the level of dopamine in their students through good classroom environments or specific activities.

Where the Myth Comes From

This myth stems from the belief that there is a necessary link between dopamine and motivation (sometimes there is, sometimes there isn't), between motivation and learning (sometimes there is, sometimes there isn't), and that certain teaching methodologies trigger dopamine in their students' brains (there is no evidence of this, yet). Although it is tempting to think that the creation of a good classroom environment will release dopamine and therefore increase students' motivation to learn, this belief sidesteps three important ideas. First, science has not definitively established what constitutes a "good" learning environment, making this impossible to test. Second, different students will react to different environments in different ways, meaning that even if we knew which environments were "good" for dopamine, not all students would react as expected. Third, there is not yet one study that indicates just how teachers can influence dopamine in students through a given activity, meaning evidence of dopamine release in students under specific conditions has not yet been studied. To complicate matters even further, with current technology there is no way to replicate studies of "good" environments, making the science behind the teacher's role questionable.

What We Know Now

While there is little doubt that motivation is linked to dopamine,[87] it is not clear how teachers can influence the level of dopamine in their students, or how different instructional activities influence the level of dopamine release.

We now know that learning can occur under conditions of negative motivation rather than positive;[88] that one does not have to be motivated to establish a memory, nor to learn;[89] that one can be motivated but *not* learn;[90] that fun and motivation are not one and the same (you can have fun without being motivated, and be motivated without having fun);[91] that one can learn without having fun;[92] and finally and most important, there is no evidence that teaching with specific methodologies can influence dopamine in all students.

While it is likely that rewards and shared values in decision making in classroom settings can change the motivational levels of students,[93] which could possibly modify dopamine levels,[94] there is no study to date that has proven this. Dopamine release can be linked to operant conditioning,[95] which is strongly connected to the specific individual memories, meaning not all situations will resonate with all individuals in the same way.

STUDENTS SHOULD BE GIVEN POSITIVE REINFORCEMENT TO SPEED LEARNING PROCESSES

Positive reinforcement means praising students for their efforts or giving rewards for behaviors, which can benefit learning in some situations, but not in all. Sometimes positive reinforcement can actually have a negative outcome.[96] Initially, positive reinforcement was based on core operant conditioning, in which good behavior is rewarded,[97] and bad behavior is punished.

The pendulum of classroom disciplinary practices has swung back and forth for centuries—or even millennia.[98] Around 2,300 years ago, Plato was in favor of positive discipline, in a way that presages the current trend in education toward restorative discipline: "Do not train a child to learn by force or harshness; but direct them to it by what amuses their minds, so that you may be better able to discover with accuracy the peculiar bent of the genius of each."[99] In the interim, educators have often adopted more punitive methods that echoed contemporaneous child-rearing wisdom—i.e., Butler's 1663 admonition "spare the rod and spoil the child"[100]—and the pendulum continues to swing back and forth. Views now are slightly more even-handed and look toward the balance between positive and negative, and extrinsic and extrinsic motivators. The current thinking about classroom management and school discipline also reflects a new emphasis on the importance of the quality of feedback that teachers provide, whether positive or negative.

Lam, Cheng and Yang's research on higher education students in Hong Kong "suggested that formative feedback leads to increases in intrinsic motivation to attend the courses and students' overall positive emotions. It also exerts a 'protecting' effect on their extrinsic motivation to attend the courses."[101] This means that, rather than being positive or negative, it is more important that feedback exists at all, as it drives motivation.

While it might seem intuitive, there is evidence that positive reinforcement can, indeed, serve to change problem behavior that had been "maintained by negative reinforcement"[102] and that differentiated reinforcement based on student behaviors is better than unconditional positive reinforcement.[103] This means that while the back-and-forth between positive and negative reinforcement has continued for centuries, it is more important to *guide* learning with feedback, rather than to be always positive. It is also clear that constant positive reinforcement is not as useful as sincere and moderate positive feedback.

Where the Myth Comes From

Recent research by John Hattie[104] indicates that a student's own self-perception as a learner makes a big difference in his likelihood of learning. This is echoed by multiple studies[105] leading to the conclusion that how teachers make a student feel is important in predicting learning outcomes. While this seems to be true, a student's sense of self-efficacy is born of more than just positive reinforcement. Students develop self-efficacy by overcoming obstacles and persisting,[106] not because people give them continual praise. The myth that all positive reinforcement is the right way to go comes from the misunderstanding that self-esteem is dependent on extrinsic positive reinforcements.

What We Know Now

It would be easy to tell teachers they just have to be positive and nice to their students, and *voilà!* they will learn, but the truth is not this simple or direct. Positive reinforcement will often work, but not all the time and not with all students. While some animal studies seem to show a correlation related to operant conditioning, humans are more complex, and motivators are often not intuitive. As with the giving of rewards to students, what we know now is that too much extrinsic reinforcement in the form of praise can reduce a student's intrinsic desire to learn.[107] Honest, constructive feedback, rather than unconditional praise, helps build up a student's self-perception as a successful learner, which in turn influences learning outcomes.[108]

STUDENTS MUST BE EXPOSED TO NEW INFORMATION BETWEEN THREE AND SEVEN TIMES TO LEARN IT EFFECTIVELY

Repetition is necessary in learning processes, but precisely how much repetition is necessary depends on prior knowledge.[109] The more prior experience you have with a concept (*prerequisite knowledge*), the less repetition is needed to build off of that concept to construct new knowledge. This means that someone with a lot of prior experience with a concept might need only a handful of repetitions to "know" the new concept (1 to 10 repetitions), but a person who has little prior knowledge might need many more exposures[110] over time[111] and with deliberate practice.[112] Physical changes in the brain (increases in white matter tracts, for example) are evidence of neural plasticity thanks to repetition[113] or experience, and they correlate with the speed of retrieval. That is, the thicker the white matter tract, the quicker the recall and the stronger the evidence for new learning.[114]

Where the Myth Comes From

Early research on memory by Hermann Ebbinghaus[115] showed that people experience a clear learning curve when faced with unknown information. He showed that distributed learning over time is more effective than massed practice, and also showed that there was such a thing as a "forgetting curve" in which fewer repetitions over time lead to faster forgetting than lots of repetition over longer periods of time.[115] He was one of the first to suggest that there was a minimum number of repetitions needed before learning occurred, and that this varied with the familiarity of the information.

Others suggested *"Why Three Exposures May Be Enough"*[116] and this became a mantra in advertising until *"The Rule of Seven"* replaced it.[117] The belief was that people need to be exposed three to seven times before the product sticks in their minds, and was known as "effective frequency."[118]

It would be easy for teachers to work three to seven repetitions of a concept into each class situation and call it a day, but this will not guarantee learning. While there is argument for multiple exposures, precisely how much repetition is needed in class contexts depends heavily on how much exposure students have already had to the new learning content in other contexts, and on human variance. While there are multiple studies that show how rats learn a maze after a handful of exposures, we can't assume that children need the same amounts of exposure as rats to learn how to read, interact socially, construct a math problem, or understand overarching themes in human history. The "magic number" (whether three or seven) might work for product recognition in advertisements or rats in a maze, but is not a reliable guide for teachers.

What We Know Now

Thanks to confirmation of Ebbinhaus's work, we now know that the more complex the concept, the more repetition is needed over time in order to learn it. Prescribing a set number of times for any new learning by all students makes no sense. If a student has more prior knowledge of a topic, less repetition is needed. Teachers need to know their students' past experiences and how to provide flexible access to resources, so students get the exposure they need.

UNSTRUCTURED DISCOVERY LEARNING IS PREFERABLE TO STRUCTURED, TEACHER-CENTERED INSTRUCTION

Calls for "unstructured" and "discovery" learning are popular these days, even though they originated back with Dewey,[119] Piaget,[120] and Vygotsky,[121] and were expanded by Rogers at the turn of the 21st century.[122] The premise is that when children are allowed to learn freely and without the restraints of adult guidance, they will learn better. *Guided play*, *problem-based learning*, *experiential or inquiry learning*, *scaffolded discovery*, and *child-led or student-centered learning* are all versions of unstructured discovery learning, which are touted as superior to teacher-centered instruction.

At first blush, it is easy to see how focusing on student-centered activities and interests might be effective. However, the optimal choice of pedagogy—whether discovery, Socratic method, or direct instruction—actually depends upon the learning goal. Different learning objectives require different methodologies. Sometimes student-led, unstructured discovery is better, and sometimes teacher-centered, explicit instruction is better. The choice of teaching tools depends on the learning objective.

Where the Myth Comes From

It is possible that the rejection of teacher-centered instruction became popular in the 1980s as the backlash against standardized tests emerged and in the 2010s, when people began to question the worth of a university education.[123] It was thought that kids spend too much time in class memorizing teacher- and text-generated context, and not enough time exploring their environment, the world around them, and their own ideas. Some studies also showed that children's free discovery permitted the achievement of self-regulation and even deeper learning, though it was harder to manage.[124] But while student-centered learning has multiple merits, its popularity across instructional contexts rested more on bandwagonitis than on research.

What We Know Now

We now know that the decision about what kind of methodology, activity, or strategy to use should be made based on the objective. This planning structure is based on Backward Design,[125] in which teachers first determine objectives, followed by evaluation criteria, and lastly, activities. If the goals are student independence, inquiry, and discovery, then permitting students to explore freely is beneficial. Unstructured play is great for children's autonomy, and student-led inquiry can be very effective for engaging students in problem solving, particularly in math and science. However, if the goal is explicit conceptual instruction, then teacher-centered education, including lecturing, can be superior.[126]

INTELLIGENCE TESTS MEASURE INTELLIGENCE

Humans have always been fascinated with comparative measures—*who is the tallest, fastest, smartest?* This competitiveness, as applied to intelligence, most likely has come about as a byproduct of human evolution; being smart, after all, extends one's life span and is thus a factor in the "survival of the fittest".[127] The desire to develop good tools to measure intelligence has existed for centuries, with roots in the work of Francis Dalton,[128] who attempted to measure heritable traits related to intelligence (which he abandoned after data did not bear out his theory). The science of measurement was extended by James McKeen Cattell, who developed *mental testing*,[129] and was succeeded by Johann Friedrich Herbart, who helped conceptualize new tools to measure the mind. Wilhelm Wundt, the first person to call himself a psychologist, joined Ernst Heinrich Weber and Gustav Fechner in defining psychometrics itself, or the measurement of the mind. It wasn't until 1905, however, that French psychologists Alfred Binet, Victor Henri, and Théodore Simon published a test that used verbal abilities as a proxy for intelligence.

The Binet-Simon Test was modified by Lewis Terman[130] at Stanford in 1906 and generated the Stanford-Binet Intelligence Test, which remains in use today. Louis Leon Thurston[131] was one of the first to suggest a multivariate aspect of intelligence, believing there were seven aspects to human intelligence (verbal comprehension, word fluency, number facility, spatial visualization, associative memory, perceptual speed, and reasoning). In 1939, David Wechsler produced his own test, which built upon Thurston's ideas and today includes 10+ subtests that further diversify the way we interpret intelligence.

Whereas Thurston and Wechsler suggested multifaceted ways that intelligence could be manifested, there was another line of thinking. People like Raymond Cattell,[132] John Horn,[133] and John Carroll[134] suggested that rather than a single intelligence or multiple intelligences (as Gardner was to propose in the early 1980s), there were two types of cognitive abilities: fluid intelligence (Gf) and crystallized intelligence (Gc). Cattell, Horn, and Carroll's view was that intelligence is highly malleable and depends on life experiences. Later versions of their test considered hierarchical models with different "strata." These levels broke down intelligence into over 70 sub-abilities,[135] making it more complete but less testable.

The most popular tests today include the Wechsler Intelligence Scale for Children and the Wechsler Adult Intelligence Scale[136] the Stanford-Binet,[137] Woodcock-Johnson Tests of Cognitive Abilities,[138] Raven's Progressive Matrices,[139] the Kaufman Assessment Battery for Children,[140] and the Differential Ability Scales.[141]

While the Stanford-Binet is arguably the standard-bearer in the field thanks to its longevity, the Wechsler IQ Test—currently the most complex structure in history—has 10 core subtests and 5 supplemental tests, each of which has two sub-elements (verbal and performance). The core test, which takes 60 to 90 minutes, measures abstract (a) verbal reasoning; (b) semantic knowledge; (c) verbal comprehension and expression; (d) the ability to express abstract social conventions, rules, and expressions; (e) visual spatial processing and problem solving; (f) visual motor construction; (g) nonverbal abstract problem solving; (h) inductive reasoning; (j) working memory; (k) attention, encoding; (l) auditory processing; (m) concentration; (n) mental manipulation; (o) associative memory; and (p) graphomotor speed. The five optional tests cover (q) the degree of general information acquired from culture; (r) the ability to quickly perceive visual details; (s) quantitative reasoning; (t) mental control; and (u) processing speed. Despite the numerous areas covered by the Wechsler, there are criticisms that it is *still limited* in considering all areas of intelligence.[142] Aside from its content limitations, it is criticized for administration and correction time; reliability related to the long-term stability of scores post test; and validity. Having said that, proponents argue that without such tests, we have no measure to gauge students' potential. Additionally, some argue that they are adequate *enough*, making them a worthwhile activity.

In addition to these intelligence tests, there are international standardized achievement exams including the Programme for International Student Assessment (PISA);

Trends in International Mathematics and Science Study (TIMSS); and the Progress in International Reading Literacy Study (PERLS). These break with the idea of measuring intelligence and instead focus on measuring skills. PISA is "a triennial international survey which aims to evaluate education systems worldwide by testing the skills and knowledge of 15-year-old students."[143] In 2017, 72 countries and 8 country regions measured through the PISA exam "whether students can apply in real life situations what they have learned in school." Students are asked to "interpret texts, solve mathematics problems, or explain a phenomenon scientifically using their knowledge and reasoning skills," and to display "social and emotional skills" as well as "work and communicate with others" rather than dates or formulas.[144] TIMSS is run by the International Association for the Evaluation of Educational Achievement and studies 4th and 8th grade math and science achievement in 57 different countries.[145] PIRLS is a study by the International Association for the Evaluation of Educational Achievement and taken by 50 countries.[146] These international standardized exams do not measure intelligence, nor are they designed to do so. This means that, independent of all the hype, results on these kinds of tests do not answer questions like whether China is the world's cleverest country.[147] Such international comparisons, often based on misinterpretations of the exams or of their results, promote myths about the purpose and applicability of standardized testing.

In the United States, "a typical student takes 112 mandated standardized tests between pre-kindergarten classes and 12th grade."[148] "Standardized tests have been a scourge of student life in America for more than 50 years, but it's fair to say they're more pressure-packed and ubiquitous than ever before" says *Time* magazine's Dan Fletcher.[149] *The Washington Post* headline summarizes that "Study Says Standardized Testing is Overwhelming Nation's Public Schools."[150] Critics of standardized tests agree that "many tests created for national use may not include content emphasized at the state level, resulting in students being tested on material they have not been taught."[151] Intelligence tests, standardized state and local exams, as well as international comparative assessments all contribute to a better understanding of an individual's abilities, but no single measure tells us the whole story of a person's full aptitude and acumen. Many suggest developing K-12 e-portfolios, which document learning over time as measured by student-generated artifacts as a more authentic and effective way of measuring intelligence.

Where the Myth Comes From

Intelligence testing has been around for so long that it leads us to mistakenly believe that the tools must be legitimate or that their use is inevitable. To make matters worse, we humans are also notorious for expecting external confirmation of our abilities,[152] rather than devoting time to learn to self-assess. Unless the boss says we are doing a good job or the teacher gives us a good grade, we seem to have a hard time evaluating our own performance.

To make matters worse, students are constantly evaluated against a "myth of average,"[153] as high school drop-out turned Harvard faculty member Todd Rose says, and every parent's dream is that their child is "above" that average.

> *Most of us know intuitively that a score on a personality test, a rank on a stan-dardized assessment, a grade point average, or a rating on a performance review doesn't reflect your, or your child's, or your students', or your employees' abilities. Yet the concept of average as a yardstick for measuring individuals has been so thoroughly ingrained in our minds that we rarely question it seriously.*[153]

In addition to their frequency, many critics of standardized tests object to their content: "many tests created for national use may not include content emphasized at the state level, resulting in students being tested on material they have not been taught."[154]

The test-making industry is a profitable one in the U.S. In 1995, standardized testing in schools was a $7 million industry. By 1997, in the wake of No Child Left Behind, it was worth $263 million, and in 2014 it was estimated at $400 million annually, spread out among just four providers: Harcourt Educational Measurement, CTB McGraw-Hill, Riverside Publishing (a Houghton Mifflin company), and NCS Pearson.[155] Since testing is legally binding in many states, the investment in the business is nonnegotiable; so test after test is added on and packaged in well-designed marketing campaigns that swamp schools, educational conferences, and direct (e)mailings.

What We Know Now

The Wechsler, Stanford-Binet, Raven's and other aforementioned tools measure *some* aspects of human intelligence, but no test covers all elements. We now know that Binet's original idea to use language as a *proxy* for intelligence created most of the problems we still have today with testing. Proxies are only *substitutes* for the real thing. Unfortunately, no test to date, independent of how well designed, measures intelligence in all its facets. The idea that human intelligence is easily measurable is attractive—but at least as of today, illusive. The complexities of thinking and the measurement of "smarts" are limited by the tools we have. Intelligence tests measure what they measure and nothing more. It would be nice if a 10- to 45-minute, or even a 4-hour test (like the SATs) could assess an individual with accuracy, but it is just not that simple. A thorough evaluation of a person's intelligence would take days or weeks of observation and testing on multiple areas of aptitude. As this is not cost-effective, and multiple-choice (online) tests are, the likelihood of convincing schools and governments to change their evaluation tools is low. To test the complexities of human intelligence, you need complex tools; we have less than adequate methods at hand.

There are severe limits to standardized tests. First, multiple-choice tests can only measure knowledge, or basic "Googleable" facts. Rarely can they measure skills, attitudes, or values in any detail, except by proxy or when a separate questionnaire is applied, as in the case of PISA. PISA collects data on social and emotional development, the value of teamwork, and whether or not a student feels engaged in school or not,[156] which may point to new trends in testing in which the broader spectrum of human skills is measured, as Naglieri suggests in his article on the "second-generation intelligence tests"[157] which are beginning to emerge.

Second, intelligence is highly complex, and its definition is debatable. Many nebulous terms used to describe intelligence tend to confound rather than clarify. If we agree with Einstein that "the true sign of intelligence is not knowledge but imagination," or with Socrates, who said, "I know that I am intelligent, because I know that I know nothing," we would have to ask ourselves: How do we measure "imagination" and "nothing"? If we agree that there are multiple intelligences, how can we justify using multiple-choice tests to measure music, kinesthetic, and interpersonal understanding? Depending on what we value, the definition of intelligence changes, and based on that definition, the evaluation tools must then also change.

If the stranglehold on time dedicated to standardized tests is lifted, teachers will once again be free to teach to individual mastery needs, rather than to the test. Without the pressure of standardized tests, teachers will be allowed to teach beyond the small number of core subjects tested in the curriculum, and to pay more attention to music, the arts, sports, and more social and nonverbal types of learning that are currently all but ignored in the curriculum because they are harder to test. According to Strauss, "Schools and school systems that point with pride to their high scores on standardized tests are advertising their willingness to limit students' thought to a couple of low-level thought processes."[158] The general consensus is that standardized tests may serve policy makers, but at what price to learners?

WHY THIS IS GOOD NEWS FOR TEACHING

It is wonderful to eliminate the idea of learning styles from the classroom context; teachers' time is much better spent working with what we know for certain about the brain, in a way that can really influence students' learning outcomes.

The fact that multiple intelligences cannot be proved in neuroscience without deciphering the complex sub-processes of each intelligence is cause for celebration rather than lament. One of the best things that the Theory of Multiple Intelligences has done for education is to motivate teachers to vary their instructional patterns and to teach with multiple entry points for each class topic. While not the main objective of the theory, this strengthens access to information by rehearsing distinct neural pathways to the same mental schema. Distinct schemata reinforce different types of memory networks for the same concept (i.e., learning that an apple is a fruit that grows from seeds that turn into trees, that has a specific shape and taste and can be used to bake certain recipes, comes in red, green, and yellow hues, can be sliced into quarters and eighths and shared . . .). The result is a broadened understanding of each concept.[159] Another piece of good news is that teachers can still be motivated to use Gardner's theory, but to do so to provide entry points into topics, rather than be-all-end-all content or classification of learner types. Author and psychologist Carlo Cerrti argues in "Building a Functional Multiple Intelligence Theory to Advance Educational Neuroscience,"[160] that helping teachers understand the complexities of how the brain works, rather than teaching and testing toward multiple intelligences, will make educational efforts more successful.

Knowing that learning cannot be separated from the socio-emotional context is important for teachers, and a relief to many. Emotions influence what and how we can think. Great teachers use emotional leverages to get students interested in the topic at hand. When we talk about "authentic" learning, we mean learning that has meaning and importance for the student, which is generated in great part by emotion. Teachers have been told for years that they should help kids believe in themselves as learners, as this has one of the strongest effect on student learning outcomes,[161] and at the least this means that the learner feels that the teacher cares about his or her learning.[161] Understanding how emotions and cognition are linked gives teachers more reason that ever to apply the advice to enhance authentic learning, create good environments, improve communication, and build student self-efficacy.

Great teachers know there is no decision, learning, or cognition without emotion. The way students feel about their peers, their teachers, the classroom environment, the schoolyard, and themselves can all influence learning outcomes.

Great teachers understand social contagion and the direct influence they have on student learning outcomes. They realize that they influence learning through their relationships with students, and in this way, are responsible for the classroom environment.

The brain is the organ of the teaching profession. It is good news for teachers to know that the brain is also responsible for feelings, not just cognition and thinking. Information gets into long-term memory and becomes learned material when it has survival value, is easy to associate with prior knowledge, or if it has personal value. Transmitting that we care about their learning can motivate students. It's good news that teachers can rethink mantras like, "head, heart, hand" with an understanding that the brain is the generator of cognition, emotions, and action. Finally, it is important for teachers to know that emotional states influence cognitive states. This is great news for teachers, who can use both cognitive as well as affective strategies to help kids learn.

A better understanding about the relationship of motivation to learning is also great news, for two reasons. First, knowledge about intrinsic motivation takes the burden off teachers as the sole motivators of students and places responsibility with the students themselves. Second, it gives teachers permission to make teaching the personal interaction it was always meant to be. It's great for teachers to know that authentic interactions with students, rather than scripted, all-positive responses, are actually more effective in influencing learning outcomes.

Teachers cannot help students identify their own motivators if they do not know the students well. There is little doubt that good student-teacher relationships enhance student engagement,[162] and now there is also evidence that this engagement translates into better learning.[163] Teachers can now spend more time getting to know their students, rather than scheming on rewards systems.

Better understanding of motivation also helps teachers understand how "time on task" enhances learning, which is not the same for all students. A simple formula might sound attractive—"repeat three to seven times"—but humans are too complex to be served by such a one-size-fits-all rule. Students vary widely based on their unique prior experiences, and some will need more practice and repetition than others to grasp a concept or master a skill.

Finally, teachers should celebrate the fact that their students are learning both inside and outside the classroom and try to take advantage of prior knowledge they might have to transfer students' understanding from one context to another. We often forget how easy and natural it is for people to learn when it is authentic and in a recognizable context. Teachers can take advantage of multiple authentic learning contexts to get across the more lasting ideas and goals of education (critical and creative thinking, perseverance, honesty, good communication skills,

Practical Application of MBE:
Differentiate Homework by Leveraging Technology

Homework, which provides students with the opportunity to extend their learning outside the classroom, offers the repetition needed to strengthen neural networks, making recall and thereby learning possible. However, not all students need the same amount of homework to learn.

One way to differentiate homework is to take advantage of virtual platforms. Different students need different amounts of repetition at different times for different subjects. Teachers can provide different types and quantities of resources for students online. For example, virtual classrooms provide space for extra rehearsal for students who need more practice through self-correcting quizzes, optional readings at higher- and lower-than-average levels, and space for students to voice specific concerns the moment they have trouble, rather than waiting for the next class. Great teachers can learn to create online access to differentiated reinforcement by planning homework options that meet every student's personal needs.

solidarity, intellectual curiosity, and teamwork, among other things), rather than limiting our instruction to content-specific ideas (such as grammatical rules and math formulas). This reminds us that shaping lifelong learners has priority over the next standardized test, as people will spend more time out of classroom contexts than within them.

We now turn to Myths about Human Development.

4 • MYTHS ABOUT

HUMAN DEVELOPMENT

HUMANS ARE BORN WITH A "BLANK SLATE" AND THEY WILL LEARN IF KNOWLEDGE IS SIMPLY PROVIDED

The concept of *tabula rasa*, Latin for blank slate, is based on the idea that all creatures are born equal, or at least under equal conditions, and that humans are shaped uniquely by their environments.[1] Being born with a blank slate means that babies can have anything deposited into the "empty vessels" of their heads, and that a person becomes, in essence, what they are exposed or taught. A blank slate suggests a type of naiveté about the world, but from a positive angle, it can also mean someone without prejudgments. The concept of *tabula rasa* as John Locke explained in the 17th century, suggests children begin their lives "morally neutral" and are made either good or bad by the environment, as "all ideas come from sensation or reflection."[2] This means that the quality of a child's upbringing would be the paramount input into her character and personality. It also means that all knowledge is constructed from perceptions of the world or life experiences, without influence from a child's internal, natural, or genetic structures.

Does this make the search for meaning innate? Certainly, learning is natural for humans. Learning, however, is not necessarily aimed at finding meaning. Humans learn things that help them survive and manage their environments, but this is not always through meaning making. If the search for meaning were innate, this would signal that humans were naturally rational (rather than socio-emotional), which is a philosophical debate.

Where the Myth Comes From

Aristotle first mentioned the concept of *tabula rasa* in what can be argued was the first psychological text ever written, *DeAnima*.[3] Aristotle suggests that all living creatures have sense perception, and it is primarily through their senses that they "know" their world. He writes that "perception is the capacity of the soul which distinguishes animals from plants," which also establishes a kind of hierarchy in nature among creatures.[3] The concept of *tabula rasa* was made famous by Locke in *An Essay Concerning Human Understanding*; it was his belief that children were born with blank slates and are all potentially good, but that society corrupts this natural purity. He suggested that being surrounded by loving parents and family members would protect children from the harshness and evils of society; an individual's environment, rather than his genetic makeup, is responsible for his personality and knowledge.

Locke can be forgiven for suggesting something we now know was intelligent speculation; after all, babies are born nearly helpless in all ways, so why not also in terms of thinking skills? Babies cannot feed themselves, clean themselves, nor at times even calm themselves without the help of adults. It is intelligent speculation to presume that children would not be able to learn or think without external assistance. The belief in the human blank slate was prevalent for nearly 200 years, through the Victorian age, and only in modern times has a clearer understanding emerged of how complex the brain is, and how much has already been "poured" into the human vessel of the mind before birth.

What We Know Now

We now know that people are born with some knowledge thanks to experiences in the womb and to their genetic makeup. The combination of nature (genes) and nurture (the environmental experiences that potentiate genes) results in a person's phenotype, or their observable behavior, including who they "are" and what they can potentially become. This combines with free will to determine intellectual potential.

There are strong arguments against blank slate beliefs, many articulated by Steven Pinker.[4] These stem from several sources, including common sense, the study of human universals, genetics, and neuroscience. Common sense suggests there are visible examples in society of how creatures are born with some innate traits, including the language instinct, and perhaps even morality.[4] Human universals suggest that all people are more alike than they are different, with inborn qualities uniting the species. Pinker argues that while culture and environment mediate approaches to the world, the core of *humanness* is the same. Genetic and neuroscientific evidence shows that identical twins separated at birth are more alike than fraternal twins separated at birth, suggesting that more than environment shapes the individual. Taken together, these arguments suggest that human beings are not born with blank slates, but rather with a combination of what they inherit both from their commonalities as members of the species and from their genetic makeup as individuals from their parents.

HUMANS ARE BORN WITH ALL OF THE NEURONS THEY WILL EVER HAVE

The precise number of neurons in the human brain at birth in not definitively known, but we think there are about 86 billion, give or take 8 billion,[5] though glial cells—those that surround and insulate the neurons—increase over the life span. Over the course of an individual's life, some of these cells will die and some new cells will be born. Synaptic pruning is the way the brain trims off excess neurons. Neurogenesis is the birth of new neurons, which come from progenitor cells and neural stem cells.

Neurogenesis occurs in all animals, but was only discovered in human beings in 1998.[6] Thus, it is understandable that this myth—that humans are born with all the neurons we will ever have—would hold sway before advances in technology made it possible to know otherwise. Nevertheless, articles about dying brain cells still make the headlines with some frequency. The idea that "New 'Wonder-Drug' May Prevent Brain Cells from Dying"[7] or that "Exercise Makes You Grow New Brain Cells–But Only the Right Kind of Exercise"[8] is common in the popular press.

Where the Myth Comes From

This is one of the more easy-to-understand myths, which arises from speculation in the absence of information. It is only in recent years that we have proof of neurogenesis thanks to advances in technology. But even now, we are unsure what this means, exactly, for learning potential. Is the gain or loss of brain cells over time good or bad? And we have yet to accurately count neurons in the brain, in part because it is not yet clear just what counts as a "cell." In a summary of the research on this topic, "The Search for True Numbers of Neurons and Glial Cells in the Human Brain: A Review of 150 Years of Cell Counting,"[9] the authors question whether the glial cells, which outnumber other types of cells in the brain, are in fact the "glue" binding other cells. That is, perhaps these are not new cells at all, but rather new links between cells.

What We Know Now

We now know that neurogenesis occurs not only as the brain is forming and throughout childhood, but also in adults, and that there are more types of cells in the brain than in all the other body's organs combined. At the time of this writing, there are 352 different cell types in the brain, based on 62,304 different digital reconstructions, which are divided by form and function.[10]

> *For a long time, it was thought that the nervous system is fixed and incapable of regeneration. Although it is indeed true that most neurons in the brain are generated before birth and are never exchanged, it is now well established that new neurons are continuously generated by stem cells . . .* [11]

According to one study,[12] "in adult humans about 700 new neurons are added in the hippocampus every day."

Scientists have organized the cells that make up the nervous system into two broad groups: *neurons*, which are the primary signaling cells, and *glia*, which support neurons in various ways. The human brain contains around 100 billion neurons and, by most estimates, somewhere between 10 to 50 times as many glial cells.[13] Of all of the different types, places, forms, and functions of neurons, there is documentation of neurogenesis in only a few areas of the brain (precisely, the subgranular zone in the dentate gyrus of the hippocampus, the striatum, and the olfactory bulb).[14] We now know that "adult-born hippocampal neurons are more likely to be lost than the neurons born during development in humans,"[15] meaning that these new neurons are fragile in comparison with those developed before birth.

EVERYTHING IMPORTANT ABOUT THE BRAIN IS DETERMINED BY THE AGE OF THREE

John Bruer, president emeritus of the James S. McDonnell Foundation, is a staunch critic of overreaching statements in education with claims to neuroscientific backing. He is best known for his article "A Bridge Too Far,"[16] in which he proclaimed that information from neuroscience and education managed such distinct variables and levels of analysis (neurons and classrooms, for example) that transferring data from one field to the other would be irresponsible. He later modified his position slightly, acknowledging that there had been some advances that teachers could now use.[17] His program in Latin America has helped a generation of educators improve practice based on evidence-backed findings. Bruer is less known for his book *The Myth of the First Three Years*[18] in which he meticulously dismantles the many popular press claims that children must receive extra stimulation in the first three years or they will not live up to their potential. The OECD[19] echoed how this neuromyth has caused a flurry of commercially motivated products—which likely will not hurt, but also not likely help—small children develop intellectual prowess.

Bruer is joined in his critique of what some have come to call "the first three years movement" in which parenting journals, some businesses, child welfare advocates, and politicians draws on the authority of neuroscience to argue that social problems such as inequality, poverty, educational underachievement, violence, and mental illness are best addressed through "'early intervention' programmes to protect or enhance emotional and cognitive aspects of children's brain development. . ."[20]

This *bandwagonitis* mentality grows out of sincere and legitimate social and parental interest to do everything possible to ensure that children succeed in life, including appropriate activities in the "critical" zero-to-three age range. Dedication to providing children with the best environment possible is admirable, but good parents and reasonable citizens can be made to feel inadequate when they are berated into buying products to help toddlers get ahead.

Where the Myth Comes From

Programs originally designed to help children born with problems often turn out to be somewhat beneficial for the general population. For example, after establishing that massage could help preterm infants whose mothers had used cocaine,[21] it was speculated that preterm babies without cocaine exposure would also benefit from massage.[22] Then it was also suggested that *any* baby would benefit from massage,[23] which turned into the recommendation that *all* babies should be massaged.[24] While it is generally correct that everyone can benefit from a massage now and then, and that receiving a massage is better than not receiving a massage (though some of the benefits are actually more pronounced in mothers, not their infants,[25] it is not clear that it is better than many other things you could be doing with the baby, like playing, reading or talking. These kinds of interventions, originally meant for special populations alone, became adopted by the general population based on the presumptions that it might help, and "it couldn't hurt."

Stories of neglect and abuse of small children helped fuel the myth, as did contemporaneous research on rats. Research conducted by Rosenzweig, Diamond, and colleagues[26] found that rats in impoverished environments had smaller brain volume, mainly due to fewer dendrites and synaptic connections caused by fewer stimuli. This study, combined with horror stories about real children such as

Genie,[27] who was strapped to a toilet seat for 14 years and, once released, was incapable of learning much more than basic language and social skills, shocked parents into action.[28] Many well-marketed early stimulation programs pushed parents into the "everything important is learned by the age of three" craze, which still holds sway today. And many well-known international agencies emphasized the urgency of intervention in this "crucial" or "critical" age, which is indeed correct if we are discussing children in extreme poverty who are malnourished, victims of war, and who suffer parental neglect—but not necessarily so for well-off children whose parents are chastised into buying early stimulation toys.

What We Know Now

After the tightly compacted cortex of the brain has passed through the narrow birth canal, the human skull grows dramatically in the first years of life.[29] This rapid growth of the head during the early years,[30] as well as its subsequent slowing around three years,[31] contributes to the idea that everything important is learned by the first three years.

Jerome Kagan suggests in his book *Three Seductive Ideas*[32] that there is a "long-standing appeal of deterministic ideas about the early years of life."[33] Macvarish and colleagues sum up Bruer's and Kagan's criticisms of the importance attributed to the first three years of brain growth as being scientifically faulty on three claims:

1. The infant brain can be characterized as undergoing a period of 'explosive synaptic connectivity,' that is, brain growth is most dynamic during gestation and during the early years of life. This is interpreted by the "first three years" movement to mean that the early years represent a "use it or lose it" opportunity to shape infant brains. Many have disputed these claims to truth, arguing that more synapses do not mean more brain power, that increased dendritic density occurs at any age, and that only certain areas of the brain showed increased density during the early years.

2. This period of intensive synaptic growth constitutes a "critical" or "sensitive" period during which particular aspects of development must be nurtured, lest permanent damage to the child's cognitive and emotional potential occurs. Bruer contends that critical periods are the exception, not the norm, in human development, and that although there seems to be evidence that language acquisition and visual development are particularly rooted in the early years, this is atypical of the development of other human faculties.

3. "Enriched" or "stimulating" environments produce better infant brains that will, in turn, create cleverer, more emotionally attuned infants, children, and adults. Bruer argues that human brains develop in massively varying but essentially "ordinary" environments, which are sufficient to stimulate brain development.[34]

There is no doubt that abuse, neglect, and lack of good nutrition and basic social exchanges, including language, can damage brain architecture over the life span. However, children do not require *extra* stimulation, but rather *adequate* stimulation, in order to develop normally. Like all creatures, children respond to their environments. Each person's individual genetic makeup combines with ambient experiences to form the unique personality and knowledge of that person. People can and do learn across the life span, not just until three years of age.

BRAIN DEVELOPMENT IS COMPLETE BY THE TIME A PERSON REACHES SECONDARY SCHOOL

Many believe that critical periods box-in specific learning moments in human brain development, and that the general windows for learning close by the time people get out of high school. Adolescence is a time when humans grow emotionally, intellectually, and physically, leading some to believe that when the body stops growing, the brain stops developing. And thus, the myth emerges. People's personalities are refined during adolescence;[35] emotional maturity is solidified;[36] risky behavior is exchanged for more thoughtful decision making;[37] intellectual growth is continually enhanced;[38] and the body completes development.[39] The brain's development does not stop, however, despite these outward signs. While head size stabilizes around nine years of age, connections inside the brain continue to be made throughout the life span.[40]

While most teachers do not believe that "brain development has finished by the time children reach secondary school," a small minority say they do believe this (5.6%) or don't know (14.4%).[41] While in the minority (20%), this is still a worrisome percentage. After all, why teach at all if students' brains are already completely developed? It is likely some popularized accounts of the research create doubts in teachers' minds and can discourage optimistic teachers, who might not believe that brains are fixed by high school, but who read things like *"Inside Your Teenager's Scary Brain"*[42] and doubt their ability to intervene.

Where the Myth Comes From

In some countries, formal education ends when children are 15 and in others around 18 years old.[43] It is not clear why these are considered cut-off dates, though it can be speculated that because external physical growth ends around this time, there is a false presumption made that the brain also ends growth at this time. Since hormones and biology settle down around this time as well, it's not illogical to think that a person's brain also stops developing.

Second, neuroimaging studies indicate that when a brain learns something new it takes a lot of rehearsal before the learning becomes more automated, but once automated, the brain's efficiency means it uses less space, real estate, and energy.[44] "In older adults, fluency or experience with a task can reduce brain activity levels—in one sense this is greater processing efficiency."[45] Belief that brain development is finished by the time a kid enters high school is likely due in part to the fact that *less* activity is seen for many skills right around this time. People presume that less activity means less learning, when in fact it means the brain has become more efficient.

What We Know Now

We now know that people can and do learn throughout the life span, which means that brain development occurs well past secondary school.[46] "Plasticity is a core feature of the brain throughout life. . . Neuroimaging of adolescents now shows us that the adolescent brain is far from mature, and undergoes extensive structural changes well past puberty."[47]

There are a host of studies on human brain development, including longitudinal studies in changes in brain development from childhood to adolescents[48] and research about brain structure in healthy individuals aged 5–32.[49] There are also major meta-analyses that consider numerous longitudinal studies of people 4 to 87 years old[50] and that document brain developmental changes across the life span. All conclude that the brain does not complete development by the time a person reaches high school.

HUMAN LEARNING PROGRESSES LINEARLY

We'd like to think curriculum planners have done a rigorous job of deciding what our children should learn at what age based on an orderly developmental path, and this is largely true. But do humans follow that path in as linear a way as the planners intended? Both the order of conceptual learning and the mental maturity of an individual are important in selecting curriculum at different stages of education. But what about the chronological age of a person?

There are numerous theories of human development, all of which postulate a logical order of development in different spheres—social-emotional (attachment); physical (biology, sexual); linguistic, behavioral (psychological); moral; and cognitive or mental—albeit not necessarily along precisely the same timeline for every individual, nor factoring in individuals' prior experiences. Lerner's *Concepts and Theories of Human Development*[51] covers more than 100 different theories. While there is general agreement that certain skills develop within certain age ranges, there is overwhelming agreement that prior experiences play a key role in what a person can learn.

Psychologist Jean Piaget[52] laid out his theory of cognitive development in stages with broad timeframes: sensorimotor stage (0–24 months); pre-operational stage (2–7 years); concrete operational stage (7–11 years); and formal operational stage (11–20 years). Michael Commons also suggested a *model of hierarchical complexity*, though without attaching age ranges, dividing his stages into sixteen levels: automatic, sensory, and motor; circular sensorimotor; sensorimotor; nominal; sentential; preoperational; primary; concrete; abstract; formal; and the five postformal: systematic; metasystematic; paradigmatic; cross-paradigmatic; and meta-cross-paradigmatic.[53] Both Commons and Piaget based their theories on a natural progression through different stages, and were careful not to emphasize specific ages.

Other learning theories emphasize the phases of learning even more than the particular conceptual knowledge acquired in each phase. Fischer and Bidell's *dynamic skill theory* suggests that current theories of human development are unnecessarily rigid: "Concepts like universal stages, innate linguistic modules, and innate cognitive competencies portray psychological organization as fixed and unchanging, insulated from variation in context and feedback from activity."[54] Instead, they believe, "human activity is both organized and variable, dynamically changing in principled ways."[54] The dynamic nature of human development and learning is thanks to both human variability and to the fact that no two people live identical experiences in their lives.

Jerome Bruner foresaw in education what Fischer was suggesting in psychology and later neuroscience. In 1960, Bruner wrote *The Process of Education*, in which he suggested a "spiral curriculum" that would methodologically return to core concepts over and over again, in order to provide new contexts to reinforce the same concepts. It is clear that both Bruner and Fischer view the steps in a process as more important than the age of the individual.

Where the Myth Comes From

The myth that cognitive development occurs linearly comes from an attempt to develop clear parenting and educational guidelines; in the process, several complex theories are often simplified and reduced into simple age groupings to fit into one-page handouts in the pediatrician's office. *"What's Normal (Kinda Annoying) 3-Year-Old Behavior and What's Not"*[55]; *"7th Grade: The Worst Year Ever"*[56]; and *"Is 25 the New Cut-Off Point for Adulthood?"*[57] are examples that box individuals and abilities into age-groupings that initially sound convincing but which are not always correct.

Consistent with this linear view of development is the way we divide our classrooms by age, despite the fact that not all students are ready to undertake the same tasks or activities in a given discipline at the same age. If learning is the goal, it might make more sense to group students by mastery levels rather than by birthdate. We have lived with age groupings in schools for so long, however, that we have stopped questioning why. Mondale reminds us that Horace Mann began age divisions for classrooms in the 1840s in the U.S., based on the Prussian model.[58] Before that we used to assemble everyone together and allow people to advance at their own pace, as Socrates had done 2,500 years prior.

It is easier to think of human development as a linear process rather than as a multifaceted structure with asynchronous advances. Linear or even cyclical processes are easier to follow than processes that involve regression and reflection. Piaget's constructivist ideas get closer to the actual process of human learning, as individual elements build off one another in a kind of hierarchical conceptual model. However, perhaps even more accurate than cognitive stages would be a *neuro*constructivist model, in which hierarchies of understanding in the brain were combined with the opportunity to reinforce new learning over time.[59]

What We Know Now

The myth that human learning progresses linearly and according to chronological ages is due not only to the desire for simplicity, but also to many people's lack of scientific literacy about how the brain actually learns. While many precise mechanisms for learning pathways have yet to be discovered, we can say a handful of things for certain. For example, neural pathways need to be consolidated through repetition (reinforcement of concepts over time creates the thickening of white matter tracts needed to retrieve information).[60] This explains the nonlinear and more cyclical pattern to learning, which changes due to experience rather than age.

The practicality and logistics of designing schooling experiences based on stages rather than ages is far more complicated to structure than age-based school design, but is potentially highly beneficial: Student learning can be optimized, motivation is heightened, and learning accelerated when students can approach topics they are ready for. Montessori-style education, in which multiple age groups are joined by design to maximize individual learning by responding to each student's appropriate learning level, is an example of successful age-stage balancing.[61]

We know two other key things related to this neuromyth as well. First, the chronological age, cognitive stages of development, and prior experiences of people all play roles in whether or not they learn, with past experiences likely playing the most important role. Second, learning and development do not advance in a linear fashion, but rather move forward and retract in a more cyclical fashion. This is kind of like walking up a spiral staircase, two steps forward then one step back, rather than moving from the bottom to the top directly.

LEARNING PROBLEMS ASSOCIATED WITH DEVELOPMENTAL DIFFERENCES IN BRAIN FUNCTION CANNOT BE REMEDIATED WITH EDUCATION

Developmental differences from one individual to another—such as when a child begins to sit, walk, or talk—are often grouped into milestones by category: social-emotional; language and communicative; visual-spatial, memory-related; attention-related; motor/sensory related; or related to physical growth.[62] Meeting milestones on time or even before expected can be influenced by parents' knowledge of the expected age by which most children reach them, meaning that simple awareness that certain "norms" exists can motivate parents to "push" kids toward meeting milestones on time.[63] Developmental milestones—such as speaking full sentences, developing a sense of Theory of Mind (understanding "the other" and developing empathy), or quantitative numerical reasoning—can also be influenced by proper stimulation. This reinforces the point that age is less important than the order of skills or the experiences of the individuals.

In a series of experiments, teachers around the world examined the following statement: "Learning problems associated with developmental differences in brain function cannot be remediated by education." A surprising number of them considered it to be *true*: 7% in Spain;[64] 16% in the UK;[65] 19% in The Netherlands;[65] 22% in Turkey;[66] 23% in Peru, Argentina, and Chile;[67] 29% in Greece;[68] and 50% in China.[69] This is a worrisome finding and questions the very role of education. *If education cannot remediate learning problems, what can?*

Norman Doidge[70] reminds us that children are not condemned to the brains they are born with. Gifted children and kids with learning problems—including dyslexia, dyscalculia, ADHD, and Asperger's—can successfully be integrated into regular classrooms. If teachers do not believe in their ability to help these children learn, then there is little reason to stay in the profession. The worldwide trend is toward the integration of different kinds of brains into regular classrooms: inclusion and differentiation. However, some teachers are fearful of this expectation, as they do not believe it is actually possible for children born with a problem to work in regular classrooms.[71] One of the most cited authors on differentiated learning is Carol Ann Tomlinson, according to whom "differentiation is student-aware teaching"[72]—meaning that part of a teacher's main job is to know students well enough to help them find their individual paths toward success.

> *These teachers are flexible with time, seating arrangements, working conditions, student groupings, and other classroom elements. They assiduously study their students. They use ongoing assessment to understand what a student needs next, and they adjust their teaching in response to what they discover.*[72]

Tomlinson believes that all children, independent of the intellectual abilities they are born with, have the potential to improve over time with the right stimuli.[73] Children who are born with learning problems or limited intellectual abilities can improve, just as gifted children can continue to grow beyond expectations, with the right interventions.

Thomas Guskey's[74] 2010 article "Lessons of Mastery Learning" echoes Tomlinson's ideas and points to the benefits of mastery learning for all students, especially those who do not follow the normal learning pathways:

> *As we strive to improve achievement even further, we can continue to learn from the core elements of mastery learning. Attention to these elements will enable educators to make great strides in their efforts to close achievement gaps and help all students achieve excellence.*[74]

Perhaps if the structure of learning were based on mastery concepts, rather than on passing tests at certain ages, many more of these students would find success in our classrooms. Accommodations for children with learning problems—including those who just have slightly fewer prior experiences than the average—would create the conditions for higher levels of success. Mastery permits a more flexible time frame for learning and relies more on students' orderly acquisition of core concepts before learning higher-order ideas.

Where the Myth Comes From

The ineffectiveness of interventions for developmental learning problems is a myth with at least three origins. First, when we think of "developmental differences," people often consider the key determinant to be time; a person just has to grow in or out of a behavior or new skill set. While time can resolve many problems, interventions from the environment can influence the speed of learning.

Second, the history of formal education is short. Only recently have we moved from educating elite communities (the wealthy and clerics) to the proclaimed goal of *Education For All* by the United Nations.[75] Earlier educational social structures only permitted people who were already somewhat "educated" into schools (those who came from wealthy, well-read families), leading to both the belief that such level entry was normal, and that only those with "normal" aptitude could learn. "Average" or "normal" students were more homogeneous in earlier times, as they came from similar backgrounds, social status, races, religions, and cultures. This means that teaching was easier in past generations, as students were far more uniform.

Third, in earlier times, teachers were not expected to do much more than supply information, after which it was up to the students to learn. The change in expectations of schools to guarantee conditions in which everyone can learn is new. These three situations make it clear that this myth arises from lack of experience in differentiation. Teachers' and parents' lack of scientific knowledge about how human development occurs, especially how rates of development are influenced by experience, plays a large role in maintaining this myth. Confirmation bias also comes into play; some teachers do not expect children with delays to succeed, and this becomes a self-fulfilling prophecy as the teachers have low expectations of these learners and/or invest less effort in them.[76] Teachers who are unprepared to manage different types of learners fail to create the conditions under which they can learn successfully.

What We Know Now

We now know that children with learning problems associated with developmental differences in brain function *can* improve. There is evidence for this related to language (pronouncing words, using correct vocabulary, matching symbols to sound, spelling, counting, reading comprehension, expressive language, reading fluently, writing coherently, retelling a story),[77] math (counting, symbol to sound, magnitude estimation, reading math problems, understanding operation signs, sequencing),[78] attention (including ADHD), memory (short-term, working, and long-term),[79] reasoning (interpreting ideas, expressing ideas),[80] motor movement (running, skipping, general coordination),[81] visual processing, and auditory processing,[82] among others. Every one of these problems can be remedied by interventions, but the key is, first, good diagnosis (what, exactly, is the problem?) followed by good response (knowing which interventions will best serve the individual).

We also know that normal milestones for certain skills can be influenced by parental or teacher interventions. This means that a child can look as if he has a problem when he actually does not; delays are not the same as disorders. We also know that being labeled with a learning problem can be the start of a downward spiral toward failure. Labels have the power to harm children, who can suffer from low self-esteem, problems with peers, frustration, and distractedness, which in turn makes the learning problem a self-fulfilling prophecy as academic achievement nosedives.[83] Worse yet, children who are misdiagnosed due to poor professional assessment and labeled inaccurately can suffer the most; misdiagnosis often leads to mistreatment, which also has the potential to lead to academic failure.

THE "TERRIBLE TWOS" AND "CRAZY ADOLESCENCE" ARE INEVITABLE AND ALWAYS NEGATIVE

Human development is typically categorized into the three stages of childhood, adolescence, and adulthood;[84] a few developmental theorists also add the bookends of "infancy" and "late adulthood."[85] The precision of terms grows with our understanding of general development.

TABLE 4.1. LIFE SPAN DEVELOPMENT

Life Span Human Development							
			Adolescence				
Infancy/ Toddler	Early Childhood	Late Childhood	Teenagers	Early Adulthood	Adulthood	Late Adulthood	Old Age
0-2	3-6	7-9	10-17	18-24	25-54	55-74	75+

Source: Tokuhama-Espinosa, based on Erikson, 1959; Kail, & Cavanaugh, 2015; Sigelman & Rider, 2014

While no one disputes that humans develop over the life span, the question about whether or not behavioral responsibility can be attached to a specific age range is in debate. Does "brain immaturity" mean it is inevitable that a two-year-old will be "terrible" and that teens can't help but be out of control?

Toddlers are forgiven for acting out because their emotional distress is presumed to be too much for their small heads to handle; the terrible twos are accepted as "truth" because they are seen as an age-appropriate response to frustration.[86] However, not all kids suffer tantrums to the same degree. People with autism are more prone to tantrums for longer periods of time;[87] children with larger vocabularies have fewer tantrums;[88] and kids with parents who respond less emotionally to their outburst have shorter antisocial bouts of anger.[89] Teens are not as easily forgiven.

Many intellectual, physical, hormonal, and social changes occur during adolescence. At the heart of behavioral changes in some teenagers is the increased myelination linking different neural circuits in the brain. Mylenogenesis—an increase in white matter tracts—helps insulate and create efficient communication between synapses. Myelination is influenced by heredity, environment and stress hormones. During the teenage years, the brain "remains structurally and functionally vulnerable to impulsive sex, food, and sleep habits."[90] To top it off, some neurotransmitters increase (glutamate) while others (gamma-aminobutyric acid) "remain under construction," which "might be responsible for immature and impulsive behavior and neurobehavioral excitement during adolescent life."[91] Myelination also fine-tunes the timing and synchrony of neural fire patterns.[92]

This is important to know. While the headlines may scream that a teenager's immature frontal lobes are "a work in progress"[93] and are the cause of poor decision making, in reality the cause is actually neural circuitry that is under development and neurotransmitters that are not yet in balance, leaving "adolescents particularly vulnerable to socio-emotional influences and risk-taking behaviors."[94] Asynchronous development of maturing emotional regulation, reasoning processes, and reward systems makes some teens seem unpredictable at times. Additionally, environmental influences as well as culture can influence adolescent development.[95]

The intolerable toddler and crazy teen myths suggest that the behaviors associated with these ages are inevitable. Headlines like "5 Toddler Tantrum and Hissy Fit Fixers"[96] make it seem that *all* small children have fits with regularity, and titles like "Experts Link Teen Brains' Immaturity, Juvenile Crime"[97] generalize the idea that *all* adolescents are prone to reckless or unlawful behavior.

This raises some legal questions: Are teenagers responsible for their actions if their brains are still "a work in progress?"[98] Are brains really like "a car with a good accelerator but a weak brake?"[99] And does this lack of socially designated maturity release them from responsibility for their acts during this stage of development, including murder? In 2005, the U.S. Supreme Court outlawed the death penalty for crimes committed before age 18, based on the belief that teens were not in control of their actions.[100] In *Roper v. Simmons,* the Supreme Court ruled that capital punishment could not be used for people under the age of 18, as it violated their Eighth Amendment constitutional right against cruel and unusual punishment: "juveniles should not be held to the same standards of criminal responsibility as adults, because adolescents' decision-making capacity is diminished, they are less able to resist coercive influence, and their character is still undergoing change."[101] The myth that individuals are not responsible for behavior associated with developmental differences in brain functions seems to be backed by law, at least where teenagers are concerned. This creates an interesting neuroethical dilemma. Similarly, toddlers are often forgiven for "irrational" fits, as their brains seem to be as immature as their bodies and, in general, it's believed that "Kids from about 18 months to 4 years are simply hardwired to misbehave."[102] Are these statements justified?

Where the Myth Comes From

Most brain development studies have been focused on emotion-to-frontal-lobe links, rather than on the roles of myelination, neurotransmitters, and the multiple environmental factors that play a role in risk taking, decision making, peer motivation, and other social factors. The myth stems from cherry-picking studies that exaggerate certain aspects of human development over others. Many in the field of adolescent health are now calling for a more transdisciplinary view to better understand teen behavior. For instance, Suleiman and Dahl note the incomplete practice of looking just at brain studies, or social tendencies, or mental health issues in vacuums, and recommend a more collaborative review of the literature.[103]

Adolescence is not specific to humans[104] and is associated across species with novelty seeking, peer interactions, and distancing from parents in all animals.[105] Stretching the novelty seeking to risk taking, and the distancing from parents to rebellion, are not illogical steps. This makes it easy to (a) think that all teens act this way, and (b) that it is excusable as a "normal" developmental trait. Neither is true. Not all teenagers commit murder due to these physiological changes; fewer than 1% do. Just 800 of 15,696 murders in the U.S. committed in 2015 were done by teens.[106] Even those teens whose profiles would suggest they are potential murderers do not always succumb to the influence of nurture, nor their contexts (nurture), but rather use "free will" to change their destinies. Unfortunately, the Supreme Court ruling in 2005 gave ammunition to those who argue that the myth of crazy teen brains is true, and we can expect them *all* to act out.

By contrast, the belief that children pass through a phase of the "terrible twos" based on their inability to express themselves well with appropriate vocabulary is probably correct. The fact is that some children and their parents manage the toddler years better than others. The ability to manage emotions is a learned trait and responding to frustration can be handled in multiple ways. Most children learn quickly whether having a hissy fit in a supermarket will get them their desired goal in the candy section or not. The onset, cessation, frequency, and duration of tantrums varies and is influenced by parental intervention. Potegal and colleagues found that "the tantrum was likely to be shorter" when parents intervened less.[107] It was also found that children with greater verbal abilities and expressive vocabulary had fewer anger issues, including tantrums, leading to the conclusion that children who can express their frustrations in words are less likely to have to resort to physical outbursts.[108] This evidence suggests that early childhood "terrible twos"—which depends on language development, parenting, and behavioral modification—is not the same as having a "crazy teen brain"—which depends on myelination, changes in neurotransmitters, and a range of cultural norms.

What We Know Now

We now know that the "terrible twos" is a normal stage of human development in which children begin to show their independence from adults. This can often lead to frustration and temper tantrums based on inadequate language skills. Toddlers begin to determine the edges of their autonomy, make their own decisions, and develop their imaginations. They also seek to test general limits and the "limits of their language(s) are the limits of their world," as Wittgenstein[109] once said. Vocabulary is key to reducing toddler frustration. This leads us to think that toddlers are not responsible, nor should they be punished for behavior associated with developmental differences in brain functions.

There are some outliers, however. There are about 24 million children zero to 5 years old in the United States. About 8% of preschool children are referred to specialists for behavioral problems, suggesting that the majority of toddlers do not suffer from extreme cases of temper tantrums. There is evidence that social-emotional behavioral problems in the first year of life—as measured by internalizing, externalizing, and/or dysregulation domains of the Infant-Toddler Social and Emotional Assessment (ITSEA)—persist into the second year of life in 49.9% of cases, according to one study.[110] This study showed "persistence was significantly more likely when parents reported co-occurring problems . . . family life disruption, and high parenting distress"; so about half the children referred for social-emotional and behavioral problems in the first year of life (4% of all children this age) continued to have these problems, which were exacerbated by environmental life conditions, but triggered by something in the child's genetics. This means that at least a small percentage of behavior problems in children is related to genetics, to brain development, or both, which will likely extend beyond the toddler years.

It is important to note that both the terrible twos and the teen years are times of testing limits, decision making, risk taking, and emotional outbursts. The bigger the kid, however, the more complex the questions that accompany behavioral adaptations to societal norms. Most people can ignore a two-year-old crying in a supermarket when denied something he wants, but society takes notice when teens invade community spaces or behave like deviants, presumably because "they should know better". The question remains: To what extent is deviant teen behavior due to brain immaturity rather than social rebellion?

The Hamilton Project of the Brookings Institute in the United States notes that more crimes are committed by people in early adult stages of life (34%) than by adolescents (27%). Adolescent crime is most prevalent in lower socioeconomic areas and among males (72%). There are about 40 million people 11 to 20 years old in the U.S., and 1 million were criminal offenders, making 1 in 40 (2.5%) adolescents criminals.[111] This is a far cry from *all* teens. Crime in the United States has been on the decrease, and this is especially true for juveniles. The Department of Justice says that in 2015, there were 56% fewer arrests of people under 18 than there were in 2006, and "just" 800 murders committed by juveniles in 2015.[112] These figures confirm that not all teens are crazy, and the majority do not have brains that tempt them to murder.

In *The Power of the Adolescent Brain*,[113] Daniel Siegel is quoted as saying in the Common Ground Speakers Series that there are multiple myths about adolescence that should be clarified:

> **MYTH:** Adolescents go crazy due to raging hormones. • **FACT:** There is no such thing as a "raging" hormone—there are only "rising" hormones. There are indeed epigenetic changes in the body during adolescence— most noticeably in the reward circuit of the brain, which is why the experience of the sexual drive is so dramatic. However, placing blame on out-of-control hormones is destructive and incorrect.

> **MYTH:** Adolescence is a negative time of life. • **FACT:** Adolescence is the most important time of our lives. By calling adolescents lazy or crazy, and associating the adolescent years with difficulty, adolescents become disenfranchised, and disenfranchised individuals experience life differently. The truth is that you can optimize the upsides and minimize the downsides of the changes to the brain.

> **MYTH:** Adolescence is so difficult that you want to get it over as quickly as possible. • **FACT:** The best thing you can do as an adult is to keep your adolescence going as long as possible.[114]

Bad behavior is not excusable for an adolescent based solely on his age and brain. Some researchers say there is a lot of promise in using functional connectivity MRI (fcMRI) in the brain to see which networks in the teen brain develop at what times to better understand the "immaturity" of some networks, but this technology is still less than perfect and suffers from multiple problems.[115] There is little evidence that the "immaturity" of a specific network is directly related to an action like murder, for example. Overwhelming evidence shows that multiple networks coincide in specific ways to lead to a probability of violent action, but none of these accounts for "free will." This means that even if all genetic, neuroscientific, and psychological readings indicate the makings of a deviant, an individual can still override his own profile.[116] "With neuroscience, we can begin to understand why this developmental group behaves uniquely. However, this does not exonerate adolescents from guilt by reason of immaturity."[117] "Neurological images 'are powerful, but images are not causes' of behaviour, says Tomas Paus, a professor of psychology and psychiatry at the University of Toronto."[118]

WHY THIS IS GOOD NEWS FOR TEACHING

Debunking the myth that we are born as blank slates helps teachers celebrate the early learning of their students and value their life experiences. As educators, we can celebrate human variability based on both genes and experience. It is good news for teachers and parents alike to know that their efforts with children across the life span have value. It is also a relief to many parents who did not invest in flash cards in the early years and the many teachers who work with older children to know that there is still time to make a difference.

The debunking of multiple myths about "critical periods" for learning in childhood and adolescence not only expands the potential for teachers to help students at all levels of achievement, but also opens the door to greater learning across the life span. Several universities now encourage older people to return to university and complete their studies or take courses to stay mentally fit. Just as pedagogy aided teachers in understanding the best teaching tactics for children, andragogy is shaping adult education, and it is possible that a whole new teaching field can develop for older students.

If we accept that learning is not linear, we can reduce the number of students who are labeled failures for not meeting age-appropriate deadlines. Teachers can feel empowered to take control of the learning environment in their classrooms, rather than feeling powerless in the face of a fixed situation, and celebrate their roles as change makers in children's lives.

It is wonderful for early childhood educators and parents to know that the

---

Practical Application of MBE:
The More You Know, the More You Can Know

The brain is efficient. Before spending energy on learning something new, it always searches for any related concept it can find. Experiences throughout the life span build off one another, and every point of new learning potentiates future learning. The greater the variety of life experiences a child has as reference points, the greater his or her potential to learn new things in the future: The more you know, the more you can know.

Great teachers and parents take the opportunity to help children and teens interact with their world at all levels, through language, emotional management, social norms, values, physical development, and cognitive challenges.

---

terrible twos are a sign of growing independence, and for middle and high school teachers to know that most of their students are maturing normally, and that they can play a positive role in this developmental process. It is especially important for teachers and parents to remember that students live up to expectations placed upon them.[119] If teachers have low expectations of students because they believe that they are incapacitated due to their age, maturity or development, then students will perform accordingly. Labels that imply a handicap or deficit, including the "terrible twos" and "crazy teens," give students justification to underperform or act irresponsibly. It's great news that just a small percentage of kids need additional attention and help at these special stages of development.

5 • MYTHS ABOUT
LEARNING ENVIRONMENTS

HUMANS NEED ENRICHED ENVIRONMENTS IN ORDER TO DEVELOP THEIR NATURAL POTENTIAL

Early childhood stimulation classes aimed at parents and their newborns are all the rage. What parent, given the opportunity and resources, would not want to offer his or her child every possibility of getting ahead? The belief that stimulation in the early years is key to later life success pushes many parents to seek out the most competitive preschools, get kids to memorize flashcards, and place musical instruments into tiny hands even before kids can walk. Titles such as "Enriched Environments Build Better Brains"[1] and *Raising Smarter Children Creating an Enriched Learning Environment*[2] make parents feel remiss if they skip the chance to help their kids get ahead. New parents are often reminded of the ominous responsibility they have to provide enriched environments for their children, even though the definition of "enriched" is relative to individual learners.

Where the Myth Comes From

In 1962, when Mark Rosenzweig and Marion Diamond discovered that "environmental complexity" changed rats' brains, the supposition arose that this must also be true for humans. And to a certain extent, it is. William Greenough and colleagues echoed these exciting findings in the early 1970s[3] and Diamond's work into the 1980s showed that crowded and complex environments actually enhanced dendritic connections and synapses in rats.[4] Extra stimulation classes for newborns soon came into fashion, and parents were pushed to ensure exceptional development any way they could.[5] The high-quality rodent studies never made claims beyond their rigorous design and reporting, but the popular press did. The OECD writes that: "This rigorous, scientifically established experimental data on rodents has been combined by non-specialists with basic human development to assert that educational intervention, to be most effective, should be timed with synaptogenesis"[6] and misinterpreted by the public at large.

Many publications since the 1990s used these original rat studies to advance the important agenda of early childhood education, including the use of rat synaptogenesis images in place of human neuroimaging.[7] The importance of early childhood education has merits based on economics, psychology, and biology. However, the argument is perceived to be even stronger when claims about the brain can also be made, despite the lack of human evidence. The argument is that kids are born in unequal circumstances, including parental household makeup (some with single parents, others with extended families, and so on), parental education, socioeconomic status, knowledge, and access to good nutrition, as well as cultural beliefs about what babies are actually capable of learning (some believe, as the Victorians did, that an infant is incapable of learning until he begins to speak. Little do they know that learning to speak is dependent in part on being spoken to!).[8] Kids are also born with different genetic potential. Many of the arguments in favor of funding high-quality early childhood education programs are related to parent education and a better understanding of the impact of *adequate* stimulation. Heckman writes: ". . . in particular, we should address the inequity in the resources families have to properly develop their children's potential"[9] by creating safe environments, sharing meals, and talking to children. This is excellent advice, and very similar to the rat situation, in which the focus is on *avoiding impoverished environments*, not extra stimulation.

The message that *enriched* environments are necessary for normal human growth is different than the message that *destructive* environments are harmful. However, the lines become blurred in propaganda. UNESCO, the World Health Organization, and other important international agencies champion the needs of the most impoverished populations. They continually remind the world of the impact that starvation, lack of immunization, poor nutrition, and violence can have on developing brains, which is excellent, important, and, some would argue, even moral work. This is not the same as giving a "normal" child extra stimulation with flash cards or violin lessons.

TABLE 5.1. CONTINUUM OF CHILDREN'S SOCIOECONOMIC STATUS

Continuum of Children's Socioeconomic Status				
Extreme poverty, neglect, abuse, ill health, violence, and/or malnutrition	Slight poverty, neglect, abuse, ill health, violence, and/or malnutrition	"Normal" children	Slightly privileged environment	Extremely privileged environment
Of particular interest in UNESCO, WHO campaigns				

Source: Author

What We Know Now

We now know at least five important things about enriched environments. First, earlier experimentation with rats was focused on rodents in cages, some with "enriched" environments consisting of being with other rats and sometimes with "toys" like walking wheels. Stimulated rats did better on maze activities than rats that were alone in an empty cage. It is now clear that the conclusions drawn from these studies should have been that *impoverished environments cause poorer results*, not that complex environments increase synapses and therefore learning potential. After all, being isolated in a cage without company and few distractions— similar to an impoverished human home environment—the rats performed worse than counterparts with company and distractions. Further evidence comes from cases of extreme neglect and/or child abuse, which do, indeed, show an impact on normal brain development in the early years,[10] and indicate that *negative environments do harm*, but this does not mean that extra stimulation is a benefit.

Second, natural stimulation (hugs, playing, talking) with children is enough. *Parents* magazine suggests "50 Ways to Make Your Baby Smarter,"[11] which include "make eye contact"; "stick out your tongue" "blab away [talk]"; "sing; "tickle toes"; "make a funny face"; and "breast feed." These are all activities that seem normal in daily interaction with small children, found in both low socioeconomic countries as well as in wealthy nations. One study conducted in 2016 between the Swiss and Peruvians found that children 6 to 35 months old whose mothers played with them for just half an hour a day performed up to 23% better at expressing feelings and emotions, fine motor skills, and communication than those whose mothers did not play with them.[12] This means basic human interactions—caring, sensory stimulations, and developmentally appropriate language—are enough to stimulate children cross culturally. Other studies go so far as to say that normal, positive parent-child interactions not only help cognitive abilities, but may also break the cycle of poverty and increase income over the life span.[13] At the other extreme, there is even concern that overstimulation can be damaging.[14]

Third, we also know that while it seems logical that more synapses should equate to greater intelligence, and that evidence from rodent studies seems to show that their ability to maneuver mazes is correlated with more synaptic activity, researchers now point out that selective pruning of synaptic connections is actually of equal or greater importance. More connections can often mean inefficient attempts at learning, while fewer, precise connections can be an indication of expert learning. According to the OECD's first look at neuromyths,[15] "the neuromyth logic is that the more synapses available, the higher the potential nerve activity and communication, thus making better learning possible."[16] But Usa Goswami cautions: "these demonstrations do not mean that greater synaptic density predicts a greater capacity to learn."[16] And even if it were correct, "there is not yet much neuroscientific evidence in humans about the predictive relationship between synaptic densities early in life and densities later in life,"[17] as in the role that early synaptic density in toddler brains plays in adult brains.

Fourth, nearly all studies that show increased synaptic activity have been conducted posthumously and on rats. This means that in order to prove that a specific kind of enrichment was beneficial to humans, a highly unethical experiment would have to occur: It would be necessary to identify a group of babies with similar characteristics (parental educational, socioeconomic status, living conditions, nutrition, and so on), divide them into experimental and control groups, stimulate (or deprive) the experimental group, perform autopsies, and see if there was, indeed, correlational additional synaptogenesis.[18] Avants and colleagues found "that cortical thickness in early adulthood is reduced (independently from parental IQ) by increased quality of the home environment,"[19] indicating that less density and more refined connections between areas of the brain are more valuable than high synaptic density.

Finally, most studies that promote the idea that enriched environments are necessary in the early years forget that "enriched" is relative to the learner. That is, a child who lives in a home in which both parents and multiple siblings are always stimulating conversation, playing patty-cake, modeling social norms, reading stories, cooking, and exploring natural phenomena will likely find attending a local early childhood stimulation course boring, unlike a child brought up in a family setting where the single parent has little time to play, read books, or even talk with him. What is known is that the combination of interventions—those that include balanced nutrition and parenting classes, as well as different types of stimulation (language, physical, cognitive, socioemotional)—are the most effective.[20]

VIOLENT VIDEO GAMES HAVE NO EFFECT ON BEHAVIOR

Video gaming is a thriving, multibillion-dollar business and the largest area of media growth globally.[21] Gaming has been around as long as humans. But as a relatively new technology, video gaming has stirred new interest in the entertainment field. There was initial concern that violent video games would disrupt "normal" behavior in schoolkids, but mixed reviews have lowered the level of angst. Headlines like "Violent Video Games DO NOT Cause Anti-Social or Aggressive Behavior, Study Finds"[22] lead parents and teachers to lower their guard. However, this singling out of evidence in order to draw attention to counterintuitive findings—citing only studies that show little or no correlation between violent games and aggressive behavior—is confirmation bias and fails to give a balanced view.

Where the Myth Comes From

The myth emerges from the mixed bag of studies. A Google Scholar search finds there are almost equal numbers of studies that say violent video games cause violent behavior as there are studies that say they do not.[23] The difference is that there are more high-quality meta-analyses and longitudinal studies on the side of studies that say they *do* cause violent behavior. While a thorough review of the thousands of studies on this topic finds the balance of the evidence on the side of behavioral changes, there are multiple studies available to support the idea that violent video games have no effect on behavior, leading many people to believe in the myth.

What We Know Now

Studies from around the world indicate that violent video games have two important effects on behavior. First, the frequency of exposure to violence experienced in video games dulls our initial reactions, and horrific scenes become normal due to a "neuronal desensitization to violence."[24] Second, and likely a consequence of the first point, it seems that virtual violence triggers the same areas of the brain as actual violence.[25] According to some studies, habitual violent video game play is a significant risk factor for later violent behavior.

One of the most complete studies, published in *Journal of the American Medical Association (JAMA) Pediatrics,* noted that 90% of American youths play video games, and 90% of games include depictions of violence.[26] In this three-year longitudinal panel study of 3,334 children and 8- to 17-year-old adolescents (average age 11.2 years), the authors showed that habitually playing violent video games increased aggressive behavior, regardless of "sex, age, initial aggressiveness and parental involvement."[27] In another rigorous study in 2017,[28] the American Psychological Association convened a task force to update knowledge about video games and violence. Consistent with past meta-analyses on the topic, video game exposure was associated with "an increased composite aggression score; increased aggressive behavior; increased aggressive cognitions; increased aggressive affect, increased desensitization, and decreased empathy; and increased physiological arousal." They came to the conclusion "that violent video game use is a risk factor for adverse outcomes, but found insufficient studies to examine any potential link between violent video game use and delinquency or criminal behavior."[28] While there are studies on both sides of the belief, there is more robust research showing violent video games do lead to violent behavior.

USING THE INTERNET MAKES YOU SMARTER/DUMBER

The speed with which online engagement has become so widespread among students and adults alike makes people cautious about the potential side effects of spending so much time on the web. There are multiple headlines such as "The Internet Makes Us Stupid and Here's Why"[29] that are meant to shock and awe readers into fearing or loving the Internet "Does the Internet Make You Dumber?"[30]; "13 Ways the Internet is Making Us Smarter"[31]; and even "How the Internet Makes You Think You're Smarter than You Really Are"[32] give us pause about the technology in our lives. While some argue that the world of education has never been more democratic thanks to the World Wide Web, others are fearful of the Internet's invasion into their privacy. To exacerbate matters, students' habituation to online pursuits and immersion in virtual worlds has raised uncertainty about the social and cognitive ramifications that may follow. Are people less or more social since the invention of smartphones and the explosion of social media?[33] Are kids' attention spans really shrinking due to too much screen time?[34] As with most topics in social science research, the answers are more complex than expected at first blush.

Where the Myth Comes From

The neuromyth blaming the Internet for making humans dumber or smarter hinges on the idea that the *tool* rather than its *use* is to blame for either enhancing or decreasing intellectual prowess. This is akin to blaming cars (rather than drivers) for accidents, or fast food options (rather than our decision to patronize them or not) for obesity. Personal responsibility is missing from each of these equations.

One reason this myth exists is because people have a love-hate relationship with technology. It is human nature to fear what we do not know; this enhances the chances of survival. Thus, there have been challenges to the incorporation of new technology throughout human history. It was once believed that it was suicide to get into a car when a coach and buggy would do,[35] that books and movie theaters would go out of fashion once people started watching television,[36] and that teachers would no longer be necessary when computers were invented.[37]

In fact, this last belief, despite its irrationality, contributes to the myth. Great teachers will always be needed; there is a worldwide shortage at the moment. Yet our own lack of understanding and appreciation of the Internet, as educators— what it can and cannot do, and the different roles teachers and tools play in learning outcomes—helps the myth thrive. After all, the average teacher around the world has not received formal training in technology.[38] Therefore, many teachers must rely on the handful of experts in the school who can help hook up the smartboard or get the class logged in. As educators, we need to accept and incorporate appropriate technology into classroom settings.

There are studies that show that the Internet is to blame for many things. A quick Google search on "the Internet is to blame" yields about 45 million results, including terrorism, overspending, sexual abuse, child abuse, depression, adolescent suicide, cyberbullying, relationship problems, bad parenting, and religious radicalization. In a quick search on "benefits of the Internet" there were about 330 million results, with the number one contribution being "information, access, and knowledge" items. The Internet has brought education to the fingertips of more people than ever before in history. As the newest tool on the block in terms of inventions, the Internet is an easy mark. It is easier to blame the Internet rather than cultivate personal skills or accept responsibility about using the tools. How we use our tools bears more responsibility for outcomes than the tool itself.

What We Know Now

The Internet, like any resource, is neither good nor bad. It is how it is used that determines the nature and quality of its contribution to education.

Few teachers were prepared in their preservice training for the quantity and varying levels of quality of information that bombards us every day on the Internet. Even fewer receive ongoing professional development to keep them up to date with fast-paced changes in educational technology. The integration of the flipped classroom model, virtual reality course rooms, and advanced instructional design for differentiation pose challenges to teachers who are caught unprepared. The Internet is a tool that we can choose to ignore, feel overwhelmed by, or leverage.

LEARNING IS INDEPENDENT OF THE LEARNER'S HISTORY

The belief that whole classes of students, of roughly the same age, will learn things at approximately the same pace underlies the foundation of our school systems. We group kids together mainly by age (and usually by geographical area), but rarely are they grouped by past experience or prior knowledge. This schooling structure goes back to the founding of formal education at the end of the 19th century and has become so ingrained that it is rarely questioned. After "advancing" from one-room schoolhouses in the 1750s to obligatory schooling for all (between 1852 and 1917), there arose a need to divide the larger number of students into manageably sized groups. At the time, age group divisions seemed logical.

Where the Myth Comes From

The myth that learning is independent of the learner's history is an artifact of the way we have organized schools.[39] It is perpetuated primarily because of what Ian Jukes calls "TTWWADI: that's the way we've always done it."[40] We have grouped kids by age for so long that we've largely forgotten to question the logic of doing so, as was recommended by proponents of competency-based and mastery learning models.[41] Teachers are often taught the importance of triggering prior knowledge and creating authentic learning environments, but they are not often reminded that both depend on the learner's history and context. All new learning is influenced by the learner's history and prior experience.[42]

What We Know Now

It is a fact that "the more you know, the more you can know,"[43] meaning that a person's prior experience plays a big role in his or her potential to learn new things. A learner's history includes all past experiences, and the power of these experiences deeply influences what a person can learn in the future. There are great disparities in what individuals know at different times in their lives. For example, children from more well-off homes tend to have more books and parents who read more to them than children in poorer households. The simple activity of reading to a child before he gets to school is correlated with later academic achievement.[44]

All new learning passes through the filter of prior experience.[45] Some children will enter our classrooms with more prior experience related to core concepts than others, and as a result will learn faster. In fact, prior experience, followed by cognitive development, is far more influential in determining new learning efficiency than a person's chronological age. Unfortunately, age divisions have distracted from perhaps more logical ways to guide students through the learning maze, such as mastery of concepts, which divide learners by constructivist skill set development.

"BRAIN TRAINING" IS SUPPORTED BY NEUROSCIENCE

Online computer games promise to improve "memory, problem solving, concentration, speed of thinking, language, and visual-spatial recognition."[46] They further promise that they "work your social skills, social awareness, self-awareness, and self-control" while you're having fun.[46] These are tempting offers, and this is a very lucrative and growing business in the United States as people age and many older adults seek out ways to maintain cognitive functioning.

"Brain training" grew from $600 million in annual revenues in 2009 to more than a $1 billion in 2012 and is projected to reach $4 to $10 billion by 2020, according to a 2016 promotional video by SharpBrains,[47] a brain training enterprise. Brain training programs have many audiences. Some are aimed at aging populations, others at millennials, while others cater to young schoolchildren. "Brain training" is different than educational gaming in that brain training programs usually claim to be backed by neuroscience. Brain training is also usually computer mediated and prides itself as being "playful," "fun," and "enjoyable": "Brain Training: Fun and Simple Exercises to Train Your Brain to Immediately Get Sharper, Faster, and More Powerful"[48] seems like attractive alternatives to the hard work of learning. While it is correct to presume that learning does not have to be painful and can be enjoyable, brain training through commercial ventures is not necessarily the solution.

Where the Myth Comes From

Multiple commercial as well as clinical venues sell "brain training" services. The promise of improved brains with little effort is very attractive—humans always want as much as they can get with as little effort as possible. Many "brain training" commercial ventures have neuroscientists and medical physicians on their boards, who testify to different (narrower) elements of the (broader) promise, or who are simply listed to offer the appearance of scientific backing. For example, one such business is run by a Stanford marketing graduate who identified his business as "an independent market research firm." He himself does not have any neuroscience credentials, nor does he claim to do anything but market research, but his scientific advisory board includes (in addition to other marketing professionals) four medical doctors, one of whom is a well-known author on aging. This researcher's reputation as an expert on aging lends a great deal of credibility to the company's claims. This medical doctor, however, has never published any work on brain training and is better known for his work in the 1970s and 1980s on aging populations and blood pressure, Alzheimer's onset, and maternal age, sleep and aging, and immunodeficiency in aging. The simple presence of this person on the webpage, however, is enough to convince many people that these types of companies are credible and neuroscientifically based.

What We Know Now

The term "brain training" is extremely broad, so much so that consensus about what is meant was debated in 2014 in academia, as dozens defended the concept while others criticized it. In an attempt to resolve this conflict, the Association for Psychological Sciences published a paper that showed, unsurprisingly, that:

> [b]ased on this examination, we find extensive evidence that brain-training interventions improve performance on the trained tasks, less evidence that such interventions improve performance on closely related tasks, and little evidence that training enhances performance on distantly related tasks or that training improves everyday cognitive performance.[49]

This means that if a person plays a computer game that rehearses *working memory*, *working memory* skills will likely be improved, but only for the duration of the practice. This also means that *orienting attention* might be improved (near transfer), and *self-regulation* will likely not improve (far transfer). It shouldn't come as much surprise that if a targeted skill is rehearsed, it can improve. In short, if a single cognitive sub-skill is rehearsed, such as inhibitory control, it can improve, but this doesn't mean that *all* executive functioning sub-skills will also improve, nor that the effects will last longer than the training.

We know that many studies that show positive results for brain training suffer from either sampling bias or the placebo effect.[50] One of the biggest training businesses, Luminosity, paid $2 million in fines because the Federal Trade Commission said their advertisement "preyed on consumers' fears about age-related cognitive decline."[51] Additionally, many studies cited to support brain training are too small to be statistically reliable, and others have selectively reported data. Michael Kane of the University of North Carolina in Greensboro is cited as saying: "It's astonishing how poor some of the experimental designs have been, violating many of the most fundamental principles that we regularly teach to undergraduates in introductory courses."[52]

We also know that there is not very much evidence for or against brain training in school-age children. With so little known, Ferrero and colleagues suggest:

> [t]he propagation of brain-based interventions with dubious scientific basis involves not only a substantial economic cost, but also an opportunity cost; that is, parents and children risk wasting money and time in a useless treatment when they could invest those resources on an effective solution . . . Many of these practices are unlikely to produce any benefit and can even harm schoolchildren.[53]

While there are few interventions shown to work with children, there is a rich body of research on sub-skills, with studies that are more refined and convincing. All these studies suggest that *some* aspects of cognition can be improved by *some* interventions, but most do not last long term, nor are they transferable to general cognitive benefits as seen in Table 5.2.

TABLE 5.2. EXAMPLES OF BRAIN TRAINING OF COGNITIVE SKILLS AND FINDINGS

Examples of "Brain Training" of Cognitive Skills		
Cognitive focus	**Study**	**Findings**
Working memory	Melby-Lervåg, M., & Hulme, C. (2013). Is working memory training effective? A meta-analytic review. *Developmental Psychology*, 49(2), 270.	". . . programs produced reliable **short-term improvements** in working memory skills. For verbal working memory, these **near-transfer effects were not sustained** at follow-up, whereas for visuospatial working memory, limited evidence suggested that such effects might be maintained. More importantly, there was **no convincing evidence of the generalization of working memory training to other skills** (nonverbal and verbal ability, inhibitory processes in attention, word decoding, and arithmetic) . . . "
Attention	Posner, M. I., Rothbart, M. K., & Tang, Y. Y. (2015). Enhancing attention through training. *Current Opinion in Behavioral Sciences, 4*, 1-5.	" . . . there are **no studies showing that training the executive network in children can improve adult outcomes**" "There are correlations between the executive attention network and self control or self regulation in children and adults . . . "
Inhibitory control	Karbach, J. (2015). Plasticity of executive functions in childhood and adolescence: Effects of cognitive training interventions. *Revista Argentina de Ciencias del Comportamiento, 7*(1), 64-70.	"Despite some encouraging findings revealing that executive control training benefitted untrained task and abilities, such as fluid intelligence and academic performance, **recent findings regarding the transferability of training-induced performance improvements to untrained tasks are heterogeneous.**"

ADHD	Tajik-Parvinchi, D., Wright, L., & Schachar, R. (2014). Cognitive rehabilitation for attention deficit/ hyperactivity disorder (ADHD): Promises and problems. *Journal of the Canadian Academy of Child and Adolescent Psychiatry*, 23(3), 207.	"Cognitive training **shows promise in remediating deficits in children with attention deficit/ hyperactivity disorder** (ADHD)—a disorder believed to stem from deficient cognitive processes—where the focus has been primarily on training **working memory and attention.**" "Although the overall pattern of findings from these studies is promising, the methodological and theoretical limitations associated with the literature **limit conclusions about the efficacy of cognitive training as a rehabilitation method for ADHD.**"
Decision-making	Kable, J. W., Caulfield, M. K., Falcone, M., McConnell, M., Bernardo, L., Parthasarathi, T., . . . & Diefenbach, P. (2017). No Effect of Commercial Cognitive Training on Neural Activity During Decision-Making. *Journal of Neuroscience*, 2832-16.	" . . . we found **no evidence that cognitive training influences neural activity during decision-making**, nor did we find effects of cognitive training on measures of delay discounting or risk sensitivity. Participants in the commercial training condition improved with practice on the specific tasks they performed during training, but participants in both conditions showed similar improvement on standardized cognitive measures over time. Moreover, the degree of improvement was comparable to that observed in individuals who were reassessed without any training whatsoever. **Commercial adaptive cognitive training appears to have no benefits in healthy young adults above those of standard video games for measures of brain activity, choice behavior, or cognitive performance.**"

All these examples suggest limited benefits to brain training, at best.

This information helps teachers prioritize the activities they do in class. Simple repetition of patterns (with or without technology) is excellent for extending working memory, but unless continual rehearsal occurs, the effects don't last long, as research from brain training shows us. On the other hand, simulations, case studies, and problem-based learning are extremely effective in long-term learning goals, due to the direct application, social interaction, and emotional connection to the content. These comparisons make it easier for teachers to make better decisions about successful classroom interventions.

ALL KNOWLEDGE HAS TO BE ACTIVELY CONSTRUCTED BY THE LEARNER

While all learning is (neuro)constructivist in design,[54] just *how* the building blocks of knowledge come together based on teacher instruction and student learning is less clear. The constructivists believe that human experiences create a kind of building block structure, the end result being "knowledge" and understanding about the world. This understanding permits the learner to construct (or create) subjective representations of objective reality. This makes a great deal of sense when it becomes clear that base-level concepts need to be in place before higher-order concepts can be established, literally "standing on the shoulders" of the earlier concepts. Teachers, in this sense, are like architects, who must assure the foundations and walls are in place before building the roofing.

Constructivism makes sense. The question is whether constructivism needs to be "actively" achieved, or if there is such a thing as "passive" constructivism. In other words, the old belief that "Knowledge is seen as something that is actively constructed *by learners*" may now be replaced with knowledge is seen as something that is actively constructed *by the teacher* and *for learners*.[55]

Where the Myth Comes From

The myth originates from *who* is active in the construction: the teacher or the student. In education, constructivist design relies heavily on the teacher and careful planning of activities.[56] While there is no doubt the teacher actively designs constructivist learning experiences, the myth emerges because some presume the learner is also active as a conscious participant, and knowing in this process, which is not always the case.

What We Know Now

While no one denies that human learning occurs constructively—which can also be shown *neuro*constructively in some cases—we know that some learning passes under the radar of consciousness. For example, a student can have great *"aha!"* moments in which everything clicks, and learning takes place, and the student himself might even be surprised that this occurred. Similarly, social and cultural interactions are not always consciously understood by the learner herself.[57] Learning can also occur thanks to sheer exposure and without any planning at all. This means that while teachers actively construct learning experiences, the student himself may be unconscious of the structures in play.

SELF-PERCEPTION IS LESS IMPORTANT THAN IQ IN ACADEMIC ACHIEVEMENT

There is a strong belief that "smart kids" are the ones who get ahead in the world, that being smart is a ticket to college and a good job. It is also, unfortunately, believed by some to be something that you either have or don't have. The belief that intelligence is mainly hereditary fuels the neuromyth that being born smart is just the luck of the draw. The truth is that there are also people who work very hard, and even if they don't seem to be the innately smarter students, manage to learn as well as or better than the students in the room who seem to learn effortlessly. These hard workers' self-confidence seems to carry them through. So, which has more weight, self-perception (*if I work hard, I will get ahead*) or IQ?

Where the Myth Comes From

The presumption that inherited IQ is more important than self-belief comes from the erroneous belief that nature outweighs nurture, and that the intelligence you are born with is more important than what you think about your ability to achieve. It is easier to believe that the genes you inherit are stronger than your ability to control them. This is often promoted by teachers' perceptions of how genes and environment influence classroom behavior.[58]

What We Know Now

Studies show that "there is ample empirical evidence that self-efficacy and self-concept beliefs are each related with and influence academic achievement,"[59] meaning that what a person thinks of his own ability to learn actually influences his learning. It seems that self-discipline, self-efficacy, and self-regulation all impact academic achievement.[60] Bandura[61] made it clear that motivation and behavior are mutually and reciprocally influential. Self-perception is important, and in many cases, even more important than IQ.

Angela Duckworth's work in the area of grit and stamina, along with Martin Seligman's positive psychology, has proved particularly insightful in this area. In their paper "Self-Discipline Outdoes IQ in Predicting Academic Performance of Adolescents,"[62] they showed that:

> [s]elf-discipline measured in the fall accounted for more than twice as much variance as IQ in final grades, high school selection, school attendance, hours spent doing homework, hours spent watching television (inversely), and the time of day students began their homework.[63]

Educational achievement can be measured by more than just grades on standardized tests, however. One goal of learning in the 21st century is to cultivate creative thinking.[64] A high percentage of U.S. 4th and 8th graders (67%) taking the TIMSS International Math test say they are confident in their math skills. Interestingly enough, they score only slightly above average, meaning they generally overrate themselves. However, in a strange twist, the U.S. "extended its long-standing position as the top source of international patent applications"[65] and has more indicators of innovation than other countries. It appears that the self-confidence might not translate into high standardized test scores, but perhaps correlates with creativity, innovation, and invention.

It seems that if a person thinks he can learn, he probably will, but if he doubts his ability (has low self-confidence), he will probably not even try, and this downward spiral can turn into a self-fulfilling negative prophecy. Failure begets failure; thinking you will fail leads to a higher probability of failure. And success begets success; believing you can succeed leads to a higher probability of success. Neural plasticity shows us that people are not trapped or limited by the brain they are born with, but rather can maximize their genetic potential through both strong environmental experiences and confidence in their own abilities.[66]

BRAIN ACTIVITY DEPENDS ENTIRELY ON SENSORY INPUT

Our senses—such as sight, which occupies more brain real estate in the cortex than other sense—are strong pathways to learning. Sayings such as "seeing is believing" or "you had to be there" lead us to think that without the senses and contact with the outside world, a person's brain is inactive. Herculano-Houzel[67] found that 50% of high school students, 48% of college students, and 33% of graduate students believe that the brain must be confronted with external stimuli to learn. However, the truth is that people can learn without any direct sensory input.

All learning occurs through the senses—or through the *memory* of these senses. Aristotle is credited with being the first to note that everything a human learns is triggered by one or more senses, and this does not have to be in real time.[68] We can remember how something felt, smelled, looked, tasted, or sounded, and this can trigger new learning contexts. In fact, most analogies work with such memory mechanisms.

Where the Myth Comes From

The belief that brain activity depends on sensory input grows out of a lack of scientific literacy about memory functions and learning. The introduction on the educational landscape of the Theory of Multiple Intelligences[69] gave teachers an appreciation for viewing students' smarts on different planes. But it also somehow suggested that the greater the variety of classroom activities, the better. The myth that stimulating more senses improves learning outcomes was born in part from a misunderstanding of MI theory, and a general lack of knowledge about how learning occurs in the brain.

What We Know Now

In 2001, a fascinating new element of human learning came to light. While searching for a baseline (control state) in neuroimaging, Raichle and colleagues came across consistent "brain oxygen extraction" rates across humans.[70] This was important for several reasons. First, having a baseline permits researchers to compare "active" brain states—as when a person is asked to complete a specific task—with the "resting" state, to determine precisely which areas or circuits of the brain are active. But perhaps even more interesting was that a little later that same year, Gusnard and Raichle identified "a specific set of mental operations"[71] related to this "resting" state; in other words, even when the brain is doing "nothing," it is in fact doing "something." This is now known as the default mode network (DMN). Over time, the consistency of this network across subjects confirmed that when the brain is not being stimulated from external sensory perception, it is still active;[72] it is occupied bouncing around memories, thinking of the future, reflecting inward and projecting outward. In fact, while in the DMN, the brain is still using 60-80% of the energy it would be using while doing a specific task, like reading.[73]

The fact that there is functional activity during the default mode effectively measures a kind of "mind wandering."[74] In its "resting state" the brain is actually very active in "discrete, bilateral and symmetrical cortical areas, in the medial and lateral parietal, medial prefrontal and medial and lateral temporal cortices."[75] The DMN is active when a person is not specifically focused on anything in the outside world, but rather is in a state of "wakeful rest," such as thinking of the past or the future.[75] This "looking inward" permits learning and, contrary to popular belief, is a time of great brain activity.[76] The DMN makes it clear that brain activity does not depend on the external environment.

We also now know that thinking about certain actions makes the brain look as if it is completing that same action[77] That is, a person who imagines a motor action, such as thinking about throwing a baseball (without actually throwing the baseball), has a brain that looks like it's throwing the baseball. This means the brain is capable of "experiencing" events without actually having the experience itself. Brain activity such as the default mode network, and emerging understandings of consciousness,[78] Theory of Mind,[79] and mirror neurons[80] all make it clear that brain activity does not depend on sensory input, but can also be internally generated.

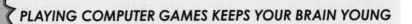

PLAYING COMPUTER GAMES KEEPS YOUR BRAIN YOUNG

People are living longer. While medicine has worked hard to keep our bodies in shape, there has been less effort expended to keep our brains in top condition.[81] It is clear that certain interventions help successful aging, including regular physical activity, good nutrition, and social engagement. Cognitive training, however, is a relative newcomer to the list of general geriatric recommendations.[82] Many entrepreneurs have launched commercial ventures to take advantage of people's desperation to stay in shape mentally, some by promoting the idea that playing computer games keeps your brain young.

While it is likely that "Video Games Can Change Your Brain"[83]—since all experiences have that potential, especially if they occur with frequency—the jury is still out on whether "Playing Video Games is Good For Your Brain."[84] Yet it is widely believed that engaging with computer games can help to maintain mental acuity as we age.

Where the Myth Comes From

People always look for the silver bullet. Aging populations put a huge burden on health care systems and the younger members of society. It would be attractive if the answer to dementia were as simple as putting grandma in front of a computer for a few minutes a day. Video gaming and brain training are new fields. Therefore, rumors abound, and wishful thinking takes over, fostering the myth that playing computer games keeps your brain young.

What We Know Now

Thinking is very complex and involves multiple cognitive sub-skills, which all need to be in sync for a person to successfully process information, resolve problems, and contemplate the world. *Some* computer games help *some* of the sub-elements of cognition, but no program attends to them *all*. An example of a computer game that does improve cognition in a specific area is *The Number Race*,[85] a game originally designed to help children with dyscalculia. The game works on symbolic numeric recognition, number-line skills, counting, and early addition and subtraction skills.[86] While these skill sets help in some aspects of math, the authors never claimed *The Number Race* improves *all* of math skills or improves an individual's grasp of mathematics as a whole. Aside from the skill sets mentioned, math also includes spatial manipulation, concepts of order, patterns, relationships, and the ability to categorize—none of which are involved in *The Number Race*.

Similarly, *FastForword* is a computer game that was originally designed to help young children with dyslexia. *FastForword* improves specific language sub-skills, such as rapid auditory temporal processing, which is thought to be at the heart of reading problems for children with difficulty in phonemic awareness.[87] One cannot say that global language facility is improved by playing *FastForword*, but rather that these specific subsets of language can be improved. Additionally, while the intervention is in place, there are gains in speaking and syntax, but longitudinal studies show these gains were not maintained over two years.[87] This means that continued rehearsal might be necessary to have an effect. (This works the same way for the elderly as it does for children.) Each of these interventions helps sub-elements of math or language, but does not improve thinking as a whole. These two examples of *The Number Race* and *FastForword* illustrate that specific sub-skills can be improved, but that general cognition cannot.

Other computer games help people improve working memory skills, which is a part of thinking, but not all of thinking. As a general rule, ". . . most evidence suggests that practicing a task only helps you get better at that particular task."[88] Most computer games can benefit some aspect of cognition, but no game improves thinking in general. In a large-scale study by Kueider and colleagues, *"Computerized Cognitive Training with Older Adults: A Systematic Review,"* computer training results were equal or better than other activities such as doing math or a maze with pencil and paper; their study suggests that "computerized training is an effective, less labor intensive alternative" than pencil and paper interventions.[89] In sum, cognitive training through video gaming has some documented benefits, but they are not as broad as promised.

It's also important to note that cognitive training does not freeze the aging process. While improving core skill sets and keeping the brain active are excellent contributions to successful aging, computer games do not put aging in reverse. Bleakley and colleagues reviewed interactive computer games in older adults and found that while there were no adverse effects, "there was preliminary evidence that ICG [interactive computer games] is a safe and effective exercise intervention,"[90] however, there was no evidence of strong cognitive benefits. In another meta-analysis by Hill and colleagues, the authors showed "small to moderate effects" for "global cognition, attention, working memory, learning, and memory, with the exception of nonverbal memory, and for psychosocial functioning, including depressive symptoms."[91] This means that, on balance, computer gaming shows small cognitive benefits, but does not reverse the effects of aging. Additionally, we know that time spent on computer games is time not spent doing other activities, such as exercising, reading, or socializing. This means that computer gaming comes with an opportunity cost. For computer gaming to become a recommended activity in regular geriatric intervention, studies would need to demonstrate that the benefits outweighed the costs.

There have been multiple studies to determine just what *can* slow the cognitive aging process, but without definitive results. Aside from good experiences in youth[92] there are few recommendations that appear to work for all populations.

WHY THIS IS GOOD NEWS FOR TEACHING

It is great news that children are not limited by their early childhood experiences; a lack of extra stimulation classes when they were toddlers does not mean students are doomed in academia. Teachers can celebrate the knowledge that they still have the power to help their students reach their potential. And both parents and teachers can rest assured that they're able to play a key role in children's potential simply by interacting with them in normal ways, without purchasing expensive toys or programs.

Teachers can celebrate the fact that constructivism is hard at work in their students' brains, but they should not expect that there are always visible or behavioral cues to the learning that is taking place. On the other hand, teachers must be fully aware of their roles in designing constructivist learning environments in order to be able to scaffold students' learning from lower- to higher-level conceptual knowledge. At the level of instructional strategies, it's good to know that teachers do not have to move their students around constantly to stimulate all their senses in order to learn. Sometimes, quiet reflection can advance learning goals just as much or more than active learning activities. While active learning is encouraged to meet some learning goals, a balance of active learning with time for reflection results in superior learning when compared with simple experiential-based learning.

Once teachers realize that the Internet is neither good nor bad but rather just another tool, they can embrace the potential benefits of its proper use. Like textbooks, collaborative learning activities, or the Socratic method, not all mediums are appropriate for all educational goals. It's great to know our toolbox for teaching activities has been expanded by the Internet, and that we have the power to decide the role it plays in our own classrooms. Likewise, the addition of virtual media like video gaming to a teacher's repertoire of options is exciting and potentially revolutionizing. As with any resource, however, video gaming is most useful when it is effective in helping students reach their learning objectives, rather than simply providing entertainment.

With regard to "brain training," it is also good for teachers to see that the brain adapts to what it does most, so the effects of training are only as good as the intensity of practice, just as rehearsal in classrooms is only as good as the activity used to practice the skill set. These discussions emphasize why certain classroom interventions are better than others in maintaining long-term learning and far transfer of abilities. Some of the best news for teachers is that we have learned that continual rehearsal over time in a variety of contexts helps cement learning and the eventual transfer far better than one-off concept introduction or short-term rehearsal.

The mixed evidence about video games also reveals some great news for teachers about the malleability of students' minds using technology. If aggressiveness can be taught through virtual media, as the evidence appears to indicate, so can positive traits and academic knowledge. Educational gaming has been shown to improve a variety of skill sets and characteristics,[93] including math,[94] reading,[95] spatial reasoning,[96] and geography,[97] as well as promoting sharing, empathy, good citizenship, and morality.[98] While gaming is still in its infancy and ripe with promise, it's helpful for teachers to know that video games can improve specific sub-skills, but not increase global intelligence.

Great teachers know they need to help their students believe in themselves. At a minimum, students need to know the teacher thinks they can learn; in the best-case scenario, teachers can be the catalysts for student self-belief and eventual academic achievement. As educators, we need to acknowledge the power of our words: "Another mistake! You just aren't trying, are you?" versus "I know this isn't the grade you wanted, but I can tell you are improving" can make all the difference in the world. Even small comments can fill a student with confidence, or with fear.[99]

Practical Application of MBE: Ages are Not as Important as Prior Experience

Not all students are ready to do the same thing in a given discipline at the same age, and oftentimes students who seem hopelessly lost in a topic early on in the school year end up excelling and even passing the early starters in the group by the end.[100] This is a strong argument in favor of mastery classes rather than grade/age divisions.

All students will need some help at some point in their academic careers. Just because a student fails to do well initially does not mean he has a learning problem or is slow. Not everyone the same age is prepared to do the same level of work in the same subject area at the same time. In several school systems around the world, there is experimentation with the idea of flexible placements, in which students can move seamlessly between levels (from "special needs" to "gifted") without the stigma of labeling.

Keeping the brain active ("use it or lose it") is helpful, but it does not *reverse* aging. The research into successfully aging brains has offered some interesting insights, not the least of which is the influence of strong education programs in youth. This is good news for teaching because it gives teachers yet another reason to do their best with young minds, as the consequences seem to extend to brain health in old age.[101]

Knowing that environmental factors can influence cognitive abilities is the essence of educational practice and great news for teachers. The fact that plasticity exists and that children are not "always stuck with the mental abilities they are born with"[102] gives teachers cause to celebrate and empowers us to create the best learning conditions possible for our students. Rather than judge a student for not being able to read at age seven (or eight or nine) because he lacks familiarity with reading due to home circumstances, something over which the teacher has no control, a teacher can focus on filling in the gaps in knowledge that are holding the student back—something she can influence. It's empowering for teachers to know they can speed up learning processes by building upon students' prior knowledge, rather than prioritizing factors like age.

6 • MYTHS ABOUT

THE MIND-BODY BALANCE

YOUR BRAIN USES 20% OF THE BODY'S CALORIES, SO SUGARY DRINKS HELP COGNITION

The brain uses more energy than any other organ in the body, meaning it is "expensive," as it "accounts for only 2% of body weight, yet the energy required to maintain brain function amounts to 20% of an individual's resting metabolic rate."[1] Brain energy is normally spent in the form of glucose to fuel electrical impulses. Glucose also regulates the delicate balance of calcium, potassium, and sodium managed by adenosine triphosphate (ATP) to maintain a general state of homeostasis in the brain. It was once thought that energy use was in proportion to the demanding nature of the task—that is, more glucose was expended in doing deep thinking than when doing easier activities. This is not completely true: ". . . any local increases in energy consumption are tiny compared with the brain's gluttonous baseline intake. So, in most cases, short periods of additional mental effort require a little more brainpower than usual, but not much more."[2] As the brain is such an energy-hungry organ and because energy is in the form of glucose, or sugar, the myth emerged that people need sugary drinks to stay focused. The idea is that if 20% of energy is used by the brain and this is in the form of glucose, then people should consume 20% of their calories in glucose. This is not true.

Where the Myth Comes From

General misunderstandings about the brain's and the body's nutritional needs lead to myths. Obsession with dieting, combined with interest in everything "neuro," leads to neuromyths about how food intake changes brain functioning. One interesting guide is to think like Socrates: "Everything in moderation." Too much (or too little) sugar is not good for the brain or the body. The World Health Organization suggests that 5% of daily caloric intake should be from sugar. However, Americans obtain an average of 13% of their calories from sugar. The myth results from the combination of generally poor nutritional habits and the belief that the brain needs extra sugar to work optimally.

What We Know Now

It is logical to presume that people should ingest lots of glucose, given the brain's need for this substance, but as all carbohydrates convert to glucose once digested, people don't need to consume sugary drinks to create the glucose needed by the brain.

Nutritional needs for optimal brain functioning change over a lifetime, depending on a number of variables, including "age, effort, personality, glucoregulation, time of day, task demand, task domain, and nature and amount of the carbohydrate."[3] *Gluconeogenesis* is the conversion of carbs into glucose. Even people with regular to low-carb diets can still produce amounts of glucose adequate for optimal brain functioning. The amount of glucose needed for optimal brain functioning does not require additional sugar intake.

Many authorities have suggestions about the best diet for your brain, and none are high in sugar. Some of the first suggestions that come up when "diet for your brain" or "brain diet" is Googled include recommendations from *BBC Good Food*, WebMD, *Scientific American*, *SHAPE*, and *Reader's Digest*. The summary of their recommendations can be found in Table 6.1.

TABLE 6.1. UNCONFIRMED POPULAR PRESS DIET RECOMMENDATIONS FOR BRAIN HEALTH

	BBC Good Food[4]	WebMD[5]	Scientific American[6]	SHAPE[7]	Reader's Digest[8]
Whole grains	X	X	X	oats, lentils	
Oily fish	X	salmon	X	sardines	salmon
Blueberries	X				X
Tomatoes	X				
Vitamin B (chicken, eggs)	X		X	eggs	eggs
Vitamin C (blackcurrant, red peppers)	X		X		
Pumpkin seeds	X				
Broccoli	X		X		
Sage	X			X	

	BBC Good Food[4]	WebMD[5]	Scientific American[6]	SHAPE[7]	Reader's Digest[8]
Nuts and seeds	X	X	X	flaxseed, walnuts	walnut
Avocados		X			X
Beans		X	X		
Pomegranate juice		X			
Freshly brewed tea		X		yerba mate	
Dark chocolate		X			
Beets				X	
(Grass-fed beef				X	
Green leafy vegetables			X	spinach	kale
Wine and Champagne			X		X

Source: Author

While there is no perfect diet for optimal brain activity, it is clear that no one recommends additional sugar as a staple.

DIETARY SUPPLEMENTS IMPROVE COGNITION

Many people don't have the time to eat right. People often think they can take supplements to replace food intake, or take a supplement rather than eat in order to lose weight ("Can You Replace Breakfast with Supplements?"[9]). Others are very conscious of their eating habits, but want to boost some mind-body functioning, like energy, stable nerves, focus, stamina, memory, and so on ("Can a Daily Pill Really Boost Your Brain Power?"[10]). And some people have habitually taken a daily vitamin their entire lives and just presume that this is the normal thing to do. Whatever the reason, more than 40% of Americans take some form of supplement daily, and this figure is rising.

People in the U.S. are taking more vitamin supplements than ever before, and "alternative medicines"—herbal formulations, for example—are also being consumed in greater quantities; so much so that chemical-induced liver damage (hepatotoxicity) has reached new heights as people overdose on the use of natural herbs.[11] There are more than 50,000 dietary supplements approved by the Office of Dietary Supplements in the United States, the most popular being vitamin and mineral supplements (43%) and botanicals (herbs) (20%).[11] There "has been a steadily rising consumption of dietary supplements by US residents over the last few decades," according to Avigan and colleagues,[12] and more than 42.6% of non-Hispanic whites take some form of vitamin or mineral supplement on a regular basis.[13] The nutritional supplements industry has very well-designed marking schemes, and people can often feel they are being negligent if they don't take *something* to enhance, prevent, or reverse different cognitive processes, after all, the more the merrier and "the earlier the better."[14]

To add to the array of options on the market, a new group of drugs have hit society with force. *Nootropics* are cognitive enhancers, or "smart drugs" that can originate from natural sources (e.g., caffeine) or be manufactured synthetically (e.g., methylphenidate). These are drugs that can be taken by people with no diagnosed needs for supplements. For example, people without attention deficit hyperactivity disorder (ADHD) who take Ritalin are, in effect, taking a cognitive enhancer. The number of website promoting the sale of these types of drugs has skyrocketed in the past decade as "cosmetic neurology" takes off.[15]

Where the Myth Comes From

Once again, people like things to be simple. It's hard to argue with the allure of the idea of just popping a pill as compared with exercising or sitting down to study to become healthy and smart. Why not? It is more complicated to plan a balanced diet and prepare food and an exercise routine than to just take a supplement. To complicate matters, there are often so many conflicting messages in the media that people can feel overwhelmed by the "advice" they receive. Smooth marketing techniques are designed to encourage the consumption of supplements, lest we be left behind, or worse yet, be accused of not doing everything possible to improve our physical and mental health (*"You're Still Not Eating Enough Vegetables"*[16]; *"Get Ahead in Silicon Valley: Take Nootropic Brain Drugs"*[17]). Well-designed commercials can make people feel that they are not doing quite enough to maximize their potential to remember, to pay attention, and to (re)act. The suggestion that "just a pill a day" can help is very tempting.

What We Know Now

Some supplements can improve sub-elements of cognition, but none have lasting effects. For example, a person might feel "extra focused and alert" after a cup of coffee, but once the effects of caffeine have worn off, their attention wanes. You cannot just pop a pill to raise your level of intelligence; enhanced attention is temporary. We also know that supplements can come at a cost, overtaxing the liver for the benefit of the brain. Some hit your pocketbook, while others are questionable, ethically speaking.

The closer to the natural source the better. Vitamin supplements are processed, and their structure changes the way that the body uses the vitamins, as compared with the way it would receive them in natural forms (from fruits, vegetables, nuts, and so on). This is complicated further by the definition of just what constitutes a "natural" source, and how much "natural" or "organic" costs, compared with the supplement option. Vitamin supplements, just like vaccinations, have done a lot to prevent problems, especially in populations in which costly foods and their natural nutrients are not an option. There is far less evidence, however, that supplements improve cognition over the long run in the school population. Most studies on supplements relate to helping malnourished children get an equal footing, or aiding pregnant mothers to prevent life-threatening diseases, rather than on helping the average student get better grades.

There are a small number of studies that look at the impact of nutrition on learning and which consider the use of dietary supplements in school-age children. One of the most famous longitudinal studies, conducted in the UK, followed more than 15,000 pregnancies from prenatal stages through 18 years of age and asked, among other things, what kinds of medications and supplements children were exposed to, as well as eating patterns. One of the most important, but not unexpected, findings was that early eating patterns had a direct influence on academic outcomes. Kids who ate more junk food did more poorly in school, a pattern established by the time the child was 3 years old.[18] Poor eating habits also correlated with slightly lower IQs.[19] Eating habits are strongly influenced by the environment, both at home and school, which requires caregivers to be aware of the influence their modeling has on young children.[20]

Other supplement-related studies show the difference between getting nutrients through pills versus through more natural sources in food. For example, there are studies that show that taking fish oil supplements during pregnancy does not influence cognitive development in children.[21] However, eating low-mercury, farm-fed fish has a slight cognitive benefit for offspring.[22] This is important because it means that nutrients from a natural source are preferable to nutrients from supplements. However, getting nutrients from supplements is preferable to not getting them at all. Crib and colleagues[23] found that a large number of children do not receive the balanced diets needed to potentiate growth, and therefore, supplements can be of help.

OMEGA-3 PILLS ENHANCE THE MENTAL CAPACITY OF CHILDREN IN THE GENERAL POPULATION

One of the most prominent dietary recommendations in the popular press as "brain food" are omega-3 fatty acids, found in oily fish such as salmon, mackerel, anchovies, bluefish, herring, sardines, sturgeon, lake trout, tuna, and cod, which provide eicosapentaenoic acid (EPA) and docosahexaenoic acid (DHA), and in chia seeds, flaxseed, walnuts, soybeans, and spinach. One of the reasons omega 3s are mentioned so much in the press is that the body does not make these essential fatty acids that affect the function of cell receptors in the brain and body, but must get them from food.[24] While omega-3s are beneficial to humans as a means of preventing heart disease (by lowering blood pressure and triglyceride cholesterol levels), they have recently been touted in the press as aiding mental capacity. Headlines like, "Omega-3 Fatty Acids and Better Brain Function . . . "[25] call attention to the "mystical powers" of omega-3s, often erroneously equated solely with fatty fish. The question is, how does this impact learning, and are the omega-3s truly cognitive enhancers that can be taken in pill form? As with other dietary supplements, it is clear that omega-3s are found in many different natural food sources, which are preferable to supplements.

Where the Myth Comes From

It was standard practice a generation ago to feed children a daily spoonful of cod liver oil as a healthy precaution. The world's most famous nanny, Mary Poppins, did this to Michael and Jane, after all, supposedly because it was known to combat depression and inflammatory diseases, improve the skin, and fight kidney diseases and other maladies, not to mention "improve brain function," all in one go.[26] Cod, along with other fatty fish, contains omega-3s. The link between the positive benefits of cod liver oil and omega-3 is one origin of this myth; people wanted the benefits of cod liver oil without its awful taste, so supplements emerged. According to the United States National Institutes of Health,[27] "fish oil was the most popular natural product used by adults in the United States in 2012. Nearly 8 million more adults used fish oil in 2012 than in 2007." Fish oil was also "the most popular natural product used by children."[28] Despite the main research on omega-3s being related to heart disease, spillover benefits to the brain are intimated in multiple publications. Explosive popular books fuel this fire (e.g., *Magnificent Mind at Any Age: Natural Ways to Unleash Your Brain's Maximum Potential*[29]) as they tout the benefits of omega-3s and suggest that they serve as cognitive enhancers.

What We Know Now

Omega-3s have been shown to be important to combat heart disease, but there is little evidence that they serve as the key to brain development, and even less evidence that school-aged populations benefit from their use, especially in supplement form as opposed to natural food sources. That is, while omega-3s can't hurt the brain, there is little evidence that they improve cognition in school-age children.

If one decides to administer omega-3s to children, however, this should be done as naturally as possible (do not follow Mary Poppins's lead here). While the popular press argues in favor of the inclusion of omega-3 fatty acids in the human diet, the United States Food and Drug Administration says that this should be consumed in fish, and only fish with low mercury levels and that has not been exposed to other contaminants.[30] This all seems like reasonable advice, but fish high in omega-3s with low mercury and caught in natural surroundings with low contamination rates costs more than supplements. Additionally, these recommendations tend to be for pregnant women, not school kids. The few studies conducted on school-age children are far less convincing.

In 2010, Kirby and colleagues[31] conducted the largest study in the United Kingdom on 450 mainstream school children 8 to 10 years old using a randomized, double-blind, placebo-controlled design, one of the most rigorous methodologies possible. Their findings were less than convincing. After 16 weeks of supplements versus placebos, there were only three differences reported in the parent, teacher, and participant questionnaires, and one of those was in favor of the placebo.[31] This means that there is inconclusive evidence in favor of omega-3 in school-age populations.

What We Know Now

Evidence about the benefits of omega-3s in school-age populations is far from compelling. "The influence of n-3 long-chain polyunsaturated fatty acids (LCP-UFA) supplementation on brain functioning is debated. Some studies have found positive effects on cognition in children with learning difficulties, elderly people with cognitive impairment and depression scores in depressed individuals."[32] while others have found no such evidence.[33] There have been more studies conducted on the elderly than on children, and on maternal influences on newborns than on school-age children, meaning there is a gap in the literature that makes it hard to reach conclusions based on evidence.

WHEN YOU SLEEP, YOUR BRAIN SHUTS DOWN

Sleep and death have been used metaphorically in literature for hundreds of years, and the likeness of deep sleep to death makes people think that the brain stops functioning while at rest. Nothing could be further from the truth, yet a large percentage of teachers from around the world believe that when you sleep, your brain shuts down.[34] Most dreaming occurs during rapid eye movement (REM) sleep, when your brain is closest to wakefulness. What's more, if you wake up naturally, you are likely waking from REM sleep and a dream. The deepest stage of sleep is when the slowest (delta) brain waves are present, which is about as inactive as your brain gets while it's alive. As you sleep, you go through four stages of sleep (each with different electrical waves) in what is called cycles, each of which lasts roughly 90 minutes, moving from near wakefulness down into deep sleep and back up again to dreaming, just before wakefulness. You go through these cycles four to six times a night, meaning you have about four to six chances to dream and four to six chances to be in deep sleep. Some believe that the brain shuts down during sleep because people do not look very active. Many people, especially students, erroneously believe that, because people look inactive as they sleep, "studying is more important than sleep."[35] These misconceptions about the role of sleep and learning lead to other assaults on potential.

"Pulling an all-nighter" might seem like a good idea when you are behind in studying and the test is just a few hours away, but the truth of the matter is that doing so will likely reduce the probability of recall and your ability to stay focused the next day.

People do not remember how they learned to sleep the way they do because sleep habits often form soon after birth. People are also generally unaware that sleeping is a behavior, and like all behaviors, can be modified and "relearned." According to a study published by the National Institutes of Health, "global public health concern over poor sleep has increased the demand for effective sleep promotion strategies that are easily accessible to the general population."[36] Simple things like a consistent bedtime routine, falling asleep independently, refraining from caffeine intake, and sleeping in bedrooms without televisions are some of the suggestions from the National Sleep Foundation[37] that sound simple enough, but are not necessarily heeded by the public.

Despite intuitively knowing the importance of good rest for learning, many adults are poor models of good sleep practices. As adults, we also promote other myths by showing kids how "we need our cup of coffee" in the morning to get going, when we should be able to start the day without stimulants if we slept sufficiently at night.

Where the Myth Comes From

People rarely remember what they dream, and most think bedtime only serves to rest the body, leading to the belief that the brain shuts down. Lack of understanding about sleep and dreaming means that few people believe anything important is occurring during sleep. People also rarely think about sleep in the context of learning, and sleep hygiene is not a typical teacher education topic.

What We Know Now

We now know that sleep and dreaming play important roles in learning. Both attention and memory are fundamental elements of learning—without both attention and memory, there is no learning.[38] Sleep helps people pay attention,[39] while dreaming consolidates memory.[40] The quality of sleep has a direct influence on the brain's ability to pay attention, and quality dreaming is important for the consolidation of memory. A memory moves from working to long-term only when the neural pathways related to it are consolidated. Memory consolidation occurs thanks to a unique combination of neurotransmitters in the brain, present only during rapid eye movement (REM) sleep.[41] We now know that getting enough sleep is vital to many aspects related to quality of life, as well as to memory.

For example, there is evidence from a handful of studies that later start times in the school day correspond better to adolescent sleep patterns, and that students do indeed perform better in all aspects of mental, physical, and academic life,[42] This includes general learning outcomes;[43] healthy decision making;[44] illness;[45] suicide;[46] school violence;[47] and standardized test scores.[48] In fact, sleep is so important for memory consolidation and attention that the National Institutes of Health published findings from the benefits of explicitly teaching sleep hygiene to students[49] We know that teaching students about the role of sleep in memory can motivate them to change behaviors that put their learning at risk.

We also know people can resolve problems when they sleep (productive sleep). Deirdre Barrette at Harvard University documented the ways in which multiple figures in history used sleep to solve problems. In fact, many leading thinkers, planners, artists, and renowned geniuses have stated that they resolved problems in their sleep, including Albert Einstein, Ludwig van Beethoven, Thomas Edison, Robert Louis Stevenson, Nobel Prize laureate Otto Loewi, pro golfer Jack Nicklaus, singer Billy Joel, writer Stephen King, and artist Salvador Dalí.[50] This is in stark contrast to what people think about sleeping—that it is a waste of time. "Sleep is overrated," Margaret Thatcher is reported to have said. *"For Successful People, Sleeping is a Waste of Time."*[51] we are told. The truth, however, is that sleep-deprived people are unproductive and even dangerous to themselves and others.[52] Lack of sleep cause accidents, depression, anxiety, obesity, forgetfulness, and impaired decision making, among other maladies. There is no upside to sleep deprivation. The sayings "let me sleep on it" or "let me consult my pillow" are likely born of the recognition that sleep adds perspective and focus to decision making.[53]

PEOPLE CAN LEARN IN THEIR SLEEP

"Wait, You **Can** Learn While You Sleep?!"[54] No, you can't, but it's easy to see how this myth has taken hold. There are multiple commercial ventures that suggest that, while sleeping, you can learn a foreign language, quit smoking, memorize the multiplication table, or go over dance routines, among other things. Can people actually learn to harness the power of sleep to conserve energy during wakefulness to learn complex information?

The promises abound: "How Much Can You Really Learn While You're Asleep?"[55] Sleep, it turns out, is vital for allowing the brain to recharge and refocus[56], while dreaming is vital for memory consolidation,[57] meaning sleep is indeed vital for learning. But does this mean people can learn new information while they snooze? The headlines seem convincing, (e.g., "How To (Really) Learn A Foreign Language While You Sleep,"[58] but the science behind such claims is not. Articles like this one, despite the enthusiastic headlines, actually go on to confess that no new learning takes place in sleep.

Where the Myth Comes From

Hypnosis and light sleep are very close. People can learn *some* aspects of foreign language,[59] to quit smoking,[60] among other things[61] under hypnosis. To many people, sleep and hypnosis are identical, contributing to the myth.

Additionally, details about sleep are fuzzy, and many people doubt their own firsthand experiences. Few people contemplate what actually goes on when they sleep, and even fewer take the time to document sleep experiences. Sleep researcher Allan J. Hobson has spent his entire career studying aspects of sleep, including the physiology of sleep,[62] sleep cycle oscillation,[63] how dreaming is a conscious state,[64] visual discrimination,[65] neuronal systems, sleep and learning,[66] sleep dependent motor learning,[67] the neurobiology of sleep and related cortical networks,[68] memory consolidation and reconsolidation,[69] and lucid dreaming,[70] to name a few. If anyone has observed sleep and dreaming, it is Hobson.

The number of commercial ventures that promise you can learn in your sleep makes people think that this is possible. These schemes, along with misleading headlines, set people up to believe that learning can occur while they are at rest. This is something we'd all like to believe, but it is a myth, and Hobson's work confirms this.

Additionally, some people wake from comas saying they have learned things while in this sleeplike state. And others say they learned to do or stop doing something while hypnotized. People presume that if you can learn while in a coma, and you can learn while under hypnosis, it is highly likely you can learn in your sleep.

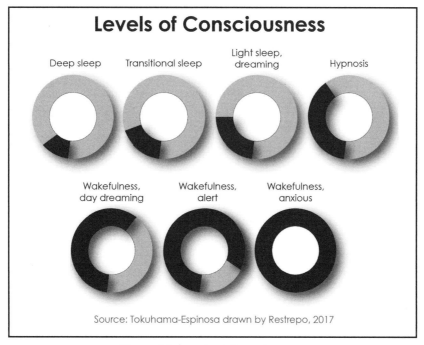

Figure 6.1: *Levels of Consciousness*

What We Know Now

Hobson knows that sleep time can be used to *rehearse* something that was already explicitly taught before sleeping, but not to learn something new. For example, if you learned how to conjugate a verb in Spanish or play a tune on the piano while awake, you can rehearse that while you are asleep. The catch is that you would have needed to pay attention during the initial learning for rehearsal to be possible. That is, there is no *new* learning in sleep, but there can be a rehearsal of information that has already been processed consciously. Hobson also established an understanding of lucid dreaming, which shows people can use tools they already know to resolve problems as they sleep (this is how Einstein reportedly made several discoveries). Some level of motor memory learning can occur during sleep as well (practicing a golf stroke, for example), as can visual rehearsal. So, we now know that nothing new can be learned in sleep, but problem solving using already-learned information can occur while dreaming.

WHY THIS IS GOOD NEWS FOR TEACHING

The truth about good nutrition and optimal brain functioning is simpler than one would think: "Everything in moderation"; "as close to the natural source as possible"; and "what's good for your heart is good for your brain," are good rules of thumb. While teachers are not directly responsible for the eating habits of their students, educating about good body-brain nutrition should be a part of everyone's education. There is a less-than-even playing field for children in our schools, with those being born into wealthy families having a leg up in the system thanks to better schooling options, but also due to the ability to pay for more nutrient-rich foods, and if needed, supplements.

It is great news that studies show that most public schools do a decent job of providing balanced meals, and that there is no difference between a home-packed lunch and a school meal in terms of cognitive payoff.[71] This means that schools that provide healthy meals have a greater influence on developing a child's potential to learn than his family's ability to pay for supplements. Having said that, government programs that provide both school meals as well as vitamin supplements for children in the early years can be beneficial, meaning certain health policy choices can also influence cognitive outcomes. This is good news for teachers because it is within their power to model and—both implicitly and explicitly— teach about the importance of good nutrition for learning.

Knowing about omega-3s is good news for teachers, for two reasons. First, research confirms that omega-3 can be found in real foods, and supplements are unneeded: The closer to the source, the better. Second, the jury is still out as to the true benefits (or not) of omega-3s, so teacher time is best spent investing in pedagogical interventions, rather than depending on "magical" pills. Teachers should understand the influence of nutrition on cognition, but use only conclusive evidence to make decisions.

The science about sleep and dreaming is good news for teaching because it adds another tool to our arsenal of interventions for struggling learners. Teachers can give students an important gift that can last a life time if they help them understand the roles of sleep and dreaming in learning. Knowing that sleep and dreaming are related to attention and memory (and that learning depends on them) is powerful. Teachers can play a role in eliminating this barrier to the conditions for good learning. Sleep hygiene education programs conducted on an experimental basis have been shown to have good results, but only if sustained over time.[72] That is, teaching kids about the role of sleep and dreaming in learning actually changes their habits and improves sleep hygiene, but they have to be reminded of good practice constantly. This suggests that the development of good sleep habits in young children is probably easier than re-educating older children or adults. Parent education programs also help families understand their role in teaching good sleep habits to young children so that correct sleep hygiene is learned early and practiced over the life span. Teachers can play a key role by modeling good sleep hygiene.

Practical Application of MBE: The Mind-Body Balance

We know that early school start times may not be conducive to learning. Research in chronobiology—the study of how different body rhythms are impacted by sleep-wake patterns—show that many students, especially teenagers, experience changes in hormonal balances and prefer later school day starts, as they tend to go to bed later.[73] Great teachers know that a slightly later school day improves not only learning outcomes, but also student attitudes toward school.

Starting the school day later is one possibility, and teaching students the basics of good sleep hygiene is another. The mind-body balance—how to take care of the body by eating, resting, and exercising right—can have a profound impact on student learning outcomes and great teachers share this with their students.

It is great news for teachers that there are no easy answers, quick paths, or gimmicks that can teach the way a good teacher can. Knowing that sleep and dreaming play a role in learning is important information and can be a powerful tool for teachers. Teachers can help students understand why studying and "sleeping on it" are good advice (rather than wishfully using textbooks as pillows). While teachers cannot manage the sleep hygiene of their students, they can share and model this information for their students.

7 • MYTHS ABOUT

BRAIN PLASTICITY

CRITICAL PERIODS LIMIT LEARNING

There are important physiological changes in the brain in childhood, adolescence, and early and late adulthood, but are they *critical* to school learning?

Some of the changes documented in the early years include glucose uptake levels, the timing of new neural connections (synaptogenesis), and pruning (refining of neural pathways). Some people have interpreted that the changes that occur in early childhood are somehow more important than at other times in a person's development. For example, the speed and density of synaptic growth in children between 3 and 10 years old has been documented at length, and often touted as *the* most important time in brain development, without differentiating the important changes that occur at other times in life.[1] Alferik and Farmer-Dougan[1] argue that there are equally important changes that have to do with pruning during adolescence that permits higher-order thinking and reasoning, which could itself be considered *the* most important time of brain development.

A worrisome number of teachers believe that there are critical periods for learning certain skills in school, and that children who miss out on these moments are unable to recuperate them in the future.[2] An example of this misunderstanding relates to the unique human ability to learn multiple languages. It is the thought that if children do not learn a foreign language before adolescence, they never will.[3] It has been shown that people can and do learn foreign languages across the life span, and that adults are actually better at doing this than children in all areas of language, with the exception of accents.[4] That is, adults can learn rules of grammar, vocabulary, syntactic structure, listening skills, reading and writing skills, and all other aspects of language better than children. However, they often do not master pronunciation and accents as well as children. The evidence shows that there is no critical period for foreign language learning, though there might be for a perfect accent when speaking. What's more, there is no evidence of a critical period for *anything* learned in school.

There are also multiple claims that critical periods limit the reaches of education: "What Are the Critical Periods in My Baby's Development"[5]; "Early Life Experience, Critical Periods, and Brain Development"[6]; "The US is Failing to Invest Enough in One of the Most Critical Periods in Children's Education."[7] While dire in their predictions, most of these warnings have to do with negative experiences in childhood, such as abuse, neglect, and how they can affect emotional attachment in later years. These are important issues, but not related to critical periods for learning in the general population, most of who do not live with traumatic stress, grossly poor nutrition or extreme situations of neglect. Childhood trauma plays a role in emotional balance in later life, but this has not been established as a critical period because of the concept of *resilience*, in which many children live through trauma and might even grow stronger through the process.[8] Other headlines have to do with unsubstantiated hypotheses or with the sensory perception ideas or physiological changes: "Is there a critical period for music perception and comprehension during which a child must be exposed to music in order to develop normal, music-specific perceptual abilities?"[9]; "0-5 Child Development is the Critical Period"[10]; or "Critical Periods in Childhood for the Development of Obesity"[11] which have not yet been proven. The prevalence of these headlines is testament to the interest and belief people have that these things are true.

There are also headlines that suggest that there are critical periods for conditions that are normally considered hereditary, such as ADHD or autism: "Mechanisms Regulating Developmental Critical Period for Establishing Attention"[12]; "Autism: A Critical Period Disorder?"[13] also to date unproven. It is interesting to note that most of these articles have to do with prenatal exposure to chemicals, trauma, neglect, malnutrition, or stress, rather than a critical period after birth.

Where the Myth Comes From

The concept of "critical periods" has been around since the 1960s, when it was used to describe limits on sensory perception in animals. Some will remember the classic experiments on kittens, in which one or both eyes were sewn shut right after birth, and then researchers measured how much time could go by before they lost sight.[14] The thought was that there were certain critical periods for visual activation before the ability to see would be lost. This study led to research on other sense perception abilities in animals, and a generalization that the same critical periods must exist for humans. The sensory perception critical periods were generalized to academic subject learning, the first "evidence" coming from second-language learners,[15] leading to further speculation and then the myth of critical periods.

What We Know Now

We now know that there are critical periods during gestation that affect organ formation. After birth, there is evidence for two critical periods: for first language[16] and for gross motor skills.[17] However, there is limited evidence for both, due to the ethical limitations of experimental research. This means we have evidence from about 240 cases of feral children who have been isolated from language for varying periods of time who recuperate it in varying degree. But we cannot design an experiment and control variables because it would be not ethical to isolate a healthy child from human contact just to see if could later develop language.

However, what is clear is that there is no critical period for things that people learn in school.[18] The specific age or period of development of a person is less important than the order of skills learned, and the neuroconstructivist development of the brain. That is, learning to read as an adult is less dependent on age and more dependent on the introduction and methodology of skill order acquisition. We also now know plasticity exists throughout the life span.[19] The brain can and does learn until it dies. This itself negates the existence of critical periods.

YOU CAN'T GROW NEW BRAIN CELLS

It was thought until recently that when brain cells died, they were gone forever. Articles and newspaper headlines today still mistakenly suggest that brain cells cannot be replaced: "Why Can't a Damaged Cell in the Brain be Replaced?"[20]; "Can Oxygen Therapy Bring Dead Brain Cells Back to Life?"[21]; "Artificial Neurons Can Now Be Used to Replace Human Brain Cells"[22]; "Are You Born with All Your Brain Cells, or Do You Grow New Ones?"[23]. It was later found that there was such a thing as "neurogenesis," or the birth of new brain cells, which was first discovered in animals in 1962[24] and then later in humans in 1998.[25]

Where the Myth Comes From

The myth might have emerged because, whereas skin cell reparation was visible to the naked eye, few were privy to seeing the brain pre- and post-trauma. Trauma in the brain sometimes causes permanent damage, leading some to believe that the replacement of cells does not occur. Whereas a cut on the hand heals as new skin cells can replace the damaged ones, the brain is insulated in the skull, and the same repair to neurons was not visible, nor was healing often apparent. The long-term damage caused by assault to the brain led many to think that there was no new cell generation in the brain. The cases of recuperation from strokes, for example, were thought to be entirely thanks to plasticity and a change in neural pathways, rather than a healing of the damaged area (which it turns out is true).

The invisible nature of the brain and the fact that brain cells appeared so complex and numerous compared to other types of cells made replacement seem unlikely. And on top of the complex-looking structure, there was a functional question about brain cells, which seemed fundamentally different from other cells in the body: "If neurons were able to divide, how would the newly created cells with their new dendrites, axons, and synapses, functionally integrate into the brain without disrupting existing circuits?"[26] These observable cell traits led to the presumption that brain cells did not replace themselves. Other cells, like blood, skin, and gut cells, replicate and are relatively simple compared to brain cells: ". . . with their highly branched dendrites and polysynaptic axonal combinations, [brain cells] were considered to be terminally differentiated and unable to re-enter the cell cycle and divide, strictly from a mechanistic view," writes Gage.[26] There are more types of cells in the brain than in all of the other organs combined. There is a total of about 85 to 86 billion neurons in the brain, and somewhere around 350 different types of neurons, depending on classification by structure, function, or their role in phenotypic continua (what role they play in potentiating genes, so they become observable behavior).[27] It is possible that the myth emerged from the sheer complexity of classifying, counting, and identifying neurons in the brain.

Additionally, the myth had been repeated so long it was considered a fact, so confronting old thinking was not just a matter of presenting new research, but rather shaking up the scientific community. Gross wrote in his article "Neurogenesis in the Adult Brain: Death of a Dogma" about how hard it was to let go of this idea. "For over 100 years a central assumption in the field of neuroscience has been that new neurons are not added to the adult mammalian brain,"[28] which made the possibility of neurogenesis seem almost sacrilegious at the time of discovery.

What We Know Now

Adult human neurogenesis exists, but has only been clearly documented in the striatum,[29] hippocampus,[30] and olfactory bulb,[31] though no one rejects the idea that it is possible to document other areas at a later time with better technology. We now know that neurogenesis in adult human brains exists and recurs throughout the life span on a regular basis and might play a key role in remembering things over time, meaning that new neurons aren't just "extra," but rather reinforce memory over time.[32]

Furthermore, there is now evidence in rat studies that there is an increase in neurogenesis when there is trauma to the brain. That is, the brain speeds its own recuperation by increasing the amount and frequency of neurogenesis when it perceives an area of the brain is in need.[33] Though there is no conclusive evidence that the same thing occurs in humans, it is possible that neurogenesis serves to heal damage in the brain in the same way as other cells heal other body parts.

BRAIN DAMAGE IS ALWAYS PERMANENT

Brain damage can be caused by trauma, stroke, tumors, or accidents. Traumatic brain injury (TBI) is particularly devastating because it is often caused by preventable circumstances, such as getting hit in the head while playing football, for example. Brain damage has broad effects, depending on where it occurs. Headway, the Brain Injury Association in the UK, suggests that consequences of getting hit on the head can range from reduced cognition, reduced awareness states (as in being in a coma), communication problems, emotional problems, executive functioning problems, physical effects, amnesia, and other behavioral problems. More than 2.5 million people suffer from some kind of brain damage each year in the United States. Recuperation from brain damage can be slow or nonexistent, leading to the myth that brain damage is always permanent.

In a recent study in New Zealand, a little fewer than 50% of the people who suffered from mild traumatic brain injury continued to have symptoms one year after their injury,[34] primarily related to sleep difficulties,[35] suggesting about half recuperate fully. Acquired brain injury (ABI) is the leading cause of disability among children and youth[36] and the "greatest contributing cause of death and disability" among children and young adults in the United States.[37] In a review of journal articles from 1989 to 2014, Lindsay and colleagues identified the efficiency rates of interventions post trauma, which ranged from 1 to 119 sessions and from 20 minutes to 4 hours each for kids 4 to 19 years old (average age 11.5 years). The sessions took place in hospitals, in schools, through media, and online and found that in 14 of 17 of the studies, there was "significant improvement in cognitive, social, psychological or behavioral functioning"[38] meaning interventions post trauma play a key role in recuperation. Other studies show that resilience plays a big role in recovery, and that this varies depending on the personal risk and protective factors of each person.[39] Despite the evidence that the majority of people do recuperate from brain damage, a large number of teachers around the world believe that brain damage is permanent.[40]

Where the Myth Comes From

There are many sources of this myth. First, since normal healing mechanisms, such as cell replacement, were thought not to exist in the brain before the discovery of neurogenesis in the late 1990s, people believed that brain damage was always permanent. Second, as brain injuries are under the skull and often not visible to the naked eye, many people cannot see improvements occur and therefore believe they are permanent. Third, changes at the cellular level often occur before behavioral changes, and so healing is not often visible to the eye until lost behaviors are reciprocated. Fourth, "the fact that brain-damaged patients could so rarely make full recoveries" with 100% of skills also makes people think brain damage is permanent.[41]

The myth rests with how little we know about the brain's capability to heal itself. Doidge relates the story of Paul Bach-y-Rita's father's stroke as illustrative of how little we really know about recovery from damage. Bach-y-Rita's father had a stroke that destroyed "ninety-seven percent of the nerves that run from the cerebral cortex to the spine."[42] He learned to walk and talk again after his stroke, thanks to intense post-trauma therapy. His sons presumed he recovered because the original damage was minor. The postmortem autopsy revealed there was actually "catastrophic damage that had caused his paralysis," stunning Bach-y-Rita's children, who realized that recuperation was due entirely to the therapy.[42] The myth emerged in part from the less-than-intensive interventions that were the norm until not long ago.

What We Know Now

We now know that, thanks to neuroplasticity, the brain is able to heal itself after brain damage, but this depends on multiple factors. The rate and speed of recovery from brain damage depends on the extent of the damage, the age of the victim, the timeliness, sophistication, length, and quality of interventions,[43] as well as to the mind frame and level of resilience of the person undergoing the recuperation.[44]

Doidge noted that "the damaged brain can often reorganize itself so that when one part fails, another can often substitute; that if brain cells die, they can at times be replaced,"[45] ideas that were considered radical at the time of writing. This has changed the way we approach therapeutic recuperation. Previously, people who suffered brain damage were treated as best as possible and sent home after a brief cycle of intervention. Now interventions are more aggressive and last longer, resulting in rates of recuperation higher than in previous decades.[46]

NEURAL PLASTICITY IS DUE TO GOOD PEDAGOGY

Plasticity can be measured on multiple scales, from individual neurons to changes in cortical restructuring or rerouting, as in the cases of injury, or by increases in white matter. When neurons grow new axons and synapses and link to other neurons, this creates a permanent change in the brain structure. White matter is the myelin sheath that insulates these connections.[47] The malleable nature of the brain reacts to the environment, and plasticity results. Plasticity can also result due to activity, as in the rehearsal of new information or actions, such as school learning.[48] Neural plasticity can be developed through recuperation of lost connections, as in the cases of people who have suffered strokes and then "relearned" a lost skill, or through new learning, either in formal or informal contexts.[49] This means when people learn from their environment, in school or out, plasticity occurs. Good pedagogy can trigger plasticity, but learning does not always happen in schools, nor is it necessarily reliant on pedagogy of any kind.

Even though teachers spend most of their waking hours promoting neural plasticity through great teaching, few teachers actually learn about how this works, leading to the misunderstanding that plasticity is due to pedagogy.

Where the Myth Comes From

Neural plasticity was originally thought to relate only to damaged brains. When the definition was broadened to cover all kinds of learning, it was believed that changes and learning only occurred with purposeful practice brought on by good pedagogy. Several "brain-based learning" books in the 1980s and 1990s promoted the idea that the best way to increase brain power was through great teaching, hence the myth that neural plasticity depends on good pedagogy.

What We Know Now

We now know that neural plasticity can come from classroom learning, therapy, rehabilitation, or simply life experiences. We also know that learning is not always positive. People can learn from bad pedagogy or negative life experiences. For example, people can learn to become racist, which changes the brain in the same neuroplastic way as teaching small children addition. The general mechanisms of plasticity are the same, independent of whether they are initiated through therapy or classroom learning and are good or bad, morally speaking.

WHY THIS IS GOOD NEWS FOR TEACHING

The fact that there are no critical periods for anything learned in schools, and that the brain has high degrees of plasticity throughout life, is liberating for teachers. Knowing that anything we learn in school can be learned at any age frees up teachers to think about the best ways to teach based on mastery of goals and the student's prior experiences.

Understanding neurogenesis reduces the mystery of the brain and makes it seem more like other organs in the body—what's good for the heart is good for the brain, for example. When damage occurs to an organ of the body, it is serious, but can sometimes be repaired, and this includes the brain. Since neurogenesis does not occur at such a pace as to replace every lost brain cell, we rely on good teaching and therapy to strengthen the architecture of the brain. Teachers, more than new brain cells (neurogenesis), make a greater difference in learning, which is a reflection of the new connections between neurons, not the quantity of neurons.

It's also great news to know that neuronal plasticity is not just determined by good pedagogy, but perhaps it is even more useful to know how plasticity works. Teachers need to understand the influence they have in shaping students' brains, and to realize that this occurs on a daily basis, thanks to everyday experiences, to therapy, or to classroom learning. This also means that brain damage is not always permanent. More aggressive and comprehensive treatments and interventions for people with traumatic brain injury shows promising results and celebrates the reaches of neuroplasticity. Stretching the brain is beneficial for all learning, from recuperation to new learning in classrooms. The lessons learned from people who recuperate from brain injuries is inspirational for teachers; if Paul Bach-y-Rita's father can learn to walk and talk again after losing so much of his brain, we should be able to teach our student with intact brains to learn all of the important things we teach at school.

8 • MYTHS ABOUT

MEMORY

THE BRAIN HAS UNLIMITED MEMORY CAPACITY

It was once thought that if you tried hard enough, you could remember anything that had occurred in your life. It was believed that the brain soaks up every detail that occurs in your surroundings. You just never consciously paid attention to it, meaning that with a little effort, you could recall that all-important algebra lesson, grammatical rule, or chemistry formula. Many people are extremely disappointed to hear that your brain does *not* take in everything it experiences, nor can you remember things just by willing yourself to do so. There is a misunderstanding that when we teach something in a classroom, everyone learns, so when anyone fails to reproduce that information at a later date it's just because of lack of retrieval to that knowledge. The truth is, they never learned it in the first place, or it was never rehearsed sufficiently to create a rapid recall path in the brain.[1] Popular press titles such as *"The Human Brain's Memory Could Store the Entire Internet,"*[2] give people the impression that the brain has unlimited capacity, which is not true.

The brain does not remember everything it has experienced, as to do so would overwhelm us. There are few documented cases of people with perfect memories[3] and most suggest that this is a distressing trait, causing extreme anxiety. Part of the efficiency of the brain is being able to link prior knowledge to new information to economize effort. A person with a perfect memory would necessarily link nearly everything to everything, which would drown him in an exhausting revival of emotions and experiences. There are several reasons why people remember, and several others why people forget.[4] However, it is a myth to think that people can be taught *"How to Remember Everything"*[5] by better encoding. The brain is a physical organ, meaning that its capacity cannot be "unlimited." While people can and do improve their memory capacity through training, no one has ever been able to remember everything.[6]

Where the Myth Comes From

The myth comes from early models about how the brain processes memories.

It was once thought that memories were formed in a simple process in which the brain received sensory input (if it paid attention), and information was passed to short-term memory. If correct encoding occurred, the information could find its way to long-term memory, where rehearsal permitted it to become a part of long-term memory. The combination of long-term memory and attention resulted in learning. This gave a highly elevated role to the process of encoding information, which many believed was conscious activity that people were aware of, but often did not employ. This meant that the myth partially originates with a misunderstanding about how much control people have over what gets to long-term memory.

Another cause of this myth has to do with the belief that the brain has an unlimited capacity, and everything that is experienced is remembered. People have always wondered, "Is there a limit to how much information my brain can store?" and, "When I make new memories or learn new things, do I forget other memories?"[7] The myth that your brain remembers everything it has ever experienced but forgets because of poor encoding is based on partial truth and people's desire for simple models.

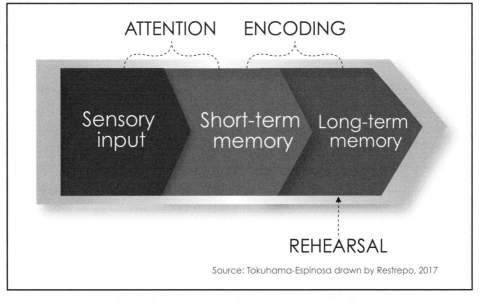

Source: Tokuhama-Espinosa drawn by Restrepo, 2017

Figure 8.1: *Old Model of Memory Consolidation*

Many of us have memories of either real-life or TV exploits in which court witnesses are asked questions about events they did not seem to recall consciously, but which they were able to recollect vividly under hypnosis. This leads the general public to presume that we all have hidden memories, rich in detail, about every situation we are faced with, but which lie deep in our unconsciousness. This can be dangerous because people can be coached, either knowingly or not, into incorporating details that they did not really experience into eyewitness testimony.[8] Initially, this appears as if people were consciously unaware of fine details that had entered their brains, but later it usually turns out that unscrupulous lawyers were actually planting *new* ideas into witnesses' minds through a convincing line of questioning. ("Just how fast was the *red* car going when it *rammed* into the sidewalk?"). People's lack of understanding about how memories are formed contributes to this myth's existence.

What We Know Now

We now know that there is so much occurring in our surroundings that our brains would be overwhelmed if we were to take in more than just a fraction of all the possible details our senses provide.[9] While the brain constantly seeks as much information as it can handle, the totality of sensory input is only a fraction of what we are exposed to. The witness can recall the color of the car that hit the woman walking next to him because the emotional surge he felt at the time locked that detail into his mind; this does not mean every other detail was also absorbed simultaneously. When people recall things, they did not remember earlier, they often report it was because the detail seemed "out of place" or "gave them a creepy feeling," meaning senses were already heightened for that particular piece of information. People do not hear,[10] see,[11] smell,[12] feel,[13] or taste[14] everything in their surroundings, even when the senses are isolated, let alone when they occur all together. Additionally, many sensory perceptions cross over and influence one another,[15] meaning that people might think they saw something because they heard something easily associated with that visual.

All this means that the complex world we live in is filtered by the brain to protect us from overstimulation, and at any given time we are paying attention to only a small percentage of possible stimuli, and therefore cannot possibly remember everything we are exposed to.

We now know people can remember things easily when they can be related to something already known (association with prior knowledge);[16] when they are of personal interest;[17] and/or when they have survival value.[18] On the other hand, people forget things due to transience (the passage of time); absent-mindedness (inattentive or shallow processing); and blocking (temporary inaccessibility to something known).[19] This means that forgetting is not only due to bad encoding procedures (inattentive or shallow processing, as Schacter says[19]), but also occurs because too much time has passed since we learned something. For example, I learned Japanese 20 years ago but have not actively used it since, meaning the passage of time reduces my access to necessary pathways.

Finally, forgetting keeps us sane. There are only a handful of documented cases of people with perfect memories, but these few accounts show they were miserable, with low quality of life. Why? Every sensory perception linked to thousands of prior experiences with the same sensation, creating chaos in their ability to link ideas and see anything as unique.

MEMORIZATION IS UNNECESSARY FOR LEARNING AND UNDESIRABLE IN MODERN EDUCATION

Pedagogical experts have coached teachers to move away from rote memory activities ("drill and kill") because these simplistic activities only dull sophisticated thinking. Mindlessly memorizing the times table, for example, is a far less efficient way of learning multiplication than by understanding the reasoning behind how 2x4 is the same as 2x (2x2). *Memorization*, on the other hand—not mindless rote memory—is a fundamental part of learning and not at all the enemy of good thinking skills. It is incorrect to think that modern education requires a choice between "Critical Thinking vs. Rote Memorization"[20] and "Deeper Learning: Moving Students Beyond Memorization."[21] Rather than calling "Rote Learning: The Pantomime Villain in Education,"[22] teachers should take the time to learn more about the complex networks in the brain to appreciate the vital role memory plays in learning. According to a Delphi panel survey of 41 experts in educational neuroscience and Mind, Brain, and Education science in 2017,

> There is no new learning without some form of memory and some form of attention. Most school learning requires well-functioning short, working and long-term memory systems and conscious attention. However, procedural learning, habituation, sensitization and even episodic memory can occur without conscious attention.[23]

Deep learning requires memory, but memory for memory's sake should not be the goal. Memorization is important for learning, but it is not all there is to education.

Where the Myth Comes From

During the No Child Left Behind initiative in the United States, starting in 2001, standardized exams became the norm. It was then that many teachers realized that multiple-choice tests could measure little beyond memorized items—dates, facts, formulas, theories, name places, concepts, and other "Googleable" information—leading to a backlash against the focus on passing the state test and a demand for higher-quality education that promoted critical thinking rather than rote memorization. At this time, many school districts, not only in the U.S. but around the world, were accused of "teaching to the test" rather than promoting deeper thinking. The results were simplistic phrases like *"No More Rote Learning in State Primary Schools"*[24] rather than a closer look at what types of memorization were actually desirable in improving student thinking skills. The myth that memorization is unnecessary and unwanted stems from falsely equating memorization and critical thinking, while believing that measuring memory on a test measures the academic worth of a child.

What We Know Now

We now know that memorization is an important part of learning, but teaching should not be limited to this mechanical aspect of the learning process. Without some form of rote memorization, people would be unable to understand the placement of the chemical elements on the periodic table, and without a deeper understanding of the codification scheme in addition to this rote memorization, there can be no conceptual understanding of how the elements are related. This is like memorizing all of the infractions possible when driving a car, without taking the time to understand why the laws exist in the first place. Rote memorization is often thought of as kids "mindlessly reciting information,"[25] which is undesirable. However, "Before students can think critically, they need to have something to think about in their brains. It is true that knowledge without comprehension is of little use, but comprehension requires knowledge and it takes time and effort to acquire,"[26] meaning not only is memorization desirable, it is necessary for new learning.

MEMORY IS A SINGLE NETWORK IN THE BRAIN

Memory is complex and made up of multiple systems. Short-term memory (keeping a phone number in mind); working memory (until dialing the number); and long-term memory (remembering distant experiences such as how you met the person you are calling); employ distinct but often overlapping neural networks.[27] Each of these subsystems of memory is, in turn, further divided into smaller substructures. For example, long-term memory is often divided into declarative memory, which are things you explicitly learned, like the name of the capital of France, and procedural memory, which involves things you learn involving processes, like walking or driving a car. These subsystems have further additional subnetworks, depending on the skill set.

Different memory systems are triggered by different classroom activities and experiences in the learning process, so teacher understanding of these systems is vital to good teaching.

Where the Myth Comes From

Over the years, knowledge about human memory has improved, but there are still a lot of unanswered questions. The substructures of memory have only recently been separated out from the umbrella concept, thanks to better neuroimaging techniques.[28] The more the brain is studied, the better the information we have about these substructures. For example, many textbooks still consider short-term and working memory to be the same, despite the evidence in neuroscience that these two types of memory have different neural signatures.[29] Think about ordering take-out. Short-term memories are the telephone number itself (digits), while working memory is recalling your order while dialing the number (process). The myth originates at least in part from a lack of scientific literacy about memory systems.

What We Know Now

We now know that there are multiple memory systems in the brain, all of which affect learning. Each memory system is developed, strengthened, and used by the brain to learn in different ways and at different stages of the learning process, and each system is triggered by different teaching interventions. Normally, information enters the brain through sensory stimuli and heads to short-term storage first. Short-term memory equates to a small amount of information (4 to 7 units of information, plus or minus two)[30] for a short period of time (seconds). If the brain decides this information has some value and it is not deceived into thinking the information is superfluous or unneeded, it will normally be passed on to working memory. Working memory is different than short-term memory because working memory is used to fulfill a process or procedure.[31] For example, keeping a math formula in your head is short-term memory at work, but keeping it in mind long enough to *apply* the formula to a homework problem is working memory. Unlike short-term memory, working memory can last minutes or even hours. For example, a student can maintain certain facts or formulas in his head long enough to take a test, but if you ask him the same questions 24 hours later, he may have no recollection of the answer. This is because he maintained the information in working memory store, but it never made it to long-term memory, which is usually dependent on sleep for consolidation. If the information has significance, is well encoded, and rehearsed sufficiently, it will move to long-term storage, where it can play a role in learning.

Long-term memory is divided into two global categories: procedural (sometimes called implicit) and declarative (sometimes called explicit).[32] Declarative memories are things you can "declare" or explain easily if I were to ask you, "How do you know X?" and you might reply, "Well, I learned that in high school English". Procedural memories are a bit trickier and much harder to explain, as they occur without conscious recall. If I were to ask you, for example, "How do you walk?" or "How do you know how to talk?" you might have a hard time responding. Declarative or explicit memories can also be broken down further into other subcategories. For example, an autobiographical memory (e.g., my grandmother's name) is stored differently in the brain than semantic memory (e.g., the dates of the American Civil War), which is stored differently than episodic memory (e.g., "Where were you on 9/11?"). There are also other theorists who believe that emotional memories are not just a subset of autobiographical memories, but a completely different kind of memory.[33] While memory in general is important for learning, long-term memory pathways in the brain permit recall, which is proof of learning.

It is also important to realize that memory and forgetting are related, but not the same. Sometimes people don't remember things because they forget them, and other times they don't remember things because they were never properly encoded in the first place and really never made it to memory storage. Schacter writes about *Sins of Memory*,[34] in which he describes memory problems and forgetting problems, both of which can lead to learning problems. For example, memories might not form due to *misattribution* of an idea to the wrong source (i.e., the student thinks the Amazon is a retailer rather than a river). Or in other instances, a memory might be created due to *suggestibility* because ideas were planted by others (i.e., if the student has been told girls are not good at math, she might presume she can't remember scientific facts). In other cases, a memory might develop due to *bias*, because prior beliefs influence the new information (i.e., if the students think Germans are historically bad people due to WWI and WWII, they will blame the Germans for the current refugee crisis in Europe). Other memories can be created due to sheer *persistence* over time, as when an idea—despite being untrue—is repeated over and over (i.e., if a child has been told by his parents that learning a foreign language is hard). These types of memories create learning, albeit in a negative sense.

Schacter also suggests that sometimes we fail to have access to memories because they are forgotten. Forgetting happens due to three primary reasons, in his view: *transience* (too much time has passed since the information was learned); *absent-mindedness* (the student wasn't really paying enough attention during the learning moment, and therefore a memory was never formed); and *blocking* (when the information is painful to retrieve—as, for example, when a student is ridiculed in front of his peers for answering a question in class incorrectly). Once teachers understand if a student's learning problems are due to memory problems (misattribution, suggestibility, bias, or persistence) or due to forgetting, (transience, absent-mindedness, or blocking), they can more precisely intervene.

THE LEARNING PYRAMID: PEOPLE ONLY REMEMBER 10% OF WHAT THEY READ

The Learning Pyramid has been a staple of many teacher education programs for several decades. Many of us can recall the easy-to-remember message that lecturing is passive and bad, while teaching others is active and good. While many of us can confirm this general idea anecdotally, it represents a myth based on a misreading of the research meant to support it.

In 1946, Edgar Dale suggested a hierarchy of learning methods for adult learners, which was converted into a now (in)famous "Cone of Experience." Dale suggested that a variety of experiences was better than single-mode learning, and he never attached a specific percentage of retention to the different types of learning, as is common today.[35] This means Dale's original work—to motivate variety in pedagogy—has been misused over time. Over the past 70 years, Dale's Cone has been used to support thousands of teacher professional development workshops, mainly because it sounds logical. But there is no apparent evidence for it.

Unfortunately, like a typical echo chamber of truths, Dale was cited as saying something he never claimed[36] which was then repeated and modified by others, including the National Training Laboratories in the early 2000s. This is akin to a game of telephone—someone citing someone incorrectly, who cites someone else slightly incorrectly—leading to an evolving model with no evidence.

Where the Myth Comes From

The myth originates from people's desire for simplicity. It would be so much easier to plan classroom activities if we could limit our choices to those things with

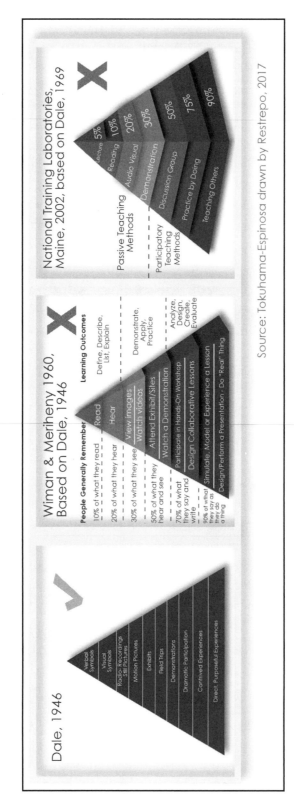

Figure 8.2: *Dale's Disgraced Cone of Experience*

the greatest retention levels. The "active learning" movement in the United States helped promote this myth as people sought justification to avoid passive classrooms, in which lecture was the norm. The general backlash to teacher-focused, lecture-based education needed a scapegoat, and Dale's Cone of Experience served that purpose. We now know that the desire for simplicity and *bandwagonitis* give life to this myth.

What We Know Now

There have been multiple rebuttals of the Cone of Experience or Learning Pyramid, on two basic grounds. The first is that there is no evidence that the percentage of retention reported is correct (and Dale never suggested any percentage at all in his study). That is, there has never been any explanation about where the very well-rounded 5%, 10%, 20%, 30%, 50%, 70%, or 90% numbers came from in subsequent interpretations of Dale's work, a point that was raised as early as 1973,[37] but which was drowned out by the enthusiasm for the idea. What is so fascinating is that the learning pyramid has taken on a life of its own with people citing one another as the main source (see Subramony and colleagues[38] for more on the historical evolution of this myth).

Second, it is now clear that the choice of learning activities should be based on the objective for the learning outcome, as suggested by Backward Design (decide objective, determine evaluation, choose activities).[39] That is, if teachers want to deliver information, lecture is one of the most efficient ways. However, if they want students to demonstrate concept mastery, getting students to teach others is probably the best method. Different objectives call for different strategies.

The learning pyramid continues to be debated passionately:

> *No qualified scholar would endorse the use of this mish-mash as a guide to either research or design of learning environments. Nevertheless, [the corrupted cone] obviously has an allure that surpasses logical considerations. Clearly, it says something that many people want to hear. It reduces the complexity of media and method selection to a simple and easy to remember formula. It can thus be used to support a bias toward whatever learning methodology might be in vogue. Users seem to employ it as pseudo-scientific justification for their own preferences about media and methods.[40]*

The *bandwagonitis* for simple and easy-to-remember formulas along with the sheer longevity of the myth explain the Cone's existence. Now armed with better information, teachers should be more wary of solutions that seem too good to be true.

WHY THIS IS GOOD NEWS FOR TEACHING

Memory and attention are the key elements in learning, without which new information cannot take hold in the brain.[41] Teachers, as designers and facilitators of learning, have the power to channel where attention is focused, and which stimuli should be prioritized for long-term memory and eventual learning. Teachers need to use classroom techniques that assure that students are paying attention to what is important in class, and to rehearse sufficiently so as to create a memory, so that new learning can occur. It's great news for teachers that the limited memory of students can be guided by good classroom routines.

Before analyzing a poem, a science problem, or the strategy for a sports game, student need to memorize. They need to remember the names of the languages spoken in Europe before questioning how this variation came about, and recollect the names of the types of cells in the brain before discussing their functions. Memorization is a fundamental aspect of cognition, without which there would be no learning. The importance of memory for learning should not be confused with the backlash against mindless memorization, which is a positive development in education.

Practical Application of MBE: Memory versus Mindless, Rote Memorization

Great teachers know that memory is a part of any learning experience, but that mindless rote memorization is not desirable. Don't be afraid of asking students to memorize poems, formulas, names, concepts, or other content information because they need to be able to discuss deeper ideas using concrete examples. What should be avoided at all costs is asking kids to memorize information for the purpose of just regurgitating it during a test.

The speed of recall of memories also facilitates how quickly a student can rely on information for problem solving. Great teachers know that memorization is a stepping stone toward deeper thinking skills, and not an end in itself.

Understanding the many reasons why students might remember or forget information is important in order to pinpoint problems and design interventions. A teacher who knows a student is forgetting for reasons of *encoding* will do one type of intervention; if he suspects the student is forgetting due to *blocking*, he can do something else; and if he thinks the student is forgetting because the information he learned was *lost over time* or was *not rehearsed* in a while, he can act accordingly. And if the teacher suspects the student never really created the memory at all, he will choose different interventions altogether.

Great teachers celebrate the complexities of the human brain, and a clear understanding of the many networks involved. For example, when a teacher understands that retrieving a word's meaning from memory involves a different neural network than understanding the order of words in a sentence, she can be more precise in her intervention with the student and help him get over his "language problem." Knowing there are different types of memory systems helps teachers choose the right interventions at the right stages of the learning process.

Finally, knowing that long-term memory is what really counts in learning keeps teachers from mistakenly believing that kids have learned something just because they can repeat it in the short term. I have seen many a teacher who believed she taught (and children learned) foreign language sentence patterns, math skills, and even social values, just because the teacher had them chant a sentence or phrase over and over. If students understand *why* and *how* to use the same concept on their own, it can be transferred to new contexts, which is the proof of real learning.

Dale's learning pyramid has a logical structure, especially in light of the critique against passive lecture formats. However, the research does not bear out the clean numbers, and teachers should always be wary of research that looks "too neat." The search for simple answers must once again give way to celebrating, rather than lamenting, the complexities of learning. This is great news for teachers who can now select activities based on how well they help reach the objective, rather than on the promise of a percentage of enhanced retention.

9 • MYTHS ABOUT

ATTENTION

THE BRAIN CAN "MULTITASK"

The vision of the modern mother who is also a high-powered executive, successfully juggling home and work responsibilities (babies, phones, dishes, and computers all in the air at once) is often invoked to describe the concept of multitasking. The belief that "Women 'Better at Multitasking' than Men"[1] is still prevalent in the popular press. The brain's attention systems, however, are not built to do this.

When one attempts to multitask, one is actually dividing attention systems in the brain.[2] Depending on the effort (*cognitive load*) needed to concentrate on one thing or another, energy is allocated to these different systems. For example, most habituated acts, such as walking, driving, or taking a shower, require a low cognitive load. Other things, like reading a technical journal, resolving a personal relationship problem, or creatively designing an original art piece, require a heavy cognitive load. The "weight" of the cognitive load is distributed between sustained (being able to concentrate for as long as the task requires), alerting (identifying where stimuli comes from), and executive function (what deserves the energy) attention systems in the brain. To burst the bubble even more forcefully, women are not better at the mythical multitasking than men. Popular press titles like "Multitasking: How to Survive the 21st Century"[3] are common and reflect what we all hope would be true. Wouldn't it be great to be able to manage more than one thing at once? Some people do, it seems, appear to multitask. *How?* This is not multitasking, but rather due to better memory.

Where the Myth Comes From

This myth comes from the sensation that we all have, at some point in our lives, managed to multitask—or at least we think so. When I simultaneously drive, use a hands-free device to talk on the phone, eat a breakfast bar, and think ahead to the ingredients for the evening meal, am I not multitasking? The truth of the matter is that some activities are habituated (such as driving and eating), while others are daydreaming (ingredients for the meal); but actually, I am focused on only one of the activities (what I am saying on the telephone). It is a different kind of situation, however, when we are faced with really *thinking* about more than one thing at once, as when air traffic controllers or emergency medical responders have to juggle multiple life-and-death decisions simultaneously.[4] These kinds of professionals have a much heavier cognitive load (the amount of mental effort required in working memory) than I do as I eat my breakfast bar. What is fascinating is that they, too, can get better at this juggling if some aspect of their work becomes habituated, thus shifting the effort from working memory to procedural or implicit (long-term) memory.[5] The emergency medical technician who responds to the car crash, attends to the victims with care, reacts to the leaking gas tank, and rescues the whole block in the nick of time is likely someone who has practiced those maneuvers so many times that they have become habituated and appear effortless due to low cognitive load. In fact, in order to increase the ability to do many things at once, simulation programs have been designed to help rescue workers reach the level of rehearsal necessary so that their actions can be taken quickly and efficiently, making it appear that they are multitasking.[6] The cognitive load of the technician has been reduced thanks to the rehearsal and near habituation of the tasks.

What We Know Now

We now know that people who appear to be multitasking are doing one of two things. They are either using working memory to compensate for divided attention,[7] or they are reducing cognitive load by incorporating one or more activities that have been habituated.[8] Using more working memory is not necessarily a bad thing, but there is a high energy toll on brains that try to multitask over too long a period,[9] which may not be worth it as both mental and physical exhaustion result. Habituating actions is not necessarily bad either, but it takes time and hundreds, if not thousands, of repetitions for an action to become automated. While the research shows that people can improve their ability to "multitask" by habituating activities or by extending working memory,[10] some suggest it would be better to stay focused on a single task alone, which tends to be more efficient in terms of accuracy. Doing several things at once that are so deeply learned they appear automated (such as walking the dog or folding laundry), is not the same thing as attempting two or more novel or unhabituated tasks at the same time (like learning something new or being faced with an unfamiliar situation). To top this all off, not only are novel situations distracting, but highly emotional situations also take their toll of attention systems. This means that the inward attention expended toward managing emotional situations doesn't leave much attention for the outside world. This is why people who are very sad, angry, or happy have a hard time doing many things at the same time.

We also now know that attention systems in the brain are as complex as memory systems. According to Michael Posner, one of the most published authors and respected researchers on attention, there are at least three global systems of attention: alerting, orienting, and executive control.[11] Each system has distinct neural circuits, though some overlap. The *alerting system* reacts as a survival mechanism to draw focus toward changes in the environment. The *orienting system* of attention helps an individual narrow in on stimuli (for example if a sound occurred, was it coming from the left or the right, was it near or far, and so on). The *executive control system* is what decides where attention energy should be directed. When people multitask, they are trying to override these natural attentional systems in the brain, which takes a great deal of energy.

LEARNING CAN OCCUR WITHOUT ATTENTION

Similar to the myth about learning in your sleep (see Chapter 6), there is a myth that people can learn without paying attention or exerting much effort. Titles like "How Can You Learn Much More Without Effort?"[12] suggest there is a trick to figuring out how to learn easily. This is misleading. Learning is, indeed, an endeavor that requires effort, and paying attention is part of the energy expended; thus, such promises of effortless learning are unfounded.

Where the Myth Comes From

When asked how they know something, people sometimes respond by saying, "I just *do*!", which seems to support what is often referred to as unconscious learning. Unconscious learning, however, does not mean you were not paying attention at the time of learning, but rather that you were not consciously aware of the cues or mental associations that prompted the learning. Much of what we know about the world occurs under the radar of consciousness. The promise and allure of effortless learning is strong, especially for people in school, who often feel their energy could be better spent on more enjoyable activities. There is a difference between attention and consciousness that leads to this myth. When kids kick a soccer ball toward you and your small baby, and you throw up your hands in defense and block the ball from bonking your child on the head, even before you are conscious that you did that, your action shows you were paying attention and perceived the threat, even if you weren't conscious of it.

It should be noted that many students who look as though they are not paying attention really *are* paying attention, and those who look as if they are paying attention are often *not* paying attention.[13] This is important for teachers to know: Sometimes we *think* kids aren't paying attention, but this is just our perception, and not necessarily true.[14]

Teachers have more influence than they might realize with regard to bringing students' wandering attention back to the topic at hand. To contribute to student engagement in class, teachers can make the content more relevant to the learner—it is impossible not to pay attention when the attention is on you. Teachers can also integrate more writing and speaking on the part of the student in class to more actively engage them, and use prompts from past information to push them toward retrieving prior knowledge to make experiences more authentic. We all know that "time flies when you're having fun," meaning that some classroom time actually whizzes by, depending on the content and its relation to the learner. Teachers who can use time to focus on gaps in student knowledge rather than just "covering" the topic ensure the attention stays on the students.

What We Know Now

We now know that humans have a finite amount of attention as measured in terms of *cognitive load*, or the energy needed to stay focused; it is a limited resource. In that way it is similar to physical strength; you were born with a genetic potential to have a certain body type, and you can do your best to maximize the potential of this, but once you have reached the outer limits, there is just no more to give. Attention can be stretched and improved through practice, but there is a maximum point.

Research to determine just how long people can pay attention is mixed at best, and in general, no controlled studies exist.[15] Thus, the widely held belief that students can only pay attention for 10 to 15 minutes[16] is unsupported by research, as are the related beliefs that attention spans have been reduced over the past decade,[17] or that in the best of cases, kids in our classrooms have "the attention span of a goldfish."[18] "Of the studies that do attempt to measure attention, many suffer from methodological flaws and subjectivity in data collection. Thus, the available primary data "do not support the concept of a 10- to 15-min attention limit."[19] Furthermore, attention spans can be extended with practice.[20] This means that even if it were true that students could pay attention for only 15 minutes, most would have learned to extend this span over time; it is rare that any classroom learning encounter is that short.

Teachers understand that attention is important for learning, but often think their students are not paying attention, though nothing could be further from the truth. In fact, it is impossible for the brain *not* to pay attention; the brain is always paying attention, but sometimes it is not paying attention to what the teacher would like.[21] Rest assured, students are paying attention to the world around them as well as to internal stimuli. As attention is spread out, it is incumbent on the teacher to help guide it.

ATTENTION IS A SINGLE NETWORK IN THE BRAIN

"Paying attention" is a catch-all phrase that appears to encompass just about any aspect of "focus," usually with meaningful intent. It is often used in singular form, despite the broad range of neural networks involved. In fact, this cognitive process, all-important in learning, takes a great deal of energy. "Pay attention!" is often heard in classrooms and in the shouts of desperate parents when they talk with their kids. This works briefly as the *alerting system* of the brain orients toward a startling cry—but only for a moment. If the shouts occur frequently, the brain will stop paying attention, as the cry no longer qualifies as different or novel. In other instances, we see children deep in the storyline of a book and try to bring them back to reality by asking, "Hello! Can you *hear* me?" but the kid seems deep into the plot and ignores us because his *sustained attention system* requires all his attention energy. We pull out a tasty snack, and his nose crinkles as he directs his attention toward the smell using his *orienting system*. While each of these scenarios is an example of attention, they use different neural circuits. It is important to break down these subsystems, because without them, our diagnosis of what a child needs to be able to pay attention is less than accurate. For example, "attention deficit disorder" is often treated as if it were a single problem with "attention," but few people take the time to ask which attention system seems to be out of sync and why.

Just as there are different memory systems in the brain, there are different attention systems.[22] Paying attention to a loud noise calls on the alerting system of the brain. Formulating a good debate question requires sustained attention and executive decisions. Becoming distracted by your friend's jokes is related to the orienting system and the executive system's choice to go off task. Since all the attention systems compete for the brain's energy, it is important to understand how to manage them well for optimal learning.

Where the Myth Comes From

This myth originates in a lack of scientific literacy about the complexities of the human brain and the multiple subsystems that can underlie aspects of cognition, such as attention. We speak of "attention" in the singular—even most psychology textbooks refer to it this way—and many of us have never had a course or even a simple explanation of all that attention entails in terms of brain networks. Unfortunately, it is precisely this lack of understanding about the multiple attention systems that generates myths. Better information about the brain and improved neuroimaging have finally allowed us to reach a point where the subtleties of the attention systems can be shared in teacher education programs.

The myth also has roots in the idea that attention is selective, and that people choose what to focus on, which is not always true. Additionally, people often confuse attention with memory, and blame faulty working memory for what are really attention problems.

What We Know Now

We now know that different attention systems in the brain are triggered by different stimuli. A loud crash calls on our alerting system, while novelty tends to pique our curiosity and our executive system chooses to follow. This is why the constant barrage of updates from friends on Facebook or through Twitter draws our attention more than the monotone of the professor at the front of the class. Additionally, as shared in Chapter 5, we now know that the default mode network—the activity of the brain when it is at "rest" or daydreaming—is another level of attention.[23]

Different sensory systems also trigger different circuits for attention in the brain. The visual attention system, for example, runs a different route in the brain than the auditory attention system, though they share hubs (important parts of the brain through which signals pass multiple times) for alerting, orienting, and executive attention aspects.

CHILDREN ARE LESS ATTENTIVE AFTER SUGARY SNACKS

There is currently a backlash against sugary snacks, but not always for the right reasons. Yes, it's true that sugary drinks like sodas cause cavities, lead to obesity, and with long-term use can irritate the stomach lining and also lead to blood sugar disorders, including diabetes. Despite what you might have read and what many teachers and parents believe, however, sugary drinks do not lower attentiveness, but rather heighten it.[24]

Where the Myth Comes From

Many people my age will remember that sodas and other sugary drinks were rarely options as we grew up. The beverage business has grown, however, and over the past three decades there are many more options on supermarket shelves. The beverage industry reports it produces 10.4 billion gallons of soda each year[25] and "on any given day, half the people in the U.S. consume sugary drinks; 1 in 4 consume at least 200 calories from such drinks; and 5% drink at least 567 calories—equivalent to four cans of soda."[26] Sound nutritional advice has lagged behind the marketing tactics of this quickly expanding industry.

What We Know Now

We know that sugary drinks give you energy: ". . . sugary drinks and snacks are associated with increases in children's ability to attend."[27] Although they are often blamed for less attentiveness, it is likely that the opposite is true because some sodas not only contain sugar, they contain caffeine (which also makes them addictive). People often worry that sugary drinks drain the body of its ability to stay focused at a consistent level. However, the body returns to a balanced state quickly and often without our noticing it. The idea of extreme sugar highs followed by crashes is often reported in parenting magazines, but this is rare.

We also know that people who drink sweetened beverages tend to have an overall lower dietary quality that those who do not drink sugary drinks.[28] This means it is likely not the intake of sugary drinks itself that makes people feel sluggish, but their generally poor diets. We also know that drinking too many sugary beverages can make people feel full, so they may forgo solid foods and regular meals. The resulting lack of food intake and key nutrients can make a person feel sluggish.

ATTENTION IS UNAFFECTED BY SLEEP

As we saw earlier, sleep is an underrated commodity in society these days, primarily due to misunderstandings about what actually occurs when one is asleep. There is a myth that attention is unaffected by sleep, though many people know from firsthand experience how this is not true. While it is easy to accept that people are more irritable,[29] aggressive,[30] and anxious[31] when they don't sleep, it is harder to accept that they can't learn as well, though this is a fact.[32]

Where the Myth Comes From

Most people report they do not sleep enough,[33] yet few people actually know why they sleep at all,[34] though the majority recognize that their general well-being is enhanced with good sleep hygiene.[35] People also think that paying attention is a matter of voluntary will, not necessarily related to cognitive energy expenditure. That is, many people think that being able to pay attention is simply a matter of deciding to do so, independent of how much sleep one has had the night before. This is not true.

What We Know Now

We now know that sleep and attention are related in both bodily and mental functions in humans. Leonie Kirszenblat and Bruno van Swinderen of the Queensland Brain Institute go so far as to write about *"The Yin and Yang of Sleep and Attention"*[36] as "sleep and attention may have co-evolved as brain states that regulate each other."[36] They believe that "although sleep and attention may outwardly appear to be very different behavioural states, they are similar in that they both involve filtering out information from our awareness."[36] Whether attention and sleep are two sides of the same coin or not, we can accept at a minimum that attention depends on sleep.

WHY THIS IS GOOD NEWS FOR TEACHING

It's great news to know some tasks can occur simultaneously that require low cognitive load, or small amounts of energy in our brains, and also important to understand that most things that require thinking and decision making cannot occur simultaneously, meaning multitasking cannot occur. Teachers will be more satisfied and efficient in their own workloads, as well as deciding those of students, if they learn how to manage expectations of what types of things can be achieved at the same time. Once teachers understand how attentional effort is managed, they can help students to do the same. A student who lies in bed listening to music while doing homework is not likely to suffer from distraction, but a student who tries to write a college essay while breaking up with his girlfriend probably will.

Practical Application of MBE: Attention Systems

Great teachers know that the brain has multiple attention systems, all of which are important for learning, and that different classroom activities call on different systems.

Teachers should remember to facilitate the right focus by saying things like, "This is particularly important, be sure and pay attention to this idea." Additionally, cognitively demanding tasks such as correcting essays or giving feedback should not be combined with other highly demanding activities like being an active listener to an emotional child, but could be combined with listening to background music or TV.

It is wonderful news that getting kids to focus on learning is largely in the hands of teachers, and that they can exercise powerful roles in directing where, how, when, and why students' attention is focused in the classroom. Knowing that different attention systems are triggered by different activities allows teachers to choose some classroom interventions and sideline others, with attention systems in mind. For example, many teachers have been told in professional development settings that they should do more hands-on activities. One of the reasons this is recommended is because shifting from a lecture to doing an experiment is novel, and things that are different get attention from the brain. Student-centered activities are also often recommended because it is impossible not to pay attention to yourself. Collaborative activities work because communication with others requires active attention skills, as compared with passively listening to a lecture.

While teachers do not often have a direct influence over their students' diets or sleep routines, they can help educate students about the many health problems associated with sugary drinks and the attention problems associated with lack of sufficient sleep. It is great to know that many attention problems can be resolved with something as simple as a good night's sleep or even a solid power nap.[37] Teachers should realize that calling students' attention to sleep problems can often be the first step toward remediating these problems.

10 • MYTHS ABOUT

LANGUAGE, BILINGUALISM, AND MULTILINGUALISM

LANGUAGE IS LOCATED IN THE LEFT HEMISPHERE OF THE BRAIN

It was once thought that language skills were located in the left hemisphere of the brain, and spatial skills in the right. Thousands of cartoon drawings of the brain depict this distinction and encourage people to believe that there is a neat anatomical separation of cerebral skill sets. The idea of being a "right-brained person" or a "left-brained person" was attached to this belief in skills dominance—if you were good at language, you were obviously "left-brained."

Where the Myth Comes From

Earlier neuroimaging studies showed that most people (about 70% of left-handed people and 95% of right-handed people), have two well-known areas related to language reception and production, Broca's and Wernicke's areas, in the left hemisphere.[1] As most people have these two areas in the left hemisphere, when brain images were taken asking people to "name all the animals you can that start with the letter 'd'" or "Tell us something about your childhood" most people's "language centers" appeared to be in the left hemisphere because signals would frequently pass through these two main hubs. Because neuroimaging was not as sophisticated as it is today, there was no visual clue that many other brain areas were also involved in that response, including those in the right hemisphere. Around the turn of the 21st century, many researchers, including Michael T. Ullman,[2] began to try to put the whole picture together to identify the locations of multiple aspects of language in the brain. This told a different story.

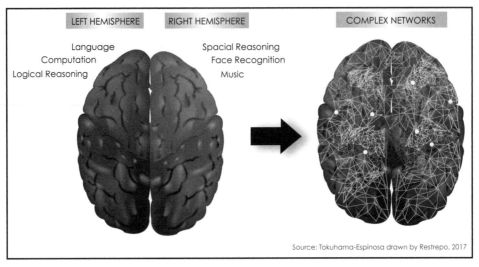

Figure 10.1: *From Mythical Division of Brain Activities to an Understanding of Complex Networks*

What We Know Now

We now know that it would be easier to say what parts of the brain are *not* involved in language than to name all the parts that *are* involved in language. If one were to overlay all the different areas of the brain involved in language and literacy, it would be clear that there are few areas of the brain that *don't* play some kind of a role. When infants enter the world and begin to learn language, we have to be sure that their hearing is intact;[3] when they are toddlers that they can grasp crayons;[4] understand abstract to tangible symbols;[5] comprehend shapes and forms;[6] and the patterns in their world.[7] Later they need to understand how the world can be classified and categorized[8] to strengthen semantic memory, and to comprehend the relationships between like concepts,[9] and the way some words are (un)like others.[10] As a child develops, he also begins to interpret humor, intonation, and sarcasm.[11] As reading is established, a child can begin to learn to write, which involves graphomotor coordination[13] that is heavily influenced by culture[13] and a more explicit understanding of grammatical order in sentence structure.[14] Each of these skill sets involves different neural pathways and crosses hemispheres.

ADULTS CANNOT LEARN A FOREIGN LANGUAGE AS FAST AS A CHILD

It is all too common to hear adults lament, "It's a pity I didn't learn a foreign language as a child." Many adults who do take on a new language feel "slow" and sense they are not as fast as children. Happily, however, adult foreign language learning is on the rise, especially in business contexts.[15] More and more people are learning languages in order to promote their companies abroad, for travel, and because of mental health benefits. The value of foreign languages is on the increase. The question is whether or not adults can learn as quickly as children.

Where the Myth Comes From

Old myths are slow to die. Starting back in the 1960s and during the arms race in the United States, there was a concern that few Americans were learning foreign languages, and that the country would fall behind its foes. Initially, research showed that there was a critical period for foreign language learning,[16] leading to further despair. After recent terrorist attacks, American authorities scrambled when they realized they did not have enough interpreters who knew Arabic, but they were sought only from immigrant populations, as it was considered too difficult to learn a language in adulthood. Former U.S. President Obama suggested that all Americans should learn another language: ". . . we should have every child speaking more than one language,"[17] but he did not say "every American" should speak another language, suggesting that children would be better than adults at this task.

Since 2010, other studies suggest that adults should be motivated to learn another language, not for cultural or commercial reasons, but because it is good for their brains.[18] This pushed the revival of the question "can adults learn a foreign language as fast as children?" The headlines still confuse the issue by questioning rather than definitively declaring this is possible: "Does It Get Harder to Learn a Language as You Get Older?"[19] The questioning nature of the headlines keeps the myth alive.

The myth of critical periods leads to the belief that adults cannot learn a foreign language as fast as a child. This belief, combined with another—that "children are like sponges" and pick up languages "effortlessly"[20]—often discourages adults, even before they start.

What We Know Now

We now know that adults can and do learn foreign languages better and faster than children, if and when they spend the same amount of time on task.[21] However, there are at least nine differences in the ways that children and adults learn languages, which explains why this fact has been hidden in plain sight.

First, adults approach language explicitly through a rules-based approach, meaning they rely on clear explanations rather than experiential learning for their foundations. Rather than habituate useful patterns in language as kids do, adults often spend a lot of time memorizing grammatical rules. This difference in the ways adults approach language can reduce the intrinsic motivation for learning and make language learning feel hard.[22]

Second, adults filter new language learning with what they know about their own native language(s). Comparing the "known" to the "unknown" makes foreign languages appear difficult. For example, when I learned Spanish I thought that assigning gender to nouns was "hard" as English only uses "the" with no equivalent to the masculine *él* or the feminine *ella*. This comparison made me initially think that Spanish was hard because it clashed with a rule base I had ingrained in my way of thinking about the world.

Third, it takes about five years for a child to become fluent in his first language.[23] Learning a second language takes about one to two years for oral fluency, and about five to seven years to come literate in another language.[23] This is a relatively long time to dominate a new task, especially when compared with learning to cook, drive, swim, or play golf. Although adults can speed this up slightly, it does take longer than most people would like and longer than other types of skill sets. The relatively long learning cycle discourages some adults.

Fourth, despite being faster at learning vocabulary, grammatical rules, and contextual aspects of language, only rarely will an adult master a foreign accent as well as a child. Accents are based on hearing—people cannot pronounce what they cannot perceive, and sounds to which a learner is not exposed early in life are harder to master as this requires new learning. This means that an adult's accent is often going to be worse than that of a child who has spent the same amount of time on the language, even if the adult is better at every other aspect of the language.[24] Because accents are among the most visible aspects of language, people jump to the conclusions that adults can't learn language as well as children. Ironically, on the world stage today, accent is the least of language worries as more people care about communicating well, not on pronouncing perfectly.

Fifth, learning as an adult is usually not as immersion-based as a child's learning. A class a few hours a week with a single teacher does not provide the regular, varied, contextualized, and realistic input needed. Children often learn languages as they use them in authentic contexts with native speakers; if adults did the same, they would learn faster than children.

Sixth, goals for children and language learning are usually related to survival ("if I don't learn the language I won't make any friends"), while adult language goals are less pressing, such as "become fluent enough to go to Italy on vacation" or "learn enough German to talk with my mother-in-law." Without the motivation provided by immediate needs, time on task is diminished and learning slows. People who have authentic goals ("If I learn Mandarin, my boss will double my salary") do learn faster than people with less pressing goals.

Seventh, little kids usually have little egos, whereas adults hate making fools of themselves, especially in front of their peers, or worse yet, their children. Children rarely blush in the face of corrections, whereas adults cringe. The person who bounces back from minor setbacks in learning tasks and who accepts corrections, rather than feeling embarrassed by them, learns faster. If the adult brain can override the adult ego, it will learn more quickly.[24]

Eighth, we now know that people can communicate when they have a lot of vocabulary, even if they have not mastered all the grammatical structures. When small children first learn to speak, they learn nouns in greater quantity than verbs (second greatest) followed by pronouns and adjectives.[25] That is, a person who knows a lot of different words (nouns and a handful of verbs) will likely be able to communicate better than a person who prioritizes the memorization of grammatical rules. Adult language learning programs usually prize grammar over vocabulary.

Finally, as with all new learning, advancing slowly but surely at a regular pace is better than erratic progress. Adults often begin language classes, then change priorities and return several weeks or months later, whereas children are often not given a choice but to learn in a more regular manner. It might appear that children are faster, but it is likely they are just more consistent.

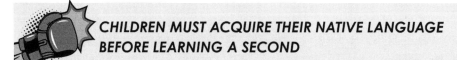

CHILDREN MUST ACQUIRE THEIR NATIVE LANGUAGE BEFORE LEARNING A SECOND

It was once thought that children should learn one language at a time, and preferably become proficient in all aspects of communication in their native language (listening, speaking, reading, and writing) before learning a second.[26] Multiple language contexts have shown, however, that kids can learn several languages at once, so long as there is a well-thought-out strategy and consistency in the way language instruction is delivered. In fact, many children benefit from learning two or more languages at once. We know from studies in neurolinguistics that students' global understanding of language (meta-linguistic awareness—being able to understand how language works) is elevated in dual-immersion settings.[27] Students who learn two or more languages simultaneously have extended executive functions compared with monolinguals.[28]

An overarching reason that Americans are not as good at foreign languages as their Asian and European counterparts is the lateness of introduction and the small number of hours devoted to languages in the curriculum. In the United States, most students are required to have one to three years of instruction in one foreign language, which normally takes place in high school, though this is slowly

changing. Some schools have begun middle school and even primary school foreign language instruction (to their credit—the earlier the better). In Europe, The
Lisbon Summit in 2000 recommended that everyone be proficient in at least two
European Community languages; and by 1998, 21 European countries required
two or three foreign languages. In 1999, the Center for Applied Linguistics
attempted to summarize the lessons learned from around the world and determined, "the results from published, longitudinal, and critical research undertaken
in varied settings throughout the world indicate clearly that the development of
multiple language proficiency is possible, and indeed that it is viewed as desirable
by educators, policy makers, and parents in many countries."[29]

It is only relatively recently that solid evidence has been used to make recommendations to U.S. schools about language learning, which may explain why so
many myths encircle multilingualism.

Where the Myth Comes From

Research in the 1970s helped establish that children should learn the structure
and grammar of their languages in a hierarchical way, with lower-level concepts
coming before higher-level concepts.[30] While this is not surprising to anyone who
subscribes to constructivist design, it was some of the first research to come out
in the field of social linguistics. The research indicated that children will show
preference for regular verbs in the past tense before irregular verbs in the past
tense, which doesn't sound like rocket science, but was groundbreaking at the
time. It also showed kids learn more nouns than any other kind of word in the
beginning stage of language, and that children learn language through imitation.[31]
The complexities of language led some to believe the brain couldn't possibly do
all this work in more than one language without giving up some other skill, but
evidence showed the brain had no problem managing this. In fact, studies from
other researchers clearly showed that errors by young children learning a foreign
language were mostly due to developmental stages and teaching strategies, rather
than language interference.[32]

Despite evidence to the contrary,[33] people continued to believe in the "native
language first" rule due to the natural desire to keep children from becoming confused, as reported in Jim Cummins's findings.[34] While it seemed to make sense to
err on the side of caution and not bombard children unnecessarily, it soon became
evident that early bilingualism, if not multilingualism, was favorable for all children[35] in terms of cognitive advantages. Despite the current views on the benefits
of bilingualism, there are still few school districts in the U.S. that promote early
foreign language acquisition or mother tongue maintenance for those who speak
a language other than English at home.

What We Know Now

We have learned a lot about bilingualism in the past 40 years. Some of the highlights of this research are the insights provided about cognitive bilingual edge, curriculum design, accents, age of learning, and perhaps most importantly, the order of skill sets when learning a new language. Each of these lessons is described in brief below.

Bilingual edge

By the early 2000s, there was finally enough evidence to support bilingual education for all—across all cultures and socioeconomic groupings.[36] The benefits of bilingualism are easily documented in culture and economics but are just now emerging in the cognitive realm.[37] We now know there are definitive benefits to bilingualism, such as extended working memory capacity, inhibitory control, and cognitive flexibility. The bilingual edge suggests there is a cognitive reserve that bilinguals enjoy,[38] and benefits that may spill over into slowing cognitive decline in old age.[39]

Curriculum design

Starting around the turn of the 21st century, researchers turned their attention from establishing the benefits of bilingualism to strategies for achieving this in the best way possible within schools.[40] There are five types of bilingual education that are most commonly implemented in the United States: (a) submersion, (b) English as a second language instruction; (c) transitional bilingual education; (d) maintenance bilingual education; and (d) two-way immersion.[41] Of these, Thomas and Collier[42] found that two-way immersion—in which students receive core academic instruction in two languages over an extended period, with at least 30% of instruction in the partner language—was superior curriculum design. This seems to confirm insights from successful European models. However, most schools in the U.S. do not use this model. Dual language immersion programs in the U.S. bring together students who are native English speakers with students whose first language is other than English—most often Spanish—and provide instruction in both languages to the whole group.

Accents

We now know that "the earlier, the better" applies as far as accents are concerned. This suggests that the way the United States approaches languages in high school is the least efficient approach if we care about accents. In order to pronounce a word, you have to be able to hear all its sounds. Humans are born able to hear all phonemes and speak any language without an accent.[43] However, at about three years of age, three small bones, called ossicles, descend into the auditory canal and slightly change the way sounds are perceived. This slight "blocking" of sounds means that the brain does not hear all the sounds, and therefore, the speaker cannot pronounce those sounds and will have an accent. That, along with the fact that the tongue is a muscle and needs to be "exercised" before it can pronounce certain sounds, means that without early exposure and practice, accents are very likely. This means that older learners have a higher probability of having an accent that younger learners.[44]

Ages

People can learn foreign languages at any age. We have known for more than 25 years that "experimental research in which children have been compared to adults in second language learning has consistently demonstrated that adolescents and adults perform better than young children under controlled conditions."[45] This mean that adults are actually better and faster at learning foreign languages, if and when they spend the same amount of time on task.

Order of languages

It is now clear that people do not need to learn one language completely before starting a subsequent language. There is evidence that people can successfully be brought up with two,[46] three,[47] or even four languages at a time,[48] so long as they are divided by person, place, and time in a good strategy.

CHILDREN LEARN SKILLS EFFORTLESSLY, INCLUDING FOREIGN LANGUAGES

Children grow quickly and change daily. Often, the rate of their learning is so fast that it seems effortless. We ask, *"Why Do Children Learn Language So Effortlessly?"*[49] While the ease of learning in childhood has been mentioned so many times in the press that it seems it must be true, there is surprisingly little evidence to support this.

Where the Myth Comes From

Children appear nonplussed as they learn to walk or learn a new language. This is deceptive, however. Children often cannot compare their learning with anything prior, and therefore cannot judge if what they are doing is "hard" or not. Adults, on the other hand, compare their own skills to children's, as well as to their own past learning, and feel much slower in relative progress. Adults are usually amazed at how quickly their children "pick up" the local language when moving to a new country, but they don't realize that there is a great deal of effort that goes into this learning. Thus, this myth originates from adults' beliefs about children's learning, rather than from the evidence.

What We Know Now

Learning takes time for all people, young or old. For example, we know that it takes about a year to learn to walk, and roughly five years for a human to learn her first language. Walking and talking take a great deal of effort and can be measured in the amount of time the child spends building up to these skills, and how long it takes to master them (practicing daily, often for hours at a time).

We know that highly motivated learners spend more time on task. One difference between children and adults is that children are often more interested in what they learn, whereas older children and adults are often *obliged* to learn. Some of the things we say are learned quickly are basically necessary for survival, including language and mobility.

We also know that children tend to put up fewer roadblocks for themselves and don't beat themselves up about getting corrected when they make errors, whereas adults have difficulty swallowing evaluations from others. We know that people (adults and children) who are open to learning from their mistakes learn faster.

ALL LANGUAGE FUNCTIONS USE THE SAME BRAIN NETWORKS

It is common to hear how the "language areas of the brain" do one thing or another, or are limited to one place or another (i.e. "localizationalism"). Despite the frequency of the comments and headlines, it is now clear that there are dozens of different networks that need to be in sync for language to function in the human brain. It is an oversimplification to tell people they "just don't have a head for language," as language is distributed throughout the brain. Just as there are different subnetworks for memory and attention, as we saw earlier, there are multiple networks related to language. Many depend on one another, but none alone is responsible for language.

Where the Myth Comes From

The myth originates from an oversimplification of brain functions. Starting with Franz Gall's phrenology and the belief that competencies rested in specific areas of the brain, people have assumed that there was a neat and clean division of labor in parts of the brain, leading to the idea that "language" must be in a particular area.

To add to the confusion, an appreciation for all the sub-elements of language is only just beginning to emerge. While many people have intuited that understanding the meaning of a word[50] is likely to be different than using the right intonation to pronounce the word,[51] it is only recently that we have the evidence in neuroscience to support this supposition. Without an appreciation of the complexities of language, it is almost impossible to choose the right classroom interventions to help all students. This is akin to being a great driver. Knowing about how to increase or decrease speed, when to shift gears, and how to keep the road in mind as you maneuver in traffic all play roles in good driving, but one skill alone will not make you a good driver. In the brain, language, just like driving, has multiple sub-elements in distinct neural pathways (some overlapping) that must all work in sync to be successful.

What We Know Now

We now know that, like all other aspects of cognition, language is complex and requires multiple neural networks. To recall the meaning of a word, a person would need to employ networks related to *semantic* memory.[52] Being able to sound out a written word[53] requires the (a) visual field to take in the symbols;[54] (b) interpret the letters as phonemes;[55] (c) consider how the phonemes connect to make a word,[56] (d) recruit the motor cortex to get the tongue to cooperate[57] to (e) say the word;[58] (and hopefully along the way semantic memory is also used to figure out the meaning of what is being said[59]). To interpret the emotional intention of a written word,[60] (which is a slightly different neural path than interpreting a spoken word),[61] the brain needs to first understand the meaning of the word (semantic memory), then consider the word in context.[62] For example, consider the statement, "I'm pregnant." Depending on who says the words to whom and in what surroundings, the tone of voice used will be different and take on very different meanings. These distinct neural pathways, which represent sub-elements of language, are new information that can inform teaching practice.

CRAWLING IS NECESSARY FOR LITERACY

In some schools, older kids who have been walking for years are told to crawl to refine the parts of their brain needed to read and write. In yet other settings, mothers and fathers are coached to get on all fours with their babies to motivate them to crawl toward them for the benefit of later academic success. These encounters presume a close link between being able to crawl and being able to read. Is there such a link? Unfortunately, many teachers seem to think so, but there is little evidence to support this.

Where the Myth Comes From

There is some research that shows a strong correlation between good, timely crawling and walking skills and later academic success.[63] Kids who don't crawl (or those who spend little time crawling) appear to have poorer reading skills than those who did crawl.[64] The theory is that the two hemispheres of the brain become more coordinated with crawling, which then leads to improved reading skills. Correlation is powerful, but it is not causation. While these studies meticulously document the correlation of crawling to academics, not one of them cites credible sources from the learning sciences to explain why this allegedly occurs. There are many statements in these studies promising a strong body of research (e.g., "There is a growing body of evidence which reveals a correlation between maturity in neuromotor skills and educational performance,"[65]), but no research is ever cited to support the link between neuromotor functioning and literacy. The belief that because two things occur together means that one of them caused the other is a logical human presumption, but it is not always true.

Some of the studies on the relation between literacy and motor skills group characteristics, making it hard to know which precise variable leads to what. For example, some state that low socioeconomic status, parents' education levels, lack of reading at home, *and* crawling (together) put children at risk of academic failure. What these studies do not seem to take into consideration is the idea that these other variables might be the causes of poor reading skills, not crawling itself.

BrainGym™ authors Dennison and Dennison suggest that children who skipped crawling are prone to having later academic problems, including with learning to read, though they cite no evidence for this claim. There is no denying that motor movement is great for childhood development and that it contributes to adequate growth,[66] but it's a leap to say that reading depends on crawling. In fact, crawling is not a prerequisite to any other developmental milestone. Kids who crawl and kids who don't crawl walk, stand, and talk around the same time.[67] Gross motor skill development, such as crawling, should be encouraged in the early months of a child's development because it helps a child be mobile and explore his world, but not because literacy depends on it.

What We Know Now

In their very thorough review of milestones in reading development, *"How to Create a Successful Reader? Milestones in Reading Development from Birth to Adolescence"*[67] written for *Acta Paediatrica*, one of the most prestigious journals for pediatricians, Horowitz-Kraus and colleagues go into the very complex nature of developing reading skills in the brain and comprehensively cover the many intrinsic and extrinsic factors influencing this particularly unique human ability. They mention crawling just once in a reference to easily observable milestones at age 12 to 24 months in a table not related to literacy, and give no importance to crawling for literacy in the rest of the extensive article.

Hansen, Joshi, and Dex's book[68] is frequently cited by articles that claim crawling is necessary, though the authors themselves do not mention "crawling," "neuromotor," or "motor skills" once in 300 pages of text. These two examples lead to the conclusion that there is a problem with circular citations, in which someone cites an article incorrectly, and then others cite that article, and so on and so on, with the end result that people have extended the interpretation of other people's research beyond the reasonable scope of their findings. This creates an echo chamber of rumors rather than facts, leading to the myth.

To counter the claim that crawling is imperative for reading, we can suggest a negative corollary: If reading was dependent on early motor movement such as crawling, we would expect to see illiteracy in quadriplegics. This is not the case.

WHY THIS IS GOOD NEWS FOR TEACHING

A better understanding of the different neural pathways involved in language will help teachers become more precise in their diagnoses of literacy problems and their classroom interventions. For example, if teachers can determine that a student has reading problems related to his ability to decode phonemes, he will do one thing, but if he thinks the child has a problem with semantic memory for the meaning of words, he will do something else. Some common reading and writing problems are indicated in Figure 10.1. While not exhaustive, the examples in Table 10.1 give an idea of the opportunities that exist for teachers who appreciate the multiple neural pathways that are involved in language.

Knowing people can learn foreign languages across the life span is great news for teachers, especially those in secondary or adult education, or those wanting to learn a new language themselves. Once artificial limits on learners are lifted, teachers can develop more realistic expectations of students' learning curves. There is a growing demand for English language teachers around the world (100,000 positions open each year), thanks to a deepening interest in quality bilingual education, and a better understanding of how to teach in multilingual contexts.

All new learning requires effort and energy, even to learn one's first language(s). This is great news for teachers; instead of mourning older students' slow progress, they can let learners know how much they understand and appreciate the effort that goes into learning and how long complex processes like foreign language learning take. It is also good for adult educators who can take advantage

Practical Application of MBE: Language

The more teachers know about language, the better for all learning outcomes in all subject areas. Each language problem relates to a very different root cause, which in turn is related to distinct interventions.

For example:

TABLE 10.1. EXAMPLE READING AND WRITING PROBLEMS

Possible Reading and Writing Problems		
Observable problem	**Root cause**	**Intervention**
Child cannot sound out words	Symbol-to-sound comprehension	Rehearsal of phonemes
Child does not understand the meaning of certain words	Semantic memory failure	Exposure to vocabulary in multiple contexts
Child cannot read sentences fluidly	Visual to motor cortex coordination	Modeling through cooperative reading (child reads one sentence, adult reads next sentence)
Child reads fluidly but does not know what he read	Working memory failure Sustained attention networks	Read shorter pieces of text (of phrases or sentences) and check for meaning comprehension
Child is dysfluent in reading but has no problem speaking or understanding	Symbol-to-sound comprehension	Decrease amount of time permitted to read a sentence correctly (build up to fluidity)
Child is fluent in speaking but cannot spell correctly	Symbol-to-sound comprehension; phonemic exceptions	Phonemic rehearsal; site word memorization
Child has many spelling errors but has coherent ideas	Symbol-to-sound comprehension; phonemic exceptions	Phonemic rehearsal; site word memorization
Child writes correctly but with poor handwriting	Graphomotor coordination is poor	Give him a computer if handwriting is not important. Practice handwriting if handwriting is important.

Source: Author

of the fact that the brain can and does learn throughout the life span, with equal effort as it did in childhood, and in some cases, with more ease than children, thanks to having substantial prior knowledge. Getting rid of this myth makes the introduction of languages more flexible, although the general rule that "the earlier the better" still stands.

As mentioned in the chapter related to sleep, while you cannot learn a new language in your sleep by placing a textbook under your pillow or playing a tape as you slumber, you can rehearse elements of language, such as vocabulary or verb conjugation, as you rest. Language learning, like all other heavy cognitive tasks, needs both conscious and unconscious processes to succeed.[69]

Crawling is among a long list of culprits blamed for poor reading skills, but thanks to more complete research, it can now be taken off that list. It's great news to know that some children in our classrooms are not doomed by "parent neglect" during the crawling stage, and that teachers do not have to make older children learn to crawl to ensure they read, as some therapists suggest.[70] It's great news that early literacy teachers can focus on the business of learning to read rather than hoping for results by getting kids down on all fours.

11

KEY TAKEAWAYS FROM THIS BOOK

HOW TO SEPARATE THE WHEAT FROM THE CHAFF

The neuromyths presented in this book demonstrate the historical evolution of the science of the brain and learning.

Neuromyths are everywhere. Classical music can make us smarter? Cognitive training keeps our brains young? Memory is unlimited? Once we know if we are right- or left-brained, we can maximize our learning style? Entertaining, but incorrect! A vital part of improving teacher education is to improve our knowledge of neuroscience.[1]

Neuromyths can be generated or disseminated for many reasons, as we've seen in previous chapters, and as depicted in Figure 11.1. The practices recommended throughout this book and brought together in this chapter can help us to recognize neuromyths and avoid applying misinformation to the brains in our classrooms. By debunking neuromyths, we can improve our teaching. Thanks to the lessons from the neuromyths, there are many things we can do, starting today, to improve teaching.

Embrace Complexity!

Human energy is at a premium, which is why humans prefer simplicity in everything from design to business to learning.[2] The first reason neuromyths exist is because humans prefer *ease and clarity* to *complexity*, which actually doesn't sound like a bad thing. General survival instincts suggest that humans want to get the most benefits with the least effort (energy). Energy conservation is a natural goal that enhances survival.[3] This means it is normal to try to reduce demands on the brain's energy by avoiding complexity.

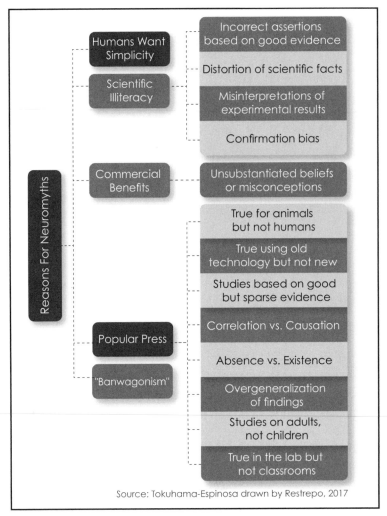

Figure 11.1: *Why Neuromyths Exist*

Therefore, it is not surprising that energy conservation spills over into educational training. Teachers enjoy learning, but they, like most people, prefer the least painful route to understanding, which is natural. This is why it is understandable to want to believe that we have learning styles, or that a fixed number of repetitions of a new concept will result in learning. However, great teachers appreciate that this comes into direct conflict with information about the brain, especially as it's "the body's most complex organ"[4] and arguably "the most complex object in the universe."[5] What many don't realize is that by embracing complexity, they also make teaching easier. Once we accept that reading, math, art, physical education, and history, as well as all other academic domains, are not located in a single part of the brain, but are rather distributed in dozens of networks throughout the brain, and that different teaching interventions strengthen and improve different networks, we can actually become more proficient in our work with students. Until we embrace complexity, we continue to see teachers gravitate toward publications dedicated to easy ways of learning.

Teacher professional development resources boast "easy" titles. Some great guides like *Teach Like a Pirate*[6] and *Teach Like a Champion 2.0*[7] have excellent content information, perhaps due to, and not in spite of, their light appearance. While the titles make teaching look easy, the contents of these books make it clear that the authors understand the complexity involved. Such titles make it appear that teachers prefer ease to difficulty, effortlessness to exertion, and simplicity to complexity. While this makes a lot of sense in terms of energy and human survival, it does not make sense for a profession whose organ of existence is the brain. There are multiple neuromyths that have been generated due to badly "digested" versions of studies, incorrect summaries of scientific advances, and the general trap of reductionism. It is attractive to think that we are right-brain dominant and have learning styles because those claims make the complexities of human learning look almost effortless. (*All we have to do is identify the style or dominant hemisphere, and teaching will be a breeze, right?*) Teachers and society as a whole need to begin to embrace complexity, especially where the brain is concerned.

Pursue Scientific Literacy!

Another big reason that neuromyths exist is related to a lack of scientific literacy on the part of many in society in general and teachers in particular.[8] One part of this deficiency means many teachers don't have *content area* knowledge about how the brain works. Another part of this "literacy" means teachers need to learn basic information about learning and the brain over time—not just brief courses— which have little or no impact.

Content area knowledge

Despite demands to the contrary, many teachers do not yet receive classes on learning and the brain in their university preparation. There are 90 million teachers in the world[9] and only a small fraction is taught anything about the brain,[10] and that instruction is limited mostly to psychological, not neurological, concepts.[11] The Deans For Impact coalition[12] acknowledges that few teacher education programs in the United States include even the most basic information about the brain, which needs to change in order to bring education into the 21st century. More teachers need to know there are multiple reasons kids might not remember information, or that competing attention systems in the brain can be harmonized with different teaching strategies. Some believe that this means creating a new structure of teacher education, while others think current systems can be modified. Zachary Stein and Kurt Fischer[13] suggest that research or a system of lab schools based on Dewey's original idea "would provide the best structure methodological symbiosis between theory, research, and practice."[14] However, the Deans For Impact believe that current education faculties can be modified through curriculum and methodological changes.[15] Whatever form it takes, the need to change teacher education is apparent.

Challenges to thinking like a scientist

Humans learn about their brains in much the same way as they learn about other things in the world, through observation and experience. The world is understood through the senses, hypotheses are made and tested about ideas, and past knowledge serves as a foundation for future learning. Learning about one's own brain also requires introspection and imagination, since we rarely have the chance to examine the working brain up close in real life. Some innovative university programs are doing their best to improve initial teacher training in this area.

In *The Neuroscience Literacy of Trainee Teachers*, Howard-Jones and colleagues[16] suggest that people develop their "theory of brain" early in life and that by about the age of four, "we consider it as an internal body part involved with a range of distinctly mental acts, but do not differentiate between mind and brain."[17] He says that as we grow and over the course of schooling, "the concepts become increasingly differentiated such that, by the age of 10-11 years old, children often consider there is some cognitive function of the brain behind sensory-motor acts" but it isn't until we are in adulthood that we realize that "the brain is essential for all behavior, including noncognitive involuntary responses such as fear and laughter."[17] This means that the understanding of our own brains evolves to the stage where we can actually think about thinking within brain structures in an orderly way in the early years, but the lack of direct contact with the brain itself makes contemplating it elusive until the college years. This does not have to be the case.

Some school programs teach children about their own brains, and find that an earlier understanding of neurological functions is helpful in getting kids to both understand and manage their own behavior.[18] It is clear that if more schools would help kids think like scientists, it would be easier to get teachers in training to do the same later in life. Thinking like a scientist means approaching problems in the classroom with an eye toward gathering information to make decisions, apply interventions, and then analyze the results to rethink the problem. Teachers have been criticized for not being able to "think like a scientist" and for believing unsubstantiated claims about the brain due to a lack of training.[19] Some neuroscientists suggest that simply understanding the scientific method and applying it to teaching practices would improve education.

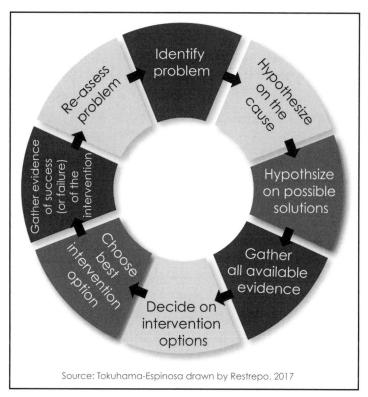

Source: Tokuhama-Espinosa drawn by Restrepo, 2017

Figure 11.2: *Problem-Solving in the Classroom with the Scientific Method*

Ironically, most teachers go through this same thinking process suggested in this scientific method wheel dozens if not hundreds of times a day as they assess their students, decide on interventions, and measure results, yet they are unaware they are applying the scientific method to their classes. The "Teacher-Researcher" model[20] or the "Research-Practitioner" model[21] formalizes this addition to current teacher education programs. Learning how to research—identify problems, pose questions, gather evidence, analyze, and reach conclusions—should be part of all teachers' professionalization. Thinking like a scientist would help eliminate myths in the classroom.

Scientific illiteracy can also lead to the misinterpretation of experimental results. An example is related to synaptic growth. While it is clear that there is a high degree of synaptic proliferation in the early years, which slows over time, it is a misinterpretation, as we saw in Chapter 4, to believe that the first three years of life determine the future limits of learning. While high stress[22] or poor nutrition in the early years[23] can have long-term negative effects on children, most normal humans can and do learn throughout their life spans.

Read More Diligently!

Lack of scientific literacy can lead to incorrect assertions based on good evidence: that is, the science is good, only if interpreted incorrectly. "Diligence" on a teacher's part would mean taking the time to search for additional sources that would help confirm or reject assertions. For example, if an article you're reading states that "since the time of the ancient Greeks, there has been an implicit belief that physical activity is linked to intellectual abilities"[24] and you make a decision to exchange class teaching time for outdoor exercise time, you are using good but incomplete information. Getting the full picture means carefully reading the *entire* article and then *others* that might present additional information or opposing viewpoints. Making a decision based on a single study, or worse yet, a single catchy sentence or headline, could do harm rather than help. It's great news that there are many new resources for teachers that permit access to high-quality, evidence-based neuroeducational concepts in summarized forms. For example, the Science of Learning Community[25] and Deans For Impact Science of Learning[26] webpages encourage teachers and school leaders to read more about how their kids learn, but to do so in a warm community atmosphere.

Humans naturally infer to fill in gaps of knowledge. This occurs from the simplest visual perception gaps[27] to the most sophisticated knowledge building in the brain[28] as it's generally beneficial to humans to guess rather than to have gaps in knowledge. But just because inferring is a natural thing to do does not mean it is the right thing to do. People naturally drift toward ideas they have read for reference, which means that reading widely and diligently is a key to staying abreast of the best information. "Diligence rather than inference" should become one of the new mantras of teacher training.

Get the Whole Story!

A lack of scientific literacy can also lead to distortions, which "stem from undue simplifications of scientific results."[29] For example, while it is true that the brain has two hemispheres, some evidence on hemispheric specialization has led to the myth that people have one hemisphere that is dominant over the other. Split-brain research by Gazzaniga, Bogen, and Sperry in the 1960s and Roger Sperry's subsequent Nobel Prize in Physiology in the early 1980s seemed to confirm this myth, by calling attention to the idea that each hemisphere was responsible for different functions. We now know, as discussed in Chapter 2, that brain functioning is more complex than intimated 40 years ago. *Localizationalism*, or the belief that a specific skill set rests in one place in the brain, has been replaced with a better understanding of the complex network systems, thanks to advances in technology. These networks have hubs that are in one hemisphere or the other, but this does not mean one hemisphere or the other is dominant. Distortion of the facts leads to myths.

Set Personal Beliefs Aside!

It is natural to seek confirmation of what we already believe. After all, who wants to find that long-held beliefs are challenged? This explains why a lack of scientific literacy can be blamed for *unwitting* confirmation bias, when a researcher mistakenly searches for or gives greater emphasis to information that supports his or her hypothesis such as "X improves Y." A lack of *academic rigor* can be blamed for a *conscious search* for confirmation bias, meaning the researcher purposefully looks only for information that confirms "X improves Y," rather than that "X hinders Y," or simply "the relationship between X and Y". For example, if I choose certain words that are framed positively or negatively, I can usually find evidence for what I hope to prove. A search on "the *benefits* of bilingualism" will only turn up good things about bilingualism, for example. It is much more time-consuming, but also more intellectually honest, to open the search for information that may contradict the hypothesis. One way to avoid confirmation bias in the social sciences is to seek answers to research questions—"What are the effects of bilingualism on cognition?"—rather than to prove or disprove hypotheses ("How does bilingualism *benefit* cognition?"). Teachers are constantly seeking new and better ways to reach their students, but asking biased questions doesn't add a lot of new knowledge to the teacher's base. For example, a teacher is likely to learn more if she researches "how and to what extent Steven's reading fluidity improves with increased small group practice" than "why small-group reading works."

Confirmation bias is even graver when related to methodological design. Studies in which participants are randomly assigned to control and experimental groups yield some of the most convincing research to come out of education. This means the researcher doesn't choose who is in which group or who gets what type of treatment. This reduces the potential biases that can come out of research, and is basic protocol when designing classroom interventions. For example, if a teacher wants to test the effectiveness of a specific teaching tool or activity, but she chooses the top kids in her group for the experiment, her results will not be as compelling as dividing the children alphabetically (which in theory mixes up the top students with those at the bottom). If a researcher's participant sampling is biased by including people who will give the answers he hopes to find or for which he has previous concurring belief, this is an assault on correct research protocol. Confirmation bias is cognitively based, and leads to a selective choice of what information to include and what information to exclude from consideration. Studies conducted with confirmation bias promote myths.

Beware the Placebo Effect!

In a different way, confirmation bias can be linked to something called the *placebo effect*. The placebo effect occurs when an intervention (a new classroom activity, for example) or substance (a vitamin supplement, for example) is given to a student "for the psychological benefit to the patient rather than for any physiological effect."[30] This produces a phenomenon in which that people can "swear" that a program or activity works because they *want* or *expect* it to work. This in turn permits the researcher to conclude that her premise is "true," thanks to the people chosen to participate, who also believe the intervention will benefit them. This is unscrupulous behavior on the part of the researchers, but teachers rarely learn about these mistakes in methodological design and end up believing the results.

Get Out of Your Comfort Zone!

Belief systems are particularly difficult to change, even in the face of hard facts. While a teacher can learn the scientific method to test hypotheses, belief systems require *un*learning a way of thinking before adapting to a new belief. People hang onto their beliefs for irrational reasons, such as because friends or family members say something, or because of cultural influences. You might not innately believe men are superior to women, but if you are brought up in a *machoist* society[31] you may find your belief system shaped by the others in your community. Beliefs are very personal and therefore hard to abandon, as people cling to them emotionally, meaning purely rational reasoning is often not enough to change someone's mind. Just because a study disproves the long-term benefits from short-term brain training does not mean people will readily abandon the idea. The longer something is around, the more likely we are to believe it is true, despite evidence to the contrary.[32] This makes it very hard for people to let go of "staples" they have referred to for many years, such as "girls are better at language and boys are better at math" or "I am a visual learner" despite the lack of evidence to prove this.

Remember Your Students Are Not Rats!

Many neuromyths grow out of well-structured studies on animals, but for which there is little or no evidence in humans. Animal studies are vital to advancing understanding, but should not be the last word where classroom learning is concerned. For example, it is exciting to of Grandma and think we can stop amnestic effects and improve memory systems with intense training, until we realize that the studies were conducted solely on rats in mazes.[33] While rodent studies are extremely helpful in advancing theories—there is less resistance to stressing rats than to stressing small children, for good reason—making conclusions about children based on them is a leap. Studies that can merge findings from rodents to humans have the best chance of proving theories with the fewest adverse effects.[34] We need to be wary of claims based solely on animal studies, which can lead to myths.

Watch Out for Sparse Evidence: One Finding Does Not a Theory Make!

Sometimes news makes headlines based on a few studies, or studies with few participants. The information and study may be of high quality, but a lack of replication or a small number of participants make them suspect. The matter of exercise and cognition in older populations is an example of sparse evidence that has led to stamped-in conclusions.

People are living longer, and there is increased interest in keeping not only their bodies, but also their minds in good shape. There has been a recent flurry of research activity on aging populations and cognition over the past decade, but few offer strong recommendations for specific types of interventions. Norman Doidge's popular book *The Brain's Way of Healing*[35] pushed a lot of people to conclude that walking was a cure for Parkinson's based on Pepper's case study. While there is nothing negative about walking in old age and there are certainly health benefits, the leap from "good for you" to "cure for Parkinson's" is a big one, and Doidge does a good job of defending this premise, citing multiple other studies. Other books are less serious, and share "anti-aging" techniques to stop time by doing crossword puzzles and jumping jacks. Many books, some authored by MDs and PhDs, substantiate the "evidence" in their books with a few testimonials rather than clinical trials, which also points to a less-than-rigorous defense of the information. The few meta-analyses that exist related to aging, cognition, and physical exercise all show that exercise is better than no exercise, but exactly what kind of exercise works best is inconclusive and probably has a lot to do with the individual. In a review of all the studies between 2002 and 2012, Kelly and colleagues[36] found that "data from epidemiological, cross-sectional, and neuroimaging research show a relationship between higher levels of exercise and reduced risk of cognitive decline but evidence from randomised controlled trials (RCTs) is less consistent," implying some physical activity is better than none, but precisely what old people should do to slow cognitive decline isn't clear. The few studies that are out there do not conclusively show that walking or any other activity reduces the probability of cognitive decline, let alone improve cognitive ability or reverse Parkinson's. Despite this evidence, there are dozens of headlines each month, such as "Taking Your Brain for a Walk: The Secret to Delaying Dementia."[37] People are much more complex that a single variable; there can be multiple reasons why a person will react well, or not at all, to an intervention.

There are also many studies with sparse evidence. The small number of studies (or small number of participants) should send out alarm bells when it comes to conclusive information. For example, there are studies on spatial rotation activities that are few in number, but that generate significant headlines. Boys tend to do better on spatial rotation activities,[38] which has led to some screaming headlines that their brains are better equipped for the challenges in math fields in general. Spatial rotation is one of dozens of sub-elements within math, and the only area for which there are a number of studies that show male superiority. Newspaper headlines, such as "Female Brains Really Are Different to Male Minds with Women Possessing Better Recall and Men Excelling at Maths"[39] appear to suggest that boys' brains are superior to girls' brains when it comes to math in general, not to spatial rotation in particular. These types of headlines only promote gender biases and demotivate female learners. The presentation of the research in the article did not consider that the evidence is high quality, but sparse, nor did it acknowledge that several controlled scientific studies showed that any differences can be reduced with training and likely have roots in boys' play with spatial-orienting toys with more frequency than girls.[40] This means that while some slight differences in spatial abilities seem evidence-based, they are not permanent conditions. We should all be wary of headlines that are based on single or small studies, which might not always have implications for the wider population or tell the whole story.

Correlation vs. Causation: Know the Difference!

The presence of more men than women in math, science, and technology fields has received a lot of attention as of late, and several countries have adopted policies to increase gender equality in these areas. While there are serious articles that try to understand why fewer women choose science careers,[41] others conflate correlation (the fact that two things happen at the same time) with causation (that one thing caused the other) and thus suggest that gender differences in the brain are to blame. The suggestion that "girls just don't have the right brains" for science and math professions can turn into a self-fulfilling prophecy.

Correlation is often pointed to as "proof" that something exists. In Ecuador, there are an average of around 70 earthquakes each year, and there is also a rainy and a dry season. People tend to believe that the rain causes the earthquakes, and actually fear the rain because of the seismic activity that might occur. There is actually no evidence that more earthquakes occur during rainy months. However, every time an earthquake does coincide with rain, TV stations, newspapers, and the average person on the street swap stories about how this "always" happens. What most people don't realize is that correlation—the fact that some earthquakes happen during the rainy season—does not imply causation, namely that the rain caused the earthquake.

Another example of correlation but not causation has to do with the Mozart effect. A teacher might play classical music and student test scores improve, so the teacher thinks the music is the reason the scores improved. This is a possibility, but it is also possible that the students studied more for that test, the topic was easier, their parents offered to reward them for good grades, or any number of other reasons. This means that the experiment did not control for variables other than the music, meaning the methodological design was flawed. Neuromyths abound with confusion of correlation and causation. Another reason neuromyths are repeated in the popular press is related to false relation and is the concept of "absence versus existence."

Find What Is, Not Just What Isn't!

In research, healthy brains are hard to come by. For many years we relied on studies of damaged brains for the vast majority of information. When a person was sick and died, an autopsy was conducted to see what areas appeared damaged, and in this way, identified areas of the brain believed to be responsible for that function. For example, one of the most famous autopsies is of the patient "Tan" and the study of what is now known as Broca's area in the brain (the patient could only say the word "Tan," hence his namesake). Paul Broca correctly identified what we now know of as "expressive aphasia" or the inability to express ideas, despite maintaining the same level of intelligence due to a stroke in that part of Tan's brain. This meant that by identifying what was *not* there—the damaged part of the brain— we could identify a crucial hub for language. This led to the general (but false) understanding that absence can prove existence. While Broca's work proved to be true in Tan's case and in those of thousands of other patients since, it turns out that it is not always true. Up to 5% of right-handed and 30% of left-handed stroke sufferers do not lose fluent speech ability with left hemisphere damage to Broca's area (because they have Broca's area in the right hemisphere). This means that the absence of a skill that coincides with damage to the brain cannot always prove that the skill is located in, or limited to, the affected part of the brain.

In another example, it was noted that "the boundary sulci are altogether missing" in Albert Einstein's parietal lobe, suggesting "structural markers for native intelligence."[42] Saying that intelligence *exists* because the sulci are *missing* is complicated and fraught with controversy, which Galaburda at the Harvard Medical School rightly challenged in a letter to *The Lancet*.[43]

A third example comes from teenage brains. There are multiple headlines that indicate that teenage brains are "not yet fully developed" and that this explains irrational behavior. This idea is born from looking at the differences between fully matured brains and adolescent brains, and drawing the conclusion that the differences in physiology (the lack of full frontal lobe maturation, for example) is the cause for teenagers' erratic behavior. What we have learned, thanks to technological advances, is that there is nothing we do that is managed by a single piece or part of the brain, but rather by networks. Any headline that shouts about how "X is missing" (mature frontal lobes) and therefore responsible for certain actions should be suspected of being a neuromyth.

Curb Your Enthusiasm for Generalizations!

Humans are both marvelously curious as well as cleverly inventive, and the search to resolve mysteries about human variation is ripe with hypotheses. Why are some people born autistic and others not? Why and how is genius nurtured? Because of our interest in the outliers, we often make unmerited blanket statements about human behavior. In an attempt to explain brains that seem to work slightly differently, we make generalizations about that population, rather than remembering that each brain is unique and uniquely organized. For example, "all geniuses . . ." or "everyone with autism . . ." or "people with ADHD . . ." suggest that individuals have no unique history or combination of learned experiences. It is both dangerous and disingenuous to pretend that *all* geniuses (autistics, people with attention problems, dyslexics, people with low socioeconomic status, girls, boys, old people, college graduates, and so on) react in the same way. It is generally good advice that studies that use the words *all* or *none*, or that make vast generalizations about large groups of people, are suspicious for some kind of neuromyth promotion (e.g., *"Girls react to warmth and boys to a firm hand"*). Similarly, blanket recommendations that "everyone" can benefit from some kind of intervention or another are also suspect (e.g., *"Want to live longer? Eat fish!"*).

Don't Assume Studies on Adults Will Apply to School-Age Children!

Other popular press neuromyths come from the fact that the vast majority of studies are conducted on adults, not children. In education, the search for effective interventions is an ongoing pursuit for a type of academic Holy Grail. Educational research publications have expanded over the years, and as of late have sought to nurture findings with other sciences, making the list of possible interventions vast. The benefit of looking at educational research is that it is almost always conducted on school-age populations, which is not always true for information from neuroscience. In neuroscience, there are not as many studies on children as there are on adults, so the popular press can mistakenly think that what was found in a study on adults can be transferred to children, leading to neuromyths.

For example, the Connectome Project is a fabulous, worldwide effort to map human neural networks. Some of the experiments teach participants to do a particular task, and then when the sampling is large enough, they can proclaim that certain networks with particular hubs (key areas) are involved in this or that type of learning. These are highly controlled and well-conducted experiments and have the world in awe of the new findings. In the vast majority of cases, however, the participants are mostly adults. This means that some conclusions being drawn by research in the Connectome Project may or may not be transferable to children.

There are differences between the ways that adults and children process information, such as reading,[44] and math,[45] but *why* they are different ranges from structural development to simply the number of life experiences that modify learning across the life span. This means that studies and findings on adults cannot be presumed similar to those that would be found on children.

Remember That True in the Lab Isn't Necessarily True in the Classroom!

Multiple research experiments are underway to determine just how people learn to read, and to devise interventions that allow them to do this even better. For example, eye-tracking machines allow a researcher to follow a person's pupils as they read sentences on a page. This helps the scientist understand what words the eyes "skip" and what parts of the sentence are returned to multiple times, in order to gauge better teaching methods. Nearly all of these experiments take place in labs, not classrooms, because labs create the optimal conditions to control experiments and reduce interference from extraneous variables, permitting the researcher to find answers to questions such as "How and to what extent does new vocabulary influence the speed of reading?" or "How and to what extent does pre-reading vocabulary review increase reading speed?" in which one variable (reviewing vocabulary before reading the passage) impacts one other variable (speed of reading). While this type of experimental research is extremely important and useful in advancing hypotheses about learning, these studies are all guilty of one big problem, namely that they rarely reflect the real conditions of learning in real classrooms, which tend to have multiple distractors occurring at the same time. This means that headlines about lab findings, such as *"Studies Show That Some Foods May Be as Addictive as Heroin and Cocaine,"*[46] should be suspicious because the single study cited took place in a lab and likely did not emulate real-life conditions (and this one was on rats!).[47] One of the reasons popular press promotions of myths catch on is *bandwagonitis*, in which people believe things because others do.

Be a Critical Consumer of Information!

The Power of Brain Images

We believe what we can see. Neuromyths have been around since people began their wonderings about the brain, and artists over the centuries have depicted what was observable about this organ. It wasn't until the 1970s, however, that safe brain imaging began to be used with frequency in experimental studies, and not until the 1990s, during the Decade of the Brain, that more money was put into this venture. Michael Posner elegantly articulates this evolution in "seeing" the brain:

> *Being able to see things has always had a dramatic impact in science. The microscope allowed people to see things too small to be observed by our senses. At the beginning of the 20th century Santiago Ramon y Cajal (1937) was able for the first time to observe individual nerve cells. Our current ability to see into the human brain depends on the operation of these nerve cells. When neurons are active, they change their own local blood supply. This makes it possible to trace areas of the brain that are active during cognitive processes . . .*[48]

Blood flow is just one way of seeing the brain in action. Better technology also allows us to measure electrical and chemical changes, as well as increased white matter tracts, which are evidence of myelination and speedier recall. Seeing the brain "in action" and in real time became a possibility, and with this came more knowledge, but also more myths.

The limitations of what we can see, however, continue to draw the parameters around what we report. The better the imaging techniques, the more accurate the information, and, thankfully, the more interest in the brain. This, along with global communication techniques, are reasons that articles on the brain continue to increase in number around the world. But widespread use does not mean accurate use. The spread of news about the brain is no longer limited to the reach of a physical newspaper article, but rather can have an audience of millions in short order, thanks to the Internet. The hunger to see a real human brain is immense, and only recently have we had the technology to allow nonspecialists to view this organ. This democratization of knowledge is powerful, but it can also be dangerous, as misinterpretations can occur, and myths as well as accurate information can be widely shared.

Neuroimages give a snapshot view of what really takes thousands of small molecular, chemical, electrical, and structural changes in the brain. The images, however, make things look much simpler than they really are. Beck suggests that "part of the allure of these data [from neuroimaging] is the deceptively simple messages they afford, as well as general, but sometimes misguided, confidence in biological data."[49] She cites multiple studies, including those by McCabe and Castel[50] and Weisberg and colleagues,[51] which offer evidence that people believe articles with fMRI scans more than logical arguments and bar graphs. This is likely because it's easier to believe that X part of the brain does Y than to delve into the complexities of the brain.

The National Institutes of Health's Human Connectome Project, which unites functional MRI, resting-state fMRI, diffusion MRI with MEG (magnetoencephalography), and EEG (electroencephalography) renders high-quality images of the most complex neural networks known to date. This permits images never before seen and changes the way we think about brain functioning. The Connectome is someplace in between the focus on molecular and cellular structures and observable behavior, creating the unique opportunity to unmask many neuromyths. These studies, however, do not often reach teachers.

The Allure of Headlines

Newspaper headlines often confirm something we already think is true or believe, which is accompanied by something else we are willing or want to believe. For example, belief that *"Eating a Full Course Seafood Meal Once a Week can Help You Stay Sharp"*[52] is a headline we'd all like to believe because we already think fish is better than red meat for our hearts, so we are willing to believe it's probably good for our brains. While newspaper reporting may offer good information, the headlines necessarily reduce the science to easily misinterpreted sound bites. If people do not read the whole article, they are left with an abbreviated version of the truth, which can be misinterpreted. If you just read the title *"Power Causes Brain Damage"*[53] and don't read the entire article to understand the two decades of serious studies underlying the article by U.C. Berkeley's Dacher Keltner, you may believe that people under the influence of power are "more impulsive, less risk-aware, and, crucially, less adept at seeing things from other people's point of view."[54] And you might think, well, that "power [electrical?] [physical?] [figurative?] [physical?] causes brain damage," as the headline says. McCall suggests that much popular press on the brain is "sensational or distorted"[55] and that many of us have a hard time discriminating information because we see only summarized headlines and not the deeper research behind the story.

Pasquinelli[56] coined the term "neurophilia" in 2012 to describe the fanatical belief in anything claiming to be brain-based, while Legrenzi and colleagues[57] warned of "neuromania" and the need to understand the limits of brain science. Headlines in the press use attractive words to bring in readership. *The Brain in the Headlines* from the OECD was a website that highlighted the absurd headlines from the popular press that misuse, misinterpret, or misunderstand the scientific articles they quoted. The OECD has tried conscientiously to educate people by placing popular press articles side by side with the original articles cited. Other websites and media, including local newspapers and television, are not as instructive. Headlines like *"'Pacemaker' for the Brain Can Help Memory, Study Finds"*[58]; *"The*

Part of Your Brain That Made You Eat That Doughnut"[59]; and *"Experts Excited by Brain 'Wonder-Drug'"*[60] excite readers about the brain, but perhaps for the wrong reasons.

If It Sounds Too Good to be True, It Probably Is!

Sometimes neuromyths come from promises that are too good to be true and are born because they are profitable. "Brain-friendly" products have become particularly sexy since the turn of the 21st century, when "neuromarketing" became popular,[61] and now any product with the word "brain" or "neuro" is attractive. Just as people believe information that is accompanied by brain scans more than the same information without brain scans,[62] the word "neuro" has a special magnetism. Koksma,[63] a particularly observant writer on this phenomenon from Radboud University in the Netherlands, notes:

> . . . *fast expansion of the neurosciences fuels an ongoing hype. The past decade has witnessed a mushrooming of 'new' disciplines trying to apply neuroscientific insights to societal domains. Such emerging fields of interdisciplinary study are invading the classroom ('neuroeducation'), the courthouse ('neurolaw'), the art gallery ('neuroesthetics'), the stock exchange ('neuroeconomics') . . .*

There are even dozens of companies around the world that earn money selling access to the "secrets" of the new neuroeconomy. It seems that just about everything from vitamins, learning to be creative or motivated, cures for dyslexia, chelation therapy for autism (TalkAboutCuringAutism), foods to boost your brainpower, and even brain-friendly cribs are currently all the rage on the Internet.

> *Enthusiasm for new information is good, but we need to avoid the allure of "quick fixes" in education unless they have solid evidence behind them. Suzanne Begley noted in her article, Beware of the cognitive brain paparazzi lurking in brain science labs,*[64] *that educators are sometimes guilty of grabbing onto cure-alls offered in the popular press without properly judging the quality of the information. Enthusiasm should partner with healthy skepticism in the careful examination of new instructional practices.*[65]

To history buffs, this is the equivalent of the "elixir" salesmen of the 1700s or the snake oil vendors of the 1800s, who tricked people into buying products that promised to cure ills and improve mental prowess. Luckily, commercial neuromyths are some of the easiest to spot. If something sounds too good to be true, it probably is. Testimonials are often used in place of data when there is not enough evidence available to back up claims. And claims about findings and the brain that are promoted by individuals with commercial interests in the product being sold should make consumers—especially teachers!—wary.

Avoid *Bandwagonitis*!

Sometimes people believe neuromyths because their friends and colleagues believe in the myth. As a 35-year teacher veteran and now a professor of education, McCall believes that some teachers suffer from *bandwagonitis*, "in this case, climbing impulsively in lemming-like fashion onto the brain-based wagon. Lack of a thorough knowledge of the brain-based approach (or any approach for that matter) before implementation leads to gross misapplication and hence developmentally inappropriate classroom practices."[66]

Bandwagonitis is often seen in learning communities, including schools and universities, in which an idea "takes off" and everyone follows, at least for a time. For example, the belief that mirror neurons were the explanation for all emotional imbalances, including autism, was all the rage for a time in the late 1990s. As *The Guardian* noted, "the discovery of mirror neurons was greeted with a great deal of excitement, and some have hailed it as one of the most important discoveries of modern neuroscience." The belief that mirror neurons were "the single most important 'unreported' (or at least, unpublicized) story of the decade"[67] was tempered, however, when they failed to live up to their promise.[68] For a few years the number of studies and claims rose steadily, until the claims just didn't seem to pan out.

Neuromyths still exist, and the many factors discussed in this chapter contribute to our willingness to believe them. This means that, despite the improvements in brain imaging tools and the number of serious studies available, it is incumbent on us, and especially those of us who are teachers, to improve their own knowledge about the brain, to use more scientific guidelines, and avoid incorrect assertions to avoid the myths. The distortion of facts, confirmation bias, and unsubstantiated beliefs will not go away on their own—we all share the responsibility to be more proactive in debunking myths.

12

CONCLUSION

Teachers matter.[1] In the Introduction we laid out the foundations of teachers' new pedagogical knowledge, including what "good" information exists—the 6 Principles and 21 Tenets agreed upon by the Delphi Panel in 2017[2]—as well as the importance of being able to identify neuromyths, their origins, and learn from the lessons they can teach us (Figure 12.1). Myths *do* harm and should be eliminated from teachers' belief systems if our profession is to thrive.

This book began as a response to the many cries for clarity about the brain and learning from the teaching community and was spurred on by the worrisome growth of the number of neuromyths touted in teacher professional development. The echo chambers of school hallways, newspapers, TV shows and magazines that promote neuro-enthusiasm for anything related to the brain, and the lack of common knowledge about this most complex organ in the universe, give life to myths that pollute educational goals. Neuromyths should be debunked so that quality information about complex teaching-learning processes can then be taught.

As we have seen throughout this book, however, debunking myths is not as easy as it might seem because it necessitates *un*learning prior beliefs, some of which we are very fond of and find hard to let go of. Luckily, neuromyths can also serve as starting points for better teacher education, and contribute to a new type of learning scientist who can transform our classrooms. The goal to rid our classrooms of myths is a first step in a new kind of teacher professionalization scheme.

The changing teacher profile in the 21st century requires new skill sets, including better knowledge of the brain and how it learns.[3] The goals of formal education have changed. We have evolved from equal access (nearly everyone goes to school) to equal quality; from teaching in silos (one subject separate from another) to transdisciplinarity; from conformity to creativity; from "passing a class" to lifelong learning; from traditional resources and tools to technology integration; from bettering the "self" to enhancing skills such as collaboration, cooperation, communication, and cultural awareness (bettering the group); from content knowledge to critical thinking; from brick-and-mortar classrooms to flipped, blended, and virtual environments. These changes demand many things, among them, a better understanding of the brain and how it learns as well as research methodologies that help us avoid neuromyths in the future described below.

CHARACTERISTICS OF MBE TEACHERS, OR LEARNING SCIENTISTS

The transdisciplinary field of Mind (psychology), Brain (neuroscience), and Education (pedagogy and didactics) science seeks to formalize a credible foundation for a new teacher knowledge base, and there are promising models emerging of how neuroscience literacy to become a part of formal teacher training programs. Until such programs are fully integrated and become a part of the background knowledge required of all teachers, there are four primary pieces of advice we can follow as individuals to avoid myths in the immediate future.

Healthy Skepticism

First and foremost, teachers need to look for as much information as possible, and to do so with a healthy skepticism. While many teachers do read peer-reviewed journals and are familiar with current research, others have little time for technical literature. We all need to read more broadly and deeply, rather than be swept away by headlines. We should not believe things just because lots of people try to sway us to do so, but rather, respect the evidence. Luckily, there are a growing number of learning science journals with digested versions of technical articles which are available to the general public. The growing availability of research in synthesized forms, such as that of the *Learning Sciences Community*, for example,[4] caters to the interest of teachers who want to learn more about quality information on the brain in learning without treading too far into their personal time or demanding too much specialist vocabulary. This type of translational research is becoming more and more readily available to teachers and increases the likelihood of core learning science ideas reaching the masses.

But teachers do not have to wait for others to interpret the information for them, they can be proactive in learning more on their own. This means we teachers also need to learn better research skills.

Accept the Evolving Nature of Science

Second, teachers should accept that science will evolve. New evidence will change the way we think about things we have taken for granted. The limits of technology once convinced us that we each had two brains (right and left) of which we only used ten percent, that were limited by styles of learning, which peaked around early childhood and on top of that, was limited by our genes. We now know better. Thanks to this information, more people can live up to greater potentials for learning than ever before because they are not shackled by these misconceptions.

As mentioned in the Introduction, the list of neuromyths has grown in the past decade and nothing identified as a myth a decade ago has suddenly become a truth thanks to new studies and technology. Rather, the more discoveries about the brain that occur, the more myths are born of the partial and incomplete data. Interestingly enough, with all the dynamic movement in neuroscience, nothing considered a Principle or "truth" has changed either. This means that in the spectrum from (a) well-established to (b) probably so; to (c) intelligent speculation; to (d) neuromyths, the "bookends" of evidence have remained relatively constant. Much of the information "in the middle"—probably so and intelligent speculation—have grown outwards towards the extremes. For example, the role of sleep and learning, once considered "probably so" has now become accepted as a Tenet of Mind, Brain, Education science (well-established), as there is finally enough evidence to support its use and justification of teaching in educator formation programs. The more we know about the brain, the more solid the "good" evidence is, and the firmer the "bad" (neuromyths) evidence becomes. This means staying up-to-date with latest findings is always the best advice for Mind, Brain and education teacher-practitioners. To do so, we need to learn core research skills.

Learn to Research

Third, teachers need to accept an expanded job description and become, at least to a certain extent, good research practitioners and learning scientists. This means at a minimum we should:

- Look for all the evidence, not just what we expect or hope to be true (review studies that test hypotheses, not just describe perceptions).
- Accept that sometimes the evidence is counterintuitive (be open to entertaining opposing ideas).
- Consider research that does not just confirm our own thinking or prior beliefs.
- Remember that just because two things occur simultaneously does not mean one caused the other (correlation vs. causation).

- Remember that information does not have to be exciting to be true.
- Remember that just because lots of people believe something does not make it true (*bandwagonitis*).
- Use only evidence-based interventions that are replicable (remembering that we might find there are different results due to methodological design).
- Remember to look for the most up-to-date studies (but don't forget the historical evolution of the science behind the recommendations).
- Remember that if something sounds too good to be true, it usually is.
- Appreciate that some studies will have different results on different people due to general human variation.
- Look at the global universe of studies, particularly those in contexts that are similar to real-life classrooms.
- Try and suspend judgement and test hypotheses rather than confirm what appears to be intelligent speculation.

In 2011, I suggested a way for teachers to follow a rigorous process to avoid neuromyths (Figure 12.1).

This figure guides research using basic questions that are easily answered after reading any "finding" in education. Is the claim supported by evidence? Was the study conducted in a context similar to your own (for example, a classroom rather than a lab?). Is the evidence offered based on an experiment with an age group similar to that of your interest (for example, school-age children rather than adults?). This series of questions is designed to identify pitfalls in research. This helps teachers themselves identify "good" from "bad" information on their own so that they can then help their students do the same.

Another guide for basic research comes from Ravitch's and Riggan's work.[5] These authors motivate teachers to read broadly and to then create their own visions of the information at hand, rather than simply adopting a conceptual framework from a single source: "Reality is always more complex than any [single] theory can completely capture."[6] This advice is crucial in gaining a well-rounded understanding of a topic rather than just buying in to the first source. Teachers should read more than the popular press and use Google Scholar (or other academic databases) rather than just Google, Yahoo, or other popular search engines when looking for information. They also recommend adopting an open-minded frame for change. Learning is a dynamic process dependent on continual revision. When new information emerges, teachers are encouraged to review it critically and think about how it does or does not fit past beliefs on the topic. This means it is crucial to keep an open mind, but this advice, too, can cause confusion.

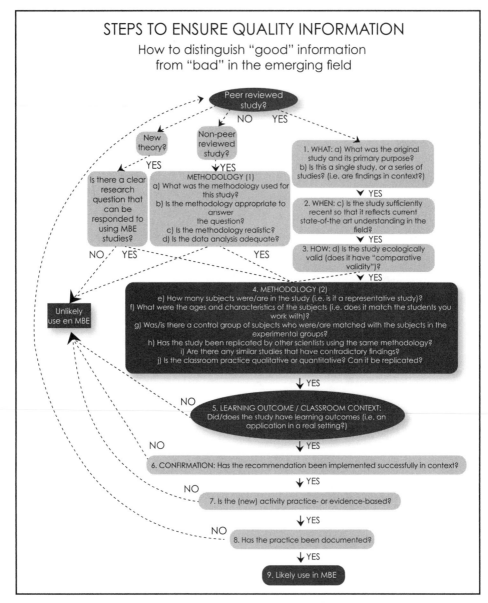

Figure 12.1: *Steps to Ensure Quality Information*

To avoid bad information in the future and spot neuromyths on their own, teachers need to be wary of studies in which the statistical results might not be of the highest relevance (subtraction method and averaging).[7] This means we should avoid studies in which information is found to be "true" but with such a small effect size that it's almost irrelevant. For example, music *does* influence student learning outcomes for some students, but the effect size is much smaller than getting a good night's sleep. This means teachers should spend more time educating about sleep hygiene than playing classical music.

We also need to be careful to avoid studies in which results on the same subject can differ due to methodological and theoretical considerations.[7] For example, the same survey with slightly different instructions, even a single word difference, can lead to different results.

We need to question studies if they rely on small laboratory reports (of single case studies or small groups) and generalize findings to apply to whole classroom applications. This means the laboratory setting might not be the appropriate place to test a skill, as it is an unnatural and contrived setting.[7] For example, teaching reading under lab conditions is very different from teaching reading with 30 small children running around in a real classroom. We should also be cautious of animal studies that generalize cognitive abilities, such as memory, as these are, too, not the same as human classroom contexts.

Another cause to be wary is when a single study tries to justify a certain classroom strategy.[7] For example, just because a grad student declares that "classical music *does* improve learning!" because she found the majority of her preschool children seemed to pay more attention after listening to Mozart, does not mean the entire school should adopt this practice.

It's important to be cautious of popular press articles, which are perhaps the most prominent sources of myths. In order to appeal to the greatest number of people, newspapers, magazines and websites often report brain research in over-simplified terms; this is the origin of a large number of misconceptions and misunderstandings about science.[7] In this book we mentioned dozens of such articles, but there are hundreds more which surround us at every turn. We must be more cautious consumers of information and protect ourselves against overgeneralizations and sensationalism of the popular press.

Red flags of poor information are when the study represents a single, isolated case rather than multiple studies. Teachers should ask themselves if this is a single study, or are there others to support the claims being made?[8] Lone studies should never be the foundation for a policy change.

Teachers should also worry if it seems that the study is *describing an event* as opposed to *testing a hypothesis*. For example, instead of responding to the research question, "How and to what extent do extra chess classes after school improve self-regulation?" the article describes the concentration on the faces of little children as they move the chess pieces. This means teachers should ask themselves if the study seems to describe what a teacher sees in a class, as opposed to the collection of data to answer a research question.[8] While learning to observe is important, documenting experiences does not constitute research if it has not followed established protocols or does not go beyond the teacher's personal recollection of events.

Another red flag is if the information seems of high quality, but has nothing to do with school-age populations. (Is the study about rats instead of school-age children?) Teachers should be wary of studies that make claims about student learning when their subjects were not students. While there are few studies on school-age populations, these are the best indicators of good information that has the potential to be applicable to real classroom contexts.[8]

Finally, it's important to consider the context. There are only a handful of new experiments taking place within real class contexts that measure neuroscientific data. These are currently the gold stars in the field and yield superior results compared to lab-only situations. For example, the Brain and Behavior Laboratory in Queensland University is currently conducting a variety of studies in which students, learning in real environments, in real time with real constraints of classrooms are being studied.[9]

Good Research: Rule of Thumb

As a rule of thumb, teachers can have confidence in studies that are current, replicated, conducted on humans (preferably school-age children), take into account the complexities of learning, and represent "real" skills and not just lab design.

Celebrate Complexity

As a final comment, it is worth stating the obvious. As educators we need to learn to celebrate the complexities of the brain. Thanks to the many sub-elements of cognition that are now visible, much of the good news about the myths presented in this book celebrates the new precision we can have as teachers. Great teachers in the modern era avoid simplistic answers, as they are generally incomplete; great teaching requires appreciating how to maximize the potential of the most complex organ in the universe, the brain.[10] This means teachers need to learn additional vocabulary that comes from neuroscience and psychology and integrate this into our regular practice. This is not as painful as it might sound, and it is more satisfying than one might imagine. To begin utilizing this information, a good starting point is with the basic Mind, Brain, and Education Science Principles and Tenets, shared in the Introduction as illustrated in Figure 12.2.

As teachers, we have the most important job in society, educating the next generation. Our art of teaching must be complemented with the learning sciences if we are to take this seriously. Neuromyths are a springboard for reflection and can teach us a lot about research, communication, marketing, social interactions, and most importantly, education. They teach us about why it's natural to want things to be easy and go along the crowd. But most of all, neuromyths show why it's necessary to resist the allure of headlines and delve into the evidence, both to honor our profession and to benefit the students in our care.

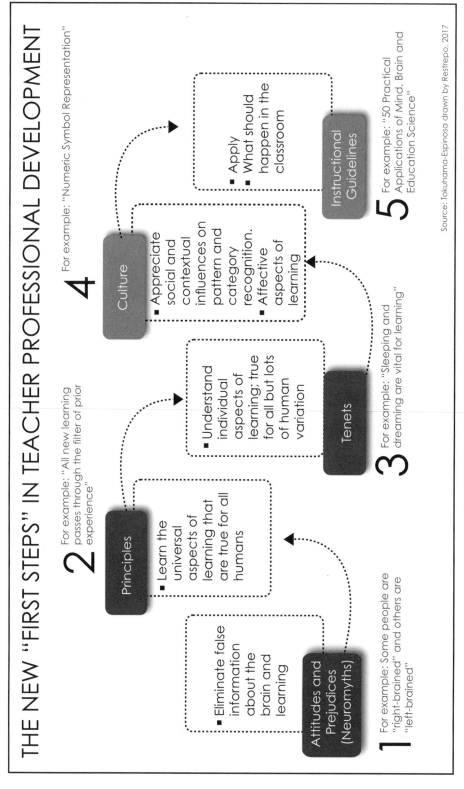

Figure 12.2: The New Teacher Training Model

ENDNOTES

Introduction

1. Bruer, 1997
2. Tokuhama-Espinosa, 2017. Link to study: https://www.researchgate.net/publication/315779095_Delphi_Panel_on_Mind_Brain_and_Education_2016_RESULTS
3. Tokuhama-Espinosa, 2017. Delphi panel mini-libraries on MBE topics. Link to mini-libraries: https://drive.google.com/file/d/1Yi5mlJidMrbgL0GMpsH4gCS4_c6O9ru1/view?usp=sharing
4. Thanks in great part to the pioneering work of Louis Pasteur (1860).
5. Goswami, 2008
6. Miescher, 1860
7. Watson & Crick, 1953
8. Waddington, 1942
9. Rabi, Millman, Kusch & Zacharias, 1939.
10. Landhuis, 2017
11. Elkhorne, 1967, p. 52
12. Carter BloodCare, 2016
13. Flynn, 1984; 1987a; 1987b; 2012
14. Clark, Lawlor-Savage & Goghari, 2016, p. 41
15. Haigh et al., 2017; Fiegerman, 2017
16. Ab Kadir, 2017
17. OECD, 2016
18. Darling-Hammond et al., 2009
19. Macdonald, Germine, Anderson, Christodoulou & McGrath, 2017
20. Society For Neuroscience, 2008
21. Howard-Jones, 2014, p. 817
22. Deans For Impact, 2015
23. Howard-Jones, 2014

24. Dekker, Lee, Howard-Jones & Jolles, 2012, para.1

25. Guerrero, 2017

26. Reynolds, 2007

27. Quart, 2006

28. Payne, 2012

29. Howard-Jones, 2014, p. 817

30. Dekker, Lee, Howard-Jones & Jolles, 2012, p. 1

31. Crockard 1996, as cited in Howard-Jones, 2014, p.817.

32. Howard-Jones, 2014, p. 817

33. Knowland, n.d.

34. McCall, 2012

35. Agarwal et al., 2012; Alferink & Farmer-Dougan, 2010; Christodoulou & Gaab, 2009; Eisenhart & DeHaan, 2005; Goswami, 2006; Hille, 2011; Howard-Jones et al., 2009

36. Jarrett, 2014, p. 5

37. Tokuhama-Espinosa, 2008

38. Tokuhama-Espinosa, 2017

39. Wellcome Trust, 2016

40. Guerrero, 2017

Chapter 1

1. Elderton, 1923

2. Bagley, 1925

3. Pickford, 1949

4. Das & Broadhurst, 1959

5. Herrnstein & Murray, 1994

6. Herrnstein & Murray, 1994, p. 109

7. Jacoby & Glauberman, 1995; Kincheloe, Steinberg, & Gresson, 1997

8. Ridley, 2003

9. Moore, 1986

10. Lavin & Hyllegard, 1996; Machin, 2006; Schuller & Desjardins, 2007

11. Willms, 2010

12. Redick, 2015

13. Ritchie, Bates, & Deary, 2015

14. Doidge, 2007, p. 26

15. Dweck, 2006, 2015, 2017

16. Knapton, 2015

17. Dweck, 2015, p. 20

18. Hattie, 2012

19. Tokuhama-Espinosa, 2014

20. Plomin & Deary, 2015

21. Polderman, Benyamin, De Leeuw, Sullivan, Van Bochoven, Visscher & Posthuma, 2015, p. 2
22. Cushman, 2017
23. Jaeggi, Buschkuehl, Jonides & Perrig, 2008, p. 6829
24. Kyllonen & Christal, 1990
25. Plomin & Dery, 2015; Polderman, Benyamin, De Leeuw, Sullivan, Van Bochoven, Visscher & Posthuma,, 2015
26. Dobbie, Fryer, & Fryer, 2011; Hanushek, 2013; Kirp, 2015
27. Swanson & McMurran, 2017
28. Eysenck, 1995
29. Galton, 1869, p. B
30. Albett, 1969
31. Ericsson, 1998; 2007; 2008; 2014
32. Kaufman, 2009
33. Alferink & Farmer-Dougan, 2010; Ansari, 2015; Boyd, 2008; Christodoulou & Gaab, 2009; Dekker, Lee, Howard-Jones & Jolles, 2012, 2012; Deligiannidi & Howard-Jones, 2015; Ferrero, Garaizar & Vadillo, 2016; Geake, 2005; Geake, 2008; Howard-Jones, 2014; Karakus, Howard-Jones & Jay 2015; OECD, 2002; OECD, 2007; Pei , Howard-Jones, Zhang, Liu & Jin, 2015; Willis, 2015
34. Higbee & Clay, 1998
35. Radford, 1999
36. Aamodt & Wang, 2009
37. Beyerstein, 1999; Myss, 1998
38. Beyerstein, 1999
39. Leng & Shaw, 1991
40. Rauscher, Shaw & Ky, 1993
41. Rauscher, Shaw & Ky, 1995, p. 4
42. Chablis, 1999
43. Krakovsky, 2005, p. 1
44. Hahne, 2012, para.1
45. Pietschnig, Voracek & Formann, 2010, p. 314
46. Rauscher, Shaw & Ky, 1995, p. 44
47. Darwin, n.d., Chapter XXI, p. 7
48. Fine, 2005
49. Kimura, 2002
50. Tokuhama-Espinosa, 2009, p. 1
51. Robert, 2005
52. Moore, 1986
53. Rose, 2009
54. Taylor, Miller, Farrington, Petropoulos, Favot-Mayaud, Li & Waight, 1999.
55. Aamodt & Wang, 2009, p. 1

56. Rosenbaum, 2017
57. Kanner, 1943
58. Aamodt & Wang, 2009, p. 1
59. Timothy, Chahrour, Coulter, Jiralerspong, Okamura-Ikeda, Ataman, . . . & D'Gama, 2013
60. Sealey, Hughes, Sriskanda, Guest, Gibson, Johnson-Williams, . . . & Bagasra, 2016
61. Williams, Woolfenden, Roberts, Rodger, Bartak & Prior, 2014
62. Hattie, 2008; 2012
63. Darling-Hammond, 2015
64. Dweck, 2011
65. Didlake & Fordham, 2014

Chapter 2

1. Dew, 1996; Leonard & Straus, 1997; Springer & Deutsch, 1993, 1998
2. Blakeslee, 1980
3. Calhoun, 2018
4. Sperry, 1961; 1968; 1975
5. Sperry, 1961, p.174
6. Banich & Heller, 1998
7. Ansari, 2015; Bruner, 1999; Carew & Magsamen, 2010; Christodoulou & Gaab, 2009; Dekker, Lee, Howard-Jones & Jolles, 2012; Deligiannidi & Howard-Jones, 2015; Ferrero, Garaizar & Vadillo, 2016; Goswami, 2014; Howard-Jones, 2014; Karakus, Howard-Jones & Jay, 2015; Leahy, Shore, & Lambert, 2017a, 2017b; McCall, 2012; Nielson, Zielinski, Ferguson, Lainhart & Anderson, 2013; OECD, 2002; OECD, 2007; Singh & O'Boyle, 2004; Smith, 1996; Weigmann, 2013
8. Zimmer, 2005
9. Bever & Chiarello, 1974
10. Kimura, 1961
11. Scovel, 1969
12. Broca, 1861; Wernicke, 1885
13. Alexandrou, et al., 2017; Gurin & Blum, 2017; Horowitz-Kraus, et al., 2015; Shibata et al., 2017
14. Groen, Whitehouse, Badcock & Bishop, 2013, p. e64876
15. Bruer, 1998; 1999
16. Freed & Parsons, 1998; Halary & Weintrayub, 1991
17. Tokuhama-Espinosa, 2009, p. 1
18. Battro, 2003
19. Immordino-Yang, 2007
20. Bach-y-Rita, 1992
21. Hyatt, 2007

22. Dekker, Lee, Howard-Jones & Jolles, 2012; Deligiannidi & Howard-Jones, 2015; Howard-Jones, 2014; Karakus, Howard-Jones & Jay, 2015; Pei, Howard-Jones, Zhang, Liu & Jin, 2015

23. Sladkey, 2013

24. Conyers & Wilson, 2014

25. Chang, Labban, Gapin & Etnier, 2012

26. van der Knaap & van der Ham, 2011

27. Active Living Research, 2013, p. 3

28. Hopkins, Davis, VanTieghem, Whalen & Bucci, 2012, p. 59

29. Nanda, Balde & Manjunatha, 2013, p. 1883

30. e.g., Jorgenson, 2015

31. ThoughtCo, 2016, para.1

32. Deligiannidi & Howard-Jones, 2015; Singh & O'Boyle, 2004; Society for Neuroscience, 2012

33. Pink, 2006

34. e.g., Hermann & Hermann-Nehdi, 2012

35. Sokolvich, 2015

36. Digital Superheroes, 2017

37. Bargmann & Marder, 2013; National Institutes of Health, 2017; Xia, Wang & He, 2013

38. Hrala, 2017

39. Deligiannidi & Howard-Jones, 2015; Pei et al., 2015

40. Tokuhama-Espinosa & Rivera, 2013

41. Tokuhama-Espinosa, 2015, p. 139

42. Xia, Wang, He, 2013, para 24

43. Semenza, Delazer, Bertella, Grana, Mori, Conti, . . . & Mauro, 2006

44. Edwards, 2012

45. Stephens, 2016

46. Caputi et al., 1995

47. Hellige, 1993

48. Gall & Spurzheim, 1810

49. Acharya et al., 2012

50. Herculano-Houzel, 2014

51. Bargmann & Marder, 2013

52. Walker & Bright, 2009

53. Salovey & Mayer, 1990

54. Goleman, 1995

55. Williamson, 2015

56. Reeve, 2014

57. Agid, 2016

58. Bechara, 2004

59. Immordino-Yang & Damasio, 2007
60. Carus, 1905
61. Damasio, 2005
62. Doidge, 2007, p. 17
63. Smart, 1959
64. LeDoux, 1998
65. Immordino-Yang, 2015
66. Gowan, 1979
67. Levy-Agresi & Sperry, 1968
68. Kimura, 1967
69. Nebes, 1974
70. Zargwill, 1961
71. Gordon, 1964
72. Harpaz, 1990, p. 161
73. Harpaz, 1990; Heilman, Nadeau & Beversdorf, 2003
74. Heilman, 2016, p. 285
75. Raichle, et al., 2001
76. Beaty et al., 2014, p. 92
77. Harvard Medical School, 2011
78. Benton & Young, 2015, p.83
79. D'Anci Constant & Rosenberg, 2006
80. Bar-David, et al., 2005
81. Benton & Young, 2015, p. 1
82. Benton & Young, 2015, p. 11
83. Roth Hursh, 2017
84. Howard-Jones, 2014, p.817
85. Valtin, 2002
86. Cheuvront & Kenefick, 2014; Masento, Golightly, Field, Butler & van Reekum, 2014
87. Howard-Jones, 2014, p.817
88. Roth Hursh, 2017
89. Mitchell, Hamilton, Steggerda, & Bean, 1945
90. Tokuhama-Espinosa, 2009, p. 1
91. Finlayson, 2010
92. Estabrooks, 1928, p. 524
93. Cheong, Anderson, Roberts, Burnett, Lee, Thompson, . . . & Wood, 2013; Pryor & Thelander, 1968
94. Belfort, Anderson, Nowak, Lee, Molesworth, Thompson, . . . & Inder, 2016
95. McDaniel, 2005; Rushton & Ankney, 1996
96. Lange, Froimowitz, Bigler, Lainhart & Brain Development Cooperative Group, 2010
97. Lange, Froimowitz, Bigler, Lainhart & Brain Development Cooperative Group, p. 296

98. Lynn & Vanhanen, 2002

99. Dickens & Flynn, 2006; Murray, 2006

100. Lechtenberg, 2014

101. Chittka & Niven, 2009; Herculano-Houzel, Manger & Kaas, 2014; Hofman, 2014

102. Cairó, 2011, p. 5

103. Montgomery, Capellini, Barton & Mundy, 2010

104. Cairó, 2011, p. 6

105. Allen, Damasio & Grabowski, 2002

106. Pietschnig, Penke, Wicherts, Zeiler & Voracek, 2015, p. 411

107. e.g., Réu, Khosravi, Bernard, Mold, Salehpour, Alkass, . . . & Frisén, 2017

108. Herculano-Houzel, 2002

109. *Daily Mail Reporter*, 2015, p. 1

110. Ghose, 2016a

111. Brueck, 2015

112. Collins, 2016

113. De Charm, 2008

114. Spreng, 2013

115. Grabianowski, 2010

116. Choi, 2013

117. see Hoffman & Morcom, 2017 for more details about this specific example

118. Anderson, Pyke & Fincham, 2016, p. 1225

119. National Institutes of Health, 2017

120. Wiggins & McTighe, 2005

Chapter 3

1. Willingham, Hughes & Dobolyi, 2015

2. Gardner, 1983

3. Pashler, McDaniel, Rohrer & Bjork, 2008

4. Coffield, Moseley, Hall & Ecclestone, 2004; Pashler, McDaniel, Rohrer & Bjork, p. 105

5. Alferink & Farmer-Dougan, 2010; Coffield, Moseley, Hall & Ecclestone, 2004; Gilmore, McCarthy & Spelke, 2007; Leahy, Shore & Lambert , 2017a; Mcdaniel, Rohrer, Bjork & Pashler, 2009; Newton, 2015; ; Riener & Willingham, 2010; Weigmann, 2013; Willis, 2015; Willingham, Hughes & Dobolyi, 2015

6. Wilson, 2011

7. Hattie, 2012

8. Deno, 1973

9. Coop & Sigel, 1971

10. Jung, 1921

11. Kendall, 2017

12. Keirsey, 1978

13. McCrea & Costa, 1989

14. Goldberg, 1990

15. Riechmann & Grasha, 1974, p.213

16. Kolb, 1981

17. Hughes, 2012

18. Pashler, McDaniel, Rohrer & Bjork, 2008, p. 106

19. Willingham, Hughes & Dobolyi, 2015, p. 268

20. Dunn, DeBello, Brennan, Krimsky & Murrain, 1981, p. 373. Also see Dunn & Dunn, 2017

21. Newton & Miah, 2017

22. Canfield, 2017; Hay Group Global, 2017; LearningRx Center, 2017

23. Pashler, McDaniel, Rohrer & Bjork, 2008, p. 105

24. Massa & Mayer, 2006

25. Royal & Stockdale, 2015

26. Hughes, 2012

27. Leahy, Shore & Lambert, 2017b

28. Gardner, 1983

29. Checkley, 1997

30. Gardner, 1999, p. 36

31. Gardner & Moran, 2006, p. 227

32. Gardner, 1999, p. 103

33. Gardner & Connell, 2000, p. 292

34. Gardner & Moran, 2006

35. Perkins, 2010

36. e.g., Allix, 2000

37. Posner, 2003, p. 3; p. 2

38. Pinel & Dehaene, 2010

39. Gardner, 1999, p. 99

40. Gardner, 1983; Gardner, 1993

41. Davis, Christodoulou, Seider & Gardner, 2011, p. 11

42. Shearer & Karanian, 2017

43. Tokuhama-Espinosa & Rivera, 2013

44. Howard-Jones, 2014, p. 818

45. Willingham, 2004, p. 19

46. Willingham, 2004, p. 23

47. Gardner & Moran, 2006

48. Cerasoli, Nicklin & Ford, 2014

49. Briggs, 1975

50. Hattie, 2012; 2015

51. Deci, Koestner & Ryan, 1999; Lepper, Henderlong & Gingras, 1999

52. Cerasoli, Nicklin & Ford, 2014

53. Mendler, 2009

54. Gruber & Gruber, 2002

55. Gershon, 2015

56. Radel, Sarrazin, Legrain & Wild, 2010

57. Hattie, 2012

58. Emmanuel, Adam, Josephine & Solomon, 2014

59. Ryan & Deci, 2016

60. Bear, Slaughter, Mantz & Farley-Ripple, 2017

61. Gotfried, 1990

62. Shernoff, Abdi, Anderson & Csikszentmihalyi, 2014; Shernoff, Csikszentmihalyi, Shneider & Shernoff, 2003

63. Hardre & Reeve, 2003; Vallerand, Pelletier, Blais, Briere, Senecal & Vallieres, 1992

64. Grant, 2008; Augustyniak, Ables, Guilford, Lujan, Cortright & DiCarlo, 2016, p. 465

65. Gess-Newsome, 2015

66. Hattie, 2008

67. Marzano, Marzano & Pickering, 2003

68. Fisher, Frey, Quaglia, Smith & Lande, 2017

69. Pekrun, 1992

70. Kim & Pekrun, 2014

71. Purkey, 1970; Hattie, 2012

72. Vicinus, 2013

73. Jussim & Harber, 2005

74. Oberle & Schonert-Reichl, 2016; Radel, Sarrazin, Legrain & Wild, 2010

75. Ochsner & Lieberman, 2001, p. 717

76. Radel, Sarrazin, Legrain & Wild, 2010

77. Ekman, 2003

78. Pavlov, 1941

79. Murphy & Cowan, 1954; Olds & Milner, 1954

80. Bell, 2013, p. 1

81. Willis, 2007

82. Banks, 2015, p. 1

83. Olds & Milner, 1954

84. Jacques, 1979

85. Adcock, Thangavel, Whitfield-Gabrieli, Knutson & Gabrieli, 2006, p. 507

86. Grogan, Bogacz, Tsivos, Whone & Coulthard, 2015, p. 2035

87. Flagel, Clark, Robinson, Mayo, Czuj, Willuhn, Akers, Clinton, Phillips & Akll, 2011; Molina-Luna, Pekanovic, Röhrich, Hertler, Schubring-Giese, Rioult-Pedotti & Luft, 2009

88. Kim & Pekrun, 2014

89. Andresen, 2017; Green, 2016; Johansen, Diaz-Mataix, Hamanaka, Ozawa, Ycu, Koivumaa, . . . & LeDoux, 2014

90. Cagniard, Balsam, Brunner & Zhuang, 2006
91. Schmidhuber, 2010
92. Brück, Di Maio & Miaari, 2014
93. Ruff & Fehr, 2014
94. Clark, 2015
95. Stein & Belluzzi, 2014
96. Maag, 2001
97. Walker & Buckley, 1968
98. Nelsen, 1996; Smith, Fisher, & Frey, 2015
99. Chu et al., 2012, p. 8
100. Butler, 1663
101. Lam, Cheng & Yang, 2017, p. 265
102. Payne & Dozier, 2013, p. 699
103. LeGray et al., 2013
104. Hattie, 2012
105. e.g., Putwain, Sander & Larkin, 2013
106. Komarraju & Nadler, 2013
107. Deci, Koestner & Ryan, 2001
108. Eppich, Hunt, Duval-Arnould, Siddall & Cheng, 2015
109. Morgado-Bernal, 2011; Tokuhama-Espinosa, 2017
110. Marzano, 2011
111. Ericsson, 2006
112. Pusic, Kessler, Szyld, Kalet, Pecaric & Boutis, 2012; Zollo & Winter, 2002
113. Taubert et al., 2010
114. Posner, 2016
115. Ebbinghaus, 1885
116. Krugman, 1965
117. Tutorialspoint, n.d.
118. Ebbinghaus, 1885; Krugman, 1972
119. Dewey, 1933, 1937, 1938
120. Creedon, 1974
121. Powell & Kalina, 2009
122. Rogers, Lyon & Tausch, 2013
123. Díaz-Méndez & Gummesson, 2012
124. Szybnski, 2006
125. Wiggins & McTighe, 2005
126. Luke, 2014
127. Hauser & Palloni, 2010
128. Dalton, 1883
129. Kaplan & Saccuzzo, 2010
130. Terman, 1916

131. Thurston, 1935
132. Cattell, 1941
133. Horn, 1966
134. Carroll, 1993
135. Kaufman, 2009
136. Weiss, Saklofske, Coalson & Raiford, 2010
137. Binet & Simon, 1916
138. Schrank, 2005
139. Raven, 1981
140. Bain & Jaspers, 2010
141. Elliott, 2012
142. Naglieri, 2015
143. Organisation for Economic Co-Operation and Development, 2015, para 1
144. Organisation for Economic Co-Operation and Development, 2017, para.1
145. International Association for the Evaluation of Educational Achievement, 2015
146. International Association for the Evaluation of Educational Achievement, 2016
147. Coughlan, 2012
148. Layton, 2015, p. E-1
149. Fletcher, 2009, para.1
150. Layton, 2015
151. Public Broadcasting Service, 2014, para. 1
152. Ronen, 2013
153. Rose, 2013, p. ix
154. Public Broadcasting Service, 2014, para. 1
155. Public Broadcasting Service, 2014;
156. Organisation for Economic Co-Operation and Development, 2013
157. Naglieri, 2015
158. Strauss, 2017, para. 14
159. Schnotz & Bannert, 2003; van Kesteren et al., 2012
160. Cerrti, 2013
161. Hattie, 2012
162. Kit, Liem, Ang, Chong & Huan, 2016
163. Fisher, Frey, Quaglia, Smith & Lande, 2017; Wubbels, Brekelmans, Mainhard, den Brok & van Tartwijk, 2016

Chapter 4

1. Locke, 1690
2. Locke, 1690, para. 2
3. Aristotle, c.350 B.C.E.
4. Pinker, 2004
5. Azevedo, Carvalho, Grinberg, Farfel, Ferretti, Leite, . . . & Herculano-Houzel, 2009

6. Eriksson, Perfilieva, Björk-Eriksson, Alborn, Nordborg, Peterson & Gage, 1998

7. Business Standard, 2017

8. Peters, 2016

9. Bartheld, et al., 2016

10. NeuroMorph.Org, 2017

11. Ernst & Frisén, 2015, p. e1002045

12. Spalding, Bergmann, Alkass, Bernard, Salehpour, Huttner, Boström, Westerlund & Vial, 2013, p. 1183

13. Jabr, 2012

14. Sailor, et al., 2017

15. Spalding, Bergmann, Alkass, Bernard, Salehpour, Huttner, Boström, Westerlund & Vial, 2013; Ernst & Frisén, 2015, p. e1002045

16. Bruer, 1997

17. Bruer, 2014

18. Bruer, 1999

19. OECD, 2007

20. Macvarish, Lee & Lowe, 2014, p. 792

21. Wheeden et al., 1993

22. Field, 2001

23. McClure, 2010

24. Moore, 2014

25. Roberts & Glover, 2008

26. Rosenzweig, Bennett, Diamond, Wu, Slagle & Saffran, 1969

27. Curtiss, 1977

28. Gordon, 1971

29. Lapeer & Prager, 2001

30. Volpe, 2008

31. Nellhaus, 1968

32. Kagan, 1998

33. Macvarish, Lee & Lowe, 2014, p. 793

34. Macvarish, Lee & Lowe, 2014, p. 794

35. Syed & Seiffge-Krenke, 2013

36. Spear, 2014

37. Arain, Haque, Johal, Mathur, Nel, Rais, . . . & Sharma, 2013

38. Reyna, Chapman, Dougherty & Confrey, 2012

39. Kail & Cavanaugh, 2015

40. Hedman, van Haren, Schnack, Kahn, Pol & Hilleke, 2012

41. Ferrero, Garaizar & Vadillo, 2016

42. McMahon, 2015

43. Organisation for Economic Co-Operation and Development, 2016

44. Chang, 2014; Petrini, Pollick, Dahl, McAleer, McKay, Rocchesso, . . . & Puce, 2011; Yang, 2015

45. Organisation for Economic Co-Operation and Development, 2007, p. 2

46. Pujol et al., 1993

47. Organisation for Economic Co-Operation and Development, 2007, p. 1

48. Khundrakpam, Lewis, Zhao, Chouinard-Decorte & Evans, 2016

49. Lebel & Beaulieu, 2011

50. Sowell, E. R., Peterson, B. S., Kan, E., Woods, R. P., Yoshii, J., Bansal, R., . . . & Toga, A. W., 2006

51. Lerner, 2001

52. Piaget, 1971

53. Commons & Rodriguez, 1993; Commons, Trudeau, Stein, Richards & Krause, 1998

54. Fischer & Bidell, 2006, p. 313

55. Stewart, 2016

56. Crawford, 2016

57. Wallis, 2013

58. Mondale, 2011

59. Karmiloff-Smith, 2012; Mareschal, 2007

60. Murre & Dros, 2015; Voelker et al., 2017

61. Tokuhama-Espinosa, 2014, p. 258

62. Green & Piel, 2015

63. Eaton, Bodnarchuk & McKeen, 2014

64. Ferrero, Garaizar & Vadillo, 2016

65. Dekker, Lee, Howard-Jones & Jolle, 2012

66. Karakus & Howard-Jones, 2014

67. Gleichgerrcht, Luttges, Salvarezza & Campos, 2015

68. Deligiannidi & Howard-Jones, 2015

69. Pei, Howard-Jones, Zhang, Liu & Jin, 2014

70. Doidge, 2007

71. Armstrong, Armstrong & Barton, 2016

72. Tomlinson & Imbeau, 2010, p. 3

73. Tomlinson & Imbeau, 2010

74. Guskey, 2010, p. 57

75. United Nations, 2015

76. Staats, 2016

77. Norbury & Sonuga-Barke, 2017

78. Lee & Bull, 2016

79. Moll et al., 2016

80. Kail, et al., 2016

81. Payne & Isaacs, 2017

82. Nesayan, et al., 2018

83. Sharma & Sharma, 2015

84. Galván, 2017

85. Tanner & Arnett, 2016

86. Benaroch, 2007

87. Bennie, 2016

88. Roben, Cole & Armstrong, 2013

89. Potegal & Davidson, 2003; Potegal, Kosorok, & Davidson, 2003

90. Arain, Haque, Johal, Mathur, Nel, Rais, . . . & Sharma, 2013, p. 449

91. Arain, Haque, Johal, Mathur, Nel, Rais, . . . & Sharma, 2013, p. 449

92. Fields & Stevens-Graham 2002; Giedd, 2015

93. Talukder, 2013

94. Smith, Chein & Steinberg, 2013, p. 323

95. Blakemore, 2007

96. *Parenting*, 2015

97. Ritter, 2017

98. Veciana-Suarez, 2015

99. Ritter, 2017

100. Bhabha, 2014; Steinberg, 2013

101. Steinberg & Scott, 2003, p. 109

102. Onderko, 2017, para. 3; Potegal & Davidson, 2003

103. Suleiman & Dahl, 2017

104. Ernst, Pine & Hardin, 2006

105. Cohen & Casey, 2014

106. Williams & Davey, 2016

107. Potegal, Kosorok & Davidson, 2003, p. 148

108. Roben, Cole & Armstrong, 2013

109. Wittgenstein, 1922

110. Briggs-Gowan, Carter, Bosson-Heenan, Guyer & Horwitz, 2006, p. 849

111. U.S. Census Bureau, 2010; U.S. Census Bureau, 2015

112. U.S. Department of Justice, 2015; Office of Juvenile Justice and Delinquency Prevention, 2017

113. Siegel, 2015

114. Siegel, 2014, para. 4-9

115. Dosenbach, Petersen & Schlaggar,, 2013

116. Gazzaniga, 2012

117. Cohen & Casey, 2014, p. 64

118. Allan, 2014, para. 16

119. Rubie-Davies, Hattie & Hamilton, 2006

Chapter 5

1. Bergland, 2012

2. Kagan & Kagan, 2005

3. Greenough & Volkmar, 1973; West & Greenough, 1972

4. Diamond, Greer, York, Lewis, Barton & Lin, 1987
5. Fowler, 1969
6. OECD, 2002, p. 73
7. Samms-Vaughan, 2015, slide 9
8. Hart & Risley, 2003
9. Heckman, 2011, p. 32
10. Perry & Pollard, 1997; Perry, 2002
11. *Parents*, 2017
12. Hartinger, Lanata, Hattendorf, Wolf, Gil, Ortiz Obando, Noblega, Verastegui & Mäusezahl, 2016
13. Gertler, Heckman, Pinto, Zanolini, Vermeersch, Walker, . . . & Grantham-McGregor, 2014
14. Carey, 2014
15. OCED, 2002
16. Goswami, cited in OCED, 2004, p. 11
17. OCED, 2002, p. 74
18. Farah, 2012
19. Avants, Betancourt, Giannetta, Lawson, Gee, Farah & Hurt, 2012, p. 3159
20. Baker-Henningham & Lopez Boo, 2010
21. Albarran, 2016
22. Parsons, 2017
23. Google Scholar, 2010–2017: DOES cause violent behavior n=449 in 2017; n=7,000 between 2010 and 2017; DOES NOT cause violent behavior n=423 in 2017; n=6,520 between 2010 and 2017
24. Engelhardt, Bartholow, Kerr & Bushman, , 2011
25. Weber, Ritterfeld & Mathiak, 2006
26. Gentile, Li, Khoo, Prot & Anderson, 2014
27. Gentile, Li, Khoo, Prot & Anderson, 2014, p. 456
28. Calvert, Appelbaum, Dodge, Graham, Nagayama Hall, Hamby, . . . & Hedges, 2017, p. 126
29. Sehgal, 2016
30. Carr, 2010
31. Weinberger, 2012
32. Kaplan, 2015
33. Wellman, Haase, Witte & Hampton, 2001
34. Mills, 2014
35. Kenner, 1905
36. Maccoby, 1951
37. Becker, 1990
38. Berk & Weil, 2015
39. Kelly, McCain, & Jukes, 2008

40. Jukes, 2010
41. Bloom, 1971
42. Tokuhama-Espinosa, 2017
43. Tokuhama-Espinosa, 2015, p. 1
44. Duncan, Dowsett, Claessens, Magnuson, Huston, Klebanov, . . . & Sexton, 2007
45. Tokuhama-Espinosa, 2010
46. Rosetta Stone, 2017
47. SharpBrain, 2016
48. Ledger, 2015
49. Simons, Boot, Charness, Gathercole, Chabris, Hambrick & Stine-Morrow, 2016, para. 3
50. Foroughi, Monfort, Paczynski, McKnight & Greenwood, 2016
51. Federal Trade Commission, 2016. para. 3
52. Young, 2016
53. Ferrero, Garaizar, & Vadillo, 2016, p. 496
54. Piaget, 1969; Mareschal, 2007; Rinaldi & Karmiloff-Smith, 2017
55. GSI, Berkeley Graduate Division, 2017, para. 2
56. Singh & Yaduvanshi, 2015
57. Taylor, 2017
58. Walker & Plomin, 2005
59. Pajares & Schunk, 2001, para 27
60. Zimmerman, 1989, 1990, 1994; Zimmerman & Bandura, 1994; Zimmerman & Martinez-Pons, 1990
61. Bandura, 1986
62. Duckworth & Seligman, 2005
63. Duckworth & Seligman, 2005, p. 939
64. Robinson & Aronica, 2015
65. WIPO, 2016, para. 1
66. Doidge, 2007; Duckworth & Seligman, 2005
67. Herculano-Houzel, 2002
68. Sorabji, 1971
69. Gardner, 1983
70. Raichle et. al., 2001, p. 676
71. Gusnard & Raichle, 2001, p. 685
72. Damoiseaux, Rombouts, Barkhof, Scheltens, Stam, Smith & Beckmann, 2006
73. Simon & Engström, 2015
74. Greicius, Krasnow, Reiss & Menon, 2003
75. Raichle, 2015, p. 433
76. Horn, Ostwald, Reisert & Blankenburg, 2014
77. Caramazza, Anzellotti, Strnad & Lingnau, 2014
78. Hohwy & Frith, 2004

79. Schurz, Radua, Aichhorn, Richlan & Perner, 2014
80. Lamm & Majdandžić, 2015
81. Goodwin, 2017
82. Williams & Kemper, 2010
83. Frontiers, 2017
84. Griffiths, 2014
85. Wilson & Deheane, 2004
86. Wilson, Revkin, Cohen, Cohen & Dehaene, 2006
87. Strong, Torgerson, Torgerson & Hulme, 2011
88. Aamodt & Wang, 2009, p. 1
89. Kueider, Parisi, Gross & Rebok, 2012, para. 1
90. Bleakley, Charles, Porter-Armstrong, McNeill, McDonough & McCormack, 2015
91. Hill, Mowszowski, Naismith, Chadwick, Valenzuela & Lampit, 2016, p. 329
92. Stowe & Cooney, 2014
93. Hamari, Shernoff, Rowe, Coller, Asbell-Clarke & Edwards, 2016
94. Castellar, All, De Marez & Van Looy, 2015
95. Ronimus, Kujala, Tolvanen & Lyytinen, 2014
96. Martin-Dorta, Sanchez-Berriel, Bravo, Hernandez, Saorin & Contero, 2014
97. Favier & van der Schee, 2014
98. Bachen, Hernández-Ramos & Raphael, C. (2012
99. Giordano, 2004
100. Chittleborough, Mittinty, & Lynch, 2013; Welsh, Nix, Blair, Bierman, & Nelson, 2010
101. Stowe & Cooney, 2014.
102. Doidge, 2007, p. xv

Chapter 6

1. Brady, Siegel, Albers & Price, 2005, p. 352
2. Swaminathan, 2008, para. 2
3. Gibson, 2007, p. 71
4. Lewin, 2016
5. Sorgen, 2008
6. Steka, 2016
7. Kedley, 2017
8. Kelly, 2017
9. Schuna, n.d
10. *The Guardian*, 2009
11. Brown, 2016
12. Avigan, Mozersky & Seeff, 2016
13. Balluz, Kieszak, Philen & Mulinare, 2000
14. Leibing, 2014

15. Cakic, 2009

16. Fox, 2015, *NBC News*

17. Corbyn, 2015, *The Guardian*

18. Feinstein, Sabates, Sorhaindo, Rogers, Herrick, Northstone & Emmett, 2008

19. Northstone, Joinson, Emmett, Ness & Paus, 2012

20. Patrick & Nicklas, 2005

21. Campoy, Escolano-Margarit, Ramos, Parrilla-Roure, Csábi, Beyer, . . . & Koletzko, 2011

22. Daniels, Longnecker, Rowland, Golding & ALSPAC Study Team, 2004

23. Dwyer, Nahin, Rogers, Barnes, Jacques, Sempos & Bailey, 2013

24. Harvard University School of Public Health, 2007

25. McGregor, 2017

26. Axe, 2015

27. United States National Institutes of Health, 2015, para.1

28. Black, Clarke, Barnes, Stussman & Nahin, 2015

29. Amen, 2009

30. Wenstrom, 2014

31. Kirby, Woodward, Jackson, Wang & Crawford, 2010

32. van der Wurff, von Schacky, Berge, Kirschner & de Groot, 2016, para. 1

33. Campoy, Escolano-Margarit, Ramos, Parrilla-Roure, Csábi, Beyer, . . . & Koletzko, 2011

34. Añazco Hermosilla, Contreras Novoa, Millafilo Antilef & Rodríguez Rodríguez, 2016; Dündar & Gündüz, 2016; Deligiannidi & Howard-Jones, 2015; Gleichgerrcht, Luttges, Salvarezza & Campos, 2015; Howard-Jones, 2014; Hermida, Segretin, Soni García & Lipina, 2016; Murtaugh, 2016; Papadatou-Pastou, Haliou & Vlachos, 2017; Pei, Howard-Jones, Zhang, Liu & Jin, 2015; Rato, Abreu & Castro-Caldas, 2013

35. Kelly, 2017. p. 1

36. Irish, Kline, Gunn, Buysse & Hall, 2015, p. 23

37. Mindell, et al., 2009

38. Tokuhama-Espinosa, 2017

39. Lim & Dinges, 2008; Pilcher, Band, Odle-Dusseau & Muth, 2007

40. Landmann, Kuhn, Piosczyk, Feige, Baglioni, Spiegelhalder, . . . & Nissen, 2014; Spencer, Walker & Stickgold, 2017; Tononi & Cirelli, 2014

41. Feld, Lange, Gais & Born, 2013

42. Fuligni, Arruda, Krull & Gonzales, 2017

43. Boergers, Gable & Owens, 2014

44. Watson, Martin, Wise, Carden, Kirsch, Kristo, . . . & Rowley, 2017

45. Orzech, Acebo, Seifer, Barker & Carskadon, 2014

46. Bernert & Nadorff, 2015

47. Hildenbrand, Daly, Nicholls, Brooks-Holliday & Kloss, 2013

48. Sievertsen, Gino & Piovesan, 2016

49. Blunden & Rigney, 2015

50. Barrett, 2001; Stickgold & Ellenbogen, 2008; Szegedy-Maszak, 2006; Zink & Pietrowsky, 2015
51. Redaktion, 2015
52. Coren, 2012
53. Cote, 2017
54. Villarica, 2012
55. Gaines Lewis, 2015
56. Kerkhof & Van Dongen, 2010
57. Spencer, Walker, & Stickgold, 2017
58. DiSalvo, 2014
59. Çetin, Çimen & Yetkiner, 2016
60. Hasan, Zagarins, Pischke, Saiyed, Bettencourt, Beal, . . . & McCleary, 2014
61. Nemeth, Janacsek, Polner & Kovacs, 2013
62. Snyder, Hobson, Morrison & Goldfrank, 1964
63. Hobson, McCarley & Wyzinski, 1975
64. Hobson, Pace-Schott & Stickgold, 2000
65. Stickgold, LaTanya & Hobson, 2000
66. Hobson & Pace-Schott, 2002
67. Walker, Brakefield, Morgan, Hobson & Stickgold, 2002
68. Pace-Schott & Hobson, 2002
69. Walker, Brakefield, Hobson & Stickgold, 2003
70. Voss, Holzmann, Tuin & Hobson, 2009
71. Patrick & Nicklas, 2005
72. Azevedo, Sousa, Paul, MacLeish, Mondejar, Sarabia, . . . & Madrid, 2008; Dewald-Kaufmann, Oor, & Meijer, 2014; Kloss, Nash, Walsh, Culnan, Horsey & Sexton-Radek, 2016; Rigney, Blunden, Maher, Dollman, Parvazian, Matricciani & Olds, 2015
73. Menna-Barreto & Wey, 2008

Chapter 7

1. Alferink & Farmer-Dougan, 2010
2. Dekker, Lee, Howard-Jones & Jolles, 2012; Deligiannidi & Howard-Jones, 2015; Karakus, Howard-Jones & Jay, 2015; Pei, Howard-Jones, Zhang, Liu & Jin, 2015; OECD, 2007; Weigmann, 2013; Worden, Hinton & Fischer, 2011
3. Birdsong, 1999
4. Bongaerts, Planken & Schils, 1995
5. Iovinelli, 2011
6. Sukel, 2015
7. Anderson, 2016
8. Barker, 2017; Masten, 2011; Sciaraffa, Zeanah & Zeanah, 2017
9. Hauser & McDermott, 2003, P.664
10. Prevent Child Abuse Arizona, 2009
11. Dietz, 1994

12. Hirofumi, 2015
13. LeBlanc & Fagiolini, 2011
14. Wiesel & Hubbel, 1963
15. Lennenberg, 1967
16. Friedmann & Rusou, 2015
17. Payne & Isaacs, 2017
18. Tokuhama-Espinosa, 2008; Tokuhama-Espinosa, 2017
19. Society For Neuroscience, 2008
20. Reference.com, 2018
21. Sears, 2017
22. Bilal, 2015
23. Society for Neuroscience, 2012
24. Altman, 1962
25. Eriksson, Perfilieva, Björk-Eriksson, Alborn, Nordborg, Peterson & Gage, 1998; Murrell, Bushell, Livesey, McGrath, MacDonald, Bates & Mackay-Sim, 1996; Rakic, 1998
26. Gage, 2002, p. 612
27. Poulin, Tasic, Hjerling-Leffler, Trimarchi & Awatramani, 2016
28. Gross, 2000, p. 67
29. Ernst, Alkass, Bernard, Salehpour, Perl, Tisdale, . . . & Frisén, 2014
30. Eriksson, Perfilieva, Björk-Eriksson, Alborn, Nordborg, Peterson, & Gage, 1998
31. Murrell, Bushell, Livesey, McGrath, MacDonald, Bates, & Mackay-Sim, 1996
32. Deng, Aimone & Gage, 2010; Winocur, Wojtowicz, Sekeres, Snyder & Wang, 2006
33. Deng, Aimone & Gage, 2010; Lu, Mahmood, Qu, Goussev, Schallert & Chopp, 2005
34. Theadom, Parag, Dowell, McPherson,Starkey, Barker-Collo, . . . & BIONIC Research Group, 2016
35. Theadom, Cropley, Parmar, Barker-Collo, Starkey, Jones, . . . & BIONIC Research Group, 2015
36. Lindsay, Hartman, Reed, Gan, Thomson & Solomon, 2015
37. Holland & Schmidt, 2015, p. 1
38. Lindsay, Hartman, Reed, Gan, Thomson & Solomon, 2015, para. 2
39. Holland & Schmidt, 2015
40. Ferrero, Garaizar & Vadillo, 2016
41. Doidge, 2007, p. 5
42. Doidge, 2007, p. 23
43. Nudo, 2013
44. Holland & Schmidt, 2015
45. Doidge, 2007, p. 6
46. Bernhardt, Borschmann, Boyd, Thomas Carmichael, Corbett, Cramer, . . . & Walker, 2016

47. Bach-y-Rita, 1992
48. Chang, 2014
49. Bernhardt et al., 2016

Chapter 8

1. Basar, 2016
2. Ghose, 2016b
3. Luria, 1968
4. Schacter, 1999
5. Anderson, 2016
6. Miller & Buschman, 2015
7. AskScience blog, 2013
8. Smalarz, Greathouse, Wells & Newirth, 2016
9. Etchells, 2015
10. Gaver, 1993
11. Fei-Fei, Iyer, Koch & Perona, 2007
12. Köster, 2002
13. Heller, 2013
14. Bartoshuk, 2000
15. Driver & Noesselt, 2008
16. Anderson & Bower, 2014
17. Tournier, Jordan & Ferring, 2016
18. Nairne, Thompson & Pandeirada, 2007
19. Schacter, 1999
20. APass Education, 2013
21. Towler, 2014
22. Stripp, 2015
23. Tokuhama-Espinosa, 2017 p. 46
24. Sharma, 2012
25. Orlin, 2013
26. Johnson, 2010, p. 1
27. Squire & Dede, 2015
28. Squire & Dede, 2015
29. Kundu et al., 2013
30. Miller, 1989
31. Baddeley, 2012
32. Squire, 2004
33. Christianson, 2014
34. Schacter, 1999
35. Lalley & Miller, 2007
36. Wiman & Meriheny, 1960

37. Curl, 1973
38. Subramony, Molenda, Betrus & Thalheimer, 2014a
39. Wiggins & McTighe, 2005
40. Subramony, Molenda, Betrus & Thalheimer, 2014c, p. 15
41. Tokuhama-Espinosa, 2017

Chapter 9

1. Morgan, 2013
2. Crenshaw, 2008; Goldstein, 2011; Hamilton, 2008; Loukopoulos, Dismukes & Barshi, 2009; Rosen, 2008; Young, 2010
3. Harford, 2015
4. Lebiere, Anderson & Bothell, 2001
5. Chiappe, Conger, Liao, Caldwell & Vu, 2013
6. Adams & Rho, 2017; Rosen, 2008
7. Bühner, König, Pick & Krumm, 2006; Konig, Buhner & Murling, 2005; Meiran & Cohen-Kdoshay, 2012
8. Just & Buchweitz, 2016; Walsh, Albright, Apperley, Beach, Beavis, Black, . . . & Carrington, 2014
9. Andrade, Bohn & Huang, 2014; Kiesel & Dignath, 2017
10. Dux, Tombu, Harrison, Rogers, Tong & Marois, 2009; Laxmisan, Hakimzada, Sayan, Green, Zhang & Patel, 2007
11. Petersen & Posner, 2012
12. Byskov, 2014
13. Hakala, 2015
14. Fisher, Frey, Quaglia, Smith & Landem 2017
15. Wilson & Korn, 2007
16. Rehn, 2016
17. Smith, 2015
18. Watson, 2015
19. Bradbury, 2016, p. 509
20. Bradbury, 2015, para 1
21. Garrison, Santoyo, Davis, Thornhill IV, Kerr & Brewer, 2013
22. Posner, 2007
23. Horn, Ostwald, Reisert & Blankenburg, 2014
24. Dekker, Lee, Howard-Jones & Jolles, 2012; Deligiannidi & Howard-Jones, 2015; Howard-Jones, 2014; Karakus, Howard-Jones & Jay, 2015; Pei, Howard-Jones, Zhang, Liu & Jin, 2015
25. Ogden, Kit, Carroll, & Park, 2011
26. Ogden, Kit, Carroll, Park, 2011; Harvard School of Public Health, n.d., para.1
27. Howard-Jones, 2009, pp. 25–26
28. Piernas, Barquera & Popkin, 2014; Harvard University School of Public Health, n.d.

29. Paiva, Gaspar & Matos, 2015
30. O'Reilly, 1995
31. Pires, Bezerra, Tufik & Andersen, 2016
32. Doran, Van Dongen & Dinges, 2001
33. World Health Organization, 2004
34. Mastin, Bryson & Corwyn, 2006
35. Sano, Phillips, McHill, Taylor, Barger, Czeisler & Picard, 2017
36. Kirszenblat & van Swinderen, 2015, pp. 776-779
37. Mednick, Nakayama & Stickgold, 2003

Chapter 10

1. Broca, 1861; 2. Wernicke, 1874
2. Ullman, 2000
3. Sininger, Doyle & Moore, 1999
4. Planton, Jucla, Roux & Démonet, 2013
5. Gaillard, Balsamo, Ibrahim, Sachs & Xu, 2003
6. Nakamura, Kuo, Pegado, Cohen, Tzeng & Dehaene, 2012
7. Kuhl, 2004
8. Regier & Kay, 2009
9. Binder, Westbury, McKiernan, Possing & Medler, 2005
10. Mills, Prat, Zangl, Stager, Neville & Werker, 2004
11. Jung-Beeman, 2005
12. Berninger, Winn, MacArthur, Graham & Fitzgerald, 2006
13. Bolger, Perfetti & Schneider, 2005
14. Abbott, Berninger & Fayol, 2010
15. Eurostat, 2016
16. Lennenberg, 1967
17. Obama, 2008
18. Antoniou, Gunasekera & Wong, 2013; Chertkow, Whitehead, Phillips, Wolfson, Atherton & Bergman, 2010; Li, Legault & Litcofsky, 2014
19. Hammond, 2014
20. Van Patten, 2012
21. Harley & Wang, 1997; McLaughlin, 1992; Tokuhama-Espinosa, 2008
22. DeKeyser, 2008
23. Cummins, 1999
24. Tokuhama-Espinosa, 2008
25. McWhinney & Snow, 1990
26. O'Rourke, 1972
27. Berens, Kovelman & Petitto, 2013
28. Bialystok, 2011
29. Tucker, 1999, p. 1

30. Slobin, 1973

31. Newport, 1974

32. Dulay & Burt, 1974

33. Hakuta, 1986

34. Cummins, 1981

35. Bialystok, 2005

36. Abutalebi & Clahsen, 2015; Bialystok, 2011b; Giambo & Szecsi, 2015

37. Antón et al., 2014; Bialystok, 2015; Paap et al., 2014; Valian, 2015

38. Bialystok, 1992

39. Abutalebi & Clahsen, 2015; 40. Perani & Abutalebi, 2015

40. De Houwer, 1999

41. Thomas & Collier, 2002

42. Thomas & Collier, 2004; (30-70, 40-60 and 50-50 models exist and while the 50-50 model is superior, schools using the 30-70 can also meet with success)

43. Werker, Yeung & Yoshida, 2012

44. Tokuhama-Espinosa, 2008

45. McLaughlin, 1992, p. 2

46. De Houwer, 2017

47. Braun & Cline, 2014;. Zabrodskaja, 2016

48. Conteh & Meier, 2014

49. Van Patten, 2012

50. Kutas & Federmeier, 2000

51. Buchanan, Lutz, Mirzazade, Specht, Shah, Zilles, & Jänke, 2000

52. Ralph, Jefferies, Patterson & Rogers, 2017

53. Shaywitz & Shaywitz, 2004

54. Hannagan, Amedi, Cohen, Dehaene-Lambertz & Dehaene, 2015

55. Madec, Le Goff, Anton, Longcamp, Velay, Nazarian, . . . & Rey, 2016

56. Gow & Olson, 2015

57. Berken, Gracco, Chen, Watkins, Baum, Callahan & Klein, 2015

58. Timmer & Schiller, 2014

59. Franklin, Mooneyham, Baird & Schooler, 2014

60. Citron, Gray, Critchley, Weekes & Ferstl, 2014

61. Rohr & Rahman, 2015

62. Lupyan & Clark, 2015

63. John, 2014

64. Bornfreund, Cook, Lieberman & Loewenberg, 2015

65. Blythe, 2013, p. 3

66. Haynes, 2016

67. Horowitz-Kraus, Schmitz, Hutton & Schumacher, 2017

68. Hansen, Joshi & Dex, 2010

69. Tokuhama-Espinosa, 2017

70. Hyatt, 2007

Chapter 11

1. Dubinsky, Roehrig & Varma, 2013; Howard-Jones, 2010

2. Maeda, 2006

3. Hyder, Rothman & Bennett, 2013

4. Society for Neuroscience, 2008, slide 7

5. Stam, & Reijneveld, 2007, p. 3

6. Burgess, 2012

7. Lemov & Atkins, 2014

8. Busso & Pollack, 2014; Dubinksky, 2010; Lindell & Kidd, 2011; Lilienfeld, Ammirati & David, 2012; McCabe & Castel, 2008; Weisberg, Keil, Goodstein, Rawson & Gray, 2008

9. World Bank, 2017

10. Guerriero, 2017

11. Clement & Lovat, 2012; Dubinsky, 2010; Dubinsky, Roehrig & Varma, 2013; Geake, 2009; Geake & Cooper, 2003; Guerriero, 2017; Glisczinski, 2011; Hook & Farah, 2013; MacNabb, Schmitt, Michlin, Harris, Thomas, Chittendon, . . . & Dubinsky, 2006; Pickering & Howard-Jones, 2007

12. Leahy, Shore & Lambert, 2017b

13. Stein & Fischer, 2011

14. Stein & Fischer, 2011, p. 2

15. Riley, 2015

16. Howard-Jones, Franey, Mashmoushi & Liau , 2009

17. Howard-Jones, Franey, Mashmoushi & Liau, 2009, p. 4

18. All Kinds of Minds, 2017; Marshall & Comalli, 2012

19. Lilienfeld, Ammirati & David, 2012

20. Megowan-Romanowicz, 2010; Mills, 2006

21. Shaw, 2005

22. McEwen & McEwen, 2017

23. Prado & Dewey, 2014

24. Tomporowski, Davis, Miller & Naglieri, 2008, p. 111

25. https://www.nature.com/npjscilearn/

26. https://deansforimpact.org/resources/the-science-of-learning/

27. Komatsu, 2006

28. Ehrenstein, Spillmann & Sarris, 2003

29. Pasquinelli, 2012, p. 90

30. Oxford Dictionary, 2017, para. 1

31. Shermer, 2011

32. Schatcher, 1999

33. Garín-Aguilar, Medina, Quirarte, McGaugh & Prado-Alcalá, 2014

34. Hermans, Henckens, Joëls & Fernández, 2014

35. Doidge, 2016

36. Kelly, Loughrey, Lawlor, Robertson, Walsh & Brennan, 2014, p.12

37. Sample, 2014

38. Maeda & Yoon, 2013

39. Macrae, 2014

40. Tzuriel & Egozi, 2010; Uttal, Meadow, Tipton, Hand, Alden, Warren & Newcombe, 2013

41. Cheema & Galluzzo, 2013; Miller & Halpern, 2014

42. Salvatori, 1999, p.1821; Wiltelson, et al., 1999

43. Galaburda, 1999, p. 1821

44. Martin, Schurz, Kronbichler & Richlan, 2015

45. Ansari, Garcia, Lucas, Hamon & Dhital, 2005

46. *Forbes*, 2016

47. Johnson & Kenny, 2010

48. Posner, 2003, p. 4

49. Beck, 2010, p. 762

50. McCabe & Castel, 2008

51. Weisberg, Keil, Goodstein, Rawson & Gray, 2008

52. *Indian Express, The*, 2017

53. Useem, 2017

54. Useem, 2017, para. 4

55. McCall, 2012, p. 42

56. Pasquinelli, 2012

57. Legrenzi, Umilta & Anderson, 2014

58. Carey, 2017

59. Kluger, 2014

60. Gallagher, 2017

61. Pasquinelli, 2012

62. Weisberg, Keil, Goodstein, Rawson & Gray, 2008

63. Koksma, 2014

64. Begley, 2005

65. Tokuhama-Espinosa, 2009, p. 1

66. McCall, 2012, p. 45

67. Edge,1995

68. Costandi, 2013

Conclusion

1. Darling-Hammond, 2000

2. Tokuhama-Espinosa, 2017

3. Guerriero, 2017

4. Nature Partner Journals, 2018

5. Ravitch & Riggan, 2016

6. Ravitch & Riggan, 2016, p. 1
7. OECD, 2002, p. 71
8. OECD, 2002, p. 72
9. Sah, 2018. University information: https://qbi.uq.edu.au/).
10. Society For Neuroscience, 2008

REFERENCES

Aamodt, S., & Wang, S. (2009). *Six myths about your brain*. Excerpt from Aamodt and Wang (2008). Retrieved 27 May 2017 from http://synapse.princeton.edu/~sam/Six_Myths_About_The_Brain.pdf

Ab Kadir, M. A. (2017). What teacher knowledge matters in effectively developing critical thinkers in the 21st century curriculum?. *Thinking Skills and Creativity, 23*, 79–90.

Abbott, R. D., Berninger, V. W., & Fayol, M. (2010). Longitudinal relationships of levels of language in writing and between writing and reading in grades 1 to 7. *Journal of Educational Psychology, 102*(2), 281.

Abutalebi, J., & Clahsen, H. (2015). Bilingualism, cognition, and aging. *Bilingualism: Language and Cognition, 18*(1), 1-2.

Acharya, S., Shukla, S., Mahajan, S. N. & Siwan, S. K. (2012). Localizationism to neuroplasticity—the evolution of metaphysical neuroscience. *The Journal of the Associations of Physicians of India, 60*, 38–46.

Active Living Research. (2013). Building evidence to prevent childhood obesity and support active communities. *Research Brief February*. Retrieved 17 July 2017 from http://activelivingresearch.org/files/ALR_Brief_ActivityBreaks_Feb2013.pdf

Adams, T. N., & Rho, J. C. (2017). Multitasking simulation: Present application and future directions. *Medical Teacher, 39*(2), 120–122.

Adcock, R. A., Thangavel, A., Whitfield-Gabrieli, S., Knutson, B., & Gabrieli, J. D. (2006). Reward-motivated learning: mesolimbic activation precedes memory formation. *Neuron, 50*(3), 507–517.

Agarwal, P. K., Bain, P. M., & Chamberlain, R. W. (2012). The value of applied research: Retrieval practice improves classroom learning and recommendations from a teacher, a principal, and a scientist. *Educational Psychology Review, 24*(3), 437–448.

Agid, Y. (2016). Consciousness, emotions and basal ganglia. *European Journal of Neurology, 23*, 900.

Albarran, A. B. (2016). *The media economy*. London, UK: Taylor & Francis Group.

Albett, R. S. (1969). Genius: present-day status of the concept and its implications for the study of creativity and giftedness. *American Psychologist, 24*(8), 743.

Alexandrou, A. M., Saarinen, T., Mäkelä, S., Kujala, J., & Salmelin, R. (2017). The right hemisphere is highlighted in connected natural speech production and perception. *NeuroImage, 152*, 628-638.

Alferink, L. A., & Farmer-Dougan, V. (2010). Brain-(not) based education: Dangers of misunderstanding and misapplication of neuroscience research. *Exceptionality, 18*(1), 42–52.

All Kinds of Minds. (2017). *Spark the learning revolution*. Retrieved 21 July 2017 from www.allkindsofminds.org/spark-the-learning-revolution

Allan, A. (2014). Wild teenage behaviour linked to rapid cognitive change in the brain. *The Guardian* (September 5). Retrieved 26 June 2017 from www.theguardian.com/science/2014/sep/05/teenage-brain-behaviour-prefrontal-cortex

Allen, J. S., Damasio, H. & Grabowski, T. J. (2002). Normal neuroanatomical variation in the human brain: An MRI-volumetric study. *American Journal of Physical Anthropology, 118*(4), 341–58. doi:10.1002/ajpa.10092. PMID 12124914.

Allix, N. M. (2000). The theory of multiple intelligences: A case of missing cognitive matter. *Australian Journal of Education, 44*(3), 272–288.

Altman, J. (1962). Are new neurons formed in the brains of adult mammals? *Science, 135*(3509), 1127–1128.

Amen, D. G. (2009). *Magnificent mind at any age: Natural ways to unleash your brain's maximum potential*. New York: Harmony Books.

Amstutz, L. S. (2015). *The little book of restorative discipline for schools: Teaching responsibility; creating caring climates*. New York: Skyhorse Publishing, Inc.

Añazco Hermosilla, L., Contreras Novoa, T., Millafilo Antilef, C., & Rodríguez Rodríguez, A. (2016). *Prevalence of neuromyths amongst student-teachers from Chile* (Doctoral dissertation). Santiago, Chile: Universidad Católica de la Santísima Concepción.

Anderson, J. (2016). The U.S. is failing to invest enough in one of the most critical periods in children's education. *Quartz*. Retrieved 13 July 2017 from https://qz.com/787226/the-us-is-failing-to-invest-enough-in-early-childhood-education-one-of-the-most-critical-periods-in-childrens-development-says-the-oecd

Anderson, J. R., & Bower, G. H. (2014). *Human associative memory*. Abingdon, UK: Psychology Press.

Anderson, J. R., Pyke, A. A., & Fincham, J. M. (2016). Hidden stages of cognition revealed in patterns of brain activation. *Psychological Science*, 0956797616654912.

Anderson, R. (2016). How to remember everything: The method of Loci. *Psychology Today* (September 13). Retrieved 14 July 2017 from www.psychologytoday.com/blog/the-mating-game/201609/how-remember-everything

Andrade, J., Bohn, D., & Huang, W. D. (2014, October). Multimedia, multitasking, and content type and their impact on college students' perceived mental effort. In *E-Learn: World Conference on E-Learning in Corporate, Government, Healthcare, and Higher Education* (pp. 97–102). Association for the Advancement of Computing in Education (AACE).

Andresen, B. B. (2017). The missing link between student capabilities and motivation: Perceived self-efficacy. *GSTF Journal on Education, 4*(2).

Ansari, D. (2015). Number symbols in the brain. *Mathematical Cognition and Learning, 2,* 27–46.

Ansari, D., Garcia, N., Lucas, E., Hamon, K., & Dhital, B. (2005). Neural correlates of symbolic number processing in children and adults. *Neuroreport, 16*(16), 1769–1773.

Antón, E., Duñabeitia, J. A., Estévez, A., Hernández, J. A., Castillo, A., Fuentes, L. J., ... & Carreiras, M. (2014). Is there a bilingual advantage in the ANT task? Evidence from children. *Frontiers in Psychology, 5.*

Antoniou, M., Gunasekera, G. M., & Wong, P. C. (2013). Foreign language training as cognitive therapy for age-related cognitive decline: A hypothesis for future research. *Neuroscience & Biobehavioral Reviews, 37*(10), 2689–2698.

APass Education. (2013). Critical thinking vs. rote memory. *APasseducation* (July 2). Retrieved 14 July 2017 from http://apasseducation.com/critical-thinking-vs-rote-memorization

Arain, M., Haque, M., Johal, L., Mathur, P., Nel, W., Rais, A., ... & Sharma, S. (2013). Maturation of the adolescent brain. *Neuropsychiatric Disease and Treatment, 9,* 449.

Aristotle. (c.350 B.C.E). De Sensu, 1. In Aristotle's *De Anima* (436b10–12). London, UK: Aeterna Press.

Armstrong, F., Armstrong, D., & Barton, L. (Eds.). (2016). *Inclusive education: Policy, contexts and comparative perspectives.* Abingdon, UK: Routledge.

Armstrong, T. (2017). *The myth of the ADHD child: 101 ways to improve your child's behavior and attention span without drugs, labels, or coercion.* New York: The Penguin Press.

ASkScIeNCe blog. (2013). Is there a limit to how much information my brain can store? When I make new memories or learn new things, do I forget other memories?. *AskScience* blog (May 11). Retrieved 24 July 2017 from www.reddit.com/r/askscience/comments/1e4e0d/is_there_a_limit_to_how_much_information_my_brain

Augustyniak, R. A., Ables, A. Z., Guilford, P., Lujan, H. L., Cortright, R. N., & DiCarlo, S. E. (2016). Intrinsic motivation: an overlooked component for student success. *Advances in Physiology Education, 40*(4), 465–466.

Avants, B., Betancourt, L., Giannetta, J., Lawson, G., Gee, J., Farah, M., & Hurt, H. (2012, October). Early childhood home environment predicts frontal and temporal cortical thickness in the young adult brain. In *Society for Neuroscience Annual Meeting* (Oct 13-17, 2012). Ernest N. Morial Convention Center in New Orleans, LA

Avigan, M. I., Mozersky, R. P., & Seeff, L. B. (2016). Scientific and regulatory perspectives in herbal and dietary supplement associated hepatotoxicity in the United States. *International Journal of Molecular Sciences, 17*(3), 331.

Axe, J. (2015 Sept 13). 11 benefits of cod liver oil: The anti-inflammatory disease fighter. *Dr. Axe Food is Medicine.* Retrieved 10 July 2017 from https://draxe.com/cod-liver-oil

Azevedo, C. V., Sousa, I., Paul, K., MacLeish, M. Y., Mondejar, M. T., Sarabia, J. A., ... & Madrid, J. A. (2008). Teaching chronobiology and sleep habits in school and university. *Mind, Brain, and Education, 2*(1), 34–47.

Azevedo, F. A., Carvalho, L. R., Grinberg, L. T., Farfel, J. M., Ferretti, R. E., Leite, R. E., ... & Herculano-Houzel, S. (2009). Equal numbers of neuronal and nonneuronal cells make the human brain an isometrically scaled-up primate brain. *Journal of Comparative Neurology, 513*(5), 532–541.

Bach-y-Rita, P. (1992). Applications of principles of brain plasticity and training to restore function. In R.R. Young & P.J. Delwaide's (Eds.). (2013). *Principles and practice of restorative neurology: Butterworth's international medical reviews* (pp. 54-65). Jordan Hill, Oxford, UK: Butterworth-Heinemann.

Bachen, C. M., Hernández-Ramos, P. F., & Raphael, C. (2012). Simulating REAL LIVES: Promoting global empathy and interest in learning through simulation games. *Simulation & Gaming, 43*(4), 437-460.

Baddeley, A. (2012 Jan). Working memory: theories, models, and controversies. *Annual Review of Psychology, 63,* 1-29.

Bagley, W. C. (1925). Determinism in education: A series of papers on the relative influence of inherited and acquired traits in determining intelligence, achievement, and character. Baltimore, MD: Warwick & York.

Bain, S. K. & Jaspers, K. E. (2010). Test review: Review of Kaufman Brief Intelligence Test, (2nd. Ed.). *Journal of Psychoeducational Assessment, 28*(2), 167–174.

Baker-Henningham, H., & Lopez Boo, F. (2010). *Early childhood stimulation interventions in developing countries: a comprehensive literature review.* Washington (DC): International Development Bank, *Social Protection and Health Division.*

Balluz, L. S., Kieszak, S. M., Philen, R. M., & Mulinare, J. (2000). Vitamin and mineral supplement use in the United States: results from the third National Health and Nutrition Examination Survey. *Archives of Family Medicine, 9*(3), 258.

Bandura, A. (1986). *Social foundations of thought and action: A social cognitive theory.* Englewood Cliffs, NJ: Prentice Hall.

Banich, M. T., & Heller, W. (1998). Evolving perspectives on lateralization of function. *Current Directions in Psychological Science, 7*(1), 1–2.

Banks, A. (2015). The dopamine reward system: Friend or foe? *Psychology Today* (12 July). Retrieved 4 June 2017 from www.psychologytoday.com/blog/wired-love/201507/the-dopamine-reward-system-friend-or-foe

Bar-David Y, Urkin J, & Kozminsky E. (2005). The effect of voluntary dehydration on cognitive functions of elementary school children. *Acta Paediatria, 94,*1667–1673.

Bargmann, C. I., & Marder, E. (2013). From the connectome to brain function. *Nature Methods, 10*(6), 483–490.

Barker, G. (2017). From stability to norm transformation: lessons about resilience, for development, from ecology. *Phenomenology and the Cognitive Sciences, 16*(4), 571-584.

Barrett, D. (2001). *The committee of sleep: How artists, scientists and athletes use dreams for creative problem-solving and how you can too.* New York: Crown, Random House.

Bartheld, C. S., Bahney, J., & Herculano-Houzel, S. (2016). The search for true numbers of neurons and glial cells in the human brain: a review of 150 years of cell counting. *Journal of Comparative Neurology, 524*(18), 3865–3895.

Bartoshuk, L. M. (2000). Comparing sensory experiences across individuals: recent psychophysical advances illuminate genetic variation in taste perception. *Chemical Senses, 25*(4), 447–460.

Basar, E. (2016). *Memory and brain dynamics: Oscillations integrating attention, perception, learning, and memory*. Boca Raton, FL: CRC press.

Bathelt, J., Gathercole, S., Butterfield, S. & Astle, D. (2017, February 15). *The role of the structural connectome in literacy and numeracy development in children*. Retrieved 4 June 2017 from osf.io/preprints/psyarxiv/jk6yb

Battro, A. (2003). *Half a brain is enough: The story of Nico*. Paris, France: Odile Jacob.

Bear, G. G., Slaughter, J. C., Mantz, L. S., & Farley-Ripple, E. (2017). Rewards, praise, and punitive consequences: Relations with intrinsic and extrinsic motivation. *Teaching and Teacher Education, 65*, 10–20.

Beaty, R. E., Benedek, M., Wilkins, R. W., Jauk, E., Fink, A., Silvia, P. J., ... & Neubauer, A. C. (2014). Creativity and the default network: A functional connectivity analysis of the creative brain at rest. *Neuropsychologia, 64*, 92–98.

Bechara, A. (2004). The role of emotion in decision-making: evidence from neurological patients with orbitofrontal damage. *Brain and Cognition, 55*(1), 30–40.

Beck, D. M. (2010). The appeal of the brain in the popular press. *Perspectives in Psychological Science 5*, 762–766.

Becker, H. J. (1990). When powerful tools meet conventional beliefs and institutional constraints. *National survey findings on computer use by American teachers. Report No. 49*. Washington, DC: Office of Educational Research and Improvement.

Begley, S. (2005 Mar 18). Beware of the cognitive brain paparazzi lurking in brain science labs. *Wall Street Journal*, Science section.

Belfort, M. B., Anderson, P. J., Nowak, V. A., Lee, K. J., Molesworth, C., Thompson, D. K., . . . & Inder, T. E. (2016). Breast milk feeding, brain development, and neurocognitive outcomes: a 7-year longitudinal study in infants born at less than 30 weeks' gestation. *The Journal of Pediatrics, 177*, 133–139.

Bell, V. (2013 Feb 2). The unsexy truth about dopamine. *The Observer* [online]. Retrieved 20 June 2017 from www.theguardian.com/ science/2013/feb/03/ dopamine-the-unsexy-truth

Benaroch, R. (2007). *Solving health and behavioral problems from birth through preschool*. Westport, CT: Praeger.

Benevolent. (2017). *Brain-body mass ratio*. Retrieved 3 June 2017 from file:///Users/admin/ Downloads/Brain-body_mass_ratio_for_some_animals_diagram.svg

Bennie, M. (2016 Feb 2). Tantrum vs autistic meltdown: What is the difference?. *Autism Awareness*. Autism Awareness Centre Inc. Retrieved 27 June 2017 from https:// autismawarenesscentre.com/what-is-the-difference-between-a-tantrum-and-an -autistic-meltdown.

Benton, D., & Young, H. A. (2015). Do small differences in hydration status affect mood and mental performance? *Nutrition Reviews, 73*(suppl. 2), 83–96.

Berens, M. S., Kovelman, I., & Petitto, L. A. (2013). Should bilingual children learn reading in two languages at the same time or in sequence?. *Bilingual Research Journal, 36*(1), 35–60.

Bergland, C. (2012). Enriched environments build better brains. *Psychology Today* (March 7). Retrieved 22 July 2017 from www.psychologytoday.com/blog/the-athletes-way/201203/enriched-environments-build-better-brains

Berk, J., & Weil, D. N. (2015). Old teachers, old ideas, and the effect of population aging on economic growth. *Research in Economics, 69*(4), 661–670.

Berken, J. A., Gracco, V. L., Chen, J. K., Watkins, K. E., Baum, S., Callahan, M., & Klein, D. (2015). Neural activation in speech production and reading aloud in native and non-native languages. *Neuroimage, 112*, 208–217.

Bernert, R. A., & Nadorff, M. R. (2015). Sleep disturbances and suicide risk. *Sleep Medicine Clinics, 10*(1), 35–39.

Bernhardt, J., Borschmann, K., Boyd, L., Thomas Carmichael, S., Corbett, D., Cramer, S. C., ... & Walker, M. (2016). Moving rehabilitation research forward: Developing consensus statements for rehabilitation and recovery research. *International Journal of Stroke, 11*(4), 454–458.

Berninger, V. W., Winn, W., MacArthur, C. A., Graham, S., & Fitzgerald, J. (2006). Implications of advancements in brain research and technology for writing development, writing instruction, and educational evolution. In C. A. MacArthur, S. Graham, J. Fitzgerald's (Eds.) *Handbook of writing research*, (pp. 96–114). New York: Guilford Press.

Bever, T. G., & Chiarello, R. J. (1974). Cerebral dominance in musicians and nonmusicians. *Science, 185*(4150), 537-539.

Beyerstein, B. (1999). Whence cometh the myth that we only use ten percent of our brains. In S. Della Salla (Ed.). *Mind myths: Exploring popular assumptions about the mind and brain* (pp. 59–82). Hoboken, NJ: John Wiley & Sons.

Bhabha, J. (Ed.). (2014). *Human rights and adolescence*. Philadelphia, PA: University of Pennsylvania Press.

Bialystok, E. (1992). Selective attention in cognitive processing: The bilingual edge. *Advances in Psychology, 83*, 501–513.

Bialystok, E. (2005). Consequences of bilingualism for cognitive development. In J.R. Kroll & A. de Groot (Eds.), *Handbook of bilingualism: Psycholinguistic approaches* (pp. 417–432). Oxford: Oxford University Press.

Bialystok, E. (2011a). Coordination of executive functions in monolingual and bilingual children. *Journal of Experimental Child Psychology, 110*(3), 461–468.

Bialystok, E. (2011b). Reshaping the mind: The benefits of bilingualism. *Canadian Journal of Experimental Psychology/Revue canadienne de psychologie expérimentale, 65*(4), 229.

Bialystok, E. (2015). Bilingualism and the development of executive function: The role of attention. *Child Development Perspectives, 9*(2), 117–121.

Bilal, A. (2015). Artificial neurons can now be used to replace human brain cells. *WCCFTECH* (June 30). Retrieved 13 July 2017 from http://wccftech.com/scientists-artificial-neurons-mimics-human-brain-cells

Binder, J. R., Westbury, C. F., McKiernan, K. A., Possing, E. T., & Medler, D. A. (2005). Distinct brain systems for processing concrete and abstract concepts. *Journal of Cognitive Neuroscience, 17*(6), 905–917.

Binet, Alfred & Simon, Th. (1916). *The development of intelligence in children: The Binet–Simon Scale*. Publications of the Training School at Vineland New Jersey, Department of Research No. 11. E. S. Kite (Trans.). Baltimore: Williams & Wilkins.

Birdsong, D. (Ed.). (1999). *Second language acquisition and the critical period hypothesis*. Abingdon-on-Thames, UK: Routledge.

Black, L. I., Clarke, T. C., Barnes, P. M., Stussman, B. J., & Nahin, R. L. (2015). Use of complementary health approaches among children aged 4–17 years in the United States: National Health Interview Survey, 2007–2012. *National Health Statistics Reports*, (78), 1.

Blakemore, S. J. (2007 Spring). Brain development during adolescence. *Education Review*.

Blakeslee, S. (2006 Jan 10). Cells that read minds. *The New York Times* (January 10). Retrieved 24 June 2017 from www.nytimes.com/2006/01/10/science/cells-that-read-minds.html

Blakeslee, T. R. (1980). *Right brain: A new understanding of our unconscious mind and its creative power*. New York, NY: Doubleday

Bleakley, C. M., Charles, D., Porter-Armstrong, A., McNeill, M. D., McDonough, S. M., & McCormack, B. (2015). Gaming for health: A systematic review of the physical and cognitive effects of interactive computer games in older adults. *Journal of Applied Gerontology*, 34(3), NP166-NP189.

Bloom, B. S. (1971). Mastery learning and its implications for curriculum development. *EW Eisner: Confronting Curriculum Reform. Boston: Little, Brown and Co*, 17, 49.

Blunden, S., & Rigney, G. (2015). Lessons learned from sleep education in schools: a review of dos and don'ts. *Journal of clinical sleep medicine: JCSM: official publication of the American Academy of Sleep Medicine*, 11(6), 671.

Blythe, S. G. (2013 Oct). The importance of movement in early development–the foundation of developing physical literacy. Bulletin 65 *Presidents Message 12*, 15. Retrieved 17 July 2017 from www.icsspe.org/sites/default/files/bulletin65_0.pdf#page=98

Boergers, J., Gable, C. J., & Owens, J. A. (2014). Later school start time is associated with improved sleep and daytime functioning in adolescents. *Journal of Developmental & Behavioral Pediatrics*, 35(1), 11–17.

Bolger, D. J., Perfetti, C. A., & Schneider, W. (2005). Cross-cultural effect on the brain revisited: Universal structures plus writing system variation. *Human Brain Mapping*, 25(1), 92–104.

Bongaerts, T., Planken, B., & Schils, E. (1995). Can late starters attain a native accent in a foreign language? A test of the critical period hypothesis. In D. M. Singleton and Z. Lengyel's *The age factor in second language acquisition*, (pp.30–50). Bristol, UK: Multilingual Matters.

Bornfreund, L., Cook, S., Lieberman, A., & Loewenberg, A. (2015). From crawling to walking: Ranking states on birth-3rd grade policies that support strong readers. *New America*.

Boyd, R. (2008, February 7). Do people only use 10 percent of their brains? *Scientific American*. Retrieved March 7, 2015, from: www. scientificamerican.com/article/do- people-only-use-10-percent-of-their- brains

Bradbury, N. A. (2016 Nov 8). Attention span during lectures: 8 seconds, 10 minutes, or more?. *Advances in Physiology Education.* https://doi.org/10.1152/advan.00109.2016

Brady, S., Siegel, G., Albers, W. & Price, D. (2005). *Basic neurochemistry: Molecular, cellular and medical aspects* (7th ed.). Cambridge, MA: Academic Press.

Braun, A., & Cline, T. (2014). *Language strategies for trilingual families: parents' perspectives* (No. 17). Bristol, UK: Multilingual Matters.

Briggs-Gowan, M. J., Carter, A. S., Bosson-Heenan, J., Guyer, A. E., & Horwitz, S. M. (2006). Are infant-toddler social-emotional and behavioral problems transient?. *Journal of the American Academy of Child and Adolescent Psychiatry, 45*(7), 849–858.

Briggs, D. C. (1975). *Your child's self-esteem: The key to life.* Mansfield, OH: Main Street Books.

Broca, P. (1861). Sur le principe des localisations cérébrales. *Bulletin de la Société d''Anthropologie 2*, 190–204.

Brown, A. C. (2016). An overview of herb and dietary supplement efficacy, safety and government regulations in the United States with suggested improvements. Part 1 of 5 series. *Food and Chemical Toxicology.*

Brück, T., Di Maio, M., & Miaari, S. H. (2014). *Learning the hard way: The effect of violent conflict on student academic achievement.* IZA Discussion Papers, No. 8543. EconStor.

Brueck, H. (2015). This camera records the thinking brain. *Forbes* (31 Oct). Retrieved 3 June 2017 from www.forbes.com/sites/hilarybrueck/2015/10/31/this-camera-records-the-thinking-brain/#72d114172e82

Bruer, J. T. (1997). Education and the brain: a bridge too far. *Educational Researcher, 26*(8), 4–16. doi: 10.3102/0013189X026008004

Bruer, J. T. (1998). Brain science, brain fiction. *Educational Leadership, 56*(3), 14–18.

Bruer, J. T. (1999). *The myth of the first three years: A new understanding of early brain development and lifelong learning.* New York: Simon & Schuster.

Bruer, J. T. (2014). The Latin American School on Education and the Cognitive and Neural Sciences: Goals and challenges. *Trends in Neuroscience and Education, 3*(1), 1–3.

Bruner, J. S. (1960). *The process of education.* Cambridge, MA: Harvard University Press.

Buchanan, T. W., Lutz, K., Mirzazade, S., Specht, K., Shah, N. J., Zilles, K., & Jäncke, L. (2000). Recognition of emotional prosody and verbal components of spoken language: an fMRI study. *Cognitive Brain Research, 9*(3), 227–238.

Bühner, M., König, C. J., Pick, M., & Krumm, S. (2006). Working memory dimensions as differential predictors of the speed and error aspect of multitasking performance. *Human Performance, 19*(3), 253–275.

Burgess, D. (2012). *Teach like a pirate.* San Diego, CA: Dave Burgess Consulting, Inc.

Business Standard. (2017 Apr 20). *New "wonder-drug" may prevent brain cells from dying.* Retrieved 7 June 2017 from www.business-standard.com/article/current-affairs/new-wonder-drug-may-prevent-brain-cells-from-dying-117042000359_1.html

Busso, D. S., & Pollack, C. (2014). No brain left behind: consequences of neuroscience discourse for education. *Learning, Media and Technology 40*, 1–19. doi: 10.1080/17439884.2014.908908

Byskov, B. (2014). How can you learn more and without much effort? *Quora* (December 12). Retrieved 17 July 2017 from www.quora.com/How-can-you-learn-more-and-without-much-effort

Cagniard, B., Balsam, P. D., Brunner, D., & Zhuang, X. (2006). Mice with chronically elevated dopamine exhibit enhanced motivation, but not learning, for a food reward. *Neuropsychopharmacology*, 31(7), 1362–1370.

Cairó, O. (2011). External measures of cognition. *Frontiers in Human Neuroscience*, 5, 108.

Cakic, V. (2009). Smart drugs for cognitive enhancement: ethical and pragmatic considerations in the era of cosmetic neurology. *Journal of Medical Ethics*, 35(10), 611–615.

Calhoun, C. (2018, Jan 12). *The U.S. is a left-brained society for right-brained people.* Miami, FL: Owlcitation, Hub Pages Inc.

Calvert, S. L., Appelbaum, M., Dodge, K. A., Graham, S., Nagayama Hall, G. C., Hamby, S., ... & Hedges, L. V. (2017). The American Psychological Association Task Force assessment of violent video games: Science in the service of public interest. *American Psychologist*, 72(2), 126.

Campoy, C., Escolano-Margarit, M. V., Ramos, R., Parrilla-Roure, M., Csábi, G., Beyer, J., ... & Koletzko, B. V. (2011). Effects of prenatal fish-oil and 5-methyltetrahydrofolate supplementation on cognitive development of children at 6.5 y of age. *The American Journal of Clinical Nutrition*, 94(6 Suppl), 1880S–1888S.

Canfield, A. A. (2017). *Learning Styles Inventory TM.* Torrance, CA: WPS. Retrieved 4 June 2017 from www.wpspublish.com/store/p/2853/learning-styles-inventory-lsi

Caputi F., Spaziante, R., de Divitiis, E., Nashold, B.S. (1995). Luigi Rolando and his pioneering efforts to relate structure to function in the nervous system. *Journal of Neurosurgery* 83(5), 933–7. doi:10.3171/jns.1995.83.5.0933. PMID 7472570

Caramazza, A., Anzellotti, S., Strnad, L., & Lingnau, A. (2014). Embodied cognition and mirror neurons: a critical assessment. *Annual Review of Neuroscience*, 37, 1–15.

Carey, B. (2017 Apr 20). 'Pacemaker' for the brain can help memory, study finds. The *New York Times*. Retrieved 4 March 2018 from https://www.nytimes.com/2017/04/20/health/brain-memory-dementia-epilepsy-treatments.html

Carey, T. (2014). *Taming the tiger parent: How to put your child's well-being first in a competitive world.* New York: Little, Brown Book Group.

Carr, N. (2010). Does the Internet make you dumber? *Wall Street Journal* (June 5). Retrieved 7 July 2017 from www.wsj.com/articles/SB10001424052748704025304575284981644790098

Carroll, J. (1993). *Human cognitive abilities: A survey of factor-analytic studies.* Cambridge, UK: Cambridge University Press.

Carter BloodCare. (2016). *Debunking blood types myth.* Bedford, TX: Author. Retrieved 23 June 2017 from www.carterbloodcare.org/debunking-blood-type-myths

Carus, P. (1905). The conception of the soul and the belief in resurrection among the Egyptians. *The Monist*, 409-428.

Castellar, E. N., All, A., De Marez, L., & Van Looy, J. (2015). Cognitive abilities, digital games and arithmetic performance enhancement: A study comparing the effects of a math game and paper exercises. *Computers & Education*, *85*, 123–133.

Cattell, R. B. (1941). Some theoretical issues in adult intelligence testing. *Psychological Bulletin, 38*(592), 10.

Cerasoli, C. P., Nicklin, J. M., & Ford, M. T. (2014). Intrinsic motivation and extrinsic incentives jointly predict performance: A 40-year meta-analysis. *Psychological Bulletin, 140*(4), 980.

Çetin, Y., Çimen, O. A., & Yetkiner, Z. E. (2016). Using Hypnosis to Enhance Learning Second Language Vocabulary. *American Journal of Clinical Hypnosis*, *58*(4), 399–410.

Chabris, C. F. (1999). Prelude or requiem for the 'Mozart effect'?. *Nature*, *400*(6747), 826–827.

Chang, Y. (2014). Reorganization and plastic changes of the human brain associated with skill learning and expertise. *Frontiers in Human Neuroscience*, *8*.

Chang, Y. K., Labban, J. D., Gapin, J. I., & Etnier, J. L. (2012). The effects of acute exercise on cognitive performance: a meta-analysis. *Brain Research*, *1453*, 87–101.

Checkley, K. (1997). The first seven... and the eighth a conversation with Howard Gardner. *Educational Leadership*, *55*, 8–13.

Cheema, J., & Galluzzo, G. (2013). Analyzing the gender gap in math achievement: Evidence from a large-scale US sample. *Research in Education*, *90*(1), 98–112.

Cheong, J. L., Anderson, P. J., Roberts, G., Burnett, A. C., Lee, K. J., Thompson, D. K., . . . & Wood, S. J. (2013). Contribution of brain size to IQ and educational underperformance in extremely preterm adolescents. *PLoS One*, *8*(10), e77475.

Chertkow, H., Whitehead, V., Phillips, N., Wolfson, C., Atherton, J., & Bergman, H. (2010). Multilingualism (but not always bilingualism) delays the onset of Alzheimer disease: evidence from a bilingual community. *Alzheimer Disease & Associated Disorders*, *24*(2), 118–125.

Cheuvront, S. N. & Kenefick, R. W. (2014). Dehydration: physiology, assessment, and performance effects. *Comparative Physiology, 4*, 257–285.

Chiappe, D., Conger, M., Liao, J., Caldwell, J. L., & Vu, K. P. L. (2013). Improving multi-tasking ability through action videogames. *Applied Ergonomics*, *44*(2), 278–284.

Chittka, L., & Niven, J. (2009). Are bigger brains better?. *Current Biology*, *19*(21), R995–R1008.

Choi, C.Q. (2013). Brain researchers can detect who we are thinking about. *Scientific American*, (14 Mar). Retrieved 3 June 2017 from www.scientificamerican.com/article/brain-researchers-can-detect-who-we-are-thinking-about

Christianson, S. A. (Ed.). (2014). *The handbook of emotion and memory: Research and theory*. Hove, UK: Psychology Press.

Christodoulou, J. A., & Gaab, N. (2009). Using and misusing neuroscience in education-related research. *Cortex 45*, 555–557. doi: 10.1016/j.cortex.2008.06.004

Chu, S. K. W., Tavares, N. J., Chu, D., Ho, S. Y., Chow, K., Siu, F. L. C., & Wong, M. (2012). *Developing upper primary students' 21st century skills: inquiry learning through collaborative teaching and Web 2.0 technology*. Hong Kong: Centre for Information Technology in Education.

Citron, F. M., Gray, M. A., Critchley, H. D., Weekes, B. S., & Ferstl, E. C. (2014). Emotional valence and arousal affect reading in an interactive way: neuroimaging evidence for an approach-withdrawal framework. *Neuropsychologia, 56,* 79–89.

Clark, C. M., Lawlor-Savage, L., & Goghari, V. M. (2016). The Flynn effect: A quantitative commentary on modernity and human intelligence. *Measurement: Interdisciplinary Research and Perspectives, 14*(2), 39–53.

Clark, I. (2015). What motivates us to learn? Collaborative peer-learning and the recruitment of the mesolimbic dopamine reward system. *NUCB Journal of Language Culture and Communication, 16*(2), 35–40.

Clement, N. D., & Lovat, T. (2012). Neuroscience and education: Issues and challenges for curriculum. *Curriculum Inquiry, 42*(4), 534–557.

Coffield, F., Moseley, D., Hall, E., & Ecclestone, K. (2004). *Learning styles and pedagogy in post-16 learning. A systematic and critical review.* London, UK: Learning and Skills Research Centre.

Cohen, A. O., & Casey, B. J. (2014). Rewiring juvenile justice: The intersection of developmental neuroscience and legal policy. *Trends in Cognitive Sciences, 18*(2), 63–65.

Collins, N. (2016). Can a brain scan tell what you're thinking? *Pacific Standard* (July 25). Retrieved 4 March 2018 from https://psmag.com/news/can-a-brain-scan-tell-what-youre-thinking

Commons, M. L., Rodriguez, J. A. (1993). The development of hierarchically complex equivalence classes. *Psychological Record, 43,* 667–697.

Commons, M. L., Trudeau, E. J., Stein, S. A., Richards, F. A., & Krause, S. R. (1998). Hierarchical complexity of tasks shows the existence of developmental stages. *Developmental Review, 8*(3), 237–278.

Conteh, J., & Meier, G. (Eds.). (2014). *The multilingual turn in languages education: Opportunities and challenges* (Vol. 40). Bristol, UK: Multilingual Matters.

Conyers, M. & Wilson, D. (2014). Move your body, grow your brain. *Edutopia* (March 12). Retrieved 17 July 2017 from www.edutopia.org/blog/move-body-grow-brain-donna-wilson

Coop, R. H., & Sigel, I. E. (1971). Cognitive style: Implications for learning and instruction. *Psychology in the Schools, 8*(2), 152-161.

Corbyn, Z. (2015). Get ahead in Silicon Valley: Take nootropic brain drugs. Technology, *The Observer* (July 11). Retrieved 11 July 2017 from www.theguardian.com/technology/2015/jul/11/hack-yourself-nootropic-drugs-upgrade-mind

Coren, S. (2012). *Sleep thieves.* New York: Simon & Schuster.

Costandi, M. (2013). Reflecting on mirror neurons. *The Guardian* (August 23). Retrieved 25 May 2017 from www.theguardian.com/science/neurophilosophy/2013/aug/23/mirror-neurons

Cote, K. A. (2017). Sleep on it: Everything will look better in the morning. *Sleep Medicine Reviews,* 31, 3–5

Coughlan, S. (2012). China: The world's cleverest country. *BBC News* (May 9). Retrieved 7 June 2017 from

Crawford, L. (2016). 7th grade: The worst year ever. *Great!schools*. Retrieved 7 June 2017 from www.greatschools.org/gk/articles/seventh-grade-worst-year-ever

Creedon, L. P. (1974). *A student centered learning system: An overview*. Quincy, MA: Quincy Public Schools.

Crenshaw, D. (2008). *The myth of multitasking: How "doing it all" gets nothing done*. Hoboken, NJ: John Wiley & Sons.

Crockard, A. (1996). Confessions of a brain surgeon. *New Scientist 2061*, 68.

Cummins, J. (1981). Empirical and theoretical underpinnings of bilingual education. *Journal of Education*, 16–29.

Cummins, J. (1999). *BICS and CALP: Clarifying the Distinction*. ERIC Database. Retrieved from http://files.eric.ed.gov/fulltext/ED438551.pdf on 7 November 2017.

Curl, D. H. (1973). AV Training AECT's. *Training in Business and Industry* (June 10), 15–16.

Curtiss, S. (1977). Genie: *A psycholinguistic study of a modern-day: Wild child*. Cambridge, MA: Academic Press.

Cushman, M. (2017). Science: Intelligence is mostly inherited. *Occidental Dissent: Nationalism, Popularism, Reaction* (May 23). Retrieved 7 July 2017 from www.occidentaldissent.com/2017/05/23/science-intelligence-is-mostly-inherited

D'Anci, K. E., Constant, F., & Rosenberg, I. H. (2006). Hydration and cognitive function in children. *Nutrition Review*, 64, 457–464.

Daily Mail Reporter. (2013). Brain scan that shows researchers what you are THINKING about. *Daily Mail Reporter*, (15 March). www.dailymail.co.uk/sciencetech/article-2293683/Brain-scan-breakthrough-researches-just-youre-thinking-lead-treatment-disorders-like-autism.html

Damasio, A. R. (2005). *Descartes' error: Emotion, rationality and the human brain*. New York: The Penguin Press.

Damoiseaux, J. S., Rombouts, S. A. R. B., Barkhof, F., Scheltens, P., Stam, C. J., Smith, S. M., & Beckmann, C. F. (2006). Consistent resting-state networks across healthy subjects. *Proceedings of the National Academy of Sciences*, *103*(37), 13848–13853.

Daniels, J. L., Longnecker, M. P., Rowland, A. S., Golding, J., & ALSPAC Study Team. (2004). Fish intake during pregnancy and early cognitive development of offspring. *Epidemiology*, *15*(4), 394–402.

Darling-Hammond, L. (2000). How teacher education matters. *Journal of Teacher Education*, *51*(3), 166–173.

Darling-Hammond, L. (2015). Want to close the achievement gap? Close the teaching gap. *American Educator*, *38*(4), 14–18.

Darling-Hammond, L., Wei, R. C., Andree, A., Richardson, N., & Orphanos, S. (2009). *Professional learning in the learning profession*. Washington, DC: National Staff Development Council.

Darwin, C. (1888). *The descent of man and selection in relation to sex (Vol. 1)*. London, UK: Murray.

Das, G., & Broadhurst, P. L. (1959). The effect of inherited differences in emotional reactivity on a measure of intelligence in the rat. *Journal of Comparative and Physiological Psychology*, *52*(3), 300.

Davis, K., Christodoulou, J., Seider, S., & Gardner, H. (2011). The theory of multiple intelligences. In R. Sternberg and Scott Barry Kaufman's *The Cambridge handbook of intelligence*, (pp.485–503). Cambridge, UK: Cambridge University Press.

De Charms, C. (2008). *A look inside the brain in real time*. TED Talks. Retrieved 3 June 2017 from www.ted.com/talks/christopher_decharms_scans_the_brain_in_real_time

De Houwer, A. (1999). Two or more languages in early childhood: Some general points and practical recommendations. *ERIC Digest*.

De Houwer, A. (2017). Bilingual language input environments, intake, maturity and practice. *Bilingualism: Language and Cognition, 20*(1), 19–20.

Deans For Impact. (2015). *The science of learning*. Austin, TX: Author.

Deci, E. L., Koestner, R., & Ryan, R. M. (1999). A meta-analytic review of experiments examining the effects of extrinsic rewards on intrinsic motivation. *Psychological Bulletin, 125*(6), 627–668.

Deci, E. L., Koestner, R., & Ryan, R. M. (2001). Extrinsic rewards and intrinsic motivation in education: Reconsidered once again. *Review of Educational Research, 71*(1), 1–27.

DeKeyser, R. (2008). Implicit and explicit learning. In C. J. Doughty & M. H. Long, M. H. (Eds.), *The handbook of second language acquisition* (Vol. 27) (pp.313–348). Hoboken, NJ: John Wiley & Sons.

Dekker, S., Lee, N. C., Howard-Jones, P. A., & Jolles, J. (2012). Neuromyths in education: Prevalence and predictors of misconceptions among teachers. *Frontiers in Psychology, 3*, 429. doi: 10.3389/fpsyg.2012.00429

Deligiannidi, K., & Howard-Jones, P. A. (2015). The neuroscience literacy of teachers in Greece. *Procedia-Social and Behavioral Sciences, 174*, 3909–3915.

Deng, W., Aimone, J. B., & Gage, F. H. (2010). New neurons and new memories: how does adult hippocampal neurogenesis affect learning and memory?. *Nature Reviews. Neuroscience, 11*(5), 339.

Deno, E. N. (1973). *Instructional alternatives for exceptional children*. Arlington, VA: Council for Exceptional Children.

Dew, J. R. (1996). Are you a right-brain or left-brain thinker?. *Quality Progress, 29*(4), 91.

Dewald-Kaufmann, J. F., Oort, F. J., & Meijer, A. M. (2014). The effects of sleep extension and sleep hygiene advice on sleep and depressive symptoms in adolescents: a randomized controlled trial. *Journal of Child Psychology and Psychiatry, 55*(3), 273–283.

Dewey, J. (1933). *How we think: A restatement of the reflective thinking to the educative process*. Boston, MA: Heath and Company.

Dewey, J. (1937). Education and social change. *Bulletin of the American Association of University Professors (1915-1955), 23*(6), 472–474.

Dewey, J. (1938). *The theory of inquiry*. New York: Holt, Rinehart & Winston.

Diamond, M. C., Greer, E. R., York, A., Lewis, D., Barton, T., & Lin, J. (1987). Rat cortical morphology following crowded-enriched living conditions. *Experimental Neurology, 96*(2), 241–247.

Díaz-Méndez, M., & Gummesson, E. (2012). Value co-creation and university teaching quality: Consequences for the European Higher Education Area (EHEA). *Journal of Service Management, 23*(4), 571-592.

Dickens, W., & Flynn, J. (2006). Black Americans reduce the racial IQ gap: evidence from standardization samples. *Psychological Science, 16*, 913–920.

Didlake, R., & Fordham, J. A. (2014). Do no harm: neurodiversity, healthcare advocacy. In A. Perry and C. Herrera's *Ethics and neurodiversity*, (pp.100-110). Newcastle Upon Tyne, UK: Cambridge Scholars Publishing.

Dietz, W. H. (1994). Critical periods in childhood for the development of obesity. *The American Journal of Clinical Nutrition, 59*(5), 955–959.

Digital Superheroes. (2017). *Whole brain teaching: Engage your students successfully in a nontraditional scientific way.* Charleston, SC: CreateSpace Independent Publishing Platform.

DiSalvo, D. (2014). How to (really) learn a foreign language while you sleep. *Forbes* (June 28). Retrieved 17 July 2017 from www.forbes.com/sites/daviddisalvo/2014/07/28/how-to-really-learn-a-foreign-language-while-you-sleep

Dobbie, W., Fryer, R. G., & Fryer Jr, G. (2011). Are high-quality schools enough to increase achievement among the poor? Evidence from the Harlem Children's Zone. *American Economic Journal: Applied Economics, 3*(3), 158–187.

Doidge, N. (2007). *The brain that changes itself: Stories of personal triumph from the frontiers of brain science.* Westminster, UK: Penguin Books.

Doidge, N. (2015). *The brain's way of healing: Remarkable discoveries and recoveries from the frontiers of neuroplasticity.* London, UK: Penguin Books.

Doran, S. M., Van Dongen, H. P. A., & Dinges, D. F. (2001). Sustained attention performance during sleep deprivation: evidence of state instability. *Archives Italiennes de Biologie, 139*(3), 253–267.

Dosenbach, N. U., Petersen, S. E., & Schlaggar, B. L. (2013). The teenage brain: Functional connectivity. *Current Directions in Psychological Science, 22*(2), 101–107.

Driver, J., & Noesselt, T. (2008). Multisensory interplay reveals crossmodal influences on 'sensory-specific' brain regions, neural responses, and judgments. *Neuron, 57*(1), 11–23.

Dubinsky, J. M. (2010). Neuroscience education for prekindergarten-12 teachers. *Journal of Neuroscience, 30*, 8057–8060.

Dubinsky, J. M., Roehrig, G., & Varma, S. (2013). Infusing neuroscience into teacher professional development. *Educational Researcher*, 0013189X13499403.

Duckworth, A. L., & Seligman, M. E. (2005). Self-discipline outdoes IQ in predicting academic performance of adolescents. *Psychological Science, 16*(12), 939–944.

Duhl, R. (2004). Adolescent brain development: A period of vulnerabilities and opportunities. *Annals New York Academy of Sciences 1021*, 1–22.

Dulay, H. C., & Burt, M. K. (1974). Errors and strategies in child second language acquisition. *TESOL Quarterly*, 129–136.

Duncan, G. J., Dowsett, C. J., Claessens, A., Magnuson, K., Huston, A. C., Klebanov, P., ... & Sexton, H. (2007). School readiness and later achievement. *Developmental Psychology, 43*(6), 1428.

Dunn, R. & Dunn, K. (2017). *International Learning Styles Network*. Retrieved 4 June 2017 from www.ilsa-learning-styles.com/About+ILSA/International+Learning+Styles+Network.html

Dunn, R., DeBello, T., Brennan, P., Krimsky, J., & Murrain, P. (1981). Learning style researchers define differences differently. *Educational Leadership, 38*(5), 372–375.

Dux, P. E., Tombu, M. N., Harrison, S., Rogers, B. P., Tong, F., & Marois, R. (2009). Training improves multitasking performance by increasing the speed of information processing in human prefrontal cortex. *Neuron, 63*(1), 127–138.

Dweck, C. (2017). *Mindset: changing the way you think to fulfil your potential*. London, UK: Hachette.

Dweck, C. S. (2006). *Mindset: The new psychology of success*. New York: Random House Digital, Inc.

Dweck, C. S. (2015). Carol Dweck revisits the 'growth mindset'. *Education Week, 35*(5), 20–4.

Dwyer, J., Nahin, R. L., Rogers, G. T., Barnes, P. M., Jacques, P. M., Sempos, C. T., & Bailey, R. (2013). Prevalence and predictors of children's dietary supplement use: the 2007 National Health Interview Survey. *The American Journal of Clinical nutrition, 97*(6), 1331-1337.

Eaton, W. O., Bodnarchuk, J. L., & McKeen, N. A. (2014). Measuring developmental differences with an age-of-attainment method. *SAGE Open, 4*(2), doi. org/10.1177/2158244014529775.

Ebbinghaus, H. (1885). *Forgetting curve. Memory: A contribution to experimental psychology*. Retrieved from http://encarta. msn. com/media, 461547609, 76157803-1.

Edge. (1995). Report of the 1995 Society For Neuroscience speech by Vilayanur Ramachandran entitled *Mirror neurons and imitation learning as the driving force behind the great leap forward in human evolution*. Retrieved 25 May 2017 from www.edge.org/conversation/mirror-neurons-and-imitation-learning-as-the-driving-force-behind-the-great-leap-forward-in-human-evolution

Edwards, B. (2012). *Drawing on the right side of the brain* (4th ed.). New York: TarcherPerigee.

Ehrenstein, W. H., Spillmann, L., & Sarris, V. (2003). Gestalt issues in modern neuroscience. *Axiomathes, 13*(3), 433–458.

Eisenhart, M., & DeHaan, R. L. (2005). Doctoral preparation of scientifically based education researchers. *Educational Researcher, 34*(4), 3–13.

Ekman, P. (2003). Darwin, deception, and facial expression. *Annals of the New York Academy of Sciences, 1000*(1), 205–221.

Elderton, E. M. (1923). A summary of the present position with regard to the inheritance of intelligence. *Biometrika*, 378–408.

Elkhorne, J. L. (March 1967). Edison: The fabulous drone, in *73 Magazine, XLVI*(3). 52–54

Elliott, C. D. (2012). *The differential ability scales* (2nd ed.). In Flanagan, D. P., Harrison, P. L. *Contemporary intellectual assessment: Theories, tests, and issues* (3rd ed.) (pp. 336–356). New York: Guilford Press.

Emmanuel, A. O., Adom, E. A., Josephine, B., & Solomon, F. K. (2014). Achievement motivation, academic self-concept and academic achievement among high school students. *European Journal of Research and Reflection in Educational Sciences* 2(2).

Engelhardt, C. R., Bartholow, B. D., Kerr, G. T., & Bushman, B. J. (2011). This is your brain on violent video games: Neural desensitization to violence predicts increased aggression following violent video game exposure. *Journal of Experimental Social Psychology, 47*(5), 1033–1036.

Eppich, W. J., Hunt, E. A., Duval-Arnould, J. M., Siddall, V. J., & Cheng, A. (2015). Structuring feedback and debriefing to achieve mastery learning goals. *Academic Medicine, 90*(11), 1501–1508.

Ericsson, K. A. (1998). The scientific study of expert levels of performance: General implications for optimal learning and creativity 1. *High Ability Studies, 9*(1), 75–100.

Ericsson, K. A. (2006). The influence of experience and deliberate practice on the development of superior expert performance. In K.A. Ericsson, N. Charness, P.J. Feltovich and R.R. Hoffman's *The Cambridge handbook of expertise and expert performance* (pp.683–704). Cambridge, UK: Cambridge University Press.

Ericsson, K. A. (2008). Deliberate practice and acquisition of expert performance: a general overview. *Academic Emergency Medicine, 15*(11), 988–994.

Ericsson, K. A. (2014). *The road to excellence: The acquisition of expert performance in the arts and sciences, sports, and games.* Hove, UK: Psychology Press.

Ericsson, K. A., Prietula, M. J., & Cokely, E. T. (2007). The making of an expert. *Harvard Business Review, 85*(7/8), 114.

Erikson, E. (1959). Theory of identity development. In G. S. Klein's (ed.) *Psychological Issues: Identity and the Life Cycle, Monograph 1, Vol. 1 No. 1.* New York: International Universities Press, Inc.

Eriksson, P. S., Perfilieva, E., Björk-Eriksson, T., Alborn, A. M., Nordborg, C., Peterson, D. A., & Gage, F. H. (1998). Neurogenesis in the adult human hippocampus. *Nature Medicine, 4*(11).

Eriksson, P. S., Perfilieva, E., Björk-Eriksson, T., et al. (1998 November). Neurogenesis in the adult human hippocampus. *Nature Medicine, 4*(11), 1313–7. doi:10.1038/3305.

Ernst, A. & Frisén, J. (2015 Jan). Adult neurogenesis in humans- common and unique traits in mammals. *PLOS Biology, 13*(1), e1002045.

Ernst, A., Alkass, K., Bernard, S., Salehpour, M., Perl, S., Tisdale, J., ... & Frisén, J. (2014). Neurogenesis in the striatum of the adult human brain. *Cell, 156*(5), 1072–1083.

Ernst, M., Pine, D. S., & Hardin, M. (2006). Triadic model of the neurobiology of motivated behavior in adolescence. *Psychological Medicine, 36*(3), 299–312.

Estabrooks, G. H. (1928). The relation between cranial capacity, relative cranial capacity and intelligence in school children. *Journal of Applied Psychology, 12*(5), 524.

Etchells, P. J. (2015). Sensation and perception. In P. Banyard, G. Dillon, C. Norman, & B. Winder (Eds.). *Essential psychology* (2nd ed) (pp.93-110). London. UK: Sage.

Eurostat. (2016). Foreign language learning statistics. *Eurostat: Statistics Explained* (January). Retrieved 24 July 2017 from http://ec.europa.eu/eurostat/statistics-explained/index.php/Foreign_language_learning_statistics

Eysenck, H. J. (1995). *Genius: The natural history of creativity* (Vol. 12). Cambridge, UK: Cambridge University Press.

Farah, M. (2002). Emerging ethical issues in neuroscience. *Nature Neuroscience, 5*, 1123–1129.

Favier, T. T., & van der Schee, J. A. (2014). The effects of geography lessons with geospatial technologies on the development of high school students' relational thinking. *Computers & Education, 76*, 225–236.

Federal Trade Commission. (2016). *Luminosity to pay $2 million to settle FTC deceptive advertising charges for its "brain training" program*. Washington, DC: Bureau of Consumer Protection. Retrieved 20 July 2017 from www.ftc.gov/news-events/press-releases/2016/01/lumosity-pay-2-million-settle-ftc-deceptive-advertising-charges

Fei-Fei, L., Iyer, A., Koch, C., & Perona, P. (2007). What do we perceive in a glance of a real-world scene?. *Journal of Vision, 7*(1), 10–10.

Feinstein, L., Sabates, R., Sorhaindo, A., Rogers, I., Herrick, D., Northstone, K., & Emmett, P. (2008). Dietary patterns related to attainment in school: the importance of early eating patterns. *Journal of Epidemiology & Community Health, 62*(8), 734–739.

Feld, G. B., Lange, T., Gais, S., & Born, J. (2013). Sleep-dependent declarative memory consolidation—unaffected after blocking NMDA or AMPA receptors but enhanced by NMDA coagonist D-cycloserine. *Neuropsychopharmacology, 38*(13), 2688.

Ferrero, M., Garaizar, P., & Vadillo, M. A. (2016). Neuromyths in education: Prevalence among Spanish teachers and an exploration of cross-cultural variation. *Frontiers in Human Neuroscience, 10*. https://doi.org/10.3389/fnhum.2016.00496

Fiegerman, S. (2017 May 9). Facebook's global fight against fake news. *CNN-Tech*. Retrieved 9 May 2017 from http://money.cnn.com/2017/05/09/technology/facebook-fake-news

Field, T. (2001). Massage therapy facilitates weight gain in preterm infants. *Current Directions in Psychological Science, 10*(2), 51–54.

Fields, R. D., & Stevens-Graham, B. (2002). New insights into neuron-glia communication. *Science, 298*(5593), 556–562.

Finlayson, C. (2010). *The humans who went extinct: Why Neanderthals died out and we survived*. New York, NY: Oxford University Press.

Fischer, K. W., & Bidell, T. R. (2006). Dynamic development of action, thought, and emotion. In *Handbook of child psychology: Theoretical models of human development* (pp.313–399). Hoboken, NJ: John Wiley & Sons.

Fischer, K., Daniel, D. B., Immordino-Yang, M. E., Stern, E., Battro, A., & Koizumi, H. (2007). Why mind, brain, and education? Why now? *Mind, Brain, and Education, 1*.

Fisher, D., Frey, N., Quaglia, R. J., Smith, D., & Lande, L. L. (2017). *Engagement by design: Creating learning environments where students thrive*. Thousand Oaks, CA: Corwin Press.

Flagel, S. B., Clark, J. J., Robinson, T. E., Mayo, L., Czuj, A., Willuhn, I., Akers, C. A., Clinton, S. M., Phillips, P. E. M., Akll, H. (2011). Dopamine is necessary for learning CS-US associations that lead to sign-tracking, but not goal-tracking. *Nature, 469*, 53–57. doi:10.1038/nature09588

Fleming, A. (1944). The discovery of penicillin. *British Medical Bulletin, 2*(1), 4–5.

Fletcher, D. (2009). Standardized testing. *Time Magazine* (Dec 11). Retrieved 7 June 2017 from http://content.time.com/time/nation/article/0,8599,1947019,00.html

Flynn, J. R. (1984). The mean IQ of Americans: Massive gains 1932 to 1978. *Psychological Bulletin, 95*(1), 29.

Flynn, J. R. (1987a). Causal factors in generational IQ gains. *Nature, 328*, 765.

Flynn, J. R. (1987b). Massive IQ gains in 14 nations: What IQ tests really measure. *Psychological Bulletin, 101*(2), 171.

Flynn, J. R., & Flynn, J. R. (2012). *Are we getting smarter?: Rising IQ in the twenty-first century*. New York: Cambridge University Press.

Forbes. (2016 Oct 13). *Studies show that some foods may be as addictive as heroin and cocaine*. Retrieved 25 May 2017 from www.forbes.com/sites/quora/2016/10/13/studies-show-that-some-foods-may-be-as-addictive-as-heroin-and-cocaine

Foroughi, C. K., Monfort, S. S., Paczynski, M., McKnight, P. E., & Greenwood, P. M. (2016). Placebo effects in cognitive training. *Proceedings of the National Academy of Sciences, 113*(27), 7470–7474.

Fowler, W. (1969). The effect of early stimulation: The problem of focus in developmental stimulation. *Merrill-Palmer Quarterly of Behavior and Development, 15*(2), 157–170.

Fox, M. (2015). You're still not getting enough vegetables. *NBC News* (July 9). Retrieved 11 July 2017 from www.nbcnews.com/health/diet-fitness/youre-still-not-eating-enough-vegetables-n389466

Franklin, M. S., Mooneyham, B. W., Baird, B., & Schooler, J. W. (2014). Thinking one thing, saying another: The behavioral correlates of mind-wandering while reading aloud. *Psychonomic Bulletin & Review, 21*(1), 205–210.

Freed, J., & Parsons, L. (1998). *Right-brained children in a left-brained world: Unlocking the potential of your ADD child*. New York: Simon & Schuster.

Friedmann, N., & Rusou, D. (2015). Critical period for first language: the crucial role of language input during the first year of life. *Current Opinion in Neurobiology, 35*, 27–34.

Frontiers. (2017). Video games can change your brain: Studies investigating how playing video games can affect the brain have shown that they can cause changes in many brain regions. *ScienceDaily* (June 22). Retrieved 9 July 2017 on www.sciencedaily.com/releases/2017/06/170622103824.htm

Fuligni, A. J., Arruda, E. H., Krull, J. L., & Gonzales, N. A. (2017). Adolescent sleep duration, variability, and peak levels of achievement and mental health. *Child Development*. Downloaded 18 May 2018 from http://adolescence.semel.ucla.edu/assets/images/2017-Fuligni-et-al.-Sleep-Duration-Variability-Peak-Achievement-and-Mental-Health.pdf

Gage, F. H. (2002). Neurogenesis in the adult brain. *Journal of Neuroscience, 22*(3), 612–613.

Gaillard, W. D., Balsamo, L. M., Ibrahim, Z., Sachs, B. C., & Xu, B. (2003). fMRI identifies regional specialization of neural networks for reading in young children. *Neurology, 60*(1), 94–100.

Gaines Lewis, J. (2015). How much can you really learn while you're asleep? *The Guardian*. (Oct 6). Retrieved 10 May 2018 from https://www.theguardian.com/education/2015/oct/06/how-much-can-you-really-learn-while-youre-asleep

Galaburda, A.M. (1999). Letter to the Editor. *The Lancet*, 354(Nov 20), 1821.

Gall, F. J., & Spurzheim, J. G. (1810). *Anatomie und Physiologie des Nervensystems im allgemeinen und des Gehirns insbesonders: mit Beobachtungen über die Möglichkeit, die Anlagen mehrerer Geistes-und Gemüthseigenschaften aus dem Baue des Kopfes der Menschen und der Thiere zu erkennen (Vol. 1)*. Paris, France: Schoell.

Gallagher, J. (2017). Experts excited by brain ‚wonder-drug'. BBC News (apr 20). Retrieved 4 March 2018 from http://www.bbc.com/news/health-39641123

Galton, F. (1869). *Hereditary genius: An inquiry into its laws and consequences* (Vol. 27). London, UK: Macmillan.

Galván, A. (2017). *The neuroscience of adolescence*. Cambridge, UK: Cambridge University Press.

Gardner, H. (1983). *Frames of mind: The theory of multiple intelligences*. New York: Basic Books.

Gardner, H. (1999). *Intelligence reframed: Multiple intelligences for the 21st century*. New York: Basic Books.

Gardner, H., & Moran, S. (2006). The science of multiple intelligences theory: A response to Lynn Waterhouse. *Educational Psychologist, 41*(4), 227–232.

Garín-Aguilar, M. E., Medina, A. C., Quirarte, G. L., McGaugh, J. L., & Prado-Alcalá, R. A. (2014). Intense aversive training protects memory from the amnestic effects of hippocampal inactivation. *Hippocampus, 24*(1), 102–112.

Garrison, K. A., Santoyo, J. F., Davis, J. H., Thornhill IV, T. A., Kerr, C. E., & Brewer, J. A. (2013). Effortless awareness: using real time neurofeedback to investigate correlates of posterior cingulate cortex activity in meditators' self-report. *Frontiers in Human Neuroscience, 7*.

Gaver, W. W. (1993). What in the world do we hear?: An ecological approach to auditory event perception. *Ecological Psychology, 5*(1), 1–29.

Gazzaniga, M. (2012). *Who's in charge?: Free will and the science of the brain*. New York, NY: Hachette.

Geake, J. (2008). Neuromythologies in education. *Educational Research 50*, 123–133.

Geake, J. (2009). *The brain at school: Educational neuroscience in the classroom: Educational neuroscience in the classroom*. London, UK: McGraw-Hill Education.

Geake, J. G. (2005). The neurological basis of intelligence: A contrast with 'brain-based' education. *Education-Line*. www.leeds.ac.uk/educol/documents/156074.htm.

Geake, J., & Cooper, P. (2003). Cognitive Neuroscience: implications for education?. *Westminster Studies in Education, 26*(1), 7–20.

Gentile, D. A., Li, D., Khoo, A., Prot, S., & Anderson, C. A. (2014). Mediators and moderators of long-term effects of violent video games on aggressive behavior: practice, thinking, and action. *JAMA Pediatrics, 168*(5), 450–457.

Gershon, M. (2015). *50 quick ways to motivate and engage your students*. North Charleston, SC: CreateSpace Independent Publishing Platform.

Gertler, P., Heckman, J., Pinto, R., Zanolini, A., Vermeersch, C., Walker, S., ... & Grantham-McGregor, S. (2014). Labor market returns to an early childhood stimulation intervention in Jamaica. *Science, 344*(6187), 998–1001.

Gess-Newsome, J. (2015). A model of teacher professional knowledge and skill including PCK. In A. Berry, P. Friedrichsen and J. Loughran (Eds). *Re-examining pedagogical content knowledge in science education*, (pp.28-42). New York: Routledge.

Ghose, T. (2016a). Mind-reading computer instantly decodes people's thoughts. *LiveScience*. Retrieved 3 June 2017 from www.livescience.com/53535-computer-reads-thoughts-instantaneously.html

Ghose, T. (2016b). The human brain's memory could store the entire Internet. *LiveScience* (February 18). Retrieved 14 July 2017 from www.livescience.com/53751-brain-could-store-internet.html

Giambo, D. A., & Szecsi, T. (2015). Promoting and maintaining bilingualism and biliteracy: Cognitive and biliteracy benefits & strategies for monolingual teachers. *The Open Communication Journal, 9* (Suppl 1: M8) 56-60.

Gibson, E. L. (2007). Carbohydrates and mental function: feeding or impeding the brain?. *Nutrition Bulletin, 32*(s1), 71–83.

Giedd, J. N. (2015). The amazing teen brain. *Scientific American, 312*(6), 32-37.

Gilmore, C. K., McCarthy, S. E., & Spelke, E. S. (2007). Symbolic arithmetic knowledge without instruction. *Nature, 447*, 589–592.

Giordano, P. J. (2004). Teaching and learning when we least expect it: The role of critical moments in student development. *Essays from e-xcellence in teaching*.

Gleichgerrcht, E., Luttges, B. L., Salvarezza, F., & Campos, A. L. (2015). Educational neuromyths among teachers in Latin America. *Mind Brain and Education 9*, 170–178. doi: 10.1111/mbe.12086

Glisczinski, D. J. (2011). Lighting up the mind: Transforming learning through the applied scholarship of cognitive neuroscience. *International Journal for the Scholarship of Teaching and Learning, 5*(1), 24.

Goldberg, L. R. (1990). An alternative "description of personality": the big-five factor structure. *Journal of Personality and Social Psychology, 59*(6), 1216.

Goldstein, A. (2011). *Our brains are evolving to multitask, not! The ill-usion of multitasking.* University of California at San Diego Center for Mindfulness. Retrieved 21 July 2017 from https://ucsdcfm.wordpress.com/2015/04/10/our-brains-are-evolving-to-multitask-not-the-ill-usion-of-multitasking

Goleman, D. P. (1995). *Emotional intelligence: Why it can matter more than IQ for character, health and lifelong achievement.* New York, NY: Bantam Books.

Goodwin, J. S. (2017). Fear of life extension. *The Journal of Gerontology: Series A, 72*(3), 353–354. https://doi.org/10.1093/gerona/glw340

Gordon, H. W., & Bogen, J. E. (1974). Hemispheric lateralization of singing after intracarotid sodium amylobarbitone. *Journal of Neurology, Neurosurgery & Psychiatry, 37*(6), 727-738.

Gordon, I. J. (1971). Early child stimulation through parent education. *International Journal of Early Childhood, 3*(1), 26–36.

Goswami, U. (2004). Neuroscience and education. *British Journal of Educational Psychology, 74*, 1–14. doi: 10.1348/000709904322848798

Goswami, U. (2006). Neuroscience and education: from research to practice?. *Nature Reviews Neuroscience, 7*(5), 406–413. Retrieved 8 Mar 2016 from www.nature.com/nrn/journal/v7/n5/full/nrn1907.html

Goswami, U. (2008). Principles of learning, implications for teaching: A cognitive neuroscience perspective. *Journal of Philosophy of Education, 42*(3-4), 381–399.

Gotfried, A.E. (1990). Academic intrinsic motivation in young elementary school children. *Journal of Educational Psychology, 82*, 522–538.

Gow, D. W., & Olson, B. B. (2015). Lexical mediation of phonotactic frequency effects on spoken word recognition: A Granger causality analysis of MRI-constrained MEG/EEG data. *Journal of Memory and Language, 82*, 41–55.

Gowan, J. C. (1979). The production of creativity through right hemisphere imagery. *The Journal of Creative Behavior, 13*(1), 39-51.

Grabianowski, E. (2010). Six ways science can see into your brain. *Io9.* Retrieved 3 June 2017 from http://io9.gizmodo.com/5495712/six-ways-science-can-see-into-your-brain

Grant, A. M. (2008). Does intrinsic motivation fuel the prosocial fire? Motivational synergy in predicting persistence, performance, and productivity. *Journal of Applied Psychology, 93*(1), 48.

Green, K. (2016). The human brain does not need high levels of motivation to learn a foreign language: Motivation has had its day. *Advances in Language and Literary Studies, 7*(5), 70–77.

Green, M. G., & Piel, J. A. (2016). *Theories of human development: A comparative approach* (2nd Ed.). New York: Routledge.

Greenough, W. T., & Volkmar, F. R. (1973). Pattern of dendritic branching in occipital cortex of rats reared in complex environments. *Experimental Neurology, 40*(2), 491–504.

Greicius, M. D., Krasnow, B., Reiss, A. L., & Menon, V. (2003). Functional connectivity in the resting brain: a network analysis of the default mode hypothesis. *Proceedings of the National Academy of Sciences, 100*(1), 253–258.

Griffiths, M. (2014). Playing video games is good for your brain – here's how. *The Conversation* (Nov 11). Retrieved 9 July 2017 from http://theconversation.com/playing-video-games-is-good-for-your-brain-heres-how-34034

Groen, M. A., Whitehouse, A. J., Badcock, N. A., & Bishop, D. V. (2013). Associations between handedness and cerebral lateralisation for language: a comparison of three measures in children. *PLoS One*, 8(5), e64876.

Grogan, J., Bogacz, R., Tsivos, D., Whone, A., & Coulthard, E. (2015). Dopamine and consolidation of episodic memory: timing is everything. *Journal of Cognitive Neuroscience*, 27(10), 2035-2050.

Gross, C. G. (2000). Opinion: Neurogenesis in the adult brain: death of a dogma. *Nature Reviews Neuroscience*, 1(1), 67.

Gruber, B. & Gruber, S. (2002). *Practical & easy ways to motivate your students (A+ teacher idea book)*. Palm Springs, CA: Practice & Learn Right Publications.

GSI (Graduate Student Instructor) Berkeley Graduate Division. *Cognitive constructivism*. Retrieved 4 December 2017 from http://gsi.berkeley.edu/gsi-guide-contents/learning-theory-research/cognitive-constructivism

Guerriero, S. (Ed.) (2017). *Pedagogical knowledge and the changing nature of the teaching profession*. Paris, France: OECD Publishing. http://dx.doi.org/10.1787/9789264270695-en

Gurin, L., & Blum, S. (2017). Delusions and the right hemisphere: a review of the case for the right hemisphere as a mediator of reality-based belief. *The Journal of Neuropsychiatry and Clinical Neurosciences*, 29(3), 225-235.

Guru Singh. (2017). Recognize your unlimited capacity. *Guru Singh blog*. Retrieved 24 July 2017 from www.gurusingh.com/recognize-your-unlimited-capicity

Guskey, T. R. (2010). Lessons of mastery learning. *Educational leadership*, 68(2), 52.

Gusnard, D. A., & Raichle, M. E. (2001). Searching for a baseline: functional imaging and the resting human brain. *Nature Reviews Neuroscience*, 2(10), 685–694.

Hahne, J. (2012). The Mozart Effect: Not so noteworthy. *Yale Scientific* (March 18). Yale University. Retrieved 25 May 2017 from www.yalescientific.org/2012/03/the-mozart-effect-not-so-noteworthy

Haigh, M., Haigh, T., & Kozak, N. I. (2017). Stopping fake news: The work practices of peer-to-peer counter propaganda. *Journalism Studies*, 1–26. https://doi.org/10.1080/1461670X.2017.1316681

Hakala, c. (2015). Why can't students just pay attention? *Faculty Focus* (May 4). Retrieved 16 July 2017 from www.facultyfocus.com/articles/effective-teaching-strategies/why-cant-students-just-pay-attention

Hakuta, K. (1986). *The mirror of language: The debate on bilingualism*. New York: Basic Books.

Halary, K. & Weintrayub, P. (1991). *Right-brain learning in 30 days*. New York: St. Martin's Press.

Hamari, J., Shernoff, D. J., Rowe, E., Coller, B., Asbell-Clarke, J., & Edwards, T. (2016). Challenging games help students learn: An empirical study on engagement, flow and immersion in game-based learning. *Computers in Human Behavior*, 54, 170–179.

Hamilton, J. (2008). Think you're multitasking? Think again. *NPR: National Public Radio: News & Analysis, World, US, Music & Arts.* Washington, DC: NPR.

Hammond, A. (2014). Does it get harder to learn a foreign language as you get older? *ESL Blog.* Retrieved 4 Mar 2018 from https://blog.esl-languages.com/blog/learn-languages/harder-to-learn-language-older-age/

Hannagan, T., Amedi, A., Cohen, L., Dehaene-Lambertz, G., & Dehaene, S. (2015). Origins of the specialization for letters and numbers in ventral occipitotemporal cortex. *Trends in Cognitive Sciences, 19*(7), 374–382.

Hansen, K., Joshi, H., & Dex, S. (Eds.). (2010). *Children of the 21st century: the first five years* (Vol. 2). Bristol, UK: Policy Press.

Hanushek, E. A. (2013). Economic growth in developing countries: The role of human capital. *Economics of Education Review, 37,* 204–212.

Hardre, P. L., & Reeve, J. (2003). A motivational model of rural students' intentions to persist in, versus drop out of, high school. *Journal of Educational Psychology, 95*(2), 347.

Harford, T. (2015). Multi-tasking: how to survive in the 21st century. *Financial Times* (September 3). Retrieved 17 July 2017 from www.ft.com/content/bbf1f84a-51c2-11e5-8642-453585f2cfcd?mhq5j=e1

Harley, B., & Wang, W. (1997). The critical period hypothesis: Where are we now. *Tutorials in bilingualism: Psycholinguistic Perspectives,* 19–51.

Harpaz, I. (1990). Asymmetry of hemispheric functions and creativity: An empirical examination. *The Journal of Creative Behavior, 24*(3), 161–170.

Hart, B., & Risley, T. R. (2003). The early catastrophe: The 30 million word gap by age 3. *American Educator, 27*(1), 4–9.

Hartinger, S. M., Lanata, C. F., Hattendorf, J., Wolf, J., Gil, A. I., Ortiz Obando, M., Noblega, M., Verastegui, H., & Mäusezahl, D. (2016). Impact of a child stimulation intervention on early child development in rural Peru: a cluster randomised trial using a reciprocal control design. *Journal of Epidemiology and Community Health.* DOI: 10.1136/jech-2015-206536

Harvard Medical School, The. (2011). *6-week plan for healthy eating.* Boston, MA: Harvard Health Publications.

Harvard University School of Public Health. (2007). Mega-3 fatty acids: An essential contribution. *The Nutrition Source.* Retrieved 10 July 2017 from www.hsph.harvard.edu/nutritionsource/omega-3-fats

Harvard University School of Public Health. (n.d.). Sugary drinks. *The Nutrition Source.* Retrieved 17 July 2017 from www.hsph.harvard.edu/nutritionsource/healthy-drinks/sugary-drinks/#ref46

Hasan, F. M., Zagarins, S. E., Pischke, K. M., Saiyed, S., Bettencourt, A. M., Beal, L., ... & McCleary, N. (2014). Hypnotherapy is more effective than nicotine replacement therapy for smoking cessation: results of a randomized controlled trial. *Complementary Therapies in Medicine, 22*(1), 1–8.

Hattie, J. (2008). *Visible learning: A synthesis of over 800 meta-analyses relating to achievement.* Abingdon-on-Thames, UK: Routledge.

Hattie, J. (2012). *Visible learning for teachers: Maximizing impact on learning*. Abingdon-on-Thames, UK: Routledge.

Hattie, J. (2015). *What works best in education: The politics of collaborative expertise*. London, UK: Pearsons.

Hauser, M. D., & McDermott, J. (2003). The evolution of the music faculty: A comparative perspective. *Nature neuroscience, 6*(7), 663.

Hauser, R., & Palloni, A. (2010). *Why intelligent people live longer*. Center for Demography and Ecology, University of Wisconsin Working Paper No. 2010-04

Hay Group Global. (2017). *Kolb learning style inventory (KLSI)*, version 4 online. Retrieved 4June 2017 from www.haygroup.com/leadershipandtalentondemand/ourproducts/item_details.aspx?itemid=118&type=2&t=2

Haynes, J. (2016). Born to move: The importance of early physical activity and interaction. *Community Practitioner, 89*(8), 37.

Heckman, J. J. (2011). The economics of inequality: The value of early childhood education. *American Educator, 35*(1), 31.

Hedman, A. M., van Haren, N. E., Schnack, H. G., Kahn, R. S., Pol, H., & Hilleke, E. (2012). Human brain changes across the life span: a review of 56 longitudinal magnetic resonance imaging studies. *Human Brain Mapping, 33*(8), 1987–2002.

Heilman, K. M. (2016). Possible brain mechanisms of creativity. *Archives of Clinical Neuropsychology, 31*(4), 285–296.

Heilman, K. M., Nadeau, S. E., & Beversdorf, D. O. (2003). Creative innovation: possible brain mechanisms. *Neurocase, 9*(5), 369-379.

Heller, M. A. (2013). *The psychology of touch*. Abingdon, UK: Psychology Press.

Hellige, J. B. (1993). *Hemispheric asymmetry: What's right and what's left* (Vol. 6). Cambridge, MA: Harvard University Press.

Herculano-Houzel, S. (2002). Do you know your brain? A survey on public neuroscience literacy at the closing of the decade of the brain. *The Neuroscientist, 8*(2), 98–110.

Herculano-Houzel, S., Manger, P. R., & Kaas, J. H. (2014). Brain scaling in mammalian evolution as a consequence of concerted and mosaic changes in numbers of neurons and average neuronal cell size. *Frontiers in Neuroanatomy, 8*, 77.

Herculano-Houzel, S. (2014). The glia/neuron ratio: how it varies uniformly across brain structures and species and what that means for brain physiology and evolution. *Glia, 62*(9), 1377–1391.

Hermann, N. & Hermann-Nehdi, A. (2012). *The whole brain business book: Unlocking the power of whole brain thinking in organizations, terms, and individuals* (2nd Ed.). New York: McGraw-Hill Education.

Hermans, E. J., Henckens, M. J., Joëls, M., & Fernández, G. (2014). Dynamic adaptation of large-scale brain networks in response to acute stressors. *Trends in Neurosciences, 37*(6), 304–314.

Hermida, M. J., Segretin, M. S., Soni García, A., & Lipina, S. J. (2016). Conceptions and misconceptions about neuroscience in preschool teachers: a study from Argentina. *Educational Research, 58*(4), 457–472.

Herrnstein, R., & Murray, C. (1994). *The bell curve.* New York: Simon & Schuster.

Higbee, K. L., & Clay, S. L. (1998). College students' beliefs in the ten-percent myth. *The Journal of Psychology, 132*(5), 469–476.

Hildenbrand, A. K., Daly, B. P., Nicholls, E., Brooks-Holliday, S., & Kloss, J. D. (2013). Increased risk for school violence-related behaviors among adolescents with insufficient sleep. *Journal of School Health, 83*(6), 408–414.

Hill, N. T., Mowszowski, L., Naismith, S. L., Chadwick, V. L., Valenzuela, M., & Lampit, A. (2016). Computerized cognitive training in older adults with mild cognitive impairment or dementia: a systematic review and meta-analysis. *American Journal of Psychiatry, 174*(4), 329-340.

Hille, K. (2011). Bringing research into educational practice: lessons learned. *Mind Brain and Education, 5,* 63–70. doi: 10.1111/j.1751-228X.2011.01111.x

Hirofumi, M. (2015). Mechanisms regulating developmental critical period for establishing attention. *Grantome.* Retrieved 13 July 2017 from http://grantome.com/grant/NIH/R21-MH106919-01A1

Hobson, J. A., & Pace-Schott, E. F. (2002). The cognitive neuroscience of sleep: neuronal systems, consciousness and learning. *Nature Reviews Neuroscience, 3*(9), 679–693.

Hobson, J. A., McCarley, R. W., & Wyzinski, P. W. (1975). Sleep cycle oscillation: reciprocal discharge by two brainstem neuronal groups. *Science, 189*(4196), 55–58.

Hobson, J. A., Pace-Schott, E. F., & Stickgold, R. (2000). Dreaming and the brain: toward a cognitive neuroscience of conscious states. *Behavioral and Brain Sciences, 23*(6), 793–842.

Hoffman, P., & Morcom, A. M. (2017). Age-related changes in the neural networks supporting semantic cognition: A meta-analysis of 47 functional neuroimaging studies. *Neuroscience & Biobehavioral Reviews.*

Hofman, M. A. (2014). Evolution of the human brain: when bigger is better. *Frontiers in Neuroanatomy, 8,* 15.

Hohwy, J., & Frith, C. (2004). Can neuroscience explain consciousness?. *Journal of Consciousness Studies, 11*(7–8), 180–198.

Holland, J. N., & Schmidt, A. T. (2015). Static and dynamic factors promoting resilience following traumatic brain injury: a brief review. *Neural Plasticity.*

Hook, C. J., & Farah, M. J. (2013). Neuroscience for educators: what are they seeking, and what are they finding? *Neuroethics, 6*(2), 331–341.doi: 10.1007/s12152-012-9159-3

Hopkins, M. E., Davis, F. C., VanTieghem, M. R., Whalen, P. J., & Bucci, D. J. (2012). Differential effects of acute and regular physical exercise on cognition and affect. *Neuroscience, 215,* 59–68.

Horn, A., Ostwald, D., Reisert, M., & Blankenburg, F. (2014). The structural–functional connectome and the default mode network of the human brain. *Neuroimage, 102,* 142–151.

Horn, J. L., & Cattell, R. B. (1966). Refinement and test of the theory of fluid and crystallized general intelligences. *Journal of Educational Psychology, 57*(5), 253.

Horowitz-Kraus, T., Schmitz, R., Hutton, J. S., & Schumacher, J. (2017). How to create a successful reader? Milestones in reading development from birth to adolescence: The contribution of language, cognition, and literacy to reading development. *Acta Paediatrica.*

Howard-Jones P., Franey L., Mashmoushi R. & Liau Y.-C. (2009). The neuroscience literacy of trainee teachers. *Paper Presented at the British Educational Research Association Annual Conference*, University of Manchester, Manchester.

Howard-Jones, P. A. (2009). Scepticism is not enough. *Cortex 45*, 550–551.

Howard-Jones, P. A. (2010). *Introducing neuroeducational research: Neuroscience, education and the brain from contexts to practice.* Abingdon, UK: Routledge.

Howard-Jones, P. A. (2014). Neuroscience and education: myths and messages. *Nature Reviews Neuroscience, 15*, 817–824. doi:10.1038/nrn3817

Howard-Jones, P. A., Demetriou, S., Bogacz, R., Yoo, J. H. & Leonards, U. (2011). Toward a science of learning games. *Mind, Brain, and Education, 5*, 33–41.

Howard-Jones, P. A., Franey, L., Mashmoushi, R., & Liao, Y. C. (2009 September). The neuroscience literacy of trainee teachers. In *British Educational Research Association Annual Conference* (pp. 1–39). Manchester, UK: University of Manchester.

Howard-Jones, P. A., Pickering, S., & Diack, A. (2007). *Perceptions of the role of neuroscience in education.* Bristol, UK: University of Bristol: The Innovation Unit. Retrieved March 27, 2012, from www.neuroeducational.net

Hrala, J. (2016). Math has its own brain region. *Science & Nonduality.* Retrieved 14 July 2017 from www.scienceandnonduality.com/math-has-its-own-brain-region

Hughes, S. (2012). The emperor's new clothes revisited: learning styles in medical education. *Education for Primary Care, 23*(2), 79–81.

Hyatt, K. J. (2007). Brain gym: Building stronger brains or wishful thinking? *Remedial and Special Education, 28*, 117–124.

Hyder, F., Rothman, D. L., & Bennett, M. R. (2013). Cortical energy demands of signaling and nonsignaling components in brain are conserved across mammalian species and activity levels. *Proceedings of the National Academy of Sciences, 110*(9), 3549–3554.

Immordino-Yang, M. H. (2015). *Emotions, learning, and the brain: Exploring the educational implications of affective neuroscience.* New York: Norton.

Immordino-Yang, M. H. (2007). A tale of two cases: Lessons for education from the study of two boys living with half their brains. *Mind, Brain, and Education, 1*(2), 66-83.

Immordino-Yang, M. H., & Damasio, A. (2007). We feel, therefore we learn: The relevance of affective and social neuroscience to education. *Mind, Brain, and Education, 1*(1), 3-10.

Indian Express, The. (2017). *Eating a full course seafood meal once a week can help you stay sharp.* Retrieved 25 May 2017 from http://indianexpress.com/about/brain/

International Association for the Evaluation of Educational Achievement. (2015). *TIMMS results.* Amsterdam, The Netherlands: Author

International Association for the Evaluation of Educational Achievement. (2016). *PIRLS results.* Amsterdam, The Netherlands: Author

Iovinelli, B.M. (2011). Q/A: What are the critical periods in my baby's development? *Babble*. Retrieved 13 July 2017 from www.babble.com/parenting/critical-periods-development

Irish, L. A., Kline, C. E., Gunn, H. E., Buysse, D. J., & Hall, M. H. (2015). The role of sleep hygiene in promoting public health: A review of empirical evidence. *Sleep Medicine Reviews, 22*, 23–36.

Jabr, F. (2012). Know your neurons: How to classify different types of neurons in the brain's forest. *Scientific American* (May 16). Retrieved 7 June 2017 from https://blogs.scientificamerican.com/brainwaves/know-your-neurons-classifying-the-many-types-of-cells-in-the-neuron-forest

Jacoby, R. & Glauberman, N. (Eds.). *The bell curve debate: History, documents, opinions*. New York: Three Rivers Press.

Jacques, S. (1979). Brain stimulation and reward: "pleasure centers" after twenty-five years. *Neurosurgery, 5*(2), 277–283.

Jaeggi, S. M., Buschkuehl, M., Jonides, J., & Perrig, W. J. (2008). Improving fluid intelligence with training on working memory. *Proceedings of the National Academy of Sciences, 105*(19), 6829–6833.

Jarrett, C. (2014). *Great myths of the brain*. Hoboken, NJ: John Wiley & Sons.

Johansen, J. P., Diaz-Mataix, L., Hamanaka, H., Ozawa, T., Ycu, E., Koivumaa, J., ... & LeDoux, J. E. (2014). Hebbian and neuromodulatory mechanisms interact to trigger associative memory formation. *Proceedings of the National Academy of Sciences, 111*(51), E5584-E5592.

John. (2014). *Benefits of crawling and your baby's development*. Woodstock, IL: Adult and Child Therapy Services.

Johnson, B. (2010). When rote learning makes sense. *Edutopia*. Retrieved 10 May 2018 from https://www.edutopia.org/rote-learning-benefits

Johnson, P. M., & Kenny, P. J. (2010). Addiction-like reward dysfunction and compulsive eating in obese rats: Role for dopamine D2 receptors. *Nature Neuroscience, 13*(5), 635.

Jorgenson, E. (2015). *Development of the open hemispheric brain dominance scale*. Retrieved 27 May 2017 from http://personality-testing.info/tests/OHBDS/development

Jukes, I. (2013). Personal conversation. Quito, Ecuador.

Jung-Beeman, M. (2005). Bilateral brain processes for comprehending natural language. *Trends in Cognitive Sciences, 9*(11), 512–518.

Jung, C. G. (1921). *Psychologische Typen*. Zurich, Switzerland: Rascher Verlag.

Jussim, L., & Harber, K. D. (2005). Teacher expectations and self-fulfilling prophecies: Knowns and unknowns, resolved and unresolved controversies. *Personality and Social Psychology Review, 9*(2), 131–155

Just, M. A., & Buchweitz, A. (2016). What brain imaging reveals about the nature of multitasking. *The Oxford Handbook of Cognitive Science*, 265.

Kable, J. W., Caulfield, M. K., Falcone, M., McConnell, M., Bernardo, L., Parthasarathi, T., ... & Diefenbach, (2017). P.57. No effect of commercial cognitive training on neural activity during decision-making. *Journal of Neuroscience*, 2832-16.

Kagan, J. (2009). *Three seductive ideas*. Cambridge, MA: Harvard University Press.

Kagan, S. & Kagan, M. (2005). *Raising smarter children Creating an enriched learning environment*. San Clemente, CA: Kagan Publishing.

Kail, R. V., & Cavanaugh, J. C. (2015). *Human development: A life-span view*. Boston, MA: Cengage Learning.

Kail, R. V., Lervåg, A., & Hulme, C. (2016). Longitudinal evidence linking processing speed to the development of reasoning. *Developmental Science, 19*(6), 1067 -1074.

Kanner, L. (1943). Autistic disturbances of affective contact. *Nerv Child Pathology. 2,* 217–250. Downloaded 18 May 2018 from http://mail.neurodiversity.com/library_kanner_1943.pdf Reprinted in Kanner, L (1968). Autistic disturbances of affective contact. *Acta Paedopsychiatr, 35*(4), 100–36.

Kaplan, R.M., & Saccuzzo, D.P. (2010). *Psychological testing: Principles, applications, and issues*. (8th ed.). Belmont, CA: Wadsworth, Cengage Learning

Kaplan, S. (2015). How the Internet makes you think you're smarter than you really are. *Washington Post* (April 1). Retrieved 7 July 2017 from www.washingtonpost.com/news/morning-mix/wp/2015/04/01/how-the-internet-makes-you-think-youre-smarter-than-you-really-are/?utm_term=.d1b740ad7615

Karakus, O., Howard-Jones, P. A., & Jay, T. (2015). Primary and secondary school teachers' knowledge and misconceptions about the brain in Turkey. *Procedia Social Behavioural Science 174*, 1933–1940. doi: 10.1016/j.sbspro.2015. 01.858

Karbach, J. (2015). J.55. Plasticity of executive functions in childhood and adolescence: Effects of cognitive training interventions. *Revista Argentina de Ciencias del Comportamiento, 7*(1), 64-70.

Karmiloff-Smith, A. (2012). From constructivism to neuroconstructivism: The activity-dependent structuring of the human brain. *After Piaget, 1*(1).

Kaufman, A. S. (2009). *IQ Testing 101*. New York: Springer Publishing.

Keirsey, D. (1998) [1978]. *Please understand me II: Temperament, character, intelligence* (1st ed.). New York: Prometheus Nemesis Book Co.

Kelly, D. (2017). The best brain food you should be eating. *Reader's Digest*. Retrieved 10 July 2017 from www.rd.com/health/conditions/best-brain-food

Kelly, F. S., McCain, T., & Jukes, I. (Eds.). (2008). *Teaching the digital generation: No more cookie-cutter high schools*. Thousand Oaks, CA: Corwin Press.

Kelly, M. E., Loughrey, D., Lawlor, B. A., Robertson, I. H., Walsh, C., & Brennan, S. (2014). The impact of exercise on the cognitive functioning of healthy older adults: a systematic review and meta-analysis. *Ageing Research Reviews, 16*, 12–31.

Kendall, B. (2017). *Myers' and Briggs' famous tool is still going strong, constantly being improved*. Oxford, UK: OPP.

Kenner, S. (1905). The legal rights of automobile drivers upon the public streets and highways. *Century Legal Journal, 61*, 464.

Kerkhof, G. A., & Van Dongen, H. P. A. (2010). Effects of sleep deprivation on cognition. *Human Sleep and Cognition: Basic Research, 185*, 105.

Khundrakpam, B. S., Lewis, J. D., Zhao, L., Chouinard-Decorte, F., & Evans, A. C. (2016). Brain connectivity in normally developing children and adolescents. *Neuro-image*, *134*, 192-203.

Kiesel, A., & Dignath, D. (2017). Effort in multitasking: Local and global assessment of effort. *Frontiers in Psychology*, *8*.

Kim, C., & Pekrun, R. (2014). Emotions and motivation in learning and performance. In *Handbook of research on educational communications and technology* (pp. 65–75). New York: Springer Science+Business Media.

Kimura, D. (1961). Cerebral dominance and the perception of verbal stimuli. *Canadian Journal of Psychology/Revue canadienne de psychologie*, *15*(3), 166.

Kincheloe, J. L., Steinberg, S. R., & Gresson III, A. D. (1997). *Measured lies: The bell curve examined*. New York: St. Martin's Press.

Kirby, A., Woodward, A., Jackson, S., Wang, Y., & Crawford, M. A. (2010). A double-blind, placebo-controlled study investigating the effects of omega-3 supplementation in children aged 8–10 years from a mainstream school population. *Research in Developmental Disabilities*, *31*(3), 718–730.

Kirp, D. L. (2015). *Improbable scholars: The rebirth of a great American school system and a strategy for America's schools*. New York: Oxford University Press.

Kirszenblat, L., & van Swinderen, B. (2015). The yin and yang of sleep and attention. *Trends in Neurosciences*, *38*(12), 776–786.

Kit, P. L., Liem, G. A. D., Ang, R. P. H., Chong, W. H., & Huan, V. S. L. (2016). Instilling educational hope to strengthen the link between the teacher-student relationship and student engagement. 77th Canadian Psychological Association (CPA) National Convention 2016, Victoria, British Columbia, 9-11 June 2016. *Canadian Psychology*. Retrieved 4 June 2017 from www.cpa.ca/docs/File/Convention/2016/CPA-Program-DIGITAL.pdf

Kloss, J. D., Nash, C. O., Walsh, C. M., Culnan, E., Horsey, S., & Sexton-Radek, K. (2016). A "Sleep 101" program for college students improves sleep hygiene knowledge and reduces maladaptive beliefs about sleep. *Behavioral Medicine*, *42*(1), 48–56.

Kluger, J. (2014 May 1). The part of your brain that made you eat that doughnut. *Time Magazine*. Retrieved 4 March 2018 from http://time.com/84689/brain-temptation-will-power/

Knapton, S. (2015). Intelligence genes discovered by scientists. *The Telegraph* (December 21). Retrieved 7 July 2017 from www.telegraph.co.uk/news/science/science-news/12061787/Intelligence-genes-discovered-by-scientists.html

Knowland, V. (n.d.). *Neuro-hit or neuromyth?* London, UK: Centre For Educational Neuroscience and the University College of London. Retrieved from www.educationalneuroscience.org.uk/neuromyth-or-neurofact on 3 May 2017.

Koksma, J. J. (2014). Narrators of Neuromyth. In Coenen, C., Dijkstra, A., Fautz, C., Guivant, J., Konrad, K., Milburn, C., & van Lente, H. (Eds.) *Innovation and responsibility: engaging with new and emerging technologies* (pp.149–163). Berlin: Akademische Verlagsgesellschaft.

Kolb, D. A. (1981). Experiential learning theory and the learning style inventory: A reply to Freedman and Stumpf. *Academy of Management Review, 6*(2), 289–296.

Komarraju, M., & Nadler, D. (2013). Self-efficacy and academic achievement: Why do implicit beliefs, goals, and effort regulation matter?. *Learning and Individual Differences, 25,* 67–72.

Komatsu, H. (2006). The neural mechanisms of perceptual filling-in. *Nature Reviews Neuroscience, 7*(3), 220–231.

Konig, C. J., Buhner, M., & Murling, G. (2005). Working memory, fluid intelligence, and attention are predictors of multitasking performance, but polychronicity and extraversion are not. *Human Performance, 18*(3), 243–266.

Köster, E. P. (2002). The specific characteristics of the sense of smell. *Olfaction, Taste and Cognition,* 27–43.

Krakovsky, M. (2005). Discredited "Mozart Effect" remains music to American ears. *Stanford Business* (February 1). Palo Alto, CA: Stanford University. Retrieved on 25 May 2017 from www.gsb.stanford.edu/insights/discredited-mozart-effect-remains-music-american-ears

Kruglanski, A. W. (2013). *Lay epistemics and human knowledge: Cognitive and motivational bases.* Berlin, Germany: Springer Science & Business Media.

Krugman, H. (1972). Why three exposures may be enough. *Journal of Advertising Research, 12*(6),11-14.

Kueider, A. M., Parisi, J. M., Gross, A. L., & Rebok, G. W. (2012). Computerized cognitive training with older adults: a systematic review. *PloS One, 7*(7), e40588.

Kuhl, P. K. (2004). Early language acquisition: cracking the speech code. *Nature Reviews. Neuroscience, 5*(11), 831.

Kundu, B., Sutterer, D. W., Emrich, S. M., & Postle, B. R. (2013). Strengthened effective connectivity underlies transfer of working memory training to tests of short-term memory and attention. *Journal of Neuroscience, 33*(20), 8705–8715.

Kutas, M., & Federmeier, K. D. (2000). Electrophysiology reveals semantic memory use in language comprehension. *Trends in Cognitive Sciences, 4*(12), 463–470.

Kyllonen, P. C., & Christal, R. E. (1990). Reasoning ability is (little more than) working-memory capacity?!. *Intelligence, 14*(4), 389–433.

Lalley, J., & Miller, R. (2007). The learning pyramid: Does it point teachers in the right direction. *Education, 128*(1), 16.

LaLopa, J. M. (2013). The difference between bigfoot and learning styles: There may be better evidence to support the existence of bigfoot. *Journal of Culinary Science & Technology, 11*(4), 356–376.

Lam, B. H., Cheng, R. W. Y., & Yang, M. (2017). Formative feedback as a global facilitator: Impact on intrinsic and extrinsic motivation and positive affect. In *Emerging practices in scholarship of learning and teaching in a digital era* (pp. 265–288). Singapore: Springer Nature.

Lamm, C., & Majdandžić, J. (2015). The role of shared neural activations, mirror neurons, and morality in empathy–a critical comment. *Neuroscience Research, 90,* 15–24.

Landhuis, E. (2017). Neuroscience: Big brain, big data. *Nature, 541*(7638), 559–561.

Landmann, N., Kuhn, M., Piosczyk, H., Feige, B., Baglioni, C., Spiegelhalder, K., ... & Nissen, C. (2014). The reorganisation of memory during sleep. *Sleep Medicine Reviews, 18*(6), 531–541.

Lange, N., Froimowitz, M. P., Bigler, E. D., Lainhart, J. E., & Brain Development Cooperative Group. (2010). Associations between IQ, total and regional brain volumes, and demography in a large normative sample of healthy children and adolescents. *Developmental Neuropsychology, 35*(3), 296–317.

Lapeer, R. J., & Prager, R. W. (2001). Fetal head moulding: finite element analysis of a fetal skull subjected to uterine pressures during the first stage of labour. *Journal of Biomechanics, 34*(9), 1125–1133.

Lavin, D. E., & Hyllegard, D. (1996). *Changing the odds. Open admissions and the life chances of the disadvantaged.* New Haven, CT: Yale University Press.

Laxmisan, A., Hakimzada, F., Sayan, O. R., Green, R. A., Zhang, J., & Patel, V. L. (2007). The multitasking clinician: decision-making and cognitive demand during and after team handoffs in emergency care. *International Journal of Medical Informatics, 76*(11), 801–811.

Layton, L. (2015). Study says standardized testing is overwhelming nation's public schools. *The Washington Post* (Oct 24). Retrieved 7 June 2017 from www.washingtonpost.com/local/education/study-says-standardized-testing-is-overwhelming-nations-public-schools/2015/10/24/8a22092c-79ae-11e5-a958-d889faf561dc_story.html?utm_term=.ab11702bcd54

Leahy, M., Shore, R., & Lambert R. (2017a). Myths or misnomers: Researched-based realities in the classroom literature review for Deans for Impact (2015). *Journal of Applied Educational and Policy Research, 3*(1), 81-89.

Leahy, M., Shore, R., & Lambert, R. (2017b). Teachers can untangle the truth from myth in the classroom: Using an interdisciplinary approach to "developing the brain." An application of Deans for Impact (2015). *Journal of Applied Educational and Policy Research, 3*(1), 90-95.

LearningRx Center. (2017). *Types of learning styles.* Retrieved 4 June 2017 from www.learningrx.com/types-of-learning-styles-faq.htm

Lebel, C., & Beaulieu, C. (2011). Longitudinal development of human brain wiring continues from childhood into adulthood. *Journal of Neuroscience, 31*(30), 10937-10947.

Lebiere, C., Anderson, J. R., & Bothell, D. (2001). *Multi-tasking and cognitive workload in an ACT-R model of a simplified air traffic control task.* Pittsburgh, PA: Carnegie Mellon University

LeBlanc, J. J., & Fagiolini, M. (2011). Autism: a "critical period" disorder?. *Neural Plasticity, 2011.*

Lechtenberg, K. (2014). *Ask a neuroscientist: Does a bigger brain make you smarter?* Stanford Neurosciences Institute. Palo Alto, CA: Stanford University. Retrieved 29 May 2017 from https://neuroscience.stanford.edu/news/ask-neuroscientist-does-bigger-brain-make-you-smarter

Ledger, B. (2015). *Brain training: Fun, simple exercises to train your brain to immediately get sharper, faster, and more powerful.* Self-published.

LeDoux, J. (1998). *The emotional brain: The mysterious underpinnings of emotional life.* New York: Simon & Schuster.

Lee, K., & Bull, R. (2016). Developmental changes in working memory, updating, and math achievement. *Journal of Educational Psychology, 108*(6), 869.

Lee, N., Broderick, A. J., & Chamberlain, L. (2007). What is "neuromarketing"? A discussion and agenda for future research. *International Journal of Psychophysiology, 63,* 199–204.

LeGray, M. W., Dufrene, B. A., Mercer, S., Olmi, D. J., & Sterling, H. (2013). Differential reinforcement of alternative behavior in center-based classrooms: Evaluation of pre-teaching the alternative behavior. *Journal of Behavioral Education, 22*(2), 85–102.

Legrenzi, P., Umilta, C., & Anderson, F. (2011). *Neuromania: On the limits of brain science.* New York: Oxford University Press.

Lehrer, J. (2010). The truth wears off. *The New Yorker* (December 3). Retrieved March 27, 2012, from www.newyorker.com/ reporting/2010/12/13/101213fa_fact_lehrer

Lehrer, J. (2011). More thoughts on the decline effect. *The New Yorker* (January 3). Retrieved March 27, 2012, from www. newyorker.com/online/blogs/newsdesk/2011/01/jonah-lehrer- more-thoughts-on-the-decline-effect.html

Lehrer, J. (2011). The mirror neuron revolution: Explaining what makes humans social. *Scientific American.* Retrieved 24 June 2017 www.scientificamerican.com/article/the-mirror-neuron-revolut

Leibing, A. (2014). The earlier the better: Alzheimer's prevention, early detection, and the quest for pharmacological interventions. *Culture, Medicine, and Psychiatry, 38*(2), 217–236.

Lemov, D. & Atkins, N. (2014). *Teach like a champion 2.0: 62 techniques that put students on the path to college.* San Francisco, CA: Jossey-Bass.

Leng, X. & Shaw, G.L. (1991). Toward a neural theory of higher brain function using music as a window. *Concepts in Neuroscience, 2,* 229–258.

Lenneberg, E. H. (1967). The biological foundations of language. *Hospital Practice, 2*(12), 59-67.

Leonard, D., & Straus, S. (1997). Putting your company's whole brain to work. *Harvard Business Review, 75,* 110–122.

Lepper, M. R., Henderlong, J., & Gingras, I. (1999 Nov). Understanding the effects of extrinsic rewards on intrinsic motivation—Uses and abuses of meta-analysis: Comment on Deci, Koestner, and Ryan (1999). *Psychological Bulletin, 125*(6), 669–676.

Lerner, R. M. (2001). *Concepts and theories of human development.* New York: Psychology Press.

Levy-Agresti, J. (1968). Ipsilateral projection systems and minor hemisphere function in man after neocommissurotomy. *Anatomical Record, 160,* 384.

Li, P., Legault, J., & Litcofsky, K. A. (2014). Neuroplasticity as a function of second language learning: anatomical changes in the human brain. *Cortex, 58*, 301–324.

Lilienfeld, S. O., Ammirati, R., & David, M. (2012). Distinguishing science from pseudoscience in school psychology: Science and scientific thinking as safeguards against human error. *Journal of School Psychology, 50*(1), 7–36.

Lim, J., & Dinges, D. F. (2008). Sleep deprivation and vigilant attention. *Annals of the New York Academy of Sciences, 1129*(1), 305–322.

Lindell, A. K., & Kidd, E. (2011). Why right-brain teaching is half witted: a critique of misapplication of neuroscience to education. *Mind, Brain, and Education 5*, 121–127. doi: 10.1111/j.1751-228X.2011.01120.x

Lindsay, S., Hartman, L. R., Reed, N., Gan, C., Thomson, N., & Solomon, B. (2015). A systematic review of hospital-to-school reintegration interventions for children and youth with acquired brain injury. *PLoS One, 10*(4), e0124679.

Locke, J. 1975 [1690]. *An essay concerning human understanding.* In P. H. Nidditch (ed.). Oxford, UK: Clarendon Press.

Loukopoulos, L. D., Dismukes, K., & Barshi, I. (2009). *The multitasking myth: Handling complexity in real-world operations.* Surrey, England, UK: Ashgate Publishing, Ltd.

Lu, D., Mahmood, A., Qu, C., Goussev, A., Schallert, T., & Chopp, M. (2005). Erythropoietin enhances neurogenesis and restores spatial memory in rats after traumatic brain injury. *Journal of Neurotrauma, 22*(9), 1011–1017.

Luke, A. (2014). On explicit and direct instruction. *Australian Literacy Association Hot Topics, 1–4.*

Lupyan, G., & Clark, A. (2015). Words and the world: Predictive coding and the language-perception-cognition interface. *Current Directions in Psychological Science, 24*(4), 279–284.

Luria, A. R. (1968). *The mind of a mnemonist: A little book about a vast memory.* Cambridge, MA: Harvard University Press.

Lynn, R., & Vanhanen, T. (2002). *IQ and the wealth of nations.* Westport, CT: Praeger Publishers.

Maag, J. W. (2001). Rewarded by punishment: Reflections on the disuse of positive reinforcement in schools. *Exceptional Children, 67*(2), 173–186.

Maccoby, E. E. (1951). Television: Its impact on school children. *Public Opinion Quarterly, 15*(3), 421–444.

Macdonald, K., Germine, L., Anderson, A., Christodoulou, J., & McGrath, L. M. (2017). Dispelling the myth: Training in education or neuroscience decreases but does not eliminate beliefs in neuromyths. *Frontiers in Psychology, 8*, 1314.

Machin, S. (2006). *Social disadvantage and education experiences.* Paris, France: OECD.

MacNabb, C., Schmitt, L., Michlin, M., Harris, I., Thomas, L., Chittendon, D., ... & Dubinsky, J. M. (2006). Neuroscience in middle schools: a professional development and resource program that models inquiry-based strategies and engages teachers in classroom implementation. *CBE-Life Sciences Education, 5*(2), 144-157.

Macrae, F. (2014 28 Jul). Female brains really ARE different to male minds with women possessing better recall and men excelling at maths. *The Daily Mail*. Retrieved 25 May 2017 from www.dailymail.co.uk/news/article-2709031/Female-brains-really-ARE-different-male-minds-women-possessing-better-recall-men-excelling-maths.html

Macvarish, J., Lee, E., & Lowe, P. (2014). The 'first three years' movement and the infant brain: A review of critiques. *Sociology Compass, 8*(6), 792–804.

Madec, S., Le Goff, K., Anton, J. L., Longcamp, M., Velay, J. L., Nazarian, B., ... & Rey, A. (2016). Brain correlates of phonological recoding of visual symbols. *NeuroImage, 132*, 359–372.

Maeda, J. (2006). *The laws of simplicity*. Cambridge, MA: MIT press.

Maeda, Y., & Yoon, S. Y. (2013). A meta-analysis on gender differences in mental rotation ability measured by the Purdue spatial visualization tests: Visualization of rotations (PSVT: R). *Educational Psychology Review, 25*(1), 69–94.

Mareschal, D. (2007). *Neuroconstructivism: How the brain constructs cognition* (Vol. 1). Oxford, UK: Oxford University Press.

Marian, V., Shook, A., & Schroeder, S. R. (2013). Bilingual two-way immersion programs benefit academic achievement. *Bilingual Research Journal, 36*(2), 167-186.

Marshall, P. J., & Comalli, C. E. (2012). Young children's changing conceptualizations of brain function: implications for teaching neuroscience in early elementary settings. *Early Education & Development, 23*(1), 4–23.

Martin-Dorta, N., Sanchez-Berriel, I., Bravo, M., Hernandez, J., Saorin, J. L., & Contero, M. (2014). Virtual Blocks: a serious game for spatial ability improvement on mobile devices. *Multimedia Tools and Applications, 73*(3), 1575.

Martin, A., Schurz, M., Kronbichler, M., & Richlan, F. (2015). Reading in the brain of children and adults: A meta-analysis of 40 functional magnetic resonance imaging studies. *Human Brain Mapping, 36*(5), 1963–1981.

Marzano, R. J. (2011). What teachers gain from deliberate practice. *Educational Leadership, 68*(4), 82–84.

Marzano, R. J., Marzano, J. S., & Pickering, D. (2003). *Classroom management that works: Research-based strategies for every teacher*. Arlington, VA: ASCD.

Masento, N. A., Golightly, M., Field, D. T., Butler, L. T. & van Reekum, C. M. (2014). Effects of hydration status on cognitive performance and mood. *British Journal of Nutrition, 111*, 1841–1852.

Massa, L. J., & Mayer, R. E. (2006). Testing the ATI hypothesis: Should multimedia instruction accommodate verbalizer-visualizer cognitive style?. *Learning and Individual Differences, 16*(4), 321–335.

Masten, A. S. (2011). Resilience in children threatened by extreme adversity: Frameworks for research, practice, and translational synergy. *Development and Psychopathology, 23*(2), 493-506.

Mastin, D. F., Bryson, J., & Corwyn, R. (2006). Assessment of sleep hygiene using the Sleep Hygiene Index. *Journal of Behavioral Medicine, 29*(3), 223–227.

McCabe, D. P., & Castel, A. D. (2008). Seeing is believing: The effect of brain images on judgments of scientific reasoning. *Cognition, 107*, 343–352.

McCall, L. A. H. (2012). Brain-based pedagogy in today's diverse classrooms: A perfect fit—But be careful!. *Delta Kappa Gamma Bulletin, 78*(3), 42–47.

McClure, V. S. (2010). *Infant massage: A handbook for loving parents*. New York: Bantam Books.

McCrae, R. R., & Costa Jr, P. T. (1989/2012). *More reasons to adopt the five-factor model*. Retrieved 10 May 2018 from https://www.researchgate.net/publication/286535058_The_Five-Factor_Model_Five-Factor_Theory_and_Interpersonal_Psychology

McDaniel, M. A. (2005). Big-brained people are smarter: A meta-analysis of the relationship between in vivo brain volume and intelligence. *Intelligence, 33*(4), 337–346.

Mcdaniel, M., Rohrer, D., Bjork, R., & Pashler, H. (2009). Learning styles: Concepts and evidence. *Individual Differences Research, 9*, 105119.

McEwen, C. A., & McEwen, B. S. (2017). Social structure, adversity, toxic stress, and intergenerational poverty: An early childhood model. *Annual Review of Sociology, 43*(1).

McGregor, A. (2017). Omega-3 fatty acids and better brain function, the power of cinnamon, and 'oral allergy syndrome'. *Inlander*. Retrieved 10 July 2017 from www.inlander.com/Bloglander/archives/2017/05/25/omega-3-fatty-acids-and-better-brain-function-the-power-of-cinnamon-and-oral-allergy-syndrome

McLaughlin, B. (1992). Myths and misconceptions about second language learning: What every teacher needs to unlearn. *Educational Practice Report 5*.

McMahon, M. (2015). Inside your teenager's scary brain. *Maclean's* (January 4). Retrieved 7 July 2017 from www.macleans.ca/society/life/inside-your-teenagers-scary-brain

McWhinney, B., & Snow, C. (1990). The child language data exchange system: An update. *Journal of Child Language, 17*, 457–472.

Mednick, S., Nakayama, K., & Stickgold, R. (2003). Sleep-dependent learning: a nap is as good as a night. *Nature Neuroscience, 6*(7), 697.

Megowan-Romanowicz, C. (2010). Inside out: Action research from the teacher–researcher perspective. *Journal of Science Teacher Education, 21*(8), 993–1011.

Meiran, N., & Cohen-Kdoshay, O. (2012). Working memory load but not multitasking eliminates the prepared reflex: Further evidence from the adapted flanker paradigm. *Acta Psychologica, 139*(2), 309–313.

Mendel, G. Corcos, A.F., Monaghan, F. V., Weber, M. C. (1993). *Gregor Mendel's experiments on plant hybrids: A guided study*. New Brunswick, NJ: Rutgers University Press.

Mendler, A. (2009). *Motivating students who don't care: Successful techniques for educators*. Bloomington, IN: Solution Tree Press.

Menna-Barreto, L., & Wey, D. (2008). Time constraints in the school environment: What does a sleepy student tell us?. *Mind, Brain, and Education, 2*(1), 24-28.

Miescher, F. (September 6, 1860). *Die medizinische Fakultät in Basel und ihr Aufschwung unter F. Plater und C. Bauhin: mit dem Lebensbilde von Felix Plater: zur vierten Säcularfeier der Universität Basel*. Basel, Switzerland: Schweighauser.

Miller, D. I., & Halpern, D. F. (2014). The new science of cognitive sex differences. *Trends in Cognitive Sciences, 18*(1), 37–45.

Miller, E. K., & Buschman, T. J. (2015). Working memory capacity: Limits on the bandwidth of cognition. *Daedalus, 144*(1), 112-122.

Miller, G. A. (1956). The magical number seven, plus or minus two: Some limits on our capacity for processing information. *Psychological Review, 63*(2), 81–97. doi:10.1037/h0043158. PMID 13310704.

Mills, D. L., Prat, C., Zangl, R., Stager, C. L., Neville, H. J., & Werker, J. F. (2004). Language experience and the organization of brain activity to phonetically similar words: ERP evidence from 14-and 20-month-olds. *Journal of Cognitive Neuroscience, 16*(8), 1452–1464.

Mills, G. E. (2006). *Guide for the teacher researcher.* New Jersey: Prentice Hall.

Mills, K. L. (2014). Effects of Internet use on the adolescent brain: despite popular claims, experimental evidence remains scarce. *Trends in Cognitive Sciences, 18*(8), 385–387.

Mindell, J. A., Meltzer, L. J., Carskadon, M. A., & Chervin, R. D. (2009). Developmental aspects of sleep hygiene: findings from the 2004 National Sleep Foundation Sleep in America Poll. *Sleep Medicine, 10*(7), 771–779.

Mitchell, H. H., Hamilton, T. S., Steggerda, F. R., & Bean, H. W. (1945). The chemical composition of the adult human body and its bearing on the biochemistry of growth. *Journal of Biological Chemistry, 158*(3), 625-637.

Molina-Luna, K., Pekanovic, A., Röhrich, S., Hertler, B., Schubring-Giese, M., Rioult-Pedotti, M. S., & Luft, A. R. (2009). Dopamine in motor cortex is necessary for skill learning and synaptic plasticity. *PloS One, 4*(9), e7082.

Moll, K., Göbel, S. M., Gooch, D., Landerl, K., & Snowling, M. J. (2016). Cognitive risk factors for specific learning disorder: processing speed, temporal processing, and working memory. *Journal of Learning Disabilities, 49*(3), 272-281.

Mondale, Sarah (2001). *School: The story of American public education.* New York: Beacon.

Montgomery, S. H., Capellini, I., Barton, R. A., & Mundy, N. I. (2010). Reconstructing the ups and downs of primate brain evolution: implications for adaptive hypotheses and Homo floresiensis. *BMC Biology, 8*(1), 9.

Moore, D. (2014). Infant and pediatric massage. *Modalities for Massage and Bodywork-E-Book,* 94.

Moore, E. G. (1986). Family socialization and the IQ test performance of traditionally and transracially adopted Black children. *Developmental Psychology, 22*(3), 317.

Morgado-Bernal, I. (2011). Learning and memory consolidation: linking molecular and behavioral data. *Neuroscience, 176,* 12–19.

Morgan, J. (2013). Women 'better at multitasking' than men, study finds. *BBC News* (October 24). Retrieved 17 July 2017 from www.bbc.com/news/science-environment-24645100

Morrison, B. E., & Vaandering, D. (2012). Restorative justice: Pedagogy, praxis, and discipline. *Journal of School Violence, 11*(2), 138-155.

Murphy, R. J., & Cowan, R. L. (1954). *Alcoholics Anonymous.* ACTS Publications.

Murray, C. (2006). Changes over time in the black–white difference on mental tests: evidence from the children of the 1979 cohort of the National Longitudinal Survey of Youth. *Intelligence* 34, 527–540.

Murre, J. M., & Dros, J. (2015). Replication and analysis of Ebbinghaus' forgetting curve. *PloS One*, *10*(7), e0120644.

Murrell, W., Bushell, G. R., Livesey, J., McGrath, J., MacDonald, K. P., Bates, P. R., & Mackay-Sim, A. (1996). Neurogenesis in adult human. *Neuroreport*, *7*(6), 1189–1194.

Murtaugh, A. L. (2016). *Myth to reality? The pedagogical connection between neuromyths and classroom instruction* (Doctoral dissertation). Baltimore, MD: Johns Hopkins University.

Myss, C. (1998). *Eye to eye with Bryant Gumbel* (July). New York: CBS News.

Naglieri, J. A. (2015). Hundred years of intelligence testing: Moving from traditional IQ to second-generation intelligence tests. In *Handbook of intelligence* (pp. 295-316). Springer, New York, NY.

Nairne, J. S., Thompson, S. R., & Pandeirada, J. N. (2007). Adaptive memory: survival processing enhances retention. *Journal of Experimental Psychology: Learning, Memory and Cognition*, *33*(2), 263.

Nakamura, K., Kuo, W. J., Pegado, F., Cohen, L., Tzeng, O. J., & Dehaene, S. (2012). Universal brain systems for recognizing word shapes and handwriting gestures during reading. *Proceedings of the National Academy of Sciences*, *109*(50), 20762–20767.

Nanda, B., Balde, J., & Manjunatha, S. (2013). The acute effects of a single bout of moderate-intensity aerobic exercise on cognitive functions in healthy adult males. *Journal of Clinical and Diagnostic Research: JCDR*, *7*(9), 1883.

National Institutes of Health. (2015). *Use of complementary health approaches in the U.S.: Most used natural products.* Washington, DC: U.S. Department of Health & Human Services.

National Institutes of Health. (2017). *Human Connectome Project.* Retrieved 27 May 2017 from www.neuroscienceblueprint.nih.gov/connectome

Nature Partner Journals. (2018). *npj Science of Learning Community.* Retrieved 5 March 2018 from https://npjscilearncommunity.nature.com/users/16553-alan-woodruff/posts/14471-what-doesn-t-work-in-education

Nellhaus, G. (1968). Head circumference from birth to eighteen years. *Pediatrics*, *41*(1), 106–114.

Nelsen, J. (1996). *Positive discipline.* New York: Ballantine Books.

Nemeth, D., Janacsek, K., Polner, B., & Kovacs, Z. A. (2013). Boosting human learning by hypnosis. *Cerebral Cortex*, *23*(4), 801–805.

Nesayan, A., Asadi Gandomani, R., Movallali, G., & Dunn, W. (2018). The relationship between sensory processing patterns and behavioral patterns in children. *Journal of Occupational Therapy, Schools, & Early Intervention*, 1-9.

NeuroMorph.org. (2018). *Anatomy: Neuronal cell types.* Retrieved on 10 May 2018 from neuromorph.org

Newport, E. (1974, September). Motherese and its relation to the child's acquisition of language. In *Conference on Language Input and Acquisition, Boston, Mass.*

Newton, P. M., & Miah, M. (2017). Evidence-based higher education—Is the learning styles 'myth' important?. *Frontiers in Psychology, 8.*

Nielson, J. A., Zielinski, B. A., Ferguson, M. A., Lainhart, J. E., & Anderson, J. S. (2013). An evaluation of the left-brain vs right-brain hypothesis with resting state functional connectivity magnetic resonance imaging. *Plos One, 8*(8).

Norbury, C. F., & Sonuga-Barke, E. (2017). New frontiers in the scientific study of developmental language disorders. *Journal of Child Psychology and Psychiatry, 58*(10), 1065-1067.

Northstone, K., Joinson, C., Emmett, P., Ness, A., & Paus, T. (2012). Are dietary patterns in childhood associated with IQ at 8 years of age? A population-based cohort study. *Journal of Epidemiology and Community Health, 66*(7), 624–628.

Nudo, R. J. (2013). Recovery after brain injury: mechanisms and principles. *Frontiers in Human Neuroscience, 7.*

O'Rourke, S. (1972). A defense of the structural approach. In *Classical Journal, 68*(2), 153-155).

O'Reilly, M. F. (1995). Functional analysis and treatment of escape-maintained aggression correlated with sleep deprivation. *Journal of Applied Behavior Analysis, 28*(2), 225–226.

Obama, B. (2008). *Children should learn another language.* Campaign speech in Power Springs, Georgia. (July 8). Retrieved 17 July 2017 from www.youtube.com/watch?v=BZprtPat1Vk

Oberle, E., & Schonert-Reichl, K. A. (2016). Stress contagion in the classroom? The link between classroom teacher burnout and morning cortisol in elementary school students. *Social Science & Medicine, 159,* 30–37.

Ochsner, K. N., & Lieberman, M. D. (2001). The emergence of social cognitive neuroscience. *American Psychologist, 56*(9), 717.

Office of Juvenile Justice and Delinquency Prevention. (2017). *OJJDP Statistical Briefing Book.* Online. Retrieved 26 June 2016 from www.ojjdp.gov/ojstatbb/crime/qa05101.asp?qaDate=2015.

Ogden, C. L., Kit, B. K., Carroll, M. D., Park, S. (2011). Consumption of sugar drinks in the United States, 2005-2008. *National Center for Health Statistics Data Brief,* 1–8.

Olds, J., & Milner, P. (1954). Positive reinforcement produced by electrical stimulation of septal area and other regions of rat brain. *Journal of Comparative and Physiological Psychology, 47*(6), 419.

Onderko, P. (2017). Why toddlers throw temper tantrums. *Parenting.* Retrieved 26 June 2017 from www.parenting.com/article/toddler-temper-tantrums

Organisation for Economic Co-operation and Development. (2002). *Understanding the brain: Towards a new learning science.* Paris, France: Author.

Organisation for Economic Co-operation and Development. (2007a). Dispelling neuromyths. In *Understanding the brain: The birth of a learning science* (pp.107-126). Paris, France: Author.

Organisation for Economic Co-operation and Development. (2013). *Results: Ready to learn-students' engagement, drive and self-beliefs* (Volume III). Paris, France: Author.

Organisation for Economic Co-Operation and Development. (2015). *What is the PISA?* Paris, France: Author.

Organisation for Economic Co-operation and Development. (2016). *Education at a glance 2016*. Paris, France: Author.

Organisation for Economic Co-operation and Development. (2017). *Programme for International Student Assessment (PISA)*. Paris, France: Author. Retrieved 7 June 2017 from www.oecd.org/pisa/aboutpisa

Organization for Economic Co-operation, and Development. (OECD). (2007b). *Understanding the brain: Birth of a new learning science*. Paris, France: Author.

Orlin, B. (2013). When memorization gets in the way of learning. *The Atlantic* (September 9). Retrieved 14 July 2017 from www.theatlantic.com/education/archive/2013/09/when-memorization-gets-in-the-way-of-learning/279425

Orzech, K. M., Acebo, C., Seifer, R., Barker, D., & Carskadon, M. A. (2014). Sleep patterns are associated with common illness in adolescents. *Journal of Sleep Research*, 23(2), 133–142.

Ozcelik, E., Cagiltay, N. E. & Ozcelik, N. S. (2013). The effect of uncertainty on learning in game-like environments. *Computers Education, 67*, 12–20.

Paap, K. R., Sawi, O. M., Dalibar, C., Darrow, J., & Johnson, H. A. (2014). The brain mechanisms underlying the cognitive benefits of bilingualism may be extraordinarily difficult to discover. *AIMS Neuroscience, 1*(3), 245–56.

Pace-Schott, E. F., & Hobson, J. A. (2002). The neurobiology of sleep: genetics, cellular physiology and subcortical networks. *Nature Reviews Neuroscience*, 3(8), 591.

Paiva, T., Gaspar, T., & Matos, M. G. (2015). Sleep deprivation in adolescents: correlations with health complaints and health-related quality of life. *Sleep Medicine, 16*(4), 521–527.

Pajares, F., & Schunk, D. H. (2001). Self-beliefs and school success: Self-efficacy, self-concept, and school achievement. In R. Riding & S. Rayner (Eds.), *Perception* (pp.239-266). London, UK: Ablex.

Papadatou-Pastou, M., Haliou, E., & Vlachos, F. (2017). Brain knowledge and the prevalence of neuromyths among prospective teachers in Greece. *Frontiers in Psychology*, 8.

Parenting. (2015). 5 toddler tantrum and hissy fit fixers. *Parenting* (November 13). Retrieved 26 June 2017 from www.kidspot.com.au/parenting/toddler/toddler-behaviour/5-toddler-tantrum-and-hissy-fit-fixers

Parents. (2017). *About us*. Retrieved 10 May 2018 from https://www.parents.com/parents-magazine/

Parsons, J. (2017). Violent video games DO NOT cause antisocial or aggressive behaviour, study finds. *Mirror* (March 9). Retrieved 7 July 2017 from www.mirror.co.uk/tech/violent-video-games-not-cause-9995091

Pashler, H., McDaniel, M., Rohrer, D., & Bjork, R. (2008). Learning styles concepts and evidence. *Psychological Science in the Public Interest, 9*(3), 105–119.

Pasquinelli, E. (2012). Neuromyths: why do they exist and persist? *Mind Brain and Education, 6*, 89–96.

Pasteur, L. (1860 May 7). De l'origine des ferments: Nouvelles expériences relatives aux générations dites spontanées. *Comptes Rendus Hebdomadaires des Séances de l'Académie des Sciences, L*, 849–854.

Patrick, H., & Nicklas, T. A. (2005). A review of family and social determinants of children's eating patterns and diet quality. *Journal of the American College of Nutrition, 24*(2), 83–92.

Pavlov, I. P. (1941). *Lectures on conditioned reflexes. Vol. II. Conditioned reflexes and psychiatry.* New York, NY, US: International Publishers.

Payne, M. A. (2012). "All gas and no brakes!": helpful metaphor or harmful stereotype? *Journal of Adolescent Research 27*, 3–17.

Payne, S. W., & Dozier, C. L. (2013). Positive reinforcement as treatment for problem behavior maintained by negative reinforcement. *Journal of Applied Behavior Analysis, 46*(3), 699–703.

Payne, V. G., & Isaacs, L. D. (2017). *Human motor development: A lifespan approach.* Abingdon, UK: Routledge.

PBS. (2014). Testing in our schools: A guide for parents. *Frontline.* Retrieved 7 June 2017 from www.pbs.org/wgbh/pages/frontline/shows/schools/etc/guide.html

Pei, X., Howard-Jones, P. A., Zhang, S., Liu, X., & Jin, Y. (2015). Teacher's understanding about the brain in East China. *Procedia Social Behavioural Science 174*, 3681–3688. doi: 10.1016/j.sbspro.2015.01.1091

Pekrun, R. (1992). The impact of emotions on learning and achievement: Towards a theory of cognitive/motivational mediators. *Applied Psychology, 41*(4), 359–376.

Perani, D., & Abutalebi, J. (2015). Bilingualism, dementia, cognitive and neural reserve. *Current Opinion in Neurology, 28*(6), 618–625.

Perkins, D. (2010). *Making learning whole: How seven principles of teaching can transform education.* Hoboken, NJ: John Wiley & Sons.

Perry, B. D. (2002). Childhood experience and the expression of genetic potential: What childhood neglect tells us about nature and nurture. *Mind, Brain and Mind, 3*(1), 79–100.

Perry, B. D., & Pollard, R. (1997, November). Altered brain development following global neglect in early childhood. In *Proceedings from the Society for Neuroscience Annual Meeting (New Orleans).*

Peters, A. (2016). Exercise makes you grow new brain cells: But only the right kind of exercise. *FastCompany* (Feb 19). Retrieved 7 June 2017 from www.fastcompany.com/3056872/exercise-makes-you-grow-new-brain-cells-but-only-the-right-kind-of-exercise

Petersen, S. E., & Posner, M. I. (2012). The attention system of the human brain: 20 years after. *Annual Review of Neuroscience, 35*, 73–89.

Petrini, K., Pollick, F. E., Dahl, S., McAleer, P., McKay, L., Rocchesso, D., ... & Puce, A. (2011). Action expertise reduces brain activity for audiovisual matching actions: an fMRI study with expert drummers. *Neuroimage, 56*(3), 1480–1492.

Piaget, J. (1964). Part I: Cognitive development in children. *Journal of Research in Science Teaching, 2*(3), 176-186.

Piaget, J. (1969). *Psichologie et pédagogie.* Paris, France: Gonthier.

Piaget, J. (1971). The theory of stages in cognitive development. In D. R. Green, M. P. Ford, & G. B. Flamer, *Measurement and Piaget.* New York: McGraw-Hill.

Pickering, S. J., & Howard-Jones, P. (2007). Educators' views on the role of neuroscience in education: Findings from a study of UK and international perspectives. *Mind, Brain, and Education, 1*(3), 109–113.

Pickford, R. W. (1949). The genetics of intelligence. *The Journal of Psychology, 28*(1), 129–145.

Piernas, C., Barquera, S., & Popkin, B. M. (2014). Current patterns of water and beverage consumption among Mexican children and adolescents aged 1–18 years: analysis of the Mexican National Health and Nutrition Survey 2012. *Public Health Nutrition, 17*(10), 2166-2175.

Pietschnig, J., Penke, L., Wicherts, J. M., Zeiler, M., & Voracek, M. (2015). Meta-analysis of associations between human brain volume and intelligence differences: How strong are they and what do they mean?. *Neuroscience & Biobehavioral Reviews, 57,* 411–432.

Pietschnig, J., Voracek, M., & Formann, A. K. (2010). Mozart effect–Shmozart effect: A meta-analysis. *Intelligence, 38*(3), 314–323.

Pilcher, J. J., Band, D., Odle-Dusseau, H. N., & Muth, E. R. (2007). Human performance under sustained operations and acute sleep deprivation conditions: toward a model of controlled attention. *Aviation, Space, and Environmental Medicine, 78*(5), B15–B24.

Pinel, P., & Dehaene, S. (2010). Beyond hemispheric dominance: brain regions underlying the joint lateralization of language and arithmetic to the left hemisphere. *Journal of Cognitive Neuroscience, 22*(1), 48–66.

Pink, D. H. (2006). *A whole new mind: Why right-brainers will rule the future.* New York: Riverhead Books/The Penguin Press.

Pinker, S. (2004). *The blank slate: The modern denial of human nature.* New York: Viking Books.

Pires, G. N., Bezerra, A. G., Tufik, S., & Andersen, M. L. (2016). Effects of experimental sleep deprivation on anxiety-like behavior in animal research: Systematic review and meta-analysis. *Neuroscience & Biobehavioral Reviews, 68,* 575-589.

Placebo effect. (2017). Oxford Dictionary. Retrieved 17 May 2017 from https://en.oxforddictionaries.com/definition/placebo_effect

Planton, S., Jucla, M., Roux, F. E., & Démonet, J. F. (2013). The "handwriting brain": a meta-analysis of neuroimaging studies of motor versus orthographic processes. *Cortex, 49*(10), 2772-2787.

Plomin, R., & Deary, I. J. (2015). Genetics and intelligence differences: five special findings. *Molecular Psychiatry*, *20*(1), 98–108.

Polderman, T. J., Benyamin, B., De Leeuw, C. A., Sullivan, P. F., Van Bochoven, A., Visscher, P. M., & Posthuma, D. (2015). Meta-analysis of the heritability of human traits based on fifty years of twin studies. *Nature Genetics*, *47*(7), 702–709.

Posner, M. I. (2003). Neural systems and individual differences: A commentary on *Frames of mind: The theory of multiple intelligences*. Paper presented at the *Annual Meeting of the American Educational Research Association* (Chicago, IL, April 21–25, 2003.

Posner, M. I. (2016). Orienting of attention: then and now. *The Quarterly Journal of Experimental Psychology*, *69*(10), 1864-1875.

Posner, M. I., & Rothbart, M. K. (2007). Research on attention networks as a model for the integration of psychological science. *Annual Review of Psychology*, *58*, 1-23.

Potegal, M., & Davidson, R. J. (2003). Temper tantrums in young children: 1. Behavioral composition. *Journal of Developmental & Behavioral Pediatrics*, *24*(3), 140–147.

Potegal, M., Kosorok, M. & Davidson, R. J. (2003). Temper tantrums in young children II: Tantrum duration and temporal organization. *Journal of Developmental and Behavioral Pediatrics 24*, 148–154.

Poulin, J-F., Tasic, B., Hjerling-Leffler, J., Trimarchi, M. & Awatramani, R. (2016). Box 1: What is a neuronal type? *Nature Neuroscience*, *19*, 1131–1141. doi:10.1038/nn.4366

Powell, K. C., & Kalina, C. J. (2009). Cognitive and social constructivism: Developing tools for an effective classroom. *Education*, *130*(2), 241-251.

Prado, E. L., & Dewey, K. G. (2014). Nutrition and brain development in early life. *Nutrition Reviews*, *72*(4), 267–284.

Prevent Childhood Abuse Arizona. (2009). *0-5 child development is the critical period: What parents do during the first five years, matters!* Author. Retrieved 11 July 2017 from www.pcaaz.org/0-5-child-development-critical-period

Pryor, H. B., & Thelander, H. (1968). Abnormally small head size and intellect in children. *The Journal of Pediatrics*, *73*(4), 593–598.

Public Broadcasting Service. (2014). The testing industry's big four. *Frontline*. Retrieved 7 June 2017 from www.pbs.org/wgbh/pages/frontline/shows/schools/testing/companies.html

Pujol, J., Vendrell, P., Junqué, C., Martí-Vilalta, J. L., & Capdevila, A. (1993). When does human brain development end? Evidence of corpus callosum growth up to adulthood. *Annals of Neurology*, *34*(1), 71–75.

Purkey, W. W. (1970). *Self concept and school achievement*. Englewood-Cliffs, NJ: Prentice-Hall, Inc.

Pusic, M. V., Kessler, D., Szyld, D., Kalet, A., Pecaric, M., & Boutis, K. (2012). Experience curves as an organizing framework for deliberate practice in emergency medicine learning. *Academic Emergency Medicine*, *19*(12), 1476–1480.

Putwain, D., Sander, P., & Larkin, D. (2013). Academic self-efficacy in study-related skills and behaviours: Relations with learning-related emotions and academic success. *British Journal of Educational Psychology*, *83*(4), 633–650.

Quart, Al. (2006). Extreme parenting: Does the baby genius edutainment complex enrigh your child's mind—or stifle it? *The Atlantic* (July/Aug). Retrieved 4 March 2018 from https://www.theatlantic.com/magazine/archive/2006/07/extreme-parenting/304982/

Rabi, I. I., Millman, S., Kusch, P., & Zacharias, J. R. (1939). The molecular beam resonance method for measuring nuclear magnetic moments. The magnetic moments of Li 6 3, Li 7 3 and F 19 9. *Physical Review, 55*(6), 526.

Radel, R., Sarrazin, P., Legrain, P., & Wild, T. C. (2010). Social contagion of motivation between teacher and student: Analyzing underlying processes. *Journal of Educational Psychology, 102*(3), 577.

Radford, (1999 Mar). The ten-percent myth. *The Skeptical Inquirer.* Retrieved 14 Feb 2018 from https://www.cuyamaca.edu/people/jr-jones/intro-psych/10_Percent_Myth_Articles.pdf

Raichle, M. E. (2015). The brain's default mode network. *Annual Review of Neuroscience, 38,* 433–447.

Raichle, M. E., MacLeod, A. M., Snyder, A. Z., Powers, W. J., Gusnard, D. A., & Shulman, G. L. (2001). A default mode of brain function. *Proceedings of the National Academy of Sciences, 98*(2), 676–682.

Rakic, P. (1998). Young neurons for old brains?. *Nature Neuroscience, 1*(8).

Ralph, M. L., Jefferies, E., Patterson, K., & Rogers, T. T. (2017). The neural and computational bases of semantic cognition. *Nature Reviews Neuroscience, 18,* 42–55.

Rato, J. R., Abreu, A. M., & Castro-Caldas, A. (2013). Neuromyths in education: what is fact and what is fiction for Portuguese teachers?. *Educational Research, 55*(4), 441–453. doi: 10.1080/00131881.2013.844947

Rauscher, F. H., Shaw, G. L., & Ky, K. N. (1995). Listening to Mozart enhances spatial-temporal reasoning: towards a neurophysiological basis. *Neuroscience Letters, 185*(1), 44-47.

Rauscher, F. H., Shaw, G.L. & Ky, K.N. (1993). Music and spatial task performance *Nature, 365*(6447), 611.

Raven, J. (1981). *Manual for Raven's Progressive Matrices and Vocabulary Scales.* Research supplement no.1: The 1979 British standardisation of the Standard Progressive Matrices and Mill Hill Vocabulary Scales, together with comparative data from earlier studies in the UK, US, Canada, Germany and Ireland. San Antonio, Texas: Harcourt Assessment.

Ravitch, S. M., & Riggan, M. (2016). *Reason & rigor: How conceptual frameworks guide research.* Thousand Oaks, CA: Sage Publications.

Redaktion. (2015). For successful people sleeping is a waste of time. *Simply. Healthy. Sleep* (November 12). Retrieved 10 July 2017 from www.simplyhealthysleep.com/general/for-successful-people-sleeping-is-a-waste-of-time

Redick, T. S. (2015). Working memory training and interpreting interactions in intelligence interventions. *Intelligence, 50,* 14–20.

Reeve, J. (2014). *Understanding motivation and emotion.* Hoboken, NJ: John Wiley & Sons.

Reference.com. (2018). *Why can't a damaged cell in the brain be replaced?* Oakland, CA: IAC Publishing. Retrieved 3 Mar 2018 from https://www.reference.com/science/can-t-damaged-cell-brain-replaced-9356a3ee3ca9af35

Reference*. (n.d.). *Why can't a damaged cell in the brain be replaced?*. IAC Publishing LLC. Retrieved 14 July 2017 from www.reference.com/science/can-t-damaged-cell-brain-replaced-9356a3ee3ca9af35

Regier, T., & Kay, P. (2009). Language, thought, and color: Whorf was half right. *Trends in Cognitive Sciences, 13*(10), 439–446.

Rehn, A. (2016). The 20-minute rule for great pubic speaking: On attention spans and keeping focused. *The Art of Keynoting* (April 11). Retrieved 24 July 2017 from https://medium.com/the-art-of-keynoting/the-20-minute-rule-for-great-public-speaking-on-attention-spans-and-keeping-focus-7370cf06b636

Réu, P., Khosravi, A., Bernard, S., Mold, J. E., Salehpour, M., Alkass, K., ... & Frisén, J. (2017). The lifespan and turnover of microglia in the human brain. *Cell Reports, 20*(4), 779-784.

Reyna, V. F., Chapman, S. B., Dougherty, M. R., & Confrey, J. E. (2012). *The adolescent brain: Learning, reasoning, and decision making.* Washington, DC: American Psychological Association.

Reynolds, G. (2007). Lobes of steel. *The New York Times* (August 19). Retrieved from www.nytimes.com/2007/08/19/ sports/playmagazine/0819play-brain.htmlRidley, M. (2003). Nature via nurture: Genes, experience, and what makes us human. New York: HarperCollins Publishers.

Riechmann, S. W., & Grasha, A. F. (1974). A rational approach to developing and assessing the construct validity of a student learning style scales instrument. *The Journal of Psychology, 87*(2), 213–223.

Riener, C., & Willingham, D. (2010). The myth of learning styles. *Change: The Magazine of Higher Learning, 42*(5), 32–35. doi.org/10.1080/00091383.2010.503139

Rigney, G., Blunden, S., Maher, C., Dollman, J., Parvazian, S., Matricciani, L., & Olds, T. (2015). Can a school-based sleep education programme improve sleep knowledge, hygiene and behaviours using a randomised controlled trial. *Sleep Medicine, 16*(6), 736–745.

Riley, D. (2015 Oct). *Deans for Impact-The Science of Learning panel discussion.* [video]. Retrieved from https://deansforimpact.org/resources/the-science-of-learning on 3 May 2017.

Rinaldi, L., & Karmiloff-Smith, A. (2017). Intelligence as a developing function: A neuroconstructivist approach. *Journal of Intelligence, 5*(2), 18.

Ritchie, S. J., Bates, T. C., & Deary, I. J. (2015). Is education associated with improvements in general cognitive ability, or in specific skills?. *Developmental Psychology, 51*(5), 573.

Ritter, M. (2017). Experts link teen brains' immaturity, juvenile crime. *ABC News.* Retrieved 23 June 2017 from http://abcnews.go.com/Technology/story?id=3943187&page=1

Roben, C. K., Cole, P. M., & Armstrong, L. M. (2013). Longitudinal relations among language skills, anger expression, and regulatory strategies in early childhood. *Child Development, 84*(3), 891–905.

Robert, M. (2005). *Size "does not matter" for brains.* BBC News (February 19). Retrieved 27 May 2017 from http://news.bbc.co.uk/2/hi/science/nature/4277359.stm

Roberts, I. S. J., & Glover, V. (2008). Postnatal depression and mother and infant outcomes after infant massage. *Journal of Affective Disorders, 109*(1), 189–192.

Robinson, K., & Aronica, L. (2016). *Creative Schools: The grassroots revolution that's transforming education.* London, UK: Penguin Books.

Rogers, C. R., Lyon, H. C., & Tausch, R. (2013). *On becoming an effective teacher: Person-centered teaching, psychology, philosophy, and dialogues with Carl R. Rogers and Harold Lyon.* London, UK: Routledge.

Rohr, L., & Rahman, R. A. (2015). Affective responses to emotional words are boosted in communicative situations. *NeuroImage, 109*, 273–282.

Ronen, S. (1993). *An underlying structure of motivational need taxonomies: A cross-cultural confirmation.* Tel Aviv University, Faculty of Management, The Leon Recanati Graduate School of Business Administration.

Ronimus, M., Kujala, J., Tolvanen, A., & Lyytinen, H. (2014). Children's engagement during digital game-based learning of reading: The effects of time, rewards, and challenge. *Computers & Education, 71*, 237–246.

Röntgen, W. C. (1895 Dec 28). On a new kind of ray, a preliminary communication. *Wurzburg Physico-Médical Society.*

Rose, S. (2009). Should scientists study race and IQ? NO: Science and society do not benefit. Commentary, *Nature, 457*, 786–788.

Rose, T. (2016). *The end of average: How to succeed in a world that values sameness.* London, UK: Penguin Books.

Rosen, C. (2008). The myth of multitasking. *The New Atlantis,* (20), 105–110.

Rosenbaum, L. (2017). Resisting the suppression of science. *New England Journal of Medicine, 376*(17), 1607–1609.

Rosenzweig, M. R., Bennett, E. L., Diamond, M. C., Wu, S. Y., Slagle, R. W., & Saffran, E. (1969). Influences of environmental complexity and visual stimulation on development of occipital cortex in rat. *Brain Research, 14*(2), 427–445.

Rosenzweig, M. R., Krech, D., Bennett, E. L., & Diamond, M. C. (1962). Effects of environmental complexity and training on brain chemistry and anatomy: a replication and extension. *Journal of Comparative and Physiological Psychology, 55*(4), 429.

Rosetta Stone. (2018). *FitBrains.* Retrieved 3 Mar 2018 from https://www.fitbrains.com/rosettastone/

Roth Hursh, L. (2017). 9 signs you're drinking too much water: Most of us could stand to drink more water—but there is too much of a good thing. *Reader's Digest.* Retrieved 27 May 2017 from www.rd.com/health/wellness/drinking-too-much-water

Royal, K. D., & Stockdale, M. R. (2015). The myth of learning styles: What medical educators need to know. *Ear, Nose and Throat Journal, 94*(4–5), 132–134.

Rubie-Davies, C., Hattie, J., & Hamilton, R. (2006). Expecting the best for students: Teacher expectations and academic outcomes. *British Journal of Educational Psychology, 76*(3), 429–444.

Ruff, C. C., & Fehr, E. (2014). The neurobiology of rewards and values in social decision making. *Nature Reviews Neuroscience, 15*(8), 549–562.

Rushton, J. P., & Ankney, C. D. (1996). Brain size and cognitive ability: Correlations with age, sex, social class, and race. *Psychonomic Bulletin & Review, 3*(1), 21–36.

Ryan, R. M., & Deci, E. L. (2016). Facilitating and hindering motivation, learning and well-being in schools: Research and observations from self-determination theory. In J. Juvonen & C.A. Knifsend's *Handbook of motivation at school*, (p.96). London, UK: Routledge.

Sah, P. (2018). Personal conversation, 5 March 2018.

Sailor, K. A., Schinder, A. F., & Lledo, P. M. (2017). Adult neurogenesis beyond the niche: its potential for driving brain plasticity. *Current Opinion in Neurobiology, 42*, 111-117.

Salovey, P., & Mayer, J. D. (1990). Emotional intelligence. *Imagination, Cognition and Personality, 9*(3), 185-211.

Salvatori, R. (1999). Albert Einstein's brain. *The Lancet, 354*(9192), 1821-1822.

Samms-Vaughan, M. (2015). The early childhood period, violence prevention and the sustainable development agenda. *Geneva, Switzerland, World Health Organization. Seventh Milestones in a Global Campaign for Violence Prevention Meeting.* Retrieved 22 July 2017 from www.who.int/violence_injury_prevention/violence/7th_milestones_meeting/Samms_Vaughan_Target_4.3_early_childhood_development.pdf?ua=1

Sample, I. (2014). Taking your brain for a walk: the secret to delaying dementia. *The Guardian* (February 17). Retrieved 24 June 2017 from www.theguardian.com/society/2014/feb/17/brain-walk-delaying-dementia-memory

Sano, A., Phillips, A. J., McHill, A. W., Taylor, S., Barger, L. K., Czeisler, C. A., & Picard, R. W. (2017). 0182 Influence of weekly sleep regularity on self-reported wellbeing. *Journal of Sleep and Sleep Disorders Research, 40*(suppl_1), A67–A68.

Scales, P. C., Benson, P. L., Roehlkepartain, E. C., Sesma Jr, A., & van Dulmen, M. (2006). The role of developmental assets in predicting academic achievement: A longitudinal study. *Journal of Adolescence, 29*(5), 691-708.

Schacter, D. L. (1999). The seven sins of memory: Insights from psychology and cognitive neuroscience. Abingdon, UK: *American Psychologist, 54*(3), 182.

Schmidhuber, J. (2010). Formal theory of creativity, fun, and intrinsic motivation (1990–2010). *IEEE Transactions on Autonomous Mental Development, 2*(3), 230–247.

Schnotz, W., & Bannert, M. (2003). Construction and interference in learning from multiple representation. *Learning and Instruction, 13*(2), 141–156.

Schrank, F. A. (2005). *Woodcock-Johnson III normative update (NU) tests of cognitive abilities.* Rolling Meadows, IL: Riverside Publishing.

Schuller, T., & Desjardins, R. (2007). *Understanding the social outcomes of learning.* Paris, France: OECD.

Schuna, C. (2017). Can you replace breakfast with supplements? Healthy Eating, *SFGate* (July 20). Retrieved 10 May 2018 from http://healthyeating.sfgate.com/can-replace-breakfast-supplements-7072.html

Schurz, M., Radua, J., Aichhorn, M., Richlan, F., & Perner, J. (2014). Fractionating theory of mind: a meta-analysis of functional brain imaging studies. *Neuroscience & Biobehavioral Reviews, 42*, 9–34.

Sciaraffa, M. A., Zeanah, P. D., & Zeanah, C. H. (2017). Understanding and Promoting Resilience in the Context of Adverse Childhood Experiences. *Early Childhood Education Journal*, 1-11.

Scovel, T. (1969). Foreign accents, language acquisition, and cerebral dominance. *Language Learning, 19*(3-4), 245-253.

Sealey, L. A., Hughes, B. W., Sriskanda, A. N., Guest, J. R., Gibson, A. D., Johnson-Williams, L., ... & Bagasra, O. (2016). Environmental factors in the development of autism spectrum disorders. *Environment International, 88*, 288–298.

Sears, A. (2017). Can oxygen therapy bring dead brain cells back to life? *AlSearsMD*. Retrieved 13 July 2017 from http://alsearsmd.com

Sehgal, K. (2016). The Internet makes us stupid and here's why. *Forbes Magazine* (Feb 3).

Semenza, C., Delazer, M., Bertella, L., Grana, A., Mori, I., Conti, F. M., ... & Mauro, A. (2006). Is math lateralised on the same side as language? Right hemisphere aphasia and mathematical abilities. *Neuroscience Letters, 406*(3), 285–288.

Sharma, N., & Sharma, K. (2015). 'Self-fulfilling prophecy': A literature review. *International Journal of Interdisciplinary and Multidisciplinary Studies, 2*(3), 41-42.

Sharma, R. (2012). No more rote learning in state primary schools. *The Indian Express* (September 12). Retrieved 14 July 2017 from http://indianexpress.com/article/cities/ahmedabad/no-more-rote-learning-in-state-primary-schools

SharpBrain. (2016). *The challenge ahead: How to develop, validate and bring to market neuroscience-based innovation*, slide 1. Author. Retrieved 20 July 2017 from https://sharpbrains.com/blog/2017/07/19/the-challenge-ahead-how-to-develop-validate-and-bring-to-market-neuroscience-based-innovation

Shaw, I. (2005). Practitioner research: evidence or critique? *British Journal of Social Work, 35*(8), 1231–1248.

Shaywitz, S. E., & Shaywitz, B. A. (2004). Reading disability and the brain. *Educational Leadership, 61*(6), 6–11.

Shearer, C. B., & Karanian, J. M. (2017). The neuroscience of intelligence: Empirical support for the theory of multiple intelligences?. *Trends in Neuroscience and Education*.

Shermer, M. (2011). The believing brain. *Scientific American, 305*(1), 85–85.

Shernoff, D. J., Abdi, B., Anderson, B., Csikszentmihalyi, M. (2014). Flow in schools revisited: cultivating engaged learners and optimal learning environments. In: *Handbook of positive psychology in schools* (pp. 211–226). New York: Routledge. Downloaded 18 May 2018 from http://citeseerx.ist.psu.edu/viewdoc/download?doi=10.1.1.454.5933&rep=rep1&type=pdf

Shernoff, D. J., Csikszentmihalyi, M., Shneider, B., & Shernoff, E. S. (2003). Student engagement in high school classrooms from the perspective of flow theory. *School Psychology Quarterly, 18*(2), 158.

Shibata, M., Terasawa, Y., Osumi, T., Masui, K., Ito, Y., Sato, A., & Umeda, S. (2017). Time course and localization of brain activity in humor comprehension: an ERP/sLORETA study. *Brain Research, 1657*, 215-222.

Siegel, D. J. (2014). Brainstorm: The power of the adolescent brain. *Common Ground Speaker Series.* Retrieved 26 June 2017 from www.commongroundspeakerseries.org/wp-content/uploads/2014/11/SiegelSummary.pdf

Siegel, D. J. (2015). *Brainstorm: The power and purpose of the teenage brain.* Westminster, UK: Penguin Books.

Sievertsen, H. H., Gino, F., & Piovesan, M. (2016). Cognitive fatigue influences students' performance on standardized tests. *Proceedings of the National Academy of Sciences, 113*(10), 2621–2624.

Sigelman, C. K., & Rider, E. A. (2014). *Life-span human development.* Boston, MA: Cengage Learning.

Simon, R., & Engström, M. (2015). The default mode network as a biomarker for monitoring the therapeutic effects of meditation. *Frontiers in Psychology, 6,* 776.

Simons, D. J., Boot, W. R., Charness, N., Gathercole, S. E., Chabris, C. F., Hambrick, D. Z., & Stine-Morrow, E. A. (2016). Do "brain-training" programs work? *Psychological Science in the Public Interest, 17*(3), 103–186.

Singh, S., & Yaduvanshi, S. (2015). Constructivism in science classroom: Why and how. *International Journal of Scientific and Research Publications, 5*(3), 1–5.

Sininger, Y. S., Doyle, K. J., & Moore, J. K. (1999). The case for early identification of hearing loss in children: auditory system development, experimental auditory deprivation, and development of speech perception and hearing. *Pediatric Clinics of North America, 46*(1), 1–14.

Sladkey, D. (2013). *Energizing brain breaks.* Thousand Oaks, CA: Corwin.

Slobin, D. I. (1973). Cognitive prerequisites for the development of grammar. *Studies of Child Language Development, 1,* 75–208.

Smalarz, L., Greathouse, S. M., Wells, G. L., & Newirth, K. A. (2016). Psychological science on eyewitness identification and the US Supreme Court: Reconsiderations in light of DNA-exonerations and the science of eyewitness identification. In *The witness stand and Lawrence S. Wrightsman, Jr.* (pp. 17–39). New York: Springer Science+Business Media.

Smart, J. J. (1959). Sensations and brain processes. *The Philosophical Review, 68*(2), 141–156.

Smith, A. R., Chein, J., & Steinberg, L. (2013). Impact of socio-emotional context, brain development, and pubertal maturation on adolescent risk-taking. *Hormones and Behavior, 64*(2), 323–332.

Smith, D., Fisher, D., & Frey, N. (2015). *Better than carrots or sticks: Restorative practices for positive classroom management.* Alexandria, VA: ASCD.

Smith, M. A. (2015). Mindfulness: An approach for learning and for life. *Proceedings of the Atlantic Universities' Teaching Showcase, 19,* 88–90.

Snyder, F., Hobson, J. A., Morrison, D. F., & Goldfrank, F. (1964). Changes in respiration, heart rate, and systolic blood pressure in human sleep. *Journal of Applied Physiology*, *19*(3), 417–422.

Society for Neuroscience. (2008). *Neuroscience core concepts. The essential principles of neuroscience.* Washington, DC: Society for Neuroscience. Retrieved 4 June 2017 from https://thelearningbraindotorg.files.wordpress.com/2012/02/sfn-neuroscience-core-concepts-powerpoint.pdf

Society For Neuroscience. (2012). Are you born with all your brain cells, or do you grow new ones? *Ask An Expert BrainFacts.org.* Retrieved 14 July 2017 from www.brainfacts.org/About-Neuroscience/Ask-an-Expert/Articles/2012/Are-you-born-with-all-your-brain-cells-or-do-you-grow-new-ones

Sokolvich, A. (2015). *How to activate your right brain: 5 electrifying tactics to jump-start your creativity.* Clinton, IA: Bent Business Marketing.

Sorabji, R. (1971). Aristotle on demarcating the five senses. *The Philosophical Review, 80*(1), 55–79.

Sorgen, C. (2008). Eat smart for a healthier brain. *WebMed* (December 18). Downloaded 10 July 2017 from www.webmd.com/diet/features/eat-smart-healthier-brain#2

Sowell, E. R., Peterson, B. S., Kan, E., Woods, R. P., Yoshii, J., Bansal, R., ... & Toga, A. W. (2006). Sex differences in cortical thickness mapped in 176 healthy individuals between 7 and 87 years of age. *Cerebral Cortex, 17*(7), 1550-1560.

Spalding, K. L., Bergmann, O., Alkass, K., Bernard, S., Salehpour, M., Huttner, H.B., Boström, E., Westerlund, I. & Vial, C. (2013). Dynamics of hippocampal neurogenesis in adult humans. *Cell, 153*(6), 1219–1227. doi: 10.106/j.cell.2013.05.002

Spear, L. P. (2013). Adolescent neurodevelopment. *Journal of Adolescent Health, 52*(2), S7–S13.

Spencer, R. M., Walker, M. P., & Stickgold, R. (2017). Sleep and memory consolidation. In S.Chokroverty's *Sleep disorders medicine* (pp. 205–223). New York: Springer Science+Business Media.

Sperry, R. W. (1961). Cerebral organization and behavior. *Science, 133*(3466), 1749–1757.

Sperry, R. W. (1968). Hemisphere deconnection and unity in conscious awareness. *American Psychologist, 23*(10), 723.

Sperry, R. W. (1975). Left-brain, right-brain. *Saturday Review, 2*(9), 30–33.

Spreng, R. N., Sepulcre, J., Turner, G. R., Stevens, W. D., & Schacter, D. L. (2013). Intrinsic architecture underlying the relations among the default, dorsal attention, and fronto-parietal control networks of the human brain. *Journal of Cognitive Neuroscience, 25*(1), 74–86.

Springer, S. P., & Deutsch, G. (1993). *Left brain, right brain.* New York: W. H. Freeman and Company.

Springer, S. P., & Deutsch, G. (1998). *Left brain, right brain: Perspectives from cognitive neuroscience.* New York, NY: W. H. Freeman and Co.,/Times Books/Henry Holt & Co.

Squire, L. R., & Dede, A. J. (2015). Conscious and unconscious memory systems. Cold Spring Harbor *Perspectives in Biology*, 7(3), a021667.

Staats, C. (2016). Understanding implicit bias: What educators should know. *American Educator*, 39(4), 29.

Stam, C. J., & Reijneveld, J. C. (2007). Graph theoretical analysis of complex networks in the brain. *Nonlinear Biomedical Physics*, 1(1), 3.

Stein, L., & Belluzzi, J. D. (2014). Operant conditioning of individual neurons. *Quantitative Analyses of Behavior*, 7, 249–264.

Stein, Z., & Fischer, K. W. (2011). Directions for mind, brain, and education: Methods, models, and morality. *Educational Philosophy and Theory*, 43(1), 56–66.

Steinberg, L. (2013). The influence of neuroscience on US Supreme Court decisions about adolescents' criminal culpability. *Nature Reviews Neuroscience*, 14(7), 513–518.

Steinberg, L. & Scott, E. S. (2003). Less guilty by reason of adolescence: Developmental immaturity, diminished responsibility, and the juvenile death penalty. *American Psychologist*, 58(12), 1009–1018 [p. 1014].

Stephens, R. (2016). *The left brain speaks, the right brain laughs*. Jersey City, NJ: Viva Editions.

Stewart, B. (2016). What's normal (kinda annoying) 3-year-old behavior and what's not. *SheKnows* (Sept 26). Retrieved 7 June 2017 from www.sheknows.com/parenting/articles/813862/your-3-year-old-development-behavior-and-parenting-tips-1

Stickgold, R., & Ellenbogen, J. M. (2008). Quiet! Sleeping brain at work. *Scientific American Mind*, 19(4), 22–29.

Stickgold, R., LaTanya, J., & Hobson, J. A. (2000). Visual discrimination learning requires sleep after training. *Nature Neuroscience*, 3(12), 1237.

Stowe, J. D., & Cooney, T. M. (2014). Examining Rowe and Kahn's concept of successful aging: Importance of taking a life course perspective. *The Gerontologist*, 55(1), 43–50.

Strauss, V. (2017). 34 problems with standardized tests. *The Washington Post* (Apr 19). Retrieved 8 June 2017 from www.washingtonpost.com/news/answer-sheet/wp/2017/04/19/34-problems-with-standardized-tests

Stripp, C. (2015). Rote learning: the pantomime villain in education *The Telegraph* (December 17). Retrieved 14 July 2017 from www.telegraph.co.uk/education/educationopinion/12054277/Rote-learning-the-pantomime-villain-in-education.html

Strong, G. K., Torgerson, C. J., Torgerson, D., & Hulme, C. (2011). A systematic meta-analytic review of evidence for the effectiveness of the 'Fast ForWord' language intervention program. *Journal of Child Psychology and Psychiatry*, 52(3), 224–235.

Subramony, D. P., Molenda, M., Betrus, A. K., & Thalheimer, W. (2014a). Previous attempts to debunk the mythical retention chart and corrupted Dale's Cone. *Educational Technology*, 54(6), 17–21.

Subramony, D. P., Molenda, M., Betrus, A. K., Thalheimer, W., Fulgham, S. M., Shaughnessy, M. F., ... & Branch, R. M. (2014b). Timeline of the mythical retention chart and corrupted Dale's Cone. *Educational Technology*, 54(6), 31–34.

Subramony, D., Molenda, M., Betrus, A., & Thalheimer, W. (2014c). The mythical retention chart and the corruption of Dale's Cone of experience. *Educational Technology*, Nov/Dec 2014, *54*(6), 6–16.

Sukel, K. (2015). Early life experience, critical periods, and brain development. *The Dana Foundation* (January 26). Retrieved 12 July 2017 from www.dana.org/News/Early_Life_Experience,_Critical_Periods,_and_Brain_Development

Suleiman, A. B., & Dahl, R. E. (2017). Leveraging neuroscience to inform adolescent health: The need for an innovative transdisciplinary developmental science of adolescence. *Journal of Adolescent Health*, *60*(3), 240–248.

Swaminathan, N. (2008). Why does the brain need so much power? *Scientific American* (April 29). Retrieved 10 July 2017 from www.scientificamerican.com/article/why-does-the-brain-need-s

Swanson, H. L., & McMurran, M. (2017). The impact of working memory training on near and far transfer measures: Is it all about fluid intelligence? *Child Neuropsychology*, 1–26.

Syed, M., & Seiffge-Krenke, I. (2013). Personality development from adolescence to emerging adulthood: linking trajectories of ego development to the family context and identity formation. *Journal of Personality and Social Psychology*, *104*(2), 371.

Szegedy-Maszak, M. (2006). What dreams are made of. *US News & World Report*, *140*, 54–64.

Szybnski, M. (2006). *Student-centered learning versus teacher-centered learning: Are students capable of directing their learning?* (Doctoral dissertation). River Falls, Wisconsin: University of Wisconsin-River Falls.

Tajik-Parvinchi, D., Wright, L., & Schachar, (2017). R.56. Cognitive rehabilitation for attention deficit/hyperactivity disorder (ADHD): Promises and problems. *Journal of the Canadian Academy of Child and Adolescent Psychiatry*, *23*(3), 207.

Talukder, G. (2013). Decision-making is still a work in progress for teenagers. *Brain Connection* (Mar 20). Retrieved 26 June 2017 from http://brainconnection.brainhq.com/2013/03/20/decision-making-is-still-a-work-in-progress-for-teenagers

Tanner, J. L., & Arnett, J. J. (2016). The new life stage between adolescence and young adulthood. In A. Furlong's *Routledge handbook of youth and young adulthood*. Abingdon, UK: Taylor and Francis.

Taubert, M., Draganski, B., Anwander, A., Müller, K., Horstmann, A., Villringer, A., & Ragert, P. (2010). Dynamic properties of human brain structure: learning-related changes in cortical areas and associated fiber connections. *Journal of Neuroscience*, *30*(35), 11670–11677.

Taylor, B., Miller, E., Farrington, C., Petropoulos, M. C., Favot-Mayaud, I., Li, J., & Waight, P. A. (1999). Autism and measles, mumps, and rubella vaccine: no epidemiological evidence for a causal association. *The Lancet*, *353*(9169), 2026–2029.

Taylor, E. W. (2017). Transformative learning theory. In *Transformative learning meets bildung* (pp. 17-29). SensePublishers, Rotterdam.

Terman, L. M. (1916). *The measurement of intelligence: An explanation of and a complete guide to the use of the Stanford revision and extension of the Binet-Simon Intelligence Scale*. Boston, MA: Houghton Mifflin.

Thalheimer, W. (2006/2014). People remember 10%, 20%...Oh really? *Will At Work Learning* (May 1). Retrieved 17 July 2017 from www.willatworklearning.com/2006/05/people_remember.html

Theadom, A., Cropley, M., Parmar, P., Barker-Collo, S., Starkey, N., Jones, K., ... & BIONIC Research Group. (2015). Sleep difficulties one year following mild traumatic brain injury in a population-based study. *Sleep Medicine, 16*(8), 926–932.

Theadom, A., Parag, V., Dowell, T., McPherson, K., Starkey, N., Barker-Collo, S., ... & BIONIC Research Group. (2016). Persistent problems 1 year after mild traumatic brain injury: a longitudinal population study in New Zealand. *British Journal General Practice, 66*(642), e16–e23.

Thomas, W. P., & Collier, V. P. (2002). *A national study of school effectiveness for language minority students' long-term academic achievement*. Washington, DC: Office of Educational Research and Improvement.

ThoughtCo. (2016). *How to tell if you are right brain dominant*. Retrieved 27 May 2017 from www.thoughtco.com/right-brain-dominant-students-1857175

Thurston, L. L., & Thurston, T. G. (1941). *Psychological examinations, 1940 Norms (No. 3)*. Washington, DC: American Council on Education.

Timmer, K., & Schiller, N. O. (2014). Neural correlates reveal sub-lexical orthography and phonology during reading aloud: a review. *Frontiers in Psychology, 5*.

Timothy, W. Y., Chahrour, M. H., Coulter, M. E., Jiralerspong, S., Okamura-Ikeda, K., Ataman, B., ... & D'Gama, A. M. (2013). Using whole-exome sequencing to identify inherited causes of autism. *Neuron, 77*(2), 259-273.

Tokuhama-Espinosa, T. (2008 Jul). *The scientifically substantiated art of teaching: A study in the development of standards in the new academic field of neuroeducation (Mind, Brain, and Education Science)*. (Doctoral Dissertation). AAT 3310716. Minneapolis, Minnesota: Capella University.

Tokuhama-Espinosa, T. (2009 Feb 10). Facts and myths about the brain and learning. *Learning Landscapes*. Baltimore, MD: Johns Hopkins University. Retrieved 17 May 2017 from https://scholarakom.wordpress.com/2009/02/10/facts-and-myths-about-the-brain-and-learning

Tokuhama-Espinosa, T. (2010). *Mind, brain, and education science: A comprehensive guide to the new brain-based teaching*. New York: Norton.

Tokuhama-Espinosa, T. (2011). *Mind, Brain, and Education Science: The new brain-based education*. New York: W.W. Norton. ISBN-10: 9780393706079

Tokuhama-Espinosa, T. (2014). *Making classrooms better: 50 practical applications of Mind, Brain, and Education science*. New York: Norton.

Tokuhama-Espinosa, T. (2015). *The neuroscience of learning: An introduction to Mind, Brain, Health and Education, PsycE1609*. Cambridge, MA: Harvard University Extension School.

Tokuhama-Espinosa, T. (2017). *Second international Delphi panel on Mind, Brain, and Education Science: What has changed 10 years later?* doi: 10.13140/RG.2.2.14259.22560. Retrieved 13 July 2017 from www.researchgate.net/publication/315779095_Delphi_Panel_on_Mind_Brain_and_Educ ation_2016_RESULTS

Tokuhama-Espinosa, T. & Rivera, M. (2013). *Estudio del arte sobre conciencia fonológica en lenguaje preescolar: El cerebro y fracaso escolar.* Contracted and published by the Government of Costa Rica and the System for Integration for Central American CECC/SICA.

Tomlinson, C. A., & Imbeau, M. B. (2010). *Leading and managing a differentiated classroom.* Alexandria, VA: ASCD.

Tomporowski, P. D., Davis, C. L., Miller, P. H., & Naglieri, J. A. (2008). Exercise and children's intelligence, cognition, and academic achievement. *Educational Psychology Review, 20*(2), 111.

Tononi, G., & Cirelli, C. (2014). Sleep and the price of plasticity: from synaptic and cellular homeostasis to memory consolidation and integration. *Neuron, 81*(1), 12–34.

Tournier, I., Jordan, O., & Ferring, D. (2016). Motivation and memory: Impact of emotional content and age relevance on recall. *The Journal of Gerontopsychology and Geriatric Psychiatry, 29*(3), 147–154. http://dx.doi.org/10.1024/1662-9647/a000153

Towler, L. (2014). Deeper learning: Moving students beyond memorization. *NEAToday* (November 25). Retrieved 14 July 2017 from http://neatoday.org/2014/11/25/deeper-learning-moving-students-beyond-memorization-2

Tucker, T.G. (1999). A global perspective on bilingualism and bilingual education. *ERIC Digest*, ED435168.

Tutorialspoint. (n.d.). *The rule of seven.* Retrieved 4 June 2017 from www.tutorialspoint.com/management_concepts/the_rule_of_seven.htm

Tzuriel, D., & Egozi, G. (2010). Gender differences in spatial ability of young children: The effects of training and processing strategies. *Child Development, 81*(5), 1417–1430.

U.S. Department of Justice (2015). *U.S. Census.* Bureau of Justice Statistics. Washington, DC: Author.

U.S. National Institutes of Health. (2015). *Use of complementary health approaches in the U.S. National Center for Complementary and Integrative Health.* Washington, DC. Author. Retrieved 10 May 2018 from https://nccih.nih.gov/research/statistics/NHIS/2012/natural-products/omega3

Ullman, M. T. (2001). A neurocognitive perspective on language: The declarative/procedural model. *Nature Reviews. Neuroscience, 2*(10), 717.

United Nations. (2015). *Education for All movement.* Geneva, Switzerland: Author. Retrieved 7 June 2017 from www.unesco.org/new/en/education/themes/leading-the-international-agenda/education-for-all.

United States Census Bureau. (2010). *Demographics.* Washington, DC: Author.

United States Census Bureau. (2015). *Demographics.* Washington, DC: Author.

Useem, J. (2017). Power causes brain damage: How leaders lose mental capacities—most notably for reading other people—that were essential to their rise. *The Atlantic* (July/August). Retrieved 24 June 2017 from www.theatlantic.com/magazine/archive/2017/07/power-causes-brain-damage/528711

Uttal, D. H., Meadow, N. G., Tipton, E., Hand, L. L., Alden, A. R., Warren, C., & Newcombe, N. S. (2013). The malleability of spatial skills: A meta-analysis of training studies. *Psychological Bulletin, 139*(2), 352–402.

Valian, V. (2015). Bilingualism and cognition. *Bilingualism: Language and Cognition, 18*(1), 3–24.

Vallerand, R. J., Pelletier, L. G., Blais, M. R., Briere, N. M., Senecal, C., & Vallieres, E. F. (1992). The Academic Motivation Scale: A measure of intrinsic, extrinsic, and amotivation in education. *Educational and Psychological Measurement, 52*(4), 1003–1017.

Valtin, H. (2002). "Drink at least eight glasses of water a day." Really? Is there scientific evidence for "8×8"? *American Journal of Regular Integral Computational Physiology, 283*, 993–1004.

van der Knaap, L. J., & van der Ham, I. J. (2011). How does the corpus callosum mediate interhemispheric transfer? A review. *Behavioural Brain Research, 223*(1), 211–221.

van der Wurff, I. S. M., von Schacky, C., Berge, K., Kirschner, P. A., & de Groot, R. H. M. (2016). A protocol for a randomised controlled trial investigating the effect of increasing Omega-3 index with krill oil supplementation on learning, cognition, behaviour and visual processing in typically developing adolescents. *British Medical Journal Open, 6*(7), e011790.

van Kesteren, M. T., Ruiter, D. J., Fernández, G., & Henson, R. N. (2012). How schema and novelty augment memory formation. *Trends in Neurosciences, 35*(4), 211–219.

Van Patten, B. (2012). *Why do children learn language so effortlessly?* Blog. Retrieved 20 July 2017 from https://billvanpatten.wordpress.com/2012/10/07/why-do-children-learn-language-so-effortlessly

Veciana-Suarez, A. (2015). The teen brain: A work in progress. *Miami Herald* (Aug 17). Retrieved 22 June 2017 from www.miamiherald.com/living/health-fitness/article32271891.html

Vicinus, M. (Ed.). (2013). *Suffer and be still (Routledge Revivals): Women in the Victorian age.* London, UK: Routledge.

Villarica, (2012). Wait, you can learn while you sleep?! *The Atlantic* (July 5). Retrieved 10 May 2018 from https://www.theatlantic.com/health/archive/2012/07/wait-you-can-learn-while-you-sleep/259434/

Voelker, P., Piscopo, D., Weible, A. P., Lynch, G., Rothbart, M. K., Posner, M. I., & Niell, C. M. (2017). How changes in white matter might underlie improved reaction time due to practice. *Cognitive Neuroscience, 8*(2), 112-118.

Volpe, J. J. (2008). *Neurology of the newborn.* Amsterdam, The Netherlands: Elsevier Health Sciences.

Voss, U., Holzmann, R., Tuin, I., & Hobson, A. J. (2009). Lucid dreaming: a state of consciousness with features of both waking and non-lucid dreaming. *Sleep, 32*(9), 1191–1200.

Waddington, C. H. (1942). The epigenotype. *Endeavour 1*, 18–20.

Walker, H. M., & Buckley, N. K. (1968). The use of positive reinforcement in conditioning attending behavior. *Journal of Applied Behavior Analysis, 1*(3), 245–250.

Walker, J. S., & Bright, J. A. (2009). Cognitive therapy for violence: reaching the parts that anger management doesn't reach. *The Journal of Forensic Psychiatry & Psychology, 20*(2), 174-201.

Walker, M. P., Brakefield, T., Hobson, J. A., & Stickgold, R. (2003). Dissociable stages of human memory consolidation and reconsolidation. *Nature, 425*(6958), 616–620.

Walker, M. P., Brakefield, T., Morgan, A., Hobson, J. A., & Stickgold, R. (2002). Practice with sleep makes perfect: sleep-dependent motor skill learning. *Neuron, 35*(1), 205–211.

Walker, S. O., & Plomin, R. (2005). The nature-nurture question: teachers' perceptions of how genes and the environment influence educationally relevant behaviour. *Educational Psychology 25*, 509–516.

Wallis, L. (2013). Is 25 the new cut-off point for adulthood. *BBC News. September, 23.*

Walsh, C., Albright, J., Apperley, T., Beach, C. L., Beavis, C., Black, R., ... & Carrington, V. (2014). Switching between productive multitasking and distraction: A case study of how users adapt to mobile tablet devices. *Digital Culture and Education* (August 12). Retrieved 17 July 2017 from www.digitalcultureandeducation.com/uncategorized/park-html

Watson, J. D., & Crick, F. H. (1953, January). The structure of DNA. *Cold Spring Harbor Symposia on Quantitative Biology, 18*, 123-131. Cold Spring Harbor Laboratory Press.

Watson, L. (2015), Humans have shorter attention span than goldfish, thanks to Smartphones. *The Telegraph*. Retrieved 17 July 2017 from www.telegraph.co.uk/science/2016/03/12/humans-have-shorter-attention-span-than-goldfish-thanks-to-smart

Watson, N. F., Martin, J. L., Wise, M. S., Carden, K., Kirsch, D., Kristo, D., ... & Rowley, J. A. (2017). Delaying middle school and high school start times promotes student health and performance: An American Academy of Sleep Medicine position statement. *Journal of Clinical Sleep Medicine, 13*(4), 623–625.

Weber, R., Ritterfeld, U., & Mathiak, K. (2006). Does playing violent video games induce aggression? Empirical evidence of a functional magnetic resonance imaging study. *Media Psychology, 8*(1), 39–60.

Weigmann, K. (2013). Educating the brain. *EMBO Reports, 14*(2), 136–139.

Weinberger, D. (2012). 13 ways the Internet is making us smarter. *Huffington Post* (March 24). Retrieved 7 July 2017 from www.huffingtonpost.com/david-weinberger/internet-makes-us-smarter_b_1225187.html

Weisberg, D. S., Keil, F. C., Goodstein, J., Rawson, E., & Gray, J. (2008). The seductive allure of neuroscience explanations. *Journal of Cognitive Neuroscience, 20*, 470–477.

Weiss, L. G., Saklofske, D. H., Coalson, D. & Raiford, S. (Eds). (2010). *WAIS-IV Clinical use and interpretation: Scientist-practitioner perspectives*. London, UK: Academic Press

Wellcome Trust. (2016). *Neuromyth busting*. London, UK: Author. Retrieved 24 May 2017 from https://wellcome.ac.uk/news/neuromyth-busting

Wellman, B., Haase, A. Q., Witte, J., & Hampton, K. (2001). Does the Internet increase, decrease, or supplement social capital? Social networks, participation, and community commitment. *American Behavioral Scientist, 45*(3), 436–455.

Welsh, J. A., Nix, R. L., Blair, C., Bierman, K. L., & Nelson, K. E. (2010). The development of cognitive skills and gains in academic school readiness for children from low-income families. *Journal of Educational Psychology, 102*(1), 43.

Wenstrom, K. (2014). The FDA's new advice on fish: It's complicated. *American Journal of Obstetrics and Gynecology, 211*(5), 475–478.

Werker, J. F., Yeung, H. H., & Yoshida, K. A. (2012). How do infants become experts at native-speech perception?. *Current Directions in Psychological Science, 21*(4), 221–226.

Wernicke, C. (1874). *Der aphasische Symptomencomplex. Eine psychologische Studie auf anatomischer Basis* [The aphasic symptom complex: a psychological study from an anatomical basis]. Breslau, Germany: M. Crohn und Weigert.

Wernicke, C. (1885). Recent works on aphasia. In G. Eggert, *Works on aphasia* (pp.173–205). The Hague, The Netherlands: Mouton Publishers.

West, R. W., & Greenough, W. T. (1972). Effect of environmental complexity on cortical synapses of rats: preliminary results. *Behavioral Biology, 7*(2), 279–284.

Wheeden, A., Scafidi, F. A., Field, T., Ironson, G., Valdeon, C., & Bandstra, E. (1993). Massage effects on cocaine-exposed preterm neonates. *Journal of Developmental & Behavioral Pediatrics, 14*(5), 318–322.

Wiesel, T. N., & Hubel, D. H. (1963). Effects of visual deprivation on morphology and physiology of cells in the cat9s lateral geniculate body. *Journal of Neurophysiology, 26*(6), 978–993.

Wiggins, G. P., & McTighe, J. (2005). *Understanding by design*. Alexandria, VA: ASCD.

Williams, K. N., & Kemper, S. (2010). Interventions to reduce cognitive decline in aging. *Journal of Psychosocial Nursing and Mental Health Services, 48*(5), 42–51.

Williams, K., Woolfenden, S., Roberts, J., Rodger, S., Bartak, L., & Prior, M. (2014). Autism in context 1: classification, counting and causes. *Journal of Paediatrics and Child Health, 50*(5), 335–340.

Williams, L. M., Barton, M. J., Kemp, A. H., Liddell, B. J., Peduto, A., Gordon, E., & Bryant, R. A. (2005). Distinct amygdala–autonomic arousal profiles in response to fear signals in healthy males and females. *Neuroimage, 28*(3), 618-626.

Williams, T. & Davey, M. (2016). U.S. murders surged in 2015, F.B.I. finds. *The New York Times* (Sept. 26). Retrieved 26 June 2017 from www.nytimes.com/2016/09/27/us/murder-crime-fbi.html

Williamson, D. (2015). Emotions, decision making, and morality. In W. Deimling's (Ed.) *Kant's theory of emotion* (pp. 59–82). New York: Palgrave Macmillan.

Willingham, D. T. (2004). Reframing the mind: Howard Gardner and the theory of multiple intelligences. *Education Next, 4*(3), 19–24.

Willingham, D. T. (2008). When and how neuroscience applies to education. *Phi Delta Kappan, 89*, 421–423.

Willingham, D. T., Hughes, E. M., & Dobolyi, D. G. (2015). The scientific status of learning styles theories. *Teaching of Psychology, 42*(3), 266–271. doi: 10.1177/00986283 15589505

Willingham, D.T. (2004 Summer). Checking the facts. Reframing the mind: Howard Gardner became a hero among educators simply by redefining talents as 'intelligences'. *EducationText*, 19–24.

Willingham, D.T. (2006 Fall). "Brain-based" learning: More fiction than fact. *American Educator*, 30–37.

Willis, J. (2007). The neuroscience of joyful education brain research tells us that when the fun stops, learning often stops too. *Educational·Leadership, 64, 1-5*.

Willis, J. (2015). The high cost of neuromyths in education. *Edutopia* (January 16). Retrieved 4 March 2018 from https://www.edutopia.org/blog/high-costs-neuromyths-in-education-judy-willis

Willms, J. D. (2010). School composition and contextual effects on student outcomes. *Teachers College Record, 112*(4), 1008–1037.

Wilson, A. & Dehaene, S. (2004). *Cognitive Neuroimaging Lab*. Retrieved 10 July 2017 from www.unicog.org/site_2016

Wilson, A. J., Revkin, S. K., Cohen, D., Cohen, L., & Dehaene, S. (2006). An open trial assessment of "The Number Race", an adaptive computer game for remediation of dyscalculia. *Behavioral and Brain Functions, 2*(1), 20.

Wilson, K., & Korn, J. H. (2007). Attention during lectures: Beyond ten minutes. *Teaching of Psychology, 34*(2), 85–89.

Wilson, M. L. (2011). *Students' learning style preferences and teachers' instructional strategies: correlations between matched styles and academic achievement*. Lynchburg, VA: Liberty University.

Wiman, R.V. & Merierhenry, W.C. (Eds.). *Educational media: Theory into practice*. Columbus, OH: Chrles E. Merrill Pubishing.

Winocur, G., Wojtowicz, J. M., Sekeres, M., Snyder, J. S., & Wang, S. (2006). Inhibition of neurogenesis interferes with hippocampus-dependent memory function. *Hippocampus, 16*(3), 296–304.

WIPO (World Intellectual Property Organization). (2016). *U.S. extends lead in international patent and trademark filings*. Geneva, Switzerland: Author. Retrieved 7 July 2017 from www.wipo.int/pressroom/en/articles/2016/article_0002.html

Witelson, S. F. Kigar, D. L. & Harvey, T. (1999). The exceptional brain of Albert Einstein. *The Lancet, 353*(June 19), 2149–2153.

Wittgenstein, L. (1922). *Tractatus Logico-Philosophicus*. In *Werkausgabe* (Vol. 1 includes the *Tractatus*). Frankfurt am Main: Suhrkamp Verlag

Worden, J. M., Hinton, C., & Fischer, K. W. (2011). What does the brain have to do with learning?. *Phi Delta Kappan, 92*(8), 8-13.

World Bank. (2017). *World development indicators.* Retrieved 24 May 2017 from http://databank.worldbank.org/data/reports.aspx?source=2&series=SE.SEC. TCHR&country=

World Health Organization. (2004). *The World Health Organization quality of life. (WHO-QOL)-BREF.* Geneva, Switzerland: Author.

Wubbels, T., Brekelmans, J. M. G., Mainhard, T., den Brok, P., & van Tartwijk, J. (2016). Teacher-student relationships and student achievement. In K. R. Wentzel and G. B. Ramani's *Handbook of social influences in school contexts: Social-emotional, motivation, and cognitive outcomes* (pp.127-145). London, UK: Routledge.

Xia, M., Wang, J., & He, Y. (2013) BrainNet Viewer: A network visualization tool for human brain connectomics. *PLoS One 8*(7): e68910. https://doi.org/10.1371/journal. pone.0068910

Yang, J. (2015). The influence of motor expertise on the brain activity of motor task performance: A meta-analysis of functional magnetic resonance imaging studies. *Cognitive, Affective & Behavioral Neuroscience, 15*(2).

Young, E. (2016). The weak evidence behind brain-training games. *The Atlantic* (October 3). Retrieved 20 July 2017 from www.theatlantic.com/science/archive/2016/10/the-weak-evidence-behind-brain-training-games/502559

Young, M. S. (2010). The multitasking myth: Handling complexity in real-world operations. *Applied Cognitive Psychology, 24*(7), 1046–1047.

Zabrodskaja, A. (2016). Language strategies for trilingual families: parents' perspectives. *International Journal of Bilingual Education and Bilingualism, 19*(3), 341–345.

Zimmer, C. (2005). *Soul made flesh: the discovery of the brain--and how it changed the world.* New York: Simon & Schuster.

Zimmerman, B. J. (1989). A social cognitive view of self-regulated academic learning. *Journal of Educational Psychology, 81*, 329–339.

Zimmerman, B. J. (1990). Self-regulating academic learning and achievement: The emergence of a social cognitive perspective. *Educational Psychology Review, 2*, 173–201.

Zimmerman, B. J. (1994). Dimensions of academic self-regulation: A conceptual framework for education. In D. H. Schunk & B. J. Zimmerman's (Eds.), *Self-regulation of learning and performance: Issues and educational implications* (pp. 3–21). Hillsdale, NJ: Lawrence Erlbaum Associates, Inc.

Zimmerman, B. J., & Bandura, A. (1994). Impact of self-regulatory influences on writing course attainment. *American Educational Research Journal, 31*, 845–862.

Zink, N., & Pietrowsky, R. (2015). Theories of dreaming and lucid dreaming: An integrative review towards sleep, dreaming and consciousness. *International Journal of Dream Research, 8*(1), 35–53.

Zollo, M., & Winter, S. G. (2002). Deliberate learning and the evolution of dynamic capabilities. *Organization Science, 13*(3), 339–351.

INDEX

Note: *Italicized* page locators refer to illustrations; tables are noted with a *t*.

ABOUT THE AUTHOR

Tracey Tokuhama-Espinosa, PhD, is a Professor at Harvard University's Extension School (The Neuroscience of Learning) and is currently an educational researcher affiliated with the Latin American Social Science Research Faculty (FLACSO) in Quito, Ecuador. She is a former member of the Organisation For Economic Co-Operation and Development (OECD) expert panel to redefine Teachers' New Pedagogical Knowledge due to contributions from Technology and Neuroscience and is the founder of Connections: The Learning Sciences Platform, which provides evidence-based resources to teachers. Conexiones and MESH, a UK-based charity, have constructed a new, free, online, evidence-based platform to help fill in gaps of pedagogical knowledge for the 21st century, which was presented to the UNESCO 10th Policy Dialogue on the Teaching Profession in September 2017.

Tracey has taught kindergarten through university and works with schools, universities, governments and NGOs in more than 40 countries around the world. She is the former Director of the Institute for Teaching and Learning (IDEA) and Director of Online Learning at the Universidad San Francisco de Quito, and founding Dean of Education at the American University in Quito. She currently heads "Conexiones," which seeks to improve the quality of education through research, teacher training and student support. Tracey's vision is to better the social, democratic and economic structures of countries through a better educated population.

Tracey's main areas of research are improved indicators to measure educational quality; the expansion of the Mind, Brain, and Education field; learning in the digital age and paradigm shifts using appropriate technologies; bilingualism and multilingualism; and the general improvement of teacher education practices.